THE CHILD ACTORS

THE CHILD ACTORS

A Chapter
In Elizabethan Stage History

BY

HAROLD NEWCOMB HILLEBRAND

NEW YORK
RUSSELL & RUSSELL · INC
1964

FIRST PUBLISHED IN 1926 AS VOLUME XI, NOS. I AND 2
UNIVERSITY OF ILLINOIS STUDIES IN LANGUAGE AND LITERATURE
REISSUED, 1964, BY RUSSELL & RUSSELL, INC.
L. C. CATALOG NO: 64—15037

PRINTED IN THE UNITED STATES OF AMERICA

PREFACE

The following history of children's companies is built chiefly on materials that have been for years in print, so that in most matters of fact the author cannot lay claim to much originality. But he thinks the subject is interesting and important enough to warrant a more comprehensive treatment than it has yet received, and on this plea he bases his *apologia* for the present book. He has found occasion to correct, or at least to combat, a number of opinions; he has been able at times to make additions to the existent corpus of fact; and he has, in the last chapter, considered questions which, strangely enough, seem never to have been raised before.

The main body of his story begins with William Cornish; and it closes about the year 1615, because by then the extraordinary and vital movement had exhausted itself and the casual appearances of children's companies afterwards are of little importance. He has omitted to review the activities of the minor Elizabethan companies—Eton, Westminster, Windsor, and the Merchant Taylors—because he has nothing to add to the very competent summaries in Mr. E. K. Chambers's *Elizabethan Stage*.

All treatises on the Elizabethan stage must be acknowledged to be imperfect and temporary—no less so in this case. For errors and omissions in a study begun many years ago and now renewed, the writer begs that the reader will mingle mercy with justice.

TABLE OF CONTENTS

Part I

Part II

CHAPTER I

CHILDREN ON THE STAGE: A PRELIMINARY SURVEY

By the end of the sixteenth century, as every student knows, London possessed two regularly established companies of child actors, while others bid from time to time for favor. And even though their popularity called forth occasional irritated or jeering comments from the adult companies, the fact of their existence caused no surprise; they were no new thing, but had a recognized place in the theatric world. This really extraordinary phenomenon, unparalleled in the history of the stage before then, and not likely to be paralleled in times to come, merits somewhat more attentive study than has hitherto been vouchsafed. To account for the appearance and rise of children's companies, to demonstrate the popularity which they enjoyed, to calculate the effect they had on the drama of their day—that is the purpose of this investigation. And to collect the miscellaneous evidences proving that even before the organization of children into commercial companies acting by children was common from the early middle ages and particularly in the sixteenth century, is the purpose of the present chapter.

These antecedent modes fall into three classes. First, the choir boys of abbeys and churches and the pupils of grammar schools from very early times were wont to act in religious plays and interludes. Secondly, the choir boys throughout England and the rest of Europe went through a curious mummery at the feast of St. Nicholas, when one of their number acted for a space as bishop, fulfilling the duties of that office. Both these modes are old stories, which must be reviewed rather to complete the record than to convey news. But the third mode is by no means so well known, namely, that in the half-dramatic pageants with which the large cities welcomed visiting sovereigns and titled guests, children were in constant use. The effect of these three modes was to make the citizens of England thoroughly familiar from early times with the spectacle of children acting in public capacities that were wholly or in part dramatic.

1. *Children in Plays, 1100-1570.*

The records of children as play-actors in the middle ages are so few and so well known that I shall spend as little time on them as

possible. Malone, on the vague authority of "the accompts of various monasteries," opines that the performance of mysteries by
choir boys was "a very ancient practice, probably coeval with the
earliest attempts at dramatick representation."[1] Certainly the first
recorded instance, that of the play of St. Catherine at Dunstable
grammar school, is very early.[2] Their schoolmaster, Geoffrey of
Maine, who became abbot of St. Albans in 1119, borrowed from
the abbey of St. Albans a number of copes, which were destroyed
by fire before he could return them. A lucky accident, whatever
Geoffrey may have thought of it, for without it the performance
would doubtless have passed unnoticed. Du Boulay,[3] in rehearsing
this story, declares that the play was not something new, but belonged
to a custom of long standing; yet he gives no authority for his
statement.

In this case the actors were grammar school boys, and it may
be that throughout the middle ages they were more active in dramatic representation than choir boys.[4] But the records are so often
ambiguous on this point, even in the late times of the sixteenth
century, that we can scarcely separate the performances of the one
class from those of the other, and must treat them as practically
the same—as indeed they were, inasmuch as the choir boys usually
attended the grammar schools of their abbeys. We do not know, for
instance, whether it was the boys of the school or of the choir of
St. Paul's who petitioned in 1378 against permitting certain in-
experienced persons to act the "history of the Old Testament,"
which they had prepared at considerable expense for the following
Christmas.[5] Here, evidently, is a case of monopoly. In the account
Rolls of Westminster for the year 1413-14 is an entry of 3s. 4d.
paid to "Pueris de Elemosinaria ludentibus coram Domino."[6] Here,
certainly, it is a question of the choir boys, the poor boys of the
almonry. Mr. E. K. Chambers has argued[7] that the reference here
is to a performance of the Boy Bishop, yet the verb "ludere,"

---

[1] Edmund Malone, *Shakespeare*, 1821, III, 24.
[2] Quoted frequently from the original account in Matthew Paris. Cf. e.g.
Hone's *Ancient Mysteries*, 1823, p. 199.
[3] *Hist. Univ. Paris.*, 1665, II, 225.
[4] Mr. Carleton Browne is of this opinion. Cf. his *English Grammar Schools*
(an unpublished thesis in the Harvard library), pp. 342, 345 ff.
[5] Cf. Malone, *Shakespeare*, III, 24; also Dodsley, *Old Plays*, 1744, I, xii.
[6] *Athenæum*, 1900, Pt. II, p. 655.
[7] *Athenæum*, 1900, Pt. II, p. 692.

while it had a loose signification, was always used when plays were meant, and may have been so used here. The same ambiguity hangs about the next two notices. The first is from Durham Abbey Account Rolls of 1416-17,[8] and records a payment of 12s. "diversis pueris ludentibus coram eodem priore" on St. Stephen's Day. The second, from the registers of St. Margaret's Southwark (later incorporated with St. Mary Overy), is dated St. Lucy's Day, 1456: "Item, paid to Harvey for his Chyldren, vpon Seynt Lucy day . . . . xxd."[9] Whether Harvey's boys acted or sang is impossible to tell, but inasmuch as notices are common in the registers of plays by parish clerks, the chances are that this was a play too.

Warton tells us that at the end of the century, in 1487, while Henry VII kept his residence at the castle of Winchester, the birth of Prince Arthur was celebrated with banquetings and revelry.[10] On Sunday during the time of dinner the king was entertained by a miracle play on Christ's descent into hell, presented by the almonry boys ("Pueri Eleemosynarii") of St. Swithin's Priory and Hyde Abbey, Winchester. Here is an indisputable instance of a religious play being acted by boys, and by choir boys too, for so far as I have been able to discover it was the invariable custom for almonry boys of abbeys and churches to pay for their support by singing in the choir.

These are all the notices of playing by children before 1500 that I have been able to find. A thorough search through churchwarden's accounts and various other records of religious establishments and households of noblemen might reveal a few more. Yet they would but add weight to what is suggested by the few notices which I have gathered above, namely, that during the middle ages the acting of religious plays was not seldom entrusted to the choir boys of an abbey or the pupils of a grammar school. The custom is known to have been in existence early in the twelfth century, there are no evidences that it met with opposition, and it is known to have been in existence in subsequent centuries. The likelihood is that it grew with the expansion of religious drama, and while we are not to suppose that children during this period ever became serious rivals with men, as they did later, nevertheless we may reasonably suppose that their performances were common and popular.

[8] Pub. by the Surtees Soc., Vol. III, p. 614.
[9] *Shakesp. Soc. Papers*, III, 46.
[10] *Hist. of Eng. Poetry*, 1871, III, 163.

If notices of acting by boys are scanty before 1500, they are plentiful enough after the turn of the century. Doubtless the great increase is due in part to the greater fullness and number of the records left us, but the real explanation, I have no doubt, lies in the multiplication of grammar schools towards the middle of the century, and still more in the greatly heightened interest in playing which grew as the century grew. We find choir boys of religious institutions playing as in the centuries before; we occasionally find also, as we have not until now, choir boys of private chapels playing; and we find a great many instances of playing by the pupils of grammar schools, whether or not connected with religious organizations. I do not propose to give a complete list of such performances, even if that were possible, or indeed of the institutions from which performances came; but only enough to show how widespread was the custom of acting among children.

The class of chorister-actors is represented early in the century by the boys of Magdalen College, Oxford. They played in 1509-10[11] and afterwards[12] and may have begun earlier. In the Household Book of the earls of Northumberland[13] (begun in 1512) it is recorded that the choristers of the chapel were accustomed to act at Easter and Christmas religious plays fitting the occasion. We are not told that the performers were children, and yet I am sure they were because with the exception of the gentlemen of the Chapel Royal, I have found no instance of plays being given by the men singers of a choir alone, while examples of playing by the children are plentiful. It seems likely that the choir boys of the chapel of the Duke of Norfolk also acted occasionally, because when the mayor dined with

[11] "Sol. pane, cibo et aliis datis pueris ludentibus in die Paschae . . . . xvijd ob." From Magdalen Coll. Acct. Books, extracted in Chambers's *Medieval Stage*, II, 249.

[12] In 1518, e. g. The entry shows the identity of the boys who played in 1509. Perrot, the master of the choristers, was paid 2s. 6d. "pro tinctura et factura tunicae eius qui ageret partem Christi et pro crinibus mulieribus." Same source and page.

[13] *Northumberland Household Book*, ed. Bishop Percy, 1827, p. 343: "Item My Lord useth and accustomyth to gyfe yearly if his Lordship kepe a Chapell and be at home them of his Lordshipes Chapell if they doo play the Play of the Nativitie uppon Cristynmes-Day in the mornynge in my Lords Chapell befor his Lordship . . . . xxs.

Item My Lord usith and accustomedith to gyfe yerely if his Lordship kepe a Chapell and is at home in rewarde to them of his Lordshipe Chapell and other his Lorshipis Servauntes that playth the Play of Resurrection upon Esturday in the Mornynge in my Lordis 'Chapell' befor his Lordshipe . . . . xxs."

the duke in 1564-5 and again in 1565-6, he gave 6s. 8d. to the children of the chapel.[14]

It is difficult to tell when the grammar schools and colleges of the sixteenth century turned seriously to giving plays. Doubtless the tradition was carried over directly from the fourteenth century by various cathedral and abbey schools. The earliest record I have found for the century is connected with Eton, and dates from 1525: "Pro expensis circa ornamenta ad duos lusus in aula tempore natalis Domini . . . . xs."[15] That is not, in all probability, to be held as the date of the initiation of plays at Eton, though it is the first year in which plays were taken notice of in the college accounts. The beginnings of the play at Westminster School are shrouded in obscurity, as are the origins of the school itself. Plays were well under way by the time of Elizabeth, and I gather that there are good evidences of their being given much earlier, though the school chronicler, Mr. Sergeaunt, is not very clear on this point.[16] It is significant of the regard which was felt for play-acting at Westminster that the statutes drawn up c. 1560 provided that one Latin play and one English be given yearly under the direction of the master of the choristers by the scholars and choristers.[17] The Latin play has survived to this day. The fact of providing carefully for annual production of plays at this particular school makes me suspect that an old and honored custom was being reaffirmed, rather than a new one established; but there are no records of these early plays extant. Mr. Sergeaunt assures us that to Alexander Nowell, headmaster from 1543 to the accession of Mary, must be ascribed the introduction of Terence into the school.[18]

At Winchester College plays were under way in 1565, and there is no telling how much earlier they may have begun.[19] The record of expenses in that year is preserved, so we are told, through the *accident* of the College bearing part of the burden. It does not appear, however, that Winchester plays were ever of great moment, or created interest outside the College. At Canterbury School, too,

[14] Cf. *Norwich Chamberlains' Accts.* in Murray, *Eng. Dramatic Companies*, II, 364-5.

[15] From *Eton Audit Books*, in Maxwell-Lyte's *Hist. of Eton Coll.*, 1899, p. 115.

[16] *Vide* John Sergeaunt, *Annals of Westminster School*, pp. 47-50.

[17] F. H. Forshall, *Westminster School Past and Present*, p. 468.

[18] *Op. cit.*, p. 48.

[19] 1565, plays at Christmas: "In exp. fact. circa ludos in feriis nataliciis . . . . xjs. vjd." Kirby, *Annals of Winchester College*, p. 287.

it is not possible to trace plays definitely beyond 1562,[20] but the chroniclers of the school, Messrs. Woodruff and Cape, surmise that plays were probably acted there at an early period, and that the revelries connected with the Boy Bishop were succeeded in the late fifteenth and early sixteenth centuries by miracle plays, mysteries, and moralities.[21] But no record of such performances exists. The sum voted by the Dean and Chapter in 1562 was enormous (£14-6-8). Possibly it was to defray expenses of costly and permanent properties. In the next year (or possibly the year before)[22] the gift was only 56s. 8d., a more reasonable sum; it was to be devoted "to the scholemaster and scholars towards such expensys as they shall be at in settyng furthe of Tragedies, Comedyes, and interludes this next Christmas." Had only tragedies and comedies been mentioned, we might be in doubt as to whether the plays were in Latin or English; but the word "interlude" assures us pretty definitely that the language was English. Plays were acted at Canterbury up to the Civil War, when Cromwell's soldiers demolished the playing place (called "the Dean's great hall") "for being profaned by the King's Scholars having acted plays there."[23]

The plays at the Merchant Taylors School in London, which, like those at Westminster and St. George's Chapel, Windsor, attained greater notoriety than others because they found their way occasionally to court, were doubtless begun soon after the school was founded in 1561.[24] But there are no notices of them until March of 1573, when because of the rowdyism attending the giving of plays in the Hall they were inhibited.[25] This order shows that plays had by that time become customary, and that the general public was admitted to them upon the payment of an admission fee. In a word, these were public performances on a commercial basis. The man who was the inspiring force in this breach of scholastic activity was the learned doctor and excellent pedagog, Richard Mulcaster.

[20] "To Mr Ruesshe (Anthony Rush, Headmaster) for rewards geven him at settyng out of his plays at Christmas *per capitulum* 14li. vjs. viijd." *Treasurer's Accts.*, 1562-3, cited in Woodruff and Cape, *Hist. of Canterbury School*, p. 80.

[21] *Op. cit.*, p. 79.

[22] *Op. cit.*, p. 80. The original record is damaged by fire so that the date of the entry is lost; it lies between 1560 and 1563.

[23] From "Gosling's Walk," quoted in Woodruff and Cape, *op. cit.*, p. 120, note.

[24] On Sept. 24, to be exact, *Vide* Clode's *Memorials of the Merchant Taylors Co.*, pp. 401 seq.

[25] Clode's *Early Hist. of the Guild of M. T.*, Pt. I, p. 234.

Numerous miscellaneous notices of performances by grammar school boys may be garnered from the transcripts of municipal records in Murray's *English Dramatic Companies*. The value of these items lies in their recording in each case the performance of a play outside the grammar school, before the dignitaries of the town. They show, in other words, that the boys of schools and choirs in those days were accustomed to act publicly, often before men of eminence, and received compensation therefor. Unfortunately little is known about these lesser school companies, more than the dates of a few performances.

From 1564 to 1574, the boys of the grammar school at Totness played before the mayors and dignitaries of the town of Plymouth.[26] Usually they are called the "boyes of Tottnes" or even simply "the plaiers of totnes," but on one occasion the usual 10s. was paid to "the scole Mr & children of Totenes."

In the Minutes of the Governors of the town of Beverley there are a number of entries from 1566 to 1572 relating to the acting of plays by the "Scolemaistres players."[27]

At Ludlow a company of schoolboys used occasionally to act plays before the town fathers. In 1562, a payment of 10s. was made "to the Chylderne which did play at the Castell." During 1575-6 an equal sum was paid "to the childerne or schollers by way of reward for playing afore us & our bretherne."[28]

The boys of a grammar school at or near Norwich are recorded in the Chamberlain's Accounts of that city as playing once in 1547. Their master was named Byrde, and they played in the chapel of the common hall on the Sunday after Twelfth Day.[29]

In the period of 1556-1568 the boys of the grammar school at Louth played on some occasions. That, at least, is the conclusion from the fact that Goodale, the headmaster, was paid 13s. 3d. in 1556 "for mony laid furthe by him at the players," and again 1s 4d. in 1558 for money laid out "for the furnishing of the play played in the markt-stede on Corpus Xpi day"; and that Pelsonne, the usher, was paid 5s. in 1568 for setting out an interlude.[30]

[26] Murray, *op. cit.*, II, 382-3.
[27] Leach, *Early Yorkshire Schools*, p. 117. Murray, who has evidently not examined the records at Beverley, does not print these notices. He has one item of August 8, 1572, of 8s. "lusoribus Magistri Richardson." (*Eng. Dram. Cos.*, II, 205)
[28] Murray, II, 324.
[29] Murray, II, 362.
[30] Murray, II, 323; Murray quotes from Goulding, *Louth Records*, p. 55.

There are a number of performances by children recorded in
Murray with no more designation than the town from which they
came. I suspect in these cases, too, that the boys were of grammar
schools, for unless they had received some kind of education they
would not be fitted to present even plays in the vernacular. In
1535-6 "certayn boyes" played in Bristol before the mayor and
aldermen;[31] in 1564 a company of unidentified children existed at
Baddow;[32] and in 1602 certain children played at Bath on Candlemas Day.[33]

The scholars of St. Paul's school of Colet's foundation, in London,
are not prominent in the history of acting in grammar schools.
Yet they must have shown skill in the art, for on one occasion at
least they were accorded a very great honor. The event has often
been commemorated in the annals of the stage, for it is sufficiently
striking. On November 10, 1527, about forty of the boys, under the
direction of their master John Rightwise, presented a Latin morality
at Greenwich before Henry VIII and the ambassadors who had been
dispatched from France on the occasion of the capture of Rome
by the Duke of Bourbon. There is no need of dwelling upon so
familiar an event in any great detail.[34] The first striking thing
about it is that although the play was written in Latin it was a
morality in form and content, or rather a moral-interlude in the
manner of Bale's *King John*. Mixed with such figures of history
as Luther, his wife, Saints Peter, Paul, and James, the dauphin
and his brother and the cardinal (Wolsey, of course,) were the
familiar personifications of the morality—Religion, Ecclesia, Veritas,
Heresy, False Interpretation, War, Lady Peace, Lady Quietness,
and Dame Tranquility. Latin interludes in the English style were
in those days a rarity. The grammar schools were accustomed to
give classic comedies and tragedies and modern Latin plays modelled
on the classics, but plays of this hybrid nature were few.

Even more striking than the play itself are the circumstances
under which it was performed. On October 20, 1527, an embassy

[31] Murray, II, 207.

[32] Chambers, *Medieval Stage*, II, 338.

[33] Murray, II, 204.

[34] *Vide* Collier, *Annals of the Stage*, 1879, I, 104 ff.; Froude, *Hist. of England*,
1856, I, 63-5; *Notes and Queries*, 2d series, II, 24, 78, for a discussion of the priority
of Collier in publishing the documents; Cavendish's *Life of Wolsey*. The list of
characters and accessories printed by Collier and Froude is one of the most interesting documents we possess of this early part of the century, for the curious
and valuable information it gives of the dresses of the actors.

arrived in England from France consisting of the Maréchal Mont-
morency, the Bishop of Bayonne, the President of Rouen, and
M. d'Humières. They were first received by Cardinal Wolsey at
Hampton Court and later by the king at Greenwich, being entertained at both places in the most sumptuous and impressive
manner. It was at Greenwich, after variously devised tourneys
in the banqueting hall and in the tilt-yard, that the play was acted.
Hall[35] gives a fairly long synopsis of it, which does not fully agree
with the *dramatis personæ* as we know them from the list of the
Master of the Revels, and is perhaps not to be taken as a wholly
accurate account, but which is probably right in the main. He
tells us that the Pope was represented in captivity and the Church
in subjection, whereupon St. Peter appeared and authorized the
cardinal to set both at liberty. So the cardinal made intercession
with the kings of England and France, who by acting in concert
accomplished the desired purpose. Then came in the French king's
children, complaining to the cardinal of how the emperor kept
them hostages and would not consent to any ransom by their father,
and beseeching him to help them. So the cardinal again worked
upon the English and French kings until he brought about a peace
with the emperor and delivered the princes. "At this play wise
men smiled; and thought that it sounded more glorious to the Cardi-
nall, then true to the matter in dede."

Collier throws aside this account of Hall with the declaration
that the writer was clearly misinformed,[36] yet his indictment is
unjustifiably severe. Hall agrees very well with the Revels Master's
list except that he makes no mention of Luther. As I have said,
doubtless Hall is not entirely accurate; yet his story has too many
circumstances of truth to be lightly discredited. The plot as he
gives it to us fits excellently the situation, for it represents England
and France acting in amity to uphold the Church and repress the
Emperor, under the wise and benign counsel of the cardinal.

It was a political move on the cardinal's part of no mean significance, this play by the boys from Paul's school. And therefore it is
especially noteworthy in our annals that such a play should be entrusted to such a company. We have seen the *pueri eleemosynarii*
of St. Swithin's and Hyde Abbeys playing a mystery before Henry
VII at the birthday feast for Prince Arthur in 1487; we shall find

[35] *Chronicle*, 1809, p. 735.
[36] *Op. cit.*, I, 108, note.

the children of Paul's acting a play called *The Abuses* before James I
and the visiting king of Denmark in 1606; we shall come upon in-
numerable occasions when boys played before royalty in less mo-
mentous fashion; but among them all there was none which partook
of statecraft and diplomacy as this one did. To be sure, it was a
piece of revelry, served up with a banquet and much wine; yet the
politic element is clearly visible in it, and even taken as a pastime
it was an event so remarkable in the annals of the court as to draw
forth the admiration of Cavendish, Stow, and Hall. And the fact
that a company of boys was preferred over all other players for
what was in reality the climax of a sumptuous entertainment, may
be taken as a prognostication of the success which boy actors were
to enjoy through the sixteenth century.

We may wonder why the boys of Colet's school were preferred to
the children of the Chapel Royal, who were at this time in the flood
tide of favor at the court revels. One reason is that so many more
players were needed than the Chapel could supply.[37] The choice
of Rightwise as the author was due, very probably, to the nature of
the occasion, for Rightwise was a more learned man than Cornish,
the Chapel master, and better able to endite a comedy in Latin,
which by the dignity of its language would be more suitable to the
event than an English interlude.[38]

Two centers of dramatic activity remain to be spoken of which
are in many respects more singular and memorable than any we
have yet touched upon—the theatres at Hitchin in Hertfordshire
and at Shrewsbury. John Bale tells us all we know about the establishment at Hitchin.[39] In 1538 one Ralph Radcliffe, a native of

---

[37] The Chapel boys at that time numbered about ten; the play called for up-
wards of forty-eight parts.

[38] Rightwise is found once again as a dramatic author; in 1564 the queen witnessed a play on Dido by him at Cambridge. Cf. Warton, *Hist. of Eng. Poetry*,
ed. Hazlitt, III, 306.

[39] *Scriptorum Illustrium Maioris Brytannie . . . . Catalogus*, 1557, p. 700. Thus
much of Bale's account concerns the theatre: "Radulphus Radclif, patria Ces-
triensis, Huchiniae in agro Hartfordiensi, & in coenobio, quod paulo ante Car-
melitarum erat, ludum literarium anno Domini 1538 aperuit, docuitque Latinas
literas. Mihi quidem aliquot dies in unis & eisdem aedibus commoranti, multa
arriserunt; eaque etiam laude dignissima. Potissimum verò theatrum, quod in
inferiori aedium parte longè pulcherrimum extruxit. Ibi solitus est quotannis
simul iucunda & honesta plebi edere spectacula, cùm ob iuuentutis, suae fidei &
institutioni comissae, inutilem pudorem exuendum; tum ad formandum os te-
nerum & balbutiens, quo clarè, eleganter, & distinctè uerba eloqui & effari con-

THE CHILD ACTORS 19

Chester, set up a school in the dissolved Carmelite Priory at Hitchin, where he taught the classics. Bale himself passed some days there with him, and speaks from personal knowledge. Radcliffe had built a stage or theatre in some lower part of the building, and there he was accustomed every year to give "merry and honest plays for the edification of the public, both to practise his charges in ease of bearing and to teach them to speak clearly and elegantly." In the library Bale saw many tragedies and comedies, particularly one on the peace between Henry VII and the King of France. The following plays (presumably in Latin) are listed as coming from his hand: comedies on *Patient Griseldis*, Chaucer's *Meliboeus*, *Titus and Gisippus*, *The Revolt of Jonah*, *Lazarus and Dives*, *The Courage of Judith*, *The Afflictions of Job*; tragedies on *The Burning of Sodom*, *The Condemnation of John Huss*, and *The Deliverance of Susanna*.

Some particulars regarding the Priory at Hitchin are supplied by the Reverend Robert Nixon in a report to the Society of Antiquaries.[40] It was surrendered to Henry VIII on May 9, aº 21, and on July 22, aº 38, was granted in fee by letters patent to Edward Watson and Henry Hendon, who conveyed it to Ralph Radcliffe, Esq. This man was the son of Thomas Radcliffe, Esq., of Radcliffe Tower, and he married a woman of the Marshall family of Hitchin. It is clear that if Nixon is right in dating the conveyance of the property to Radcliffe in 1546, Bale is wrong is saying that the school was begun in 1538. It looks as though one or the other had made the simple error of confusing 1538 and *anno* 38 H. VIII, but which is to blame I cannot say.

Radcliffe's experimental theatre was in many respects not greatly different from the efforts of other grammar schools. The plays

---

suesceret. Plurimas in eius museo uidi ac legi tragoedias & comoedias, epistolas, orationes, congratulationes . . . . Scripsit . . . .

. . . .
De patientia Griselidis, Com. 1
De Melibaeo Chauceriano, Com. 1
De Titi & Gisippi amicitia, Com. 1
De Sodomae incendio, Tra. 1
De Io. Hussi damnatione, Tra. 1
De Ionae defectione, Com. 1
De Lazaro ac diuite, Com. 1
De Iudith fortitudine, Com. 1
De Iobi afflictionibus, Com. 1
De Susannae liberatione, Tra. 1."

[40] *Archæologia*, XVIII, 446-8.

were given once a year, in Latin, and with the purpose of perfecting
the lads in behavior and declamation.[41] Yet certain facts are significant. In the first place, Radcliffe seems actually to have built
a theatre; the words "potissimum vero theatrum, quod in inferiori
aedium parte longe pulcherrimum extruxit" hardly seem to refer
to a temporary stage erected in a chapel or dormitory, as was the
custom at Westminster and elsewhere. The next point of interest
is the fact that the plays were performed before the general public,
the *plebs*; and the third is that although the plays were in Latin the
subjects were in no case classical, but ranged from Hebrew annals
to modern history in a truly catholic and English spirit. But perhaps
the most notable fact of all is that in the decade before the middle
of the century, this schoolmaster had instituted an annual performance of plays in a theatre erected in the precincts of the school,
before a public audience, on subjects of present interest (for so
Biblical themes must be counted), and wrote them himself with so
much success that Bale was impressed. This undertaking possesses
a striking quality of purpose and solidity.

Perhaps the most remarkable dramatic enterprise of all was
carried on at Shrewsbury. There from a very early period it was
customary to celebrate Whitsuntide by the performance of a
mystery or a morality in certain grounds adjoining the Severn,
known locally as "the Quarry." Previous to the foundation of the
grammar school in February of 1552, the plays were doubtless given
by the townsmen, but thereafter they seem to have passed into the
hands of the scholars. I say "seem" because the evidence for it is
only circumstantial, and depends upon· the fact that Thomas
Ashton, the first headmaster, was strongly addicted to play-giving
and wrote and managed the Whitsuntide plays during his tenure
of office. The implication is that his pupils were the actors, and
Mr. Fisher, the historian of the school, takes it for granted that
they were.[42] The inference is stronger by the fact that Ashton left
a regulation that on every Thursday the highest form should "de-
claim and play one Act of a Comedy."

These Shrewsbury Whitsun plays were famous in the land,
especially under the guidance of Ashton. The writer of a MS.

---

[41] Sir James Whitelocke, who attended the Merchant Taylors school in the
1580's, wrote that Mulcaster presented plays to teach his boys "good behaviour
and audacitye." *Vide Liber Famelicus of Sir J. W.*, ed. John Bruce for the Camden Soc., 1858, p. 12.

[42] G. W. Fisher, *Annals of Shrewsbury School*, p. 17.

chronicle[43] says that "a notable stage playe (was) played in Shros-
berie in a place called the Quarrell," and that "the chyffe auther
therof was one master Aston, beinge the head schoolemaster of
the free schoole there a godly and lernyd man who tooke marvelous
greate paynes therein." He informs us that the plays "lastid all
the hollydayes" and were attended by "great nomber of people
of noblemen and others." In 1566 Elizabeth was drawn by the fame
of Ashton's plays toward Shrewsbury, and progressed as far as
Coventry, but was too late to reach Shrewsbury in time. The play
on this occasion was *Julian the Apostate*.[44] In 1569 the Corporation
of Shrewsbury voted £10 for the maintenance of the Whitsun plays
over and above such sums as might be levied by the occupations
of the town or raised by private subscription, and in further token
of their generosity pledged themselves to pay any deficit which
Ashton might declare.[45] This was a signal mark of confidence and
an indication of how greatly the plays were esteemed. The generosity
of the Corporation was justified, for in this year Ashton produced
his "great play" on the *Passion of Christ*.

The plays, as the two titles we possess show and as the conditions
of their performance would demand, were religious in theme, and
most certainly they were given in English, or else they would not
have drawn the crowds they did. A most interesting circumstance
about them is that they were played in a permanent theatre, built
in the Quarry, or Quarrell, near the river; not a theatre like the
memorable one at Shoreditch, but a kind of amphitheatre of classic
model. The Quarrell, now a smooth and verdant lawn, was then
really the quarry from which its name has come, and doubtless
by its natural conformation lent itself to arrangement. Mr. Fisher
assures us that traces of the old structure are still to be seen. Thomas
Churchyard, among the manifold things which busied his pen,
found time to commemorate the theatre at Shrewsbury.

> "There is a ground new made theator wyse
> Both deepe ana hye in goodlie auncient guise:
> Where well may sit ten thousand men at ease,
> And yet the one the other not displease.
>
> .   .   .   .

---

[43] Fisher, *op. cit.*, p. 18. The document is known as the *Taylor MS*.
[44] Fisher, p. 18. Fisher cites Owen's *Arms of the Bailiffs*.
[45] Fisher, p. 19.

A grounde most apt, and they that sit above
At once in vewe all this may see for love;
At Ashton's playe, who hadde behelde thys then
Might well have seen there twentie thousand men."[46]

While Churchyard is more interested in metrical fluency than numerical accuracy, it is nevertheless certain that the amphitheatre was large and would accommodate several thousand spectators. We should be glad to know more about an edifice which anticipated by many years the first permanent theatres of London.

Again we find grammar school boys engaged in an interprise of bigness and importance, this time the central figures in a yearly festival of religious plays given in a permanent theatre of large capacity, financed by public and private donations, attended by great numbers of people, and so famous throughout the country that the queen undertook a special progress to see one of them. In the first half or two-thirds of the sixteenth century, grammar school boys were clearly predominant in play-acting outside London. All the truly significant performances came from them, and on one or two occasions, as we have seen, they even invaded the court. By 1570, however, these school players had shot their bolt, and from then on they appeared less and less in the chronicles of the times, while the two chorister-companies of St. Paul's and the Chapel Royal were springing into great prominence in London and were drawing to their use the talents of some of the most respected writers of their day.

2. *The Boy Bishop.*

No discussion of the relations of children to drama in the six-teenth century would be complete without at least a reference to the ceremony of the Boy Bishop. This curious form of pageantry has been frequently written about. The best account of it so far as England is concerned remains an article in *The Fortnightly Review* by A. F. Leach;[47] Chambers's résumé in *The Medieval Stage* is full of facts and bibliographical material; Gregory's old essay[48] still furnishes the most colorful and interesting reading. It is not my purpose here to go deeply into the history of the Boy Bishop, which

[46] Thos. Churchyard, *The Worthines of Wales*, 1587; in *Pub. of the Spenser Soc.*, No. 20, 1876, p. 85. Quoted in Fisher, p. 17.

[47] A.F. Leach, "The Schoolboys' Feast," in *Fortnightly Review*, Jan., 1896, p. 128.

[48] John Gregory, *Episcopus Puerorum in Die Innocentium*, in *Works*, 1665, II, 93 ff.

yet awaits definitive treatment, but simply to emphasize the essentially dramatic nature of the ceremonies which attended the celebration of this feast.[49]

One should first of all bear in mind how prevalent and how full of vitality this custom was. "It is certain," says Mr. Leach, "that the Boy Bishop was almost universal, not only in every cathedral and collegiate church, and wherever there was a school, but, in later times at least, in every parish church where there was a sufficient band of choristers to furnish forth the Boy Bishop's ceremonial." My own researches into the accounts of monasteries and churches have shown me that hardly a corner of ecclesiastical England was free from St. Nicholas's Bishop. He was in full force at Paul's,[50] was at least known in the Chapel Royal,[51] was a familiar figure at Eton,[52] Westminster,[53] Winchester,[54] Salisbury and York,[55] and hosts of less important places.[56] There is ample evidence, according to Leach, that by the first half of the sixteenth century (when the custom was at its height) every parish church in London had its Boy Bishop. In 1542 the ceremonies of St. Nicholas's Day

[49] The student who is interested in the subject of the Boy Bishop in England will find material in all these volumes: Brand's *Popular Antiquities*; Hone's *Ancient Mysteries*; Chambers's *Medieval Stage*; Rimbault's introduction to his edition of *Two Sermons preached by the Boy Bishop*, in *Camden Miscellany*, Vol. VII; Warton, *Hist. of Eng. Poetry* (ed. Hazlitt, II, 228-32, IV, 237); John Gregory, *op cit., supra*; Strutt, *Sports and Pastimes*; J. P. Malcolm, *Londinium Redivivum* (1803, III, 140); Sparrow-Simpson, *Chapters in the History of Old St. Paul's*, and *St. Paul's Cathedral and Old City Life*; Hawkins, *Hist. of Music* (II, 5); Wm. Dodsworth, *Hist. of the See and Cathedral of Salisbury*; Strype, *Eccles. Memorials* (ed. 1721, III, 202, 205-6, 387); *Durham Abbey Account Rolls*, ed. J. T. Fowler for the Surtees Soc. (Introd. and *passim*); Raines, *Hist. of Durham*.

In *Archæologia*, references to the Boy Bishop will be found in the following volumes: VII, 416; IX, 39, 43; XXVI, 342; XLIII, 244; XLV, 115; L, Pt. II, 446-7, 448, 472-3, 480; LII, Pt. I, 200, 209; LIII, Pt. I, 25, 50.

Archæologia, LXII, Pt. I, pp. 214, 218, 227 contains various statutes and evidences relating to the ceremony at St. Paul's.

[50] For the section of the Statutes relating to the Boy Bishop, *vide* A. F. Leach, "St. Paul's School before Colet," in *Archæologia*, LXII, Pt. I, 1910, p. 218.

[51] Cf. *Privy Purse of Queen Elizabeth of York*, p. 76; Dec. 1502: "Itm to the Bisshop of the Kinges Chappelle on Saint Nicholas even at Westminster xls." There are other notices in the Books of King's Payments.

[52] Maxwell-Lyte, *Eton College*, p. 156.

[53] *Archæologia*, LII, Pt. I, pp. 200, 209.

[54] Kirby, *Annals of Winchester*, p. 90.

[55] Chambers's *Medieval Stage*, II, 287, reprints the Sarum Office and the York *Computus*.

[56] They have never been even approximately listed. The *Med. Stage*, I, 358, gives a number of such places.

and kindred feasts were put down by edict,[57] to be revived for a short space under Mary. In the period just previous to the suppression the Boy Bishop seems to have flourished with especial vigor.

The remarkable prevalence of the ceremony has, I think, great significance, especially when we remember that it was popular not only with the boys who participated but also with the people. The statutes regulating the ceremony at St. Paul's in 1263, for instance, relate that it had been turned from its solemn purpose to a disgrace to the house of God "because of the insolence of the disorderly multitude following (the Bishop)."[58] In 1319 at Salisbury a statute was passed warning the people on pain of excommunication not to throng upon the procession and disturb it.[59] The pleasure which the young performers had in their feast is easily comprehended when we recollect that out of the whole school year—whether it were a grammar or a choir school—this was the only holiday the boys had, and it must have come as a blessed respite. The processions and ceremonies which attended the installation of the youthful pontiff, as well as the games and plays which were often concomitants, were what attracted the crowd. We find, in short, a great ceremony flourishing through the middle ages[60] down to the middle of the sixteenth century, in which the actors and directors were choir boys, which existed in all parts of the kingdom, and which so delighted the people that restraining orders had to be issued to hold in the enthusiasm of the mob.

Let us review briefly the conduct of this popular celebration. On St. Nicholas's Day (Dec. 6) the Bishop was elected by his fellows. Leach says that he did not officiate until Innocents' Day (Dec. 28), but there seems to be some doubt about that. Gregory,[61] for instance, tells us that "from this day (St. Nicholas's) till Innocents' Day at night . . . . the *Episcopus Puerorum* was to bear the name and hold up the state of a *Bishop*, answerably habited with a Crosier or *Pastoral-staff*, and a Mitre upon his head." But certainly no important ceremonies were entered upon until In-

---

[57] Wilkins's *Concilia*, III, 864.

[58] Leach, *Archæologia*, LXII, Pt. I, p. 218.

[59] Leach, *Fortn. Rev.*, LXV, 136.

[60] The beginnings are shrouded in mystery; that the custom was well developed by 1263 is shown in the statutes of St. Paul's.

[61] *Works*, 1665, II, 113.

nocents' Eve, Dec. 27. As the chosen chorister or school boy became Bishop, so his fellows were elevated to the ranks of prebends
and canons, and officiated duly in these capacities. From vespers
of Innocents' Eve until vespers of the following day, the children
assumed complete control over the church. They went in solemn
procession, with the usual order of precedence reversed, for now
the canons went first and the boys with their Bishop brought up
the rear. At St. Paul's previous to 1263, the adult dignitaries of
the church had been accustomed to act as candle-holders and
incense-bearers, that is, to assume the duties ordinarily fulfilled
by the acolytes and clerks, but by the ordinance of 1263 this was
done away with, and the boys were ordered to elect certain from
among their number for these offices. Forming in solemn procession,
and in the order explained above, the men and boys marched (according to the Use of Sarum, the most detailed of any that have
come down to us) to the altar of the Trinity and All Saints, chanting
the *Centum quadraginta quatuor* and *Hi empti sunt ex omnibus.*
Then while the boys sang *Sedentem in supernae majestatis arce,*
the Bishop censed the altar and afterwards the image of the Holy
Trinity. After the *Laetamini* and a short prayer, the return from
the altar was begun, to the accompaniment of *De Sancta Maria.*
The procession entered the Choir from the west door and seated
itself in such a way that the dean and canons occupied the lowest
places, the chaplains the next, and the Bishop and his fellows the
topmost rounds. Leach says that the manner of installing the Boy
Bishop in certain places had much of the picturesque; for at the
words in the *Magnificat* "He shall put down the mighty from their
seat," the bishop or dean or abbot (as the case might be) left his
seat and came down to a lower position in the Choir, while the boy
took his place. And from this moment until the end of the following
day *nullus clericorum solet gradum superiorem ascendere, cujuscumque
conditionis fuerit.* When the seats had been taken, the Bishop said
the verse *Speciosus forma* ("Thou art beautiful beyond the sons
of men"[62]); then came the *Benedicamus Domino,* and the Bishop
blessed the people according to a particular form.

Thus ended the pageantry for Innocents' Eve. A supper followed,
and the Bishop had the liberty of choosing (at St. Paul's at least)

[62] This verse made it necessary for the York statutes to require that the boy
elected Bishop should be "sufficiently good-looking." (Leath, *Fortnightly Review,*
LXV, 133.)

with which of the canons he should dine. On Innocents' Day all
the services, even including at many places the celebration of the
Mass, were performed by the Bishop. He preached a sermon, of
which two specimens have come down to us, very moral and very
dull.[63] After dinner the Bishop and his staff marched through the
city, levying contributions from the people. It does not appear,
however, that the progress was made with the dignity which should
belong to an ecclesiastical function. In Hall's *Triumphs of Rome*,[64]
these processions are thus spoken of: "What merry work it was
here in the days of our holy fathers (and I know not whether in
some places it may not be so still), that upon St. Nicholas, St.
Katherine, St. Clement, and Holy Innocents' Day, children were
wont to be arrayed in chimers, rochets, surplices, to counterfeit
Bishops and Priests, and to be led, with songs and dances, from
house to house, blessing the people, who stood girning in the way
to expect that ridiculous benediction." The writer apparently had
Henry VIII's act of suppression[65] in mind (he refers to it a few lines
after), which inveighs against "the superstitions & Chyldyshe
observations used vpon St Nicholas, St Catherine, St Clement, the
Holy Innocents, & such like, wherein Chyldren be strangelye decked
& apparelled to counterfeet Preists, Byshoppes & women, & so
ledde with songes & dances from House to House, blessing the
people, & gatheringe of money, & Boyes to singe masse & preache
in the Pulpit—rather to the derysyon, then to any true Glorye
of God." There seems always to have lingered about the Boy
Bishop a taint of the extravagances of the Feast of Fools, from which
the children's feast most probably descended. Thus we know that in
1441 at St. Swithin's monastery, Winchester, the boys of the
Almonry, together with the boys of the Chapel of St. Elizabeth,
dressed themselves like girls, dancing, singing, and performing plays
before the Abbess and the nuns of St. Mary's Abbey on the Feast
of Innocents.[66] On the continent the revels of Childermas Day
usually included the performance of stage-plays, and doubtless the
same custom obtained in England.

On the evening of Innocents' Day, the solemn procession, service,
and dinner of the preceding day were repeated. Then in some

[63] They are printed in the *Camden Miscellany*, Vol. VII.
[64] Quoted in Brand, *Popular Antiquities* (ed. Hazlitt, 1870), I, 234.
[65] In Wilkins's *Concilia*, III, 864.
[66] Leach, *Fortn. Rev.*, LXV, 139.

places came what must have delighted the heart of the young pontiff, for during the next fortnight he went the rounds of episcopal visitations, levying contributions from all parts of his diocese. A York *Computus* of 1396 gives a detailed account of the expenses and receipts incident to the visitation in that year.[67] The Bishop's train consisted of a tenor singer, a "middle voice" singer, a steward, and two or three attendants; all were mounted. They visited in turn the important abbeys and priories and the houses of the gentry, and did not disdain to accept the smaller contributions of more humble folk. The account shows that in this case the authority of the Bishop extended for over a month after Innocents' Day, for it is stated that "on the fifth Sunday and to the end of the Purification (Feb. 2)" he received nothing.

Such, then, was the festival *in die Innocentium*. Much in condemnation and in praise has been written about it, of which the greater part has been idle. Not even Leach, it seems to me, has appreciated the dual nature of the ceremonies and revels which took place. Antiquarians have been continually puzzled by the contradictions in point of view which existed in the minds of contemporaries; have been hard put to it, for example, to reconcile the praise bestowed on the custom by Dean Colet when he inserted a clause in the statutes for St. Paul's School directing that the scholars attend the sermon of the Boy Bishop and contribute each a penny, with the unqualified condemnation expressed by the proclamation of Henry VIII. The fact is that there were two sides to the festival; there were the solemn processions, services, and sermons in the church, and there were the saturnalian progresses through the town, when the Bishop and his train, dressed like women and priests, went singing and dancing from door to door, and the decorum of the cathedral ceremony gave place to unrestrained license. The processions about town, and the accompanying shows and games, were doubtless often scandalous to serious-minded people; at them were aimed the edict of Henry VIII and the numerous decrees promulgated on the continent. The sermons and services within the church were conceived in religious respect and religiously performed; it was these which won the respect of men like Colet and enabled the Church to tolerate the festival so generally and so long. Perhaps, as would be natural, the saturnalia came to overtop

---

[67] Printed in Chambers's *Medieval Stage*, II, 287, and in *Camden Miscellany*, VII, p. xi ff. According to Gregory visitations were also held at Salisbury.

the religious ceremonials, just as the secular element in the miracle plays crowded out the Biblical history. The statute of St. Paul's tells us in its preamble that the office of the Boy Bishop was established in honor of the Holy Innocents who shed their blood for Christ the Innocent, so that in this way a child might be exalted over children and an innocent rule over the innocent; but that what had been invented for the praise of sucklings had been converted to the derision of the decorum of the House of God, because of the insolence of the unruly mob which delighted in it.[68]

We should not fail to perceive the essentially dramatic nature of the ceremonies which belonged to the office of the Boy Bishop, especially of those which were performed in church. The whole affair was a glorified masquerade. With those elements of drama which exist in the assumption of disguises, in the recitation of prepared parts, in the serious pretence of being something which one is not, in losing for a time one's identity in that of a quite different person—with all these things the ceremony was replete. It was again the spirit of drama revivifying religion. This ceremony was no mummery or mere game, except in the extra-cathedral revels which attended it, but a widely popular custom, with many honorable traditions. And we should not forget that it *was* popular in the broadest sense of the word.

Again we find children playing a leading role in a really dramatic ceremonial, entertaining the three estates[69] equally, and meeting with the enthusiastic support of the people in all parts of the country.

3. *Children in Pageants.*

One mode of dramatic activity remains to consider, about which least has been written. I mean the part taken by children in the various shows and pageants with which the hospitable Englishmen of the 16th century welcomed their own and visiting sovereigns. No one, it is true, can have read much in the literature of these pageants and not have discovered that children were frequently used, but it is not understood how general was this use. True it is,

---

[68] *Vide* Leach, *Archæologia*, LXII Pt. I, p. 218.

[69] *Vide* the *Wardrobe Account of 28 Ed. I*, pub by the Soc. of Antiquaries, p. 25: "Septimo die Decembris cuidem episcopo puerorum dicenti vesperis de Sancto Nicholao coram Rege in capella sua apud Heton juxta Novum Castrum super Tynam, et quibusdam pueris venientibus et cantantibus cum episcopo predicto de elemosina ipsius Regis per manus Domini Henrici Elemosinar(ii) participantis inter pueros predictos" 40s.
The old Household books of noblemen and kings are full of payments to Boy Bishops.

nevertheless, that in these popular and often elaborate devices the
service of boys was felt to be not merely desirable or appropriate,
but even necessary.

We need not go deeply into the history of pageantry in England,[70]
nor into the nature and construction of pageants. Everyone knows
that at prominent places about London—at Fenchurch, Leadenhall,
St. Paul's, and the conduits in Cheap, Fleet Street, Cornhill, and
elsewhere—stages were erected and lavishly adorned, whereon were
arranged various groups of people in symbolical costumes, so that
the device represented some idea or story flattering to the nob e
visitor; and that usually each pageant was provided with persons
to salute the guest with an oration or a song. The actors who sat
in disguise upon the stage were often boys (rarely girls); the orators
were almost invariably boys. Sometimes the pageant bore only
singers and musicians, and here the boys of choirs were useful for
their double skill in song and instrumental playing. One might
divide the functions of boys in pageants into these three groups:
(1) musicians, singers, and players; (2) silent participants in costume;
(3) expositors (of the meaning of the pageant) or orators. With the
boys were usually, though not always, grown men; yet I have never
found, except in some cases after 1600 when professional actors were
frequently used, that men played nearly so important a part as
boys. We shall see better what these pageants were and what the
function of the boys, as we consider them more in detail.

The first beginnings of children in pageants are shrouded in
darkness. Certainly they date as early as 1487-8. At the coronation
of Elizabeth, wife of Henry VII, in the third year of his reign, "in
dyvers parts of the Citie were ordeynede wele singing Childerne.
Some arrayde like Angells, and others like Vyrgyns, to sing swete
Songes as hir Grace passed by."[71] I suspect that it was the skill
of choir boys in song, and the delightful effect of concerted singing
by boys in the open air, that first drew them into pageantry. Children were the preferred musicians, but not always the only ones.
At the reception of the Emperor Charles by Henry VIII in 1522
galleries were built at the Great Conduit in Cheap, and there "sat
children mixed with men and women singing and playing on instruments melodiously."[72] There also a welcoming address in Latin

[70] The subject has been exhaustively studied by Robert Withington, *English
Pageantry, an Historical Outline*, 2 vols., Harvard Univ. Press, 1918-20.

[71] Leland, *Collectanea*, 1770, IV, 220.

[72] Hall, *Chronicle*, reprint of 1809, 639.

meter was said by one of the children. The question, here as elsewhere, of the identity of the boys arises. We are told in some cases
that they were choir boys, and it is safe to assume that they were
such in most cases, especially when there was music. But the pageant
at St. Paul's School was always occupied by the scholars there, one
of whom delivered the Latin oration; and in other places in the city
schoolboys (of Christ's Hospital or Westminster, for example) were
the orators.

At the coronation of Anne Boleyn, the pageants were elaborate,
with their decorations and symbolical arrangement and garbing of
actors. At Fenchurch was a "pageaunt all with children apparelled
like marchauntes, whiche welcommed her to the Citie with two proper
preposicions in Frenche & Englishe."[73] She passed on to Leadenhall, "where was a goodly pageant with a type and a heauenly
roffe, ... and in the same pageant satte Saint Anne with all her
issue beneath her, and under Mari Cleoph satte her iiii children,
of the whyche children one made a goodly Oracion to the quene of
the fruitfulness of Saint Anne and of her generacion, trustyng that
like fruyte should come of her." At the east end of Paul's church-
yard, against the school, she found a scaffold, and thereon two hundred children "well apparelled," who recited "divers goodly verses
of Poetes translated into Englishe"; and on the leads of St. Martin's
church stood a choir of men and children, who sang new ballads
made in her praise.[74]

Children played an important part in the coronation ceremonies
of Edward VI, with particular appropriateness on this occasion
because the prince was also a child. At the Great Conduit in Fleet
was erected a stage "whereon sat a Childe in very riche Apparell,
which represented Truth, and was accompanied with two other
children before him in Red, representing Faith and Justice, whose
names were before him written in their Places."[75] Truth delivered
the oration. "Towards Cheap" six children saluted the king with
"divers goodly songs" and played upon their regals;[76] and at the
conduit in Cornhill, where there were various kinds of music and
singing, two boys, richly apparelled, pronounced two addresses.[77]
At the Great Conduit in Cheap was another elaborate pageant:

[73] Hall, *op. cit.*, 801.
[74] Hall, *op. cit.*, 802.
[75] Leland, *Collectanea*, IV, 321.
[76] *Same*, 318.
[77] *Same*, 313.

"nigh unto the same Fountaine did stand foure Children very richly adorned, representing Grace, Nature, Fortune, and Charity, who, the one after the other, pronounced these speeches following. .... At a certain Distance from thence .... stood eight richly apparelled other like Ladyes, representing Sapience, and the seven Liberal Sciences, which declared certaine goodly speeches."[78] At another place there was a double scaffold, an upper and a lower; on the nether one was a sumptuous throne "whereupon satt a Childe apparelled with rich Cloath of Gold, with a Robe of crymson Satten, representing the King's Majesty. The which Throne was upholden with foure other Children one representing

> Regallity having a Regall in his hand,
> Justice drawing a Sword,
> Truth having a Book
> Mercy having a little Curtain,

who speak these Speeches or Words following."[79]

Nor were children less in evidence at the entry of Elizabeth for her coronation. At the pageant near Fenchurch, which was given up to music, she was received by a lad richly dressed who welcomed her in behalf of the city with verses.[80] At the upper end of Gracious Street was a tableau representing Henry VIII, Anne Boleyn, and Elizabeth, all on different stages, in the manner of a genealogical tree—a favorite device on these occasions. "Thys Pageant nowe agaynste the Quenes Majesties comming was addressed with children representing the forenamed personages"; and a child, standing on a platform at the front, expounded the meaning to the queen as she paused before him.[81] "Against" the end of Soper Lane a pageant was built from one side of the street to the other, with three gates in it, all open. Over the middlemost were erected three stages with eight children seated thereon, one at the top, three in the middle, and four at the bottom. On a table above the head of each was written the blessing which he represented. As in the preceding pageant, a stand was built to the front, whereon a boy stood and expounded the sense of it all to the queen. "Everie one of these children was appointed and apparelled according to the blessing

---

[78] *Same*, 314-15.
[79] *Same*, 317.
[80] J. G. Nichols, *Progresses of Queen Elizabeth*, 1823, I, 39.
[81] *Same*, 41.

which he did represent. And on the forepart of the sayde Pageant
was written, in fayre letters, the name of the said Pageant in this
maner following: The eight Beatitudes expressed in the v chapter
of the Gospel of St. Matthew, applyed to our Soveraigne Lady
Quene Elizabeth."[82] Other pageants in which children served were
these: a pageant of Time, in which one character at least, Truth,
was a child, and which was expounded by a child; a pageant of
Deborah and her Estates, expounded by a child; one at Paul's
School, where one of Colet's boys pronounced a Latin oration; one
at St. Dunstan's church, where the children of Christ's Hospital
stood with their governors, and one delivered an oration; one other
given up to a "noyse of singing children," where a boy richly garbed
as a poet said farewell to the queen in the name of the city, just as
a child at the opposite end of the town had welcomed her.[83] In the
whole tract from which these descriptions are drawn, there is no
pageant mentioned which did not have at least one child in it.
In many cases the age of the actors is not told, and we therefore
have the right to suppose that many more children were used than
are actually described.[84]

It seems that girls were occasionally admitted to pageants. When
the queen was received at Norwich in 1575, there was arranged a
stage whereon stood "eyght small women chyldren spinning worsted
yarne, and at the other side as many knittyng of worsted yarne
hose; and in the midst of the stage stood a pretie boy richly apparelled, which represented the Commonwealth of the Citie. And
all the reste of the stage was furnished with men whiche made the
sayde severall workes . . . . and when she did come, the childe
which represented Commonwelth did speak to her Highnesse."[85]

If we have yet any doubt as to whether boys were the accessories of pageants or the necessaries, we are reassured by that

[82] *Same*, 46.

[83] *Same*, I, 48-56.

[84] The City took great pains in the preparation of the pageants for this coronation. The various stages were put in the charge of particular persons, with instructions to see that they were "very well and semely trymmed & deckyd for the
honour of the Cyty agyanste the commynge of our Soueraigne Lady the Quenes
Maiesty that nowe is to her Coronacion thoroughe the Cyty with pageauntes
fyne payntynge and Riche clothes of arras syluer and golde in suche and lyke manner & sorte as they were trymmed agaynst the commyng of our late Soueraigne
lady Quene Mary to her Coronacion and moche better if it convenyently may be
done." *Repertories of the Court of Common Council*, XIV, fol. 97-8.

[85] Nichols, II, 144.

industrious and capable deviser of *al fresco* revels, Thomas Church-
yard. In one of his multitudinous tracts, in which we are given an
account of the queen's entertainment in Norfolk and Suffolk,[86]
he gossips at length on the difficulties which he endured in preparing
his shows. He went down to Norwich three weeks ahead of the
court; yet when the queen arrived in the neighborhood he was not
well supplied either with men or shows. Nevertheless, determining
upon an impromptu entertainment, as he puts it himself, "I hastily
prepared my boyes and men, with all their furniture, and so sette
forward." "My boyes and men," he says, as one who speaks of his
usual equipment of helpers; his boys were as much a part of his
preparation as his men. Going further into this account we learn
that two shows of Water Nymphs and "Manhood and Dezarte"
were made ready, the first for boys and the other for men and boys,
but had to be given up on account of rain.

When noble or princely visitors came to the grammar schools,
they were usually entertained by learned orations in Latin and by
plays. But sometimes masquings and disguisings were indulged in
pageant-wise. Thus when Sir Henry Sidney visited Shrewsbury
school in 1581, the scholars delivered their addresses in the guise
of ñymphs.[87]

The function of boys in the pageants at court hardly belongs
to the present discussion. Yet it may not be amiss to note in passing
that in the brilliant tourney-pageants with which Elizabeth entertained the French ambassadors in Whitsun week of 1581, when the
"Four Foster Children of Desire" and the "Fortress of Beauty"
drew the admiration of the visitors, pages played a not inconspicious
part. The summons to the surrender of the Castle and the call to
attack of the Foster Children were sung by boys; and it is noteworthy that *all* the speeches occurring in the pageants were delivered
by pages.[88]

In the reign of James I, pageants flourished more vigorously
than ever before. In addition to the occasional reception of royalty,
there were the yearly Lord Mayor's shows. For the allegorical

[86] *A Discourse of the Queenes Majesties Entertainment in Suffolk and Norfolk. . . . .
Devised by Thomas Churchyarde, Gent. with divers shewes of his own invention, sette
out at Norwiche,* etc. Reprinted in Nichols, II, 179 ff.

[87] Nichols, II, 307.

[88] *Vide* Henry Goldwell's *Briefe Declaration of the Shews. . . . done and performed
before the Queene's Majestie and the French Ambassadours. . . . the Munday and
Tuesday in Whitsun Weeke last, Anno 1581,* in Nichols, II, 310 ff.

personages therein actors came to be used more and more, yet
they did not by any means oust the children. It is not my intention
to delve into this period of history, because it is too late for our
purposes. We have reviewed the part which children played in the
pageants of the sixteenth century so that it might be clear how close
were the bonds between children and the stage and how easy was
the passage of children from frequent acting in an informal and
semi-dramatic way to organized acting on a commercial scale. But
by 1603 this passage had been made completely, and commercial
child-companies had been long familiar to London, so that there is
no illustrative value in pursuing the history of pageants further.
Yet because the revels attending the entry of James I into London
are interesting in themselves, and because they show that boys were
still the necessary servants of these devices, I shall summarize
briefly the pageants then used.[89]

Fenchurch pageant, usually the first met by the visitor and
hence always an important one, represented a large gate bearing
houses on it and various allegorical persons, mutes and speakers,
such as Britain Monarchy, Divine Wisdom, the Genius of the City,
the River Thamesis, Gladness, Veneration, etc. Only Genius and
Thamesis were speakers, of whom the first was played by Edward
Alleyn, the actor, and the second by a boy of the company of the
Queen's Revels. Alleyn delivered the gratulatory speech "with
excellent Action, and a well tun'de voyce." The speeches of this
pageant, and also of those in the Strand and at the Temple Bar,
were composed by Ben Jonson, and indeed the whole contrivance of
them is laid to his credit.

The Queen's Revels was not the only boys' company honored with
a part in the pageantry. At Soper Lane the pageant was explained
by a person representing Circumspection, who was one of the
choristers belonging to Paul's. At the close of his speech a song accompanied by violins "and an other rare Artificiall Instrument
wherein besides sundry severall soundes effus'd, (all at one time)

[89] Good descriptions of the pageants with citations of the speeches are given in
these two tracts:

*The Whole Magnifycent Entertainment: Given to King James, Queen Anne his
wife, and Henry Frederick the Prince* . . . . *the 15. of March. 1603* . . . . Tho. Dekker
. . . . *1604*; reprinted in Somers's *Tracts* (ed. W. Scott, 1810), II, pp. 3. ff.

B. Jon. His Part of King James his Royal and Magnificent Entertainement
through his Honorable Cittie of London, Thursday the 15. of March. 1603. . . . . Printed
at London by V. S. for Edward Blount, 1604.

were also sensibly distinguisht the chirping of Birdes" was sung "by two Boyes (Choristers of *Paules*) deliuered in sweete and rauishing voyces." At the Little Conduit the King was taken by Sylvanus into the Garden of Hesperides, very beautifully built, where "a sweet pleasure likewise courted his eare in the shape of Musicke, sent from the voyces of nine Boyes (all of them Queristers of Pauls) who in that place presenting the nine Muses, sang the Dittie following to their Violles and other Instruments." At Paul's an anthem was sung "by the Quiristers," and a Latin oration given "by one of maister Mulcasters Schollers, at the dore of the free-schole founded by the Mercers." The choristers of Paul's are seen to have had a predominant part among the children of these pageants, if the chronicler is to be trusted. He cannot be accepted entirely, since the choir, which numbered then not more than twelve, could not possibly have filled all the places he has given them. But it is certain that Paul's did play an important part in pageants such as these.

From these various examples, extending from 1487 to 1603, the reader will easily see how general was the use of children in public pageants. I have said that they were actually necessary, and I have spoken advisedly. Anthony Munday, in his *Camp-Bell, or the Iron-mongers Faire Feild*,[90] prefaces his account with an apology for the haste with which the pageant was made ready, and an explanation of why he used the device of having Saints George and Andrew explain the pageants. "And the rather," says he, "haue we yeelded to this kinde of deliuery because our time for preparation hath bene so short, as neuer was the like vndertaken by any before, nor matter of such moment so expeditiously performed. Besides, the weak voyces of so many Children, which such shewes as this doe vrgently require, for personating each deuise, in a crowde of such noyse and vnciuill turmoyle, are not any way able to be vnderstood, neither their capacities to reach the full height of euery intention, in so short a limitation for study, practice, and instruction." This explanation shows conclusively that there were reasons why children were particularly suitable to pageants of this nature. Can we inter-pret them from the bare facts we possess?

In the first place, as I have hinted, the musical character of so many of the pageants made demands which choir boys, from whom

---

[90] A pageant for the installation of Sir Thos. Campbell as Lord Mayor on Oct. 29, 1609. Pub. 1609.

most of the actors were drafted, could satisfy admirably, for they were well taught in part singing and in playing on musical instruments. In this way they were useful just as we shall find the Chapel boys useful at the beginning in court masques. The Chapel youngsters began by filling supernumerary parts, in which they sang or were silent; there seems also to be evidence that children in public pageants began in the same way. Then the education of the choristers may have had something to do with it, for the parts they were required to play demanded in many cases a knowledge of Latin or French, powers of elocution, a pleasing and cultivated voice, and a graceful and contained demeanor. In those days there was not a large class of men who possessed these advantages. The sons of gentlemen could have done these things; but they would not, and where else could one go for suitable material except to the not over-abundant class of university and grammar school men? They were not always to be had when the need arose, but in the choristers of the big churches, like St. Paul's, and in the scholars of grammar schools there was a constant body of intelligent youth, perfectly able to carry off their parts and always at hand.

There was still another cause, which I think was more potent than any. As we have seen, the pageants were frequently built in the form of tiers or stages, especially when it was desired to represent an ancestral tree, and these stages were in all likelihood none too substantial. The greatly less weight of a group of children must have counted materially. In a similar way, I have supposed that the Chapel boys came into favor in court pageants partly because they could ride securely on the tops of the devices (on the battlements of castles, in many instances) where adults would endanger stability. Then, too, the size of the children may have had some influence, for they would not crowd a pageant and would be more in proportion to the scale of the construction, whereas men would seem hulking and unwieldy.

Thus far we have been busied with establishing the fact that acting by children was prevalent in England and of ancient origin, but we have not yet adequately accounted for that prevalence. How is it that a practice so strange to our modern taste flourished for several centuries? Are we to lay it to the uncritical taste of a primitive age? Or must we suppose that acting by children is a lost art, like Venetian glass making? How did the people look on these performers? Were they tolerated as a harmless frivolity, or did they enter more deeply into the life of their communities?

To account for children in pageants is easy enough, as we have seen. Likewise no mystery hangs about the plays of grammar school children. They were part of the curriculum; their performance gave practice in speaking the Latin tongue and cultivated an easy, assured bearing. Therefore, at many schools, like Eton and Westminster, such performances were established by statute, so strong was the approval of pedagogical theory. That is all clear enough. But what about the public performances of these and other children? What of Ralph Radcliffe's theatre at Hitchen, and the great amphitheatre at Shrewsbury? What of the constant visits of choir and school companies to neighboring towns and to the houses of nobility?

Before attempting to answer these questions, we must wholly clear from our minds any idea that acting by children was faddish or exotic. It became exotic before the closing of the theatres, and the "nursery" which was maintained for a time under the Restoration, as a training school for actors, while it may have had value for that purpose, was as a producing company only a passing fancy. Even more exotic was the child who, for a time early in the last century, astonished London as "Master Betty, the Young Roscius." To be sure, he was taken quite seriously; people crowded to hear him, standing in line from early morning as they do to hear a great singer, and Parliament adjourned to see him play Hamlet. But his vogue was brief, because it was built merely on curiosity. Poor Master Betty—he flourished for his nine days of wonder, and then vanished. He was the last of his line.

But in the days of great Elizabeth, things were different. Her two favorite court playwrights of the earlier years—Richard Edwards and John Lyly—devoted their talents to children. In 1566, on a visit to Oxford where she was entertained by Edwards's *Palemon and Arcite*, she was so delighted with the lad who played Emilia that she called him to her, praised his singing and acting, and gave him £4.[91] During her father's reign, William Cornish, Master of Revels, and possibly John Heywood, had likewise written largely for children. And after the turn of the century we hear Ben Jonson sing tenderly and sincerely of Salathiel Pavy, who played old men so truly that death itself was deceived. No, in the sixteenth century

---

[91] See Nichols, *Progresses of Queen Elizabeth*, I, 213.

child actors were not a fad; yet we cannot pretend that it was an unsophisticated age. Nor were they a fad in the ages preceding. Who ever heard of a fad that lived five hundred years?

On the contrary, they were a natural and legitimate part of the primitive English theatre, to the development of which they contributed not a little of importance, as we shall see. But they belonged definitely to the formative stage; when the theatre came to maturity they were forced out. Thus we find them flourishing until the close of the sixteenth century—indeed from the accession of Henry VIII until 1590 the English drama was mainly in their hands. But by 1590 the stage as a profession had ripened to such a point that great actors began to appear, and, from being half outlawed, it grew to be both honorable and profitable; and at that point the children began a rapid decline. Their extinction did not come for a half century later, but one may say that they were doomed when William Burbage drove the first nail into his playhouse in Shoreditch.

They flourished in the middle ages, accordingly, and up to the building of the London theatres because of the dearth of competition, because trained actors were few. Their rivals were bands of strolling minstrels, or minstrels retained in some lord's household, or the untrained members of trade guilds which held the monopolies on certain Biblical pageants—certainly not a formidable rivalry. In those early days when the profession of acting was wholly discreditable and even acting for pleasure was held to be scarce fitting for gentlefolk, there were not many people who had time or inclination for acting. But as grammar schools and choir schools appeared and multiplied, they offered little islands of culture, where, under the guidance of a learned master, youths were trained in speech and bearing, which are Thalia's handmaids. These schools, it seems, must have been fertile ground for histrionic seeds to fall into. Urged on by the general growing curiosity to see plays, and by the dearth of players, these boys began to act. And they must have acted not badly. For, if in point of technical adroitness they were considerably behind the professional strollers, think how well they must have shone beside the lumbering apprentices of some clothworkers' or goldsmiths' guild! They were youths of more than common alertness—they needs must in order to survive the austere grammar school training; they were scholars, hence, in their humble degree, of the elect; and they had almost no holidays. What a lark their play-acting must have been to them! With what zeal they must have thrown themselves into it! How they must have planned months beforehand, and with what furious industry did they rehearse! I dare say they rarely accomplished, even for their uncritical generation, the illusion of being actors in the real sense of the word; their piping voices, for one thing, would always be against them. But they could wear their clothes and strut the stage as bravely as their grown brothers; and there was not much in the drama of the period that was beyond their powers of expression. Undoubtedly they were heard with some indulgence, but for all that the rift between them and the adult players cannot have been so great then as now—cannot indeed have been so great as it was after the turn of the seventeenth century when the Children of the Chapel and of Paul's competed in open market with the company of Burbage and Shakespeare. The boy actor of the fifteenth century, thanks to his training, the simplicity of the medieval drama, and the disrepute of the acting profession, suffered less from his natural handicaps, so that many a man in those days must have been glad to listen to a child.

CHAPTER II

THE CHAPEL ROYAL BEFORE ELIZABETH

Among all the children's companies that which went by the name of "The Children of the Chapel Royal" had the longest and most distinguished history. In recent years their importance has been increasingly perceived, with the result that their doings have become the subject of exhaustive study. Thus Professor Charles William Wallace has published a monograph on *The Children of the Chapel at Blackfriars 1597-1603*[1] and has treated their early history in his *Evolution of the English Drama up to Shakespeare*.[2] Mrs. C. C. Stopes has investigated an important period in her *William Hunnis and the Revels of the Chapel Royal*.[3] Besides these extended monographs, there are shorter treatments of importance; for example, Professor J. M. Manly's chapter on "The Children of the Chapel Royal and their Masters" in the *Cambridge History of English Literature*, Vol. VI, and Mr. E. K. Chambers's chapter on "The Children of the Chapel and of the Queen's Revels" in his monumental history, *The Elizabethan Stage*.[4]

With the ground already so well taken up the new historian must necessarily repeat much that has been said before. Yet he may plead this justification that there is always something more to be said on every subject, and that in this instance there is a good deal to say on account of the fragmentary treatment which the Chapel children have received and the frequent inaccuracies which their historians have committed. My task shall be to give a coherent summary of their activities, avoiding as far as possible, the repetition of such details as have been fully covered elsewhere.

1. *The Constitution of the Chapel Royal.*

All that I have been able to find on matters relating purely to the organization of the Chapel Royal I have published in an article entitled "The Early History of the Chapel Royal,"[5] where besides

---

[1] Published in *Nebraska University Studies*, 1908.
[2] Berlin, 1912.
[3] In Bang's *Materialen zur Kunde* series, Vol. XXIX, 1910.
[4] Oxford University Press, 1923, 4 vols.
[5] In *Modern Philology*, Vol. XVIII, No. 5, September, 1920.

various notices of operation and personnel I printed a hitherto unknown "Register" which supplements curiously the entries of the *Old Cheque Book*.[6] For this reason, and because such details are not of immediate interest to the historian of the stage, I shall give here but a brief sketch of the Chapel organization, only enough for the purpose of background.

History does not record the time when the Royal Household did not have its Chapel. The earliest notices of it date from the reign of Henry I (1100-1135), but not until the reign of Edward IV do we meet with full particulars of its constitution.[7] Then it was composed of a dean, twenty-six chaplains and clerks, two yeomen or "pistelers" (usually appointed from the children when their voices changed), eight children, and a master of grammar. These components, although remaining essentially the same throughout the period with which we are concerned, varied in numbers from time to time. Thus the gentlemen ranged from twenty to thirty-two and the children from eight to twelve. I have never found that there were more than twelve children, and the usual number was ten.

The most important man in the Chapel, from our point of view, was the master of grammar. According to the *Liber Niger* he was to be versed in poetry and the rules of grammar, and had the duty of teaching, besides the children of the Chapel, all the men and boys about the court who might be disposed to learn. Later, as he developed into a producer of stage plays and assistant to the Master of the Revels, his general duties as court schoolmaster lapsed. It appears, although on this point the records are not quite clear, that he boarded and lodged the children. The confusion arises from the fact that in the statutes provision is made for boarding the children with the Household and clothing them from the Wardrobe. Yet the patent to William Newark, who became master in 1493, granted him forty marks annually for the teaching of ten boys and for supplying them with beds and clothing; furthermore, in 1583, when William Hunnis made his plea for restitution of the ancient perquisites of his office, the whole maintenance of the children had devolved upon the master. It is clear, at any rate, that during the

---

[6] Edited by Dr. Rimbault for the Camden Society, New Series, No. 3.

[7] Contained in the *Liber Niger Domus Regis*, a transcript of which, rather badly garbled, may be found in *A Collection of Ordinances and Regulations for the Government of the Royal Household*, printed for the Society of Antiquaries; John Nichols, Lond. 1790.

period of their dramatic activity the children were under the direct government of their masters.

The ranks of the Chapel, since at least as early as Edward IV, were kept full by a device which was afterwards notoriously abused— namely, by impressment from the choirs of other churches. This was an expedient frequently used for obtaining men of almost any kind— artificers, mechanics, musicians—to do work for the crown. It is well to bear in mind that writs of impressment were by no means confined to replenishing the royal chapels, for historians of the stage have frequently overlooked that fact and have drawn unwarrantable inferences from grants to some of the later Chapel masters. The earliest known Chapel writ was issued in 1420, when John Pyamour, clerk, was authorized to take up as many boys as were needed for the Chapel wherever he could find them.[8] In order that certain other favored choirs, like those at St. Paul's, Windsor, and Westminster, might not suffer from the depredations of Chapel masters, exemptions from conscription were often granted these institutions. The earliest of these that has yet been found is dated July 9, 1453, when, at the request of Thomas Lyseux, Dean of St. Paul's, protection was granted to all choristers and ministers of that church, with the assurance that neither the dean of the king's Chapel, nor any officer or minister of the king should take any such chorister or minister for the use and service of the king or other against his will.[9]

The future of children thus forcibly brought into the Chapel Royal was well provided for. The Chapel itself offered a career that might last until death, as numerous entries in the *Old Cheque Book of the Chapel Royal* show. Doubtless many boys remained in the Chapel as gentlemen, or went into other choirs. A few became composers of note. Others found positions at court. And all who did not choose their own careers were paternally sent to Oxford and Cambridge, where they were lodged in colleges of the king's foundation until further advancement was devised for them. This benevolent provision, expressly stated in the *Liber Niger*, seems to have lapsed sometime during the economical administration of Elizabeth, for William Hunnis, in the petition before referred to, declared that nothing was done for the children after their voices

---

[8] *Patent Rolls*, 7 Henry V, memb. 11d. Printed in full in Wallace, *Evolution*, p. 12. A similar writ was granted to John Croucher, Dean of the Chapel, in 1440. Cf. Manly, "The Chapel Royal," *Camb. Hist. of Eng. Lit.*, VI, 316.

[9] *Cal. Pat. Rolls*. 1452-61, p. 90.

had changed. It was reaffirmed by James I in 1604, in a writ of impressment to Nathaniel Gyles.

All in all, the lot of the child impressed for the Chapel Royal was an enviable one. He was comfortably housed and cared for until he was fifteen; he was well taught in music, vocal and instrumental, and in the elements of grammar; and above all he was allowed the freedom of the great court and even given a part in its most brilliant revels. The problem of his future was settled for him in the most liberal way. No doubt the youngster whom the Chapel master, armed with his writ of impressment, bore away to London with him, was regarded by his companions with the deepest envy. What luck![10]

2. *Early Masters.*

No interest of a dramatic kind attaches to John Plummer, the first Chapel master whom we can identify (appointed in 1444), nor to his successor, Henry Abyngdon (1455), and hardly more to Gilbert Banaster, who followed Abyngdon in 1478. The last named was indeed something of a literary man in his day, having written the exceedingly dull *Miracle of St. Thomas*[11] and a number of the songs in the *Fayrfax Boke.*[12] Collier has it that there were plays by the Chapel at the Christmas festivities of 1485,[13] but search has failed to find the source which Collier failed to quote,[14] and in the absence of confirmation we must be wary of trusting Collier's not always reliable transcripts. Yet though we cannot on good authority connect the Chapel with drama before 1500, we have no reason to believe that such a connection may not have existed even for some time earlier. The general custom of employing children in religious plays and the aptitude of the Chapel boys for taking part in court pageants, are reasons for suppposing the acting tradition in the Chapel to have gone farther back than our records take us.

[10] For a discussion of the Children of the Privy Chamber and their confusion with the Chapel, See *Appendix I.*

[11] See Warton, *Hist. of. Eng. Poetry*, 1871, III, 132.

[12] An interesting collection of late fifteenth and early sixteenth century songs in the British Museum, *Add. MSS.* 5465. Burney, in his *History of Music*, ed.1782, II, 540, says of the whole collection: "The Music, indeed, of these ditties, is somewhat uncouth, but it is still better than the poetry."

[13] *Hist. Eng. Dram. Poetry*, I, 46.

[14] A search by Professor Wallace in the British Museum MSS. failed to turn up Collier's source. The only documents near this date which he could find at all described the doings at Christmas of 1487-8. Cf. his *Evolution*, p. 12, note 3.

Banaster was succeeded in turn by a priest, Lawrence Squier, in September of 1486.[15] Banaster did not die until a year later, in the later part of August.[16] Beyond the fact of his appointment, and that he was a canon[17] of St. Mary's, Warwick, we know nothing of Squier. His reign was short, for he died in 1493.[18]

After him came William Newark,[19] who had been a gentleman of the Chapel since at least as early as 1480.[20] The only works of his known to be extant are a few songs in *The Fayrfax Boke*.

Newark is a man of some importance to our story, because he is the first master of whom it can be said on grounds more solid than mere conjecture that he brought the Chapel Royal on the stage. To be sure, in his day the gentlemen of the chapel, and not the children, seem to have done most if not all of the real acting, and to have organized from among their number, as we shall see presently, a company of interlude-players. But the children were making their approaches to the stage, and by a door which we have found them using elsewhere, that is to say, pageantry. For it was in the great court pageants that they served a modest apprenticeship, by riding upon the mechanical devices and singing. Thus they touched upon the confines of drama, in that they wore disguises and played at being something they were not. Furthermore, these court pageants, unlike the city shows, were themselves plays of a kind, to this extent that they told a story, however elementary, or had some moment of action. They were a queer, uncanonical genus, having a little of ballet, a little of opera, and a good deal of spectacle, but unquestionably they were akin to the *genus ludus*. By the time of Henry VII pageants had become a part of court routine, forerunners of the masque. For

---

[15] *Patent Rolls*, 2 Henry VII, Pt. 1, m. 22(6); dated Nov. 8, 1486, term to begin Michaelmas preceding. Wallace, *Evolution*, p. 25.

[16] His will (Somerset House, *Prerog. Court of Cant.*, 11 Miles) was dated Aug. 18, 1487. He died before Sept. 1 following, because on that day three corrodies vacated by his death were granted to William Newark, Edward John, and Thomas Morley. Cf. Wallace, *op. cit.*, p. 25.

[17] So called in his will.

[18] His will was dated May 29, proved June 17; in *P. C. C.*, 24 Dogett.

[19] *Patent Rolls*, 9 Hen. VII, m. 31 (7). His patent was dated September 17, 1493. It was renewed on the accession of Henry VIII; cf. *Pat. Rolls*, I Hen. VIII, Pt. 1, m. 26, Public Record Office.

[20] He was granted a corrody of Thetford Priory in that year; cf. *Pat. Rolls*, 20 Ed. IV, Pt. 2, m. 21, P. R. O. In the patent he is called gentleman of the Chapel. He also received a life annuity of £20 from Richard III in 1485 (*Pat. Rolls*, 2 Rich. III, Pt. 3, m. 11); and the corrody which Banaster resigned in 1487.

their proper manipulation children were a valuable, indeed a
necessary, adjunct, being light in weight, so that they could ride
more securely than men on the tops of the devices, having skill in
song, and through their piping voices being fitted to act the parts of
women, cupids, Virtues, and others of the common population
of pageants. Then having proved their worth in such apprenticeship to Thalia, they at length, under the lead of ambitious Cornish,
set their feet upon the stage itself.

The first of such pageants known to have employed Chapel
boys came, as I have said, in the mastership of William Newark.
The occasion was the splendid revels which attended the marriage
of Prince Arthur to Katherine of Aragon in 1501.[21] The whole
account, as given in *Harleian MS*. 69, is extraordinarily vivid and
interesting, so that I should like to quote it *in extenso* for its picture of Tudor merrymaking, but space forbids. There were several
pageants. One was a castle drama by four beasts of gold and silver;
within the castle were eight "goodly & fresh ladyes," and on each
of the four turrets thereof a "little child, apparelled like a maiden."
And so the pageant advanced, the four children singing sweetly
all the while. Next came in a full rigged ship and cast anchor
alongside the castle; from which descended Hope and Desire, "two
well beseene and goodly persons," who wooed the favor of the
ladies as ambassadors from the Knights of the Mount of Love.
But they received "small answeare" for their pains. Then entered eight noble knights, conveyed in a hill; and they assaulted
the castle and conquered without great difficulty. Whereupon
they all descended, as was usual at the ends of pageants, and danced.
Though we are not told so, I think there can be no doubt that
the four children dressed as maidens who sang so sweetly were
Chapel boys. The ultimate pageant, and the most important
because in it the Chapel boys are expressly mentioned, I shall
present in its original garb of language.

Against that his grace had supped the goodly hall was addressed and
goodly beseene and a Royall Cupborde sett thervppon in a baye windowe
of ix or x stages and haunces of height, furnished and fulfilled with rich and
goodly plate of gould and of silver and guilt and in the upper part of the hall a
Cloth of gould carpett*es* and Cushions for the King*es* noble Ma*ies*tie whither
when that his Grace was come and his welbeloved company of Nobles entred

---

[21] See Collier, *Eng. Dram. Poetry*, I, 58. Also Paul Reyher, *Les Masques Anglais*,
pp. 7, 500-504.

in a pleasant disguising conveyed and shewed by a glorious towne or tabernacle made like a goodly Chapell fenestred full of light*es* and brightnes
within this Pageant or tabernacle was another standing Cupboard of rich
and Costly plate to a great substance and quantitye this throne and pageant
was of two stories in whose longer were viij goodly disguised Lordes Knight*es*
and men of honor and in the upper story and partition viij other fresh
ladyes most strangely disguised and after most pleasurefull manner, thus when
this goodly work was aproached vnto the Kinge presence and sight drawen
and conveyed vppon wheeles by iij woddose ij before and one behind and
on either side of the said homely mermaides one of them a man mermaide the
other a woman the man in harnesse from the wast vpward*es* and in every of
the said mermaides a Childe of the Chapell singing right sweetly and with
quaint hermony descend these viij pleasant gallante men of honor and before
their coming forth they cast out many quicke conyes the which ran about the
hall and made very great disport*es*. after they daunced many divers goodly
daunces and forthwith came downe the viij disguised Ladyes and in their
apearance the let flye many white doues and byrdes that flewe about the hall
and great laughter and disport they made.   These Lordes and Laydyes
coupled together and daunced a long season many Courtly roundes and
pleasant daunces.   After that the Earle of Spaine and a Ladye of the same
Countrey daunced two base daunces and went vp againe.

Then, with a light and rich repast and gifts of value from the
king to the nobler of his guests, the revelry for that day broke
up. This was the environment in which the Chapel made their
modest beginnings as actors in the public eye. We are apt not
to keep in mind how much children were used in court festivities,
even in entertainments of great significance, when royalty entertained royalty. We shall see the Chapel boy appearing regularly
in the splendid pageants of Henry VIII; we have already seen
Henry entertaining the French ambassadors with a play on Luther,
the heretic, acted by the boys of Colet's school; and long after,
in 1606, we shall find James I entertaining his royal guest from
Denmark with a play by the children of St. Paul's. With such
constant practice in appearing before the public in dramatic situations of all kinds, is it surprising that children in the sixteenth
century grew to know the stage familiarly, and that the pubic
became as accustomed to see them wear the sock as they did the
regular players?

But the Chapel drew closer in those days to actual drama than
mere participation in pageants of this sort; we find them appearing actually as stage players. It was through the gentlemen,

however, that this first came about, not through the children.
The first of these genuinely dramatic performances that I have
been able to find took place in the year 1506. In the "Kyngs boke of
paymentis, begynnyng primo die Oct^i A° 21 Regis Henrici
vii^{mi}",[22] is the entry: "21 H vii Jan. 1. To the four players of the
kings chapell, 6l. 13s. 4d." That these were gentlemen of the Chapel
is shown pretty conclusively by the collective evidence of similar
notices of the same period. Thus a little later in the "Kyngs boke"
we read: "To the 5 gentlemen of the king's Chapell that played
in the Hall opon 12th nyght affore the kings grace in rewarde,
6l. 13s. 4d." Other entries from the same book are:
"22 H. vii Jan. 16. To 4 players of the Chapell that played affore the
king opon 12th day at nyght, 2l."
"24 H. vii Dec. 19. To Mr. Kyte Cornisshe and other of the
Chapell that played affore the king at Richmounte, 6l. 13s. 4d."
"24 H. vii Jan. 7. To diverse of the King's chapell that played
affore the King opon 12th nyght, 2l. 13s. 4d."
These entries make known to us that certain gentlemen of the
Chapel, including William Cornish and John Kyte, were at this
time playing regularly before the king and were receiving the
same fee as was assigned a professional performance—the £6-13-4
which persisted till 1642 as the standard reward for a play given at
court. Whether the "diverse of the King's Chapell" may ever have
included some of the children, is a question open to surmise. I
think it very possible that a use for them could be found in these
performances—whatever they were: moralities, interludes, débats
—just as a use was found for them in pageants; but I doubt very
much if at this time they served any higher purpose than that of
supernumeraries. The payments are always for plays by the gentlemen, not by children; and it was not until well on in the mastership
of Cornish that children began to act first in conjunction with
the gentlemen, and finally alone.
Yet if the Chapel lads had little or nothing to do with these
performances, still the moral effect of so much acting close at
home must have been considerable. To know that Cornish and his
fellows were preparing another interlude, to be present actually
at rehearsals, and to be full of the whole affair until it was over
for that time—all this must have been a stimulation of no little

[22] Collier, *op. cit.*, I, 53.

account to these boys, who knew themselves to be capable of taking a part successfully in public and even of presenting whole miracle plays, as the choristers of great abbeys did. It is not hard to understand why the gentlemen took up play-acting. The Chapel Royal contained a body of gentlemen of good family, well taught in the various arts of music, generally well educated for the times, and versed in court etiquette and demeanor. Above all, their none too arduous duties left them plenty of leisure time. They must have been interested in the interludes and moralities of one kind and another which began to appear more and more frequently at court, and might readily have become incited to rival in a gentlemanly way the professional accomplishments of English's troupe[23] and of the various visiting bands of players. That they did undertake the work seriously, and succeeded in it, is shown by the fact that they were paid for their plays the same price as the professionals.

Among the gentlemen who were in the Chapel during the mastership of Newark was one more enterprising, more brilliant in devising and carrying through dramatic entertainments than any one else. This was William Cornish. We have seen that he was one of the small company who played frequently before the king. He was more than an actor; already at this early time he was an inventor of pageants. So early as 1502 he was paid £20 for three pageants.[24] Considering what genius and industry he showed in the next reign in this same business of planning pageants, one is led strongly to suspect that even at this time it was he who was the moving factor in court festivities, not Newark. The fact that he was paid for three pageants at once is strong supporting evidence. But whatever he did at this time, it is certainly true that he is the outstanding, the great figure in the court drama and pageantry during the first and more brilliant half of the reign of Henry VIII.

3. *William Cornish, Chapel Master, 1509-1523.*

In November of 1509, William Newark died[25] and William Cornish, gentlemen of the Chapel, already distinguished for his

[23] The four professional players of interludes maintained for the special service of the king.

[24] In the account books for 17-18 Hen. VII (Collier, I, 49) are the entries: "Oct. 26 Itm to Cornysshe for 3 pagents, 20l."
Itm to John Englishe for his pagent, 6l. 13s. 4d."

[25] Buried in Greenwich Church. Cf. will in *Rochester Wills*, Bk. 6, fol. 262; dated Nov. 5, 1509, proved Dec. 13, 1509. Possibly he was the first of the group of Chapel men who settled in East Greenwich.

zeal in directing court entertainments, succeeded him.[26] Our first
notice of Cornish comes from 1493, when among the privy Purse
expenses of that year we find this payment: "To one Cornysshe
for a prophecy in rewarde, 13s. 4d."[27] From the same book comes
a notice in December, 1502, of payment of 12s. 4d. "for setting
of a carrall upon Cristmas day"; this was the year of his devising
three pageants, already spoken of. In 1504 he was imprisoned
in the Fleet for writing a satire on Sir Richard Empson,[28] and addressed theretrom a poetical petition entitled *A Treatise between
Truth and Information*, under the acrostic nom-de-plume "Nysh-
wheate."[29] We have seen that in December of 1508 he was playing with John Kyte and others in the Chapel company. He continued his work as contriver, actor, and manager in the court pageants under Henry VIII; we shall find notice of his activity as
early as 1510. Throughout Henry VIII's reign until Cornish's
death the references to him are many in the account books. Besides
acquiring various sums in connection with his duties as master
of the Chapel, he received payments which show that he was put
in charge of work of importance, and was a man to be trusted with
the carrying through of business outside his ordinary duties. For
instance, in April of 7 Henry VIII this payment was made to him:[30]
"Item to William Cornisshe gentylman of ye chapell upon a warraunt for certain Reparacions to be don in the kinges manour of
Grenewyche-Cli." There were other grants of large sums, apparently for similar work.[31]

[26] Cornish's patent of appointment has not been found. The *Exchequer of Receipt*
shows that in Easter, 1510, Cornish was paid the master's salary for the two preceding quarters; that is, since Sept. 29, 1509. Wallace, *Evolution*, p. 33. A puzzling
notice occurs in a list of Exchequer fees payable during the year ending Michaelmas
1508 of £26-13-4 to William Cornish as master of the children of the Chapel (cited
by Chambers, *Elizabethan Stage*, II, 29, note 5). Chambers thinks this is an error,
but it is quite possible that Cornish, during an illness of Newark, may have been
acting master of the children.

[27] *Excerpta Historica*, p. 95. (Household Book of Henry VII, 1491-1505, *Add.
MSS*. 7099.)

[28] Cf. Stow's *Annales*, ed. 1615.

[29] Cf. Jos. Ritson, *Bibliographia Poetica* (1802), p. 53. The poem has been edited
by F. J. Furnivall in *Archiv. für d. Stud. der n. Sprachen u. Lit.* (1908), p. cxx.

[30] *Excheq. Miscel. T. R.*, Vol. 215, p. 442. Public Record Office.

[31] The early records show a John Cornish who was a gentleman in the Chapel at
the same time as William. Chambers, on tenuous evidence, believes there was also
an older William, and that our Cornish entered the Chapel about 1503. (Cf.
Elizabethan Stage, II, 29, note 6.) I cannot accept the evidence. The John Cornish

Aside from the *Treatise between Truth and Information*, nothing now remains of Cornish's work save a few songs and some musical settings of them. Part of these are contained in the "Fayrfax Boke," already referred to, and some dozen in the rare MS. collection catalogued at the British Museum as No. 31922 of *Add. MSS*.[32] The poems by Cornish in the latter collection are light, amatory pieces in lilting measures, not bad for their day, but more praiseworthy in their aptness for musical setting, than in their intrinsic beauties.

An interesting light on Cornish's mastership in the Chapel is thrown by Pace, Wolsey's henchman, in his correspondence with the great churchman. In March of 1518 he wrote: "My lord, if it were not for the personal love that the King's highness doth bear unto your grace, surely he would have out of your Chapel, no children only, but also men; for his grace hath plainly shown unto Cornysche that your grace's Chapel is better than his, and proved the same by this reason, that if any manner of new song should be brought unto both the said Chapels to be sung *ex proviso*, then the said song should be better and more surely handled by your Chapel than by his grace's."[33] Cornish seems to have acted at once upon the king's hint, for Pace wrote Wolsey on April 1: "Cornysche doth greatly laud and praise the child of your Chapel sent hither, not only for his sure and cleanly singing, but also for his good and crafty descant, and doth in like manner extol Mr. Pygote for the teaching of him."[34] And he adds the interesting commentary that the transferred child was to be treated "honestly" by Cornish, "i.e. otherwise than he doth his own." The splendors of Wolsey's chapel were the admiration of the times; the primate lavished particular care on it, and enriched it with the plunder of Northumberland's famous and no less splendid chapel.[35]

---

seems to have taken no part in the Chapel plays. The "Kit Cornish" discovered by Mrs. Stopes (*Wm. Hunnis*, p. 141) is an error of reading which has often been exploded.

[32] Reviewed in detail in *Archæologia*, Vol. XLI, p. 371. Two songs in Chapell's *Popular Music of Olden Time*—namely, those entitled "Ah, the syghes that com fro my hart," and "Blow thy horne, hunter"— are proved by this MS. to be from Cornish. For reprints from the "Fayrfax Boke" cf. Ritson's *Ancient Songs*.

[33] Brewer and Gairdner, *Letters and Papers of Henry VIII*, II, Pt. 2, § 4024.

[34] *Same*, § 4055.

[35] For information as to Northumberland's chapel see Bishop Percy's edition of *The Regulations and Establishment of the Royal Household of Henry Algernon Percy, The Fifth Earl of Northumberland*, Lond. 1827, p. 323 ff. Wolsey's confiscation came after the death of this earl, on the accession of his son. It appears that Percy

Cornish apparently did not take orders, for the distinguishing "Sir" is never prefixed to his name. The date of his death is not absolutely certain, but it was before October 14, 1523, when his will was proved.[36] His successor, William Crane, was not formally appointed until May, 1527, but doubtless served as master in the interim. Cornish's will contains nothing of interest, except a few references to his family. He is styled "William Cornysche of Estgrenewiche gentilman and one of the gentlemen of the kinges honorable Chapell." His body is to lie in the Chapel of the Roods in East Greenwich, or somewhere else if he happens not to die there. He makes small bequests to Rochester Cathedral, and leaves everything else to Johane, his wife. All his lands and goods in East Greenwich, after the death of Johane, are to go to his son Henry and his male heirs. Perhaps the most interesting thing in this will is the indication that Cornish, like Newark, was a resident of East Greenwich, and was an early member of the colony there which was made up of Chapel masters and gentlemen.

William Cornish was the first man to set the children of the Chapel steadfastly in the road of playacting; he was also a producer of industry and ingenuity. Consequently his activities deserve respectful attention, and indeed they have already been inspected with considerable minuteness by Professor C. W. Wallace, who in his *Evolution of the English Drama* has written a chapter on "The New Drama Shaped by William Cornish." There Professor Wallace, with admirable method, has compared the two most reliable and fruitful sources we possess, the fragmentary *Revels Books* and Hall's *Chronicle*, and from them produced a full and valuable exposition. Hence I am relieved of the need of reviewing in detail Cornish's work. Yet, because of the very great importance of Cornish in the history of children's companies, and because Professor Wallace in

---

maintained all the customs current in the chapels of the court and of great abbeys. Thus we find payments for the Boy Bishop; for the "Play of the Nativitie uppon Cristynnes-Day in the mornyne in my Lords Chapelle befor his Lordship"; and for the "Play of Ressurrection uppon Esturday in the Mornynge."

[36] In Somerset House, *Prerog. Court of Cant.* 13 Bodfelde. It is dated seemingly Jan. 5, 1512, but the text has curious hiatuses, and may have meant to read 1522; thus, " . . . . a thousande fyve hundred and   xii And in the   iiijth yere* of the Reigne" &c. The blank spaces perhaps should be filled with an x. Wallace (*Evolution*, p. 61) reads the date of the will as Jan. 10, 1512, and the date of proving as Dec. 14, 1523; whereas I read Jan. 5, 1512 (or 1522) and Oct. 14, 1523.

* This is obviously wrong, anyway. January 5 of the fourth year of Henry VIII would be 1513.

the heat of enthusiasm has been seduced into making claims for
Cornish which his own cooler judgment must reject as extravagant,
I cannot pass by the work of this man without touching upon its
significant features.

The sources of information in regard to Cornish's play-producing
are four. The *Revels Books*, of which only three remain to us, give
many valuable details of pageants, in the difficult hand and astonishing spelling of Richard Gibson. Unfortunately, the condition
of the books is so bad that much cannot be deciphered.[37] Hall is
luckily full of stories of court festivities, which supplement excellently the undecipherable parts of the *Revels Books*, and make up a
good deal which is contained in the lost volumes. Some of the bare
notices of interludes and pageants in the *Books of Payments* are also
supplemented by fuller accounts in Hall. Finally, some lacunæ are
filled in by documents in Brewer and Gairdner.

The first play within our ken given by the Chapel before Henry
VIII was acted by the gentlemen of the Chapel on Twelfth Night
in the first year of Henry's reign, 1510.[38] Another performance was
given on or before Twelfth Day of the next year.[39] No particulars
are known of these interludes, but Hall[40] records a rich pageant of
Twelfth Day, 1510, "devised like a mountayne, glisteringe by night,
as though it had bene all of golde and set with stones" and adorned
with rare trees and flowers.

It is the festivities of February 12 and 13, in the second year of
Henry, which first give us pause. An elaborate pageant was then
devised by Cornish in which the Chapel children were used, and
which bore the title of "The Golden Arbor in the Orchard of Pleasure." In the White Hall of Westminster an arbor was built with
pillars of shining silver, covered by a vine of silver bearing grapes of
gold and adorned with a canopy embroidered with flowers of all
kinds. Round about was set up an orchard of orange, pomegranate,
apple, pear, and olive trees, wherein sat twelve lords and ladies
attended by eight minstrels, while on the steps stood "dyveres
persoones dysgysed," among them the subdean, Crane, and Cornish,
of the Chapel, and on the top were the children of the Chapel,

---

[37] Extracts from the *Revels Books*, somewhat impaired by inaccuracies, have
been printed in Collier's *English Dramatic Poetry* and in Brewer and Gairdner's
Letters and Papers of Henry VIII.
[38] Wallace, *Evolution*, p. 38.
[39] *Same*, p. 38.
[40] *Chronicle*, p. 516.

singing. This "mervelus wyghty" pageant was wheeled up and down the hall and turned round. Hall furnishes us a long and picturesque account of these revels, to which I refer the curious reader.[41] He tells us that they were begun with an interlude played by the gentlemen of the Chapel, with "diuers freshe songes," but the account books make no direct mention of it. The lists[42] of properties used show that Cornish played two parts. There were thirteen yards of russet satin for garments like shipmen's for two gentlemen of the Chapel who sang in the play; this would seem to refer to the interlude which preceded the pageant. Account is also given for sixteen yards of blue damask, for a garment of strange fashion, and a rolled cap like that of a Baron of the Exchequer, for Mr. Subdean, "now my Lord of Armykan."

The dancing which followed the pageant was broken in upon by one of those sudden, boisterous scenes of disorder which sometimes invaded Henry's revelry. For the "rude people," roped at one end of the hall, broke through, and running to the pageant began to despoil it, nor could the officers restrain them "excepte they shoulde haue foughten and drawen bloude." A little while after, when the king was on the point of distributing the monograms of gold which were sewn on all the costumes, the populace again made a raid, respecting not even the anointed presence of King Hal himself, and "stripped hym into his hosen and dublet, and all his compaignons in likewise." Apparently the relations of Henry to his subjects had something of the bluff, beer-bench feudalism of Heorot.

At New Year's night 1512 (aº 3) there was an elaborate pageant called the "Fortresse dangerus," an account of which is given in the *Revels Books*, but is so mutilated as to be almost illegible.[43] Hall's narrative[44] is clearer and more vivid. A castle was made in the great hall, with gates, towers, and dungeons, armed with artillery after the most warlike fashion. On the front was written *le Fortresse dangerus*; within were six ladies in russet satin, laid over with leaves of gold, and with coifs and caps of gold on their heads. When the castle had been conveyed round the hall, in came the king with five others, who assaulted the castle, until the ladies "wer content to

[41] *Chronicle*, p. 518.

[42] Added to Gibson's résumé; also given in Brewer and Gairdner, vol. II, Pt. 2, p. 1496.

[43] Some excerpts are given in Brewer and Gairdner, II, Pt. 2, p. 1497.

[44] P. 526.

solace with them, and upon farther communicacion to yeld the
castle." So they came down and danced a space; then returned to
the castle, which vanished suddenly "out of their sightes." It appears from the *Revels Accounts* that the subdean, Cornish, Crane,
seven gentlemen of the Chapel, and an indeterminate number of
children took part.

On Shrove Sunday of 1512, there was a play by the gentlemen of
the Chapel, and again on Whitsunday.[45] The next revels which
demand out attention are those of Christmas, 6 Hen. VIII (1514-15).
The text of Gibson's account in the Public Record Office is so badly
defaced that I could make little out of it. However, a recourse to
Brewer and Gairdner[46] shows that on Twelfth Day night Gibson
prepared a pageant "kawlld the wryttyng there over, the Pavyllyon
un the Plas Parlos." There was a pavilion with four towers at the
corners on a stage hung with crimson and blue damask. In each
tower was a lord dressed in purple satin embroidered with gold
wreaths and the letters H and K. Six minstrels sat on the pageant,
and at the foot two armed knights; there were also present Cornish,
Crane, "Master Harry" Kite, and one of the children. These gentlemen, or some of them, first declared the meaning and purpose of the
pageant; then entered three armed knights "with noise of drom-
byllslads in fierce manner, making a goodly tourney." After some
skirmishing the revels ended in the usual dance.

In none of the revels so far reviewed have the children appeared
as actors; nor has Cornish been designated as the deviser of pageants.
Yet we know that as early as the reign of Henry VII Cornish was
inventing them,[47] and the fact that he appears regularly in them and
sometimes has a speaking part makes it likely that many of them
were his handiwork. It was at Christmas, 1515, that Cornish and
his children first appeared, as far as our knowledge goes, in an interlude. The occasion is memorable for that alone; but it is made
doubly so by the theme of the play, which was the story of Troilus
and Cressida. This was the interlude of "Troilus and Pandor,"
which has not received from historians the attention it deserves.
Fortunately Gibson's characteristic description has come down
intact; I refer the curious reader to the *Appendix*,[48] which con-

---

[45] Wallace, *Evolution*, p. 38.
[46] Vol. II, Pt. 2, p. 1501.
[47] In the year 1502; cf. p. 48.
[48] Cf. p. 324.

tains a fuller transcription of this interesting document than he
will find anywhere else.

The king celebrated Christmas in this year at Eltham, with the
usual revelries. Among them was the Chaucerian interlude, written
by Cornish, and played by him and his children. The characters
spoken of are Troilus, Pandor, Cressida, Calchas, Diomedes, and
Ulysses (Cornish had been reading some other book of Troy besides
Chaucer's). Harry Kite, gentleman of the Chapel, played in the
pageant (also of Cornish's devising) which followed the interlude,
but we are not told that any grown actor took part in the play
except Cornish, who played Calchas in a mantle and a bishop's
surcoat. We are told definitely that Troilus, Pandor, and Ulysses
were children. Cressida was dressed "lyke a wedow of onour" in
black. Among the particular items is mention of a lady who
played Faith; and we might reasonably speculate as to whether
some relics of the Morality had got mixed in with this romantic
interlude, if it were not equally probable that Faith belonged to the
pageant which followed.

The significance of this play lies not only in the fact that here for
the first time the Chapel children were out as full fledged actors—
although for us, and for the history of the drama in England, this
event is not devoid of meaning—but in the nature of the theme.
It has been customary hitherto to date the entry of romantic inspiration into English drama with the advent of *Calisto and Meli-
bœa*, about 1530,[49] but perhaps now we must push back this date
to 1515. Furthermore, this, the first play of romantic source on
record in England, was not derived from Latin culture, but from a
native source of unchallengeable purity. That Cornish's interlude
was in the main romantic, in spite of the tendencies of his time to
broad farce and morality, the nature of the Troilus story assures us.
If we only had a copy of it!

Certain general facts should be borne in mind regarding this
interlude: that it was certainly of the "literary" class, with its
source in Chaucer, and not of the "popular" school of Heywood's
farces; that it employed a remarkably large cast of fifteen people,[50]

---

[49] "This drama became the forerunner of that ruling spirit of romance which was,
in another generation, to burst forth and carry everything before it." Schelling,
Eliz. Drama, I, p. 90.

[50] See "ye nombyr of persones" attached to the Revels account in the *Appendix*,
p. 325.

many of whom, doubtless, were no more than supernumeraries; that Cornish acted in the play, but that three parts at least—Ulysses, Troilus, and Pandor—were played by Chapel boys.

In the Christmas season of 1516-17 (a° 8), Cornish played with his children again before the king.[51] This is the second notice of a play by the Chapel boys; but unfortunately we know nothing more about it than the fact of the occurrence.

On Twelfth Night, 1517, a great pageant was enacted, devised by Cornish, who as usual had a place in it; and two of his boys took part. For the celebration of the Epiphany at Greenwich, there was constructed a "garden of Esperance," railed in and banked with flowers and trees of all kinds. The meaning thereof was interpreted by Cornish, dressed "lyk A stranger" in red sarsenet. The duties of the two children are not specified. In the garden were six knights and six ladies walking in rich and curious attire, who, after the pageant had been displayed, descended and danced.

The next performance of a play by Cornish fell on Shrove Tuesday, 1517;[52] more about it we do not know. After that we hear of nothing until July 6, 1518, when two pageants devised by Cornish were given, for which the author received £ 18-2-11. Thereafter Cornish played before the king with his children on January 1, Shrove Monday, and in the Christmas holidays of 1519, and twice between New Year's and April of 1520. Meanwhile on September 3, 1519 (a° 11), the "Meskeler of New Hall" had been celebrated. The *Revels Accounts* are in such bad shape that I must rely for information on Hall[53] and Brewer and Gairdner,[54] with a few items I have picked out of the original. Hall tells us that after a sumptuous banquet there entered eight masquers with white beards and "long and large garments of Blewe satten," who danced in a sober fashion "and communed not with the ladies after the fassion of Maskers, but behaued theimselfes sadly"; whereupon the queen plucked off their visers and disclosed them to be all old men, the youngest past fifty. Then entered the king and the four French hostages, with the Earl of Devonshire and six young gentlemen, gorgeously arrayed, and they all danced. Hall says nothing of a part of this entertainment

---

[51] Wallace, *Evolution*, p. 38.
[52] All the dates in this paragraph are taken from notices of payments in the Household Books. Cf. Wallace, *Evolution*, p. 39.
[53] P. 599.
[54] Vol. III, Pt. 2, p. 1550.

much nearer our interest—namely, a play or pageant of some kind by Cornish acted by the Chapel children, in which the actors represented elements and objects of nature. The few items we find in the *Revels Accounts* regarding this "pastime" are tantalizing. There were ten yards of green sarsenet made into bonnets and garments for the two children that played Summer and Lust in the pastime "y⁴ mast Kornyche maad"; yellow sarsenet for the child who played Moon, and for Cornish's children "y⁴ played be foor ye kyng"; and red, black, blue, and russet sarsenet for those that played Sun, Winter, Wind, and Rain. The children's garments were in keeping with their characters: one, red powdered with gold suns and clouds; one, yellow powdered with moons and clouds; one, blue powdered with drops of silver; the fourth powdered with gold primroses; the fifth with silver honeysuckles; the sixth with gold stars, and the seventh with silver snowflakes. From this list and from an item of seven girdles for Cornish's children, the number of boy actors seems to have been seven; and their names, too, were seven—Sun, Moon, Wind, Rain, Summer, Winter, Lust. This second of Cornish's dramatic works about which we have definite information is thus shown to have been an imaginative piece slightly suggestive of Heywood's *Play of the Weather*; but certainly not in the category of such folk drama as *The Four PP* and *John the Husband*.

Cornish presented a play, presumably with his usual company, in the Christmas holidays of 1520-21.[55]

On Shrove Tuesday (March 4), 1522, a particularly sumptuous pageant was held by Cardinal Wolsey, in honor of the king and the foreign ambassadors. Hall's description[56] is long and full; that of Gibson[57] is almost indecipherable. There was a castle built in the great hall, which the *Revels Accounts* tells us was called "the Schatew vert"; it had one great tower and two smaller ones flanking, adorned with banners bearing curious devices. The castle was kept "with ladies of straunge names, the first *Beautie*, the second *Honor*, the third *Perseuerance*, the fourth *Kyndnes*, the fifth *Constance*, the sixte *Bountie*, the seuenthe *Mercie*, and the eight *Pitie*; these eight ladies had Millian gounes of white sattin . . . . , on their heddes calles, and Millein bonettes of gold, with ·Iwelles." These were doubtless the children of the Chapel, for among Gibson's accounts is

⁵⁵ Wallace, *Evolution*, p. 39.
⁵⁶ P. 631.
⁵⁷ Brewer and Gairdner, Vol. III, Pt. 2, p. 1558.

a payment for eight silk cauls of diverse colors, and another item tells that three cauls were lost by the children of the Chapel by casting them out of the castle. Underneath the "basse fortresse" were eight other ladies, attired like women of India. Then came in eight lords in gorgeous apparel, headed by the king. The castle was summoned to surrender by Ardent Desire, but the ladies refused; so the knights began the attack. The ladies "defendded the castle with Rose water and comfittes, and the lordes threwe in Dates and Orenges, and other fruites made for pleasure, but at last the place was won." Then the eight ladies of India, who represented the evil passions, fled, and the knights danced with the ladies of honor. This was the last performance of a dramatic nature at court before Cornish's death.

He died before October 14, 1523, when his will was proved, and his work at court came to an end. He was the first Chapel master to enter systematically into the business of writing and producing plays; he was a figure of prominence at court, a man who had much to do with the devising and carrying through of the amusements of the king, and was trusted with important duties.[58] He is seen, then, to be a figure of prime importance. Under him the Chapel children appeared first as a regular acting company; there are eight indubitable references to plays presented by him in the *Books of King's Payments*, and if the royal accounts were preserved intact we would doubtless find many more. He used his boys not only in plays, but in the pageants and pastimes that filled so much of the holiday time at court. No master of the children of either Paul's or the Chapel will be found to be more active as author and producer of dramatic entertainments. With this in mind, the reader will hardly disagree with Wallace's estimate[59] that Cornish is worthy to rank as the earliest dramatic impresario, the first promoter of the art of the theatre, and the father of English actor-managers. But many of Wallace's contentions about Cornish are extravagant and baseless. We have no way of judging the *quality* of his work; we only know something of the quantity and versatility of it. The particulars which Hall and Gibson supply us all relate to the accoutrements of his devices, their outward trappings. The fact that the comedy of

[58] The *Books of King's Payments* show in divers places payments of large sums, as £200, to Cornish for various services; among which seem to have been supervision of reparations in the manor of Greenwich.

[59] *Evolution of the English Drama*, chap. on "The New Drama Shaped by William Cornish."

Troilus and Pandor seems clearly taken from Chaucer argues something for the intelligence and culture of its author. Then, too, we have some songs from his pen, which are good enough for the day and show the author to have been a man of culture. But this does not justify us in going into rhapsodies over Cornish's dramatic work and claiming for him a preeminence over all competitors in his own time. Still less are we justified in turning over to him the interludes which till now have been ascribed to John Heywood—*The Four PP*, *The Pardoner and the Friar*, and *John the Husband, Tyb the Wife, and Sir John the Priest*[60]—and which do not at all accord with what little we know about the bent of Cornish's dramatic genius. Let us be satisfied with bestowing on Cornish the honor of being first in the line of men who developed the drama and stage in England in the sixteenth century, and not load him with merits he does not deserve.

4. *The Mastership of William Crane, 1523-1546.*

On Cornish's death in the autumn of 1523, the charge of the boys was assumed by a gentleman of long standing in the Chapel—William Crane. His name is found on a Chapel list of the time of Newark's mastership. He had from then on, as we have seen, exhibited an interest in the dramatic part of court revels by sharing with Cornish the duties and honors of playing in pageants and interludes. Crane assumed at once command over the boys,[61] although it was not until May 12, 1526, that his patent of office was issued.[62] Therein the number of children is officially fixed at twelve, and the salary of the master is raised from forty marks to forty pounds.

Crane is of interest for the remarkable number of business enterprises he was engaged in, for which he received many royal grants. The number and value of them show that he was a man of influence at court. Among his offices he counted those of water bailiff to the town and port of Dartmouth and controller of the petty customs of the port of London. He was granted many licenses to import commodities of various kinds. In May, 1528, he was connected with a still larger affair; on that date a release was granted him of £800

[60] For a refutation of Prof. Wallace's contentions in regard to these interludes and a reconsideration of Heywood's claims upon them, see my article in *Modern Philology*, XIII, No. 5, Sept. 1915: "On the Authorship of the Interludes Attributed to John Heywood." Mr. A. W. Reed, in his important series of articles on Heywood which have appeared in *The Library* (3d. Ser., Vols. VIII, IX), also rejects the claims for Cornish.

[61] Cf. Wallace, *Evolution*, p. 61.

[62] The Privy Seal, hitherto unpublished, may be found in *Chancery Warrants, Ser. II, Privy Seals*, file 574 (May, 18 Henry VIII).

received by him to be spent in furnishing and preparing two ships called "le Caryke," alias "le Kateryn Forteleza," and "le Nicholas Rede," and the three galleys called "le Rose," "le Henry," and "le Kateryn." In November, 1531, he was given a capital messuage called "Beaumondis Inne," in the parish of St. Michael in Wood-street in Cripplegate Ward, and two other messuages adjoining, which had all formed part of the property of William, late Viscount Beaumont and Lord Bardolfe, and which came into the hands of Henry VII by the attainder and forfeiture of Francis Lovell, late Lord Lovell.[63]

Crane was married at one time and had at least a daughter. "Mr. Crane's daughter of the Chapel" is mentioned in a letter from the Archbishop of York to Christopher Draper, clerk, in January, 1535.[64] It appears that Draper, who was supposed to be in orders and had obtained a prebend in York, was in reality not in orders, and was reported to be contracted to mistress Crane. "If so," comments his grace succinctly, "you can no longer enjoy promotion." What the sequel to the romance may have been is not revealed to us. Crane's wife was named Margaret, as we learn from a grant of 1540, by which Crane received ten tenements within the close of "the late priory of St. Helen."[65]

In 1545 Richard Bower was appointed master of the Chapel boys, and presumably Crane relinquished his charge. But he did not die till some time before April of 1546;[66] and indeed was receiving augmentations in that year.[67] Doubtless he withdrew before advancing age, for if he was a gentleman during the mastership of Newark—that is, before 1509—he should be growing old by 1545. His Inquisition Post Mortem was taken in 1546; that of his wife in 1553.[68]

Our information about Crane, composed as it is mostly of dry business facts, yet goes to show that he was a man of affairs and property and a man well in favor at court. Only to one in the good

---

[63] For a full list of Crane's business affairs see Wallace's *Evolution*, p. 62.

[64] Brewer and Gairdner, VIII, p. 40.

[65] Brewer and Gairdner, XV, p. 167.

[66] His will, dated July 6, 1545, was proved in the Prerogative Court of Canterbury on April 7, 1546. It contains nothing of interest, except that the injunction to his wife to sell his house in Greenwich to pay his funeral debts shows him to have had at least a foothold in the Greenwich Chapel colony. He was to be buried in the parish church of St. Elias before the high altar—a place of honor. His property and effects went to his wife.

[67] Brewer and Gairdner, XXI, Pt. 2, p. 444.

[68] Mrs. C. C. Stopes, *William Hunnis*, 1910, p. 144.

graces of the ruling power would so many and so large concessions be made. This indirect evidence of court favor is borne out by more direct proof, which indicates that Crane was admitted to the privilege of playing games with the monarch himself, even to the extent of daring to win. "Itm the last daye paied to William Crane for so moche money as he wanne of the kinges grace at pryckes xix Angelles in money currant—vij^{li} ij^s vj^d."[69]

It is unfortunately true that nothing from the pen of William Crane has come down to us, and we are perforce ignorant of his gifts in literature and music. Unfortunately, too, our knowledge of the revels of the latter half of Henry's reign is scanty; documents are few in number and meager in details. Indeed, it is evident that the life and nature of the court had changed, as Henry grew older, and as the conflicts and heartburnings attending the royal marriage schemes and the Reformation came on. Crane himself was doubtless hampered from taking Cornish's place as contriver and promoter of pageants by the press of business affairs, which must have been considerable. Yet if we had all the documents, or even as large a percentage as we have of the preceding period, we should no doubt find a great deal of interest in the goings-on at court, and find that the Chapel children went on playing with considerable frequency.

The first recorded performance of a play by Crane and the children did not take place till Christmas holidays of 1528 (a° 20).[70] Meanwhile a performance of great significance had been held on November 10, 1527 (a° 19), when the boys of Dr. Colet's school at St. Paul's played a Latin interlude on matters of state and religion. This has been noticed elsewhere.[71] Crane played with the children at Christmases of 1529 (a° 21),[72] 1530 (a° 22),[72] and 1538,[73] and probably

[69] N. H. Nicolas, *Privy Purse Expenses of Henry VIII*, p. 227—June, 1532.

[70] Henry VIIIth's Household Books, in *Trevelyan Papers to 1551*, edit. for the Camden Soc., p. 146:— "Rewardes geven on Wednesdaye, new yeres day, at grenewich, anno xxmo. . . . . .Item, to Maister Crane, for playing before the King with the Children of the Chapell, in rewarde . . . . vi^{li} xiii^s iiii^d." Perhaps this entry, which occurs among the New Year's payments both of this year and the following, means that the gentlemen of the Chapel acted twice during each holiday season: "Item, to the gentilmen of the Chapel, for payn taking this Christmas, in rewarde . . . . xiii^{li} vi^s viii^d."

[71] Cf. p. 16.

[72] *Trevelyan Papers*, pp. 161, 174. The entries are essentially the same as the one quoted.

[73] *Privy Purse Expenses of the Princess Mary*, edit. by Sir F. Madden, 1831, p. 221:—"(Christmas, 1538) Mr. Crane, for plaing w^t the Children before ye King vj^{li} xiii^s iiii^d."

earlier in the same winter,[74] and at Christmas of 1539[75] and 1540.[76]
Meanwhile, in the early part of 1538, probably in February or
March, John Heywood had played before the princess Mary with a
company of children which may well have come from the Chapel.[77]

Although the first recorded play under Crane falls under the date
of Christmas 1528, Hall[78] tells us of revels held on May 6, 1527,
when members of the Chapel assisted in the performance of a dialogue. There came in "eight of the kynges Chappel with a song and
brought with theim one richly appareled; and in likewise at the other
side, entred eight other of the saied Chappel bryngyng with them
another persone, likewise appareled, these two persones plaied a
dialog theffect whereof was whether riches were better then loue,
and when they could not agre vpon a conclusion, eche called in thre
knightes, all armed, thre of them woulde haue entred the gate of the
Arche in the middel of the chambre, & the other .iii. resisted." So
they fought and departed; and out came an old man with a white
beard, and concluded "that loue & riches, both be necessarie for
princes (that is to saie) by loue to be obeied and serued, and with
riches to rewarde his louers and frendes."

An extended and vivid account of the whole proceeding is given
in *Calendar of State Papers, Venetian*.[79] The writer declares he could
never conceive anything so costly and well designed as the revels
which were held that night at Greenwich. After the spectators were
seated, there entered eight singers, forming two wings, singing certain English songs; among them was a handsome youth alone, clad
in blue taffeta, sown with eyes. The singers having made obeisance
and withdrawn, the youth declared himself to be Mercury, sent to
the king by Jupiter, and proceeded to deliver a Latin oration to the
glory of his majesty; after which he announced that Jupiter, having
frequently listened to disputes between Love and Riches, and being
unable to decide their superiority, had appointed the king judge, to

[74] *Arundel MSS.* 97, fol. 46. In December of 1538 (aº 30), "Sonday at Hampton
corte," the children were paid, without specification of service, £6-13-4.
[75] *Same*, fol. 53 (Newyear's day at Greenwich, aº 31): "Item to mr Crane for
playinge before yᵉ king wᵗ the children—viˡⁱ xiiiˢ iiiiᵈ."
[76] *Same*, fol. 164 b. Similar entry to last, dated "Saterday New yeres day at
Hampton Courte Anno xxxiiº."
[77] *Privy Purse Expenses of Princess Mary*, p. 62 (March, 1538): "Itm geuen to
Heywood playing an enterlude wᵗ his children bifore my ladis grace xls."
[78] P. 723. Cf. also Wallace, *Evolution of the English Drama*, p. 67; Brewer and
Gairdner, Vol. IV, Pt. 2, p. 1393.
[79] Vol. IV, pp. 57 ff.

pass final sentence in the controversy. Thereupon Mercury went off, and on came eight young choristers (the children) of the chapel, four on each side; those to the right were led by Love ("Amor") and the other wing by Riches ("la Richezza"). In the center walked a man alone, in the guise of Justice, and sang. Justice commenced narrating the substance of the dispute in English; thereupon Love and Riches began their debate, each being supported by the choristers on his side, who recited verses. The debate ended, the mimic battle began, as described by Hall.

This account is especially interesting because it gives in unusual detail a picture of the courtly revels in the latter part of Henry's reign, and because it describes the manner in which the interludes of the day were often given. We are not to understand that all plays by the Chapel were attended with such pomp as this, but only those which were united with pageants as in the present case. The interlude itself is characteristic of the times; it recalls Heywood's *Play of Love*, and in its use of Jupiter as prime mover, his *Play of the Weather*. But this general resemblance does not justify us in concluding with Wallace[80] that "the whole play . . . . is so exactly after the manner of the youthful John Heywood as to identify it as one of his numerous unpublished efforts." Before we come to such a determination, we must first show that the play was not also in the vein of William Crane, who was a more likely man to be involved in court pageants than Heywood, or John Rastell, who was at least an occasional writer of interludes, and was engaged in directing the construction of a pageant to be used some time between Frebuary 6 and May 7 of this very year, 1527.[81]

There are no particulars to be found regarding any other of the Chapel performances until that of New Year's, 1541. In relation to this occasion, there is an order among the *Loseley MSS.*[82] on Sir Anthony Browne and John Bridges for preparing certain garments for a play to be given on New Year's by the children of the Chapel. Some few items of apparel are listed, but they are unilluminating, except that from four of everything—jerkins, slops, caps—being specified, it would seem that the number of players was four.[83]

[80] *Evolution of the Eng. Drama*, p. 67.
[81] Wallace, *op. cit.*, p. 67, note 2.
[82] A. J. Kempe, *The Losely MSS.*, Lond. 1846, p. 70; also Wallace, *Evolution*, p. 69.
[83] Many of the interludes of this time demanded only three or four players. *Love and Riches* used four, so also the *Four PP*, *The Pardoner and the Friar*, and and *The Play of Love*.

Without doubt the children played in interlude or pageant some time during the year 1543-4, for the *Revels Accounts* of that year contain a payment of 7s. 4d. for "a wherry, to fetch the children's geer."[84]

This is the last scrap of information we have concerning the revels of Henry's reign which has to do with the Chapel boys. Crane died suddenly between July 6, 1545, when his will was dated, and July 7, 1546, when it was proved. The period measured by Crane's mastership was not so brilliant by any means as the earlier one when Cornish was the guiding spirit of the royal pastimes; and this despite the fact that one of the most brilliant festivities, of May 6, 1547, fell within Crane's time.[85] Yet it must not be forgotten that much of the barrenness of this period is only seeming, and is due to the scarcity of our documentary evidence.

5. The Mastership of Richard Bower, 1545-1561.

As we have seen, Richard Bower succeeded Crane before the latter's death. His patent[86] is dated October 31, 1545, but he assumed the office even earlier, on June 30, as the patent tells us, and his salary is ordered to be paid from that day. The terms of his patent were precisely the same as those of Crane's.

Of all the masters since Newark, we know least of Bower. Beyond his letters patent and notices of plays given under his direction by the Chapel boys, practically nothing remains to us. That he was looked upon with favor by Queen Mary is shown by a grant[87] to him and Thomas Tallis, also gentleman of the Chapel, of "all the site and capital messuage of our manor of Mynster . . . . in the island of Thanet in our county of Kent, once belonging and appertaining to the recently dissolved monastery of St. Augustine adjoining the walls of the city of Canterbury." One other grant, of an annuity of ten marks, is recorded as having been made in the first year of Mary's reign.[88] It would seem that Mary looked with favor upon the master of her Chapel. Indeed, the man could not be devoid of the arts of pleasing who held his post in four successive reigns, through times of unusual unrest, and only resigned it when he was compelled to give up the world altogether.

---

[84] Kempe's *Loseley MSS.*, p. 72.
[85] The *Revels Accounts* in the *Loseley MSS.* show a great falling off in the sums appropriated for the revels in the latter years of Henry's life.
[86] Brewer and Gairdner, XX, Pt. 2, p. 447.
[87] *Patent Roll* No. 465, Philip and Mary.
[88] *Excheq. of Receipt. Auditor's Patent Books*, Vol. 8, fol. 20.

He died in 1561.[89] His will shows him to have been a member of the East Greenwich colony. His children were Stephen (the heir), Ralph, Annis (or Agnes) Farrant, Katherine, Elizabeth; his wife's name was Joan. He wills his house and appurtenances in East Greenwich to his wife, to go at her death to Stephen and his heirs; also the yearly rent of £36-6-8 for a lease for a term of years yet continuing within the Isle of Thanet. Various legacies of money were assigned with elaborate care to the five children. The overseers are William Roper, Esq. of Eltham, Kent, and Thomas Tallis, of the Chapel. The will was proved on the oath of Richard Farrant, the legal representative of John Bower. Not the least interesting feature of the document is the evidence that Richard Farrant, later Chapel master, married Bower's daughter Agnes, and that the Anne Farrant who went through such trouble in the '80's in connection with the Blackfriars theatre was the "Annis" Bower of this document.

We have no information of Chapel plays during the last years of Henry's reign, after Bower took the management; and our knowledge of such performances during the reign of Edward is limited to the two years 1548-1550, because only for those years are the *Books of King's Payments* extant. Bower and his boys played during the Christmas holidays each year,[90] and doubtless if we had the means of knowing, we should find that they played regularly at the court of the young king. Though we cannot be positively certain that they had any part in the revels which were held at the coronation of the king, it seems more than likely.[91] No definite information is to be

[89] His will is in Somerset House, *Prerog. Court of Cant.*, 27 Loftes. It was dated June 18, 1561, and proved on August 25; so the date 1563 for his death in the *Cheque Book* is wrong, as has been pointed out.

[90] *Exchequer Accounts, K. R.* 426/5. fol. 63b. Jan. 1, 1 Ed. VI (1548). "Item to Richard brewyer for playing before the kinges maieste w^t the Children of the Chappell in rewarde . . . . vj^{li} xiij^s iiij^d." Fol. 30b. Jan. 1, 2 Ed. VI. "Itm to Richard Bower M^r of the Children of the kinges Chappell for playinge bifore the kinges maiestie with the said Children . . . . vj^{li} xiij^s iiij^d."

[91] *Vide* Prof. Albert Feuillerat's *Documents Relating to the Revels at Court in the Time of King Edward VI and Queen Mary.* Louvain (Bang's *Materialen* series), 1914; pp. 12, 13, 14. On April 1, 1547, an inventory of Revels stuff was taken, in which these two items occur:

"not servisable j of Twoo gownes for prestes or Cardynalles of Crimsin thes with M^r stone of damaske. Twoo hattes of Red Sarcenet to the same . . . the Kinges chappell
not servisable j with vj longe gownes of whyte damaske . . . . etc. gravesend of the Chappell

had regarding the plays given in the Christmas holidays of 1547-48.[92]
Wallace believes the second play, of Christmas 1548-9, was one
referred to, but without date, as "the playe of yeowthe at Crystmas"
on the margin of an inventory of silks and stuffs for the tailor;[93]
and he identifies the play with the well known *Interlude of Youth*.
That is a hasty guess. In the first place, the "playe of yeowthe"
may have been given in Mary's reign for all we know to the contrary.
Secondly, if it belongs to Edward's reign it cannot possibly have been
Youth, which is strongly Catholic in doctrine. It is possible that
Lusty Juventus is the play referred to, for it is soundly Protestant
and its main character is usually called *Youth*. But Professor
Feuillerat's theory[94] is doubtless to be preferred, that in the present
note we find a reference to the "play, after a talk between one that
was called Riches, and th'other Youth, wither of them was better,"
which was acted before the king on Jan. 6, 1552.

It seems that the custom of using children in pageants was kept
up under Edward VI; and when we hear of a child being so used, we
may be sure that he was in all probability a Chapel boy. In Kempe's
Loseley MSS.[95] there is a series of documents relating to the *Triumph
of Cupid*, which was performed under the direction of George Ferrers,
then Lord of Misrule, on Twelfth Night, 1553. One of them, which
describes the order and sense of the pageant, informs us that "Cupid
shalbe a letell boye howe must be tremmed, w^t a bow and arrows
blindfelde." Other actors were Mars, Venus, Idleness, Dalliance,
"the Marshall and his band"; "Venus to come in w^t a maysk of
ladies and to reskue Cupide from the Marshall."

That is the last notice except one we have of children in the reign
of Edward VI. In 1553, among plays that were "prepared . . . .

---

not ser*uisable*   j Gowne of Tawny Tilsent newe for a Boye to pley the
                            *pro*fett with a *prophett*es cappe of Tilsent."
There are other items of garments for boys. Altogether, they create at least a
strong inference that the children or gentlemen of the Chapel, or both, took part
in some of the coronation pageantry.

[92] There was a pageant like "the Tower of Babylon." More than this we cannot
with certainty derive from the Revels documents. *Vide* Feuillerat, *Revels of Edward
and Mary*, p. 26.

[93] Wallace describes the document as a list of stuffs for the tailor, made out in
1547, and annotated in the margin from time to time till 1554, as the cloth was made
up into garments. Many notes are undated, as in the present case. See Feuillerat,
Revels of Edward and Mary, p. 194, l. 21, and note.

[94] *Op. cit.*, p. 278. Feuillerat quotes from *Cotton MS. Nero* C.x. ff. 51 b.-52 a.

[95] Pp. 39 ff; also Feuillerat's *Revels of Edward and Mary*, p. 93.

ageanste Shroftyde," as the *Revels Accounts* tell us,[96] was a play "of childerne sett owte by M[r] haywood," for which twelve coats for the boys in it were requisitioned. This play with another on "the state of Ireland" by William Baldwin was "deferred tyll Easter and Maydaye folowinge." The position of Heywood at court during this time is not easy to determine. He is known to have been attached to the court since as early as 1519,[97] when he was twenty-two years old, and to have served both as singer and as player on the virginals. Occasionally, as in the case above, he is recorded as directing the efforts of a company of boy players, which has until recently been taken to be the children of the Chapel.[98] But Mr. Reed, the latest student of the problem, finds no sure evidence of connection with the Chapel, and is inclined to believe that Heywood's associations were rather with the boys of St. Paul's.[99] Heywood is known as a dramatic poet of no mean gifts, as an ardent Catholic, and as a famous wit. Bale[100] says that he was much bent on fostering vanities, such as pageants, plays, and masques. He was an especial favorite of Mary, both as princess and queen, and was the constant recipient of favors from her. But just what his relations to court drama were is hard to define. He seems to have been a free lance, lending his services and suggestions wherever they were wanted.

[96] Cf. Feuillerat's *Revels of Edward and Mary*, pp. 129, 140, 142, 145. Also Kempe's *Loseley MSS.* p. 89.

[97] Thus A. W. Reed, "John Heywood and his Friends," *Library*, 1917, Ser. 3, Vol. VIII. Mr. Reed shows that the payment of 8d. to John Heywood in January 1515, noted by Collier and elsewhere, was made to a different man of the same name, a Yeoman Usher, who was pensioned off in 1525-6.

[98] Heywood is mentioned four times in the old accounts as leader of a troupe of boys or in ways that suggest that connection.

1. March, 1538, before the Princess Mary, "w[t] his children" (see *supra*, p. 62).

2. Feb. 13, 1551, before the Princess Elizabeth (see p. 116). The connection is ambiguous here; Heywood is paid along with Sebastian Westcote and the king's drummer, perhaps all for the same service.

3. 1553, a play "of childerne sett owte by M[r] haywood." See above.

4. August, 1559, before Elizabeth at Nonsuch, "a playe of the chylderyn of Powlles and ther master S(ebastian), master Phelypes, and master Haywod" (see p. 124). The connection with Paul's is here pretty certain.

[99] "On the whole I think the evidence points to Heywood's being associated with St. Paul's or 'called in' there and elsewhere to manage, collaborate or advise. He was the author or joint author of plays and the deviser or joint deviser of pageants, and where so much is uncertain we can at least, I think, postulate his association with Redford and Westcott." A. W. Reed, "John Heywood and his Friends," *Library*, Ser. 3, Vol. VIII, p. 300.

[100] *Scriptorum Illustrium . . . . Catalogus* (1557-8), II, 110.

I am not at all sure, from the fact that he used occasionally a children's company, that he did not also employ the various men's companies for the presentation of his pieces, especially the interlude players regularly retained for the service. In fact, from the number of the pieces he seems to have composed,[101] we must feel pretty sure that had he always written for his children's company, we should have more notices of him than we do. We must not regard John Heywood as devoted to the production of plays for children until we have better proof of it.

Whatever changes Mary introduced into the ordering of her court and into the general dramatic world,[102] she did not give up the custom of Chapel plays. In fact she commanded a performance by the gentlemen of the Chapel to be prepared for her coronation, and this was done;[103] but for some reason it was deferred and not played till Christmas.[104] The children played in the Christmas holidays too,

[101] He is known to have composed the plays of *Love* and *Weather*, *The Four PP*, *Wit and Witless* (or *Wisdom and Folly*), and is credited on good grounds with *The Pardoner and the Friar*, and *John the Husband*. But his output must have been greater than that. In an epigram on himself he calls himself "Heywood that hath made many mad plays." It may be worth noting that had his genius been confined to such allegorical stuff as *Love*, *Wit and Witless*, *Spider and the Fly* and even *Weather*, he could hardly with justice have termed himself "Heywood with the mad merry wit" and spoken of his "many mad plays." Cf. Warton's *Hist. of Eng. Poetry* (1871), IV, 87.

[102] Immediately upon her accession in July, 1553, Mary issued an act prohibiting the performance of interludes and plays without the licence of the queen. The reason given is the prevalence of plays and books "concerning doctryne in matters now in question and controversye, touchynge the hyghe poyntes and misteries of christian religion." The act is dated August 16, 1553. Cf. Collier, I, 155, where so much of it is given as relates to plays. Cf. also *Acts of Privy Council* and *State Papers, Domestic, Mary*, under proper date.

[103] This was the well known *Genus Humanum*, a play no longer in existence. The queen's requisition to the Keeper of the Wardrobe of garments for the occasion is extant among the *Exchequer Accounts*, 427/5 (9), and was first printed by Mrs. Stopes in *Athenæum* of Sept. 9, 1905. Since then it has been reprinted in various places, e.g. Wallace's *Evolution*, p. 94, and Feuillerat's *Revels of Edward and Mary*, p. 289. The list is one of the most interesting of its kind that we possess; it tells us more completely than anything else how an elaborate moral play of the period was garbed for court presentation.

[104] Wallace, in *Evolution of the English Drama*, 96 note 2, cites the *Loseley MSS.*, *Revels*, No. 118, to the effect that Cawarden, under date 1 Mary, makes note of certain charges "in the Chrystenmas in A° predicto for makynge of maskers and dyuers players garmentes wythe stuff necessarye for the same"; after the word "garmentes" is interlined, "for the children of the Chappell." But Feuillerat says that various documents in referring to this play use the words "children" and "gentlemen" interchangeably.

and we may make a shrewd and safe guess when we name *Respublica* as the interlude then given.[105] This play was presented by
boys, as the prologue shows,[106] and from its title it is seen to have
been written in 1553: "A merye enterlude entitled Respublica, made
in the yeare of oure Lorde 1553, and the first yeare of the moost
prosperous Reigne of our moste gracious Soveraigne Quene Marye
the first." The prologue moreover shows the play to have been
devised for Christmas recreation,[107] and the epilogue addresses
prayers only for Queen Mary, not for Philip and Mary, as would be
the case a year later. All this gives us as good circumstantial evidence for assigning *Respublica* to the Chapel boys in their performance at Christmas, 1 Mary, as we could well wish for in this
period of scarce and puzzling documents. Mr. Magnus believes from
comparison of *Ralph Roister Doister* with *Respublica* that they were
both by the same hand, namely Nicholas Udall's. That is certainly
possible, and gains strength from the fact that Udall is known to
have served Mary in much the same way as Cornish served Henry
VIII—by devising and presenting plays and pastimes.[108]

I fear we cannot be nearly so certain that *Ralph Roister Doister*
was given on the same occasion by the same children, as Professor
Wallace would like to think.[109] The note in the *Revels Accounts*
which tells us that the boys acted then does not give us any hint of
there being two performances. There is good reason for believing
that *Ralph Roister Doister* was not written until 1552 or 1553, or at
least after 1546.[110] Thomas Wilson quotes in his 1553 edition of
The Rule of Reason the letter in *Ralph* which is made the subject in

---

[105] For a discussion of date and authorship cf. Leonard A. Magnus's edition of
the play for *E. E. T. S.*, *Extra Series*, XCIV, 1905.

[106] "But shall boyes (saith some nowe) of such high mattiers plaie?
   No not as disscussers, but yet the booke doth saie
   Ex ore infantium perfecisti Laudem."

[107] "We, that are thactours, have ourselves dedicate
   with some Christmas devise your spirites to recreate."

[108] Cf. the well known order of Mary to the Master and Yeomen of the Revels,
printed first in Kempe's *Loseley MSS.* p. 63, in which Udall is said to have "at
soondrie seasons convenient heretofore shewed, and myndeth hereafter to shewe,
his dilligence in setting foorth of Dialogues and Enterludes before us for our regell
disporte and recreation." Cf. also my review of W. H. Williams's edition of *Jack
Juggler* in *Jour. of Eng. and Germ. Philol.*, XV, No. 2, April 1916, p. 317.

[109] *Evolution*, pp. 96-97.

[110] Cf. John W. Hales's "The Date of 'The First English Comedy,' " in *Englische
Studien*, XVIII, 1893, p. 408. Mr. Hales's two main arguments I have outlined
above.

the play of two diametrically opposite interpretations, but does not quote it in the two earlier editions of his book, of 1550-1 and 1552. Ergo, it is maintained, the play appeared between 1552 and 1553. At least it came out after 1546, when Heywood's *Proverbs* appeared, for there are many close parallels between the two works. But those arguments are not quite enough to place *Ralph* with any real certainty in the first year of Mary's reign; for while the evidence afforded by Wilson's *Rule of Reason* shows pretty clearly that Wilson got hold of Udall's comedy between 1552 and 1553, it hardly shows more than that. The play may have been written a year or two, or even longer, before; it may even have come out in 1552 in an edition now lost. At any rate, we cannot be sure, even allowing that Wilson was an old pupil of Udall's, that he became at once familiar with a play acted in the comparative privacy of court. That the play should be dated much later than the various guesses ranging from 1534 to 1541 with which commentators have favored it, seems reasonable enough; that it can be definitely assigned to the Christmas of 1552 or 1553 I believe to be beyond our present knowledge. I attach no importance to a circumstance which clinches the matter for Wallace—namely, the fact that the "Queen" is referred to in the text and prayed for at the end. Of course, in a play printed after 1566 the "Queen" alluded to was Elizabeth. We shall meet elsewhere[111] with a case exactly in point, of a play in which the original references to the "King" had been changed on publication to "Queen," to the detriment of the rhyme.

The position of Nicholas Udall at court during Mary's reign is even more puzzling than Heywood's, and indeed it is precisely the relative positions of these two men that are hard to settle. Heywood by virtue of his training, his skill and reputation as a playwright, and the long partiality of Mary for him, would seem destined to fill the place of contriver of entertainments when she came to the throne. But instead we find that it was Udall who "shewed and (minded) hereafter to shew" his diligence in that behalf, while Heywood sank into the background. We can indulge in numerous suppositions as to the wherefor of this vicissitude, without being able to arrive at any definite conclusion. Perhaps Heywood's playing days were over, and he had retired from "fostering vanities," or perhaps his time was wholly given up to editing *The Spider and*

[111] Cf. p. 125. The play is *The Nice Wanton*, written presumably in the reign of Edward VI and published soon after the accession of Elizabeth.

the Fly and he had the "mad, merry wit" all choked out of him by that monumental allegory. At any rate, there was Udall in his place. Between 1541, when he was dismissed from Eton, and 1553, when he became master at Westminster, Udall's life was unsettled and is now only vaguely known. It seems he must have drifted to court and there put to good use his talents of play writer and producer, which he had doubtless gained in exercising the dramatic genius of the boys of Eton. How extensive was his success is shown by the sweeping nature of the grant made December 8, 1554,[112] permitting him to call on Cawarden for any supplies he might need. It would seem that Udall was then in absolute control of the pastimes at court.

At Christmas 1554-5 there were "certeine plaies set forthe by Nicholas Udall,"[113] but what they were we know not. He is known to have written a play called *Ezechias*,[114] and *Jacob and Esau*, on no evidence at all, has been attributed to him.[115] Since he died

---

[112] So Wallace, *Evolution*, p. 97 note 1. Kempe in the *Losely MSS.*, p. 63, prints the date as December 3, and Feuillerat, in his *Revels of Edward VI and Mary*, p. 159-160, as December 13.

[113] Feuillerat, *Revels of Edward VI and Mary*, p. 166. "(Christmas 1 and 2 Philip and Mary) . . . . charges of the said Maskes and plaies set owte by vdall *with* alteracion of garment*es* for his Actours. . . . ."

[114] J. G. Nichols, *Progresses of Queen Elizabeth*, I, 186.

[115] Wallace, *Evolution*, 101 and note 1. The sum of Wallace's hypothesis is this: "It seems remarkable that students of the drama have not long ago universally recognized Udall in this play. Even the most cursory examination of it and all related matters is convincing." With so little to go on, one can hardly tell how to judge Professor Wallace's steps of proof. One thing is certain, that not even the most cursory examination should convince even the most careless critic that the two plays are by the same hand. We have only *Ralph Roister Doister* and the somewhat dubious *Respublica* to compare it with. A cursory examination shows that *Jacob and Esau* has a theme quite different from the other two, is free from the coarseness of language and character that is common in the others, is deeply serious and religious in the main parts of the story and shows a light and playful tenderness in the characters of Mido and Abra which finds no counterpart in the others, and shows practically none of the characteristic words and phrases which Mr. Magnus (ed. of *Respublica*, E. E. T. Soc., pp. xviii ff.) has found to be common to the two others. Moreover, in dramatic art *Jacob and Esau* greatly excels; there is a feeling for character and dramatic suspense—as for example in the scenes of Rebecca's pleading for Jacob with Isaac (Act I, sc. 4), of the hunger of Esau, and of the anger of Esau—that is unmatched in any play previous to it. All this is not incompatible with Udall's having written the play long after *Roister Doister*, in the development of his powers. But Wallace, to be consistent with his own arguments, must assign the play to 1552-3, on account of the epilogue addressing *only the queen*. This is his argument with regard to *Roister Doister*. To assign both plays to Udall and to the

in 1556, his plays must necessarily fall in the pre-Elizabethan period, and it is only reasonable to suppose that the bulk of them were done when he had the greatest opportunity and incentive to exercise his powers—in Mary's reign.

One play of this period there is which I think might be proposed as Udall's work with much more reason than *Jacob and Esau*, though I dislike suggesting authorships which cannot be proved. This is *Jack Juggler*, an interlude in the style of *Thersites* written for children.[116] It was licensed in 1562-3 but the quarto is undated. This piece is not divided into acts, and retains the Vice of the old popular drama, but it is just such a working up of a hint from Plautine comedy as is *Roister Doister*; *Roister Doister* goes back to the *Miles Gloriosus* and *Jack Juggler* to *Amphitruo*, but neither is a translation or even adaptation of the original so much as a reworking of a situation from classic comedy in the manners and speech of contemporary England. This is something new in English drama; possibly the earliest example of it is *Thersites*. The names of the characters have a similar ring in the two plays, being in both cases

---

same year is preposterous. But first we must have some reason for connecting it with Udall at all. I would sooner assign it to Heywood's old age; for then I should have the weight of Heywood's known depth of religious feeling on my side.

Mrs. Stopes (*William Hunnis*, pp. 265 ff.) would like to give the play to Hunnis; but her arguments hardly carry weight, and some of them (such as the evident familiarity of the writer with church music and the palpable writing for boy actors in the parts of Mido and Abra) would apply to other men than Hunnis. Moreover, she places the play so early—as early as the reign of Edward VI—in its first rendering, that Hunnis must have been a precocious genius to have written it so young; for Mrs. Stopes fixes the date of his birth at approximately 1530. It is worth noting that *Jacob and Esau* was licensed in 1557-8, and *Roister Doister* not until 1566; our earliest copy of *Jacob* is dated 1568; the date of *Roister Doister* is lost. Mrs. Stopes does not hesitate to date *Jacob* earlier than *Roister Doister;* but that is only possible if they were written by different men, and is incompatible with what we know of the age of Hunnis. The claims of Udall and Hunnis are equally thin.

Mrs. Stopes's critical remarks on the play are just, and deserve quoting. (Cf. p. 268.) "It is the first drama of its kind that eschews all allegorical treatment; among the first that has a due regard to classical unities, and is divided into five acts and proportionate scenes . . . . . The most striking feature of the play perhaps, is the modernness of its style, a sign that the writer was one of the leaders in the literary developments of the Metropolis. The Dialogue is well-sustained; except for two lively soliloquies there are no long speeches, as were then too common. It is permeated with quiet humour that never approaches either coarseness or profanity."

[116] "A new Enterlued for Chyldren to playe, named Iacke Iugeler, both wytte and very playsent." Title page. The play has been variously reprinted. The best edition is by W. H. Williams, for the Cambridge University Press, 1914.

built on a descriptive principle. Thus in *Jack Juggler* are Dame
Coye, Mayster Boungrace, Jacke Jugeler, Jenkin Careaway, and
Ales (or Alison) Trype-and-go; in *Roister Doister* are Margerie
Mumblecrust, Tibet Talkapace, Tristram Trustie, and Tom Tru-
penie. Then some of the characteristic oaths in *Roister Doister* occur
in *Jack*: "St. George thee borrow" (or "St. George to Borowe"),
"by Cock's precious podstick," "by God's precious."

Furthermore, the prologues to the two plays are almost identical
in content. Both start off with an adjuration to men to mix decent
mirth with the serious businesses of their lives, and go on to assert
that mirth relaxes the mind and by refreshing it prolongs the life,
and that it must be joined with virtue and honesty. The classic
writers understood this very well, and especially were the Latin
comedy writers, Plautus and Terence, skilled in uniting virtue and
wit. The substance of the two prologues is thus identical, only *Jack
Juggler's* is much longer and consequently more verbose. It looks
as if Udall had been pleased to cut down one of his old prologues for
his new play of *Roister Doister*; for certainly *Jack* is the earlier piece
of the two.[117]

[117] See my review, already cited, of Williams's edition of the play in *Jour. of
Eng. and Germ. Philol.*, XV, No. 2, April 1916, p. 317.

CHAPTER III

THE CHAPEL UNDER ELIZABETH, 1558-1592

1. *1558-1576, Richard Edwards.*

It is an interesting fact that during the earlier decades of Elizabeth's reign the children of Paul's appeared more frequently at court than the children of the Chapel. The reason is hard to discover. By long custom the Chapel had come to be the company naturally in demand at court revels, yet Westcote's boys began playing directly on the accession of Elizabeth, and continued almost yearly, while the Chapel played comparatively seldom. Perhaps Westcote was *persona grata* for being an old friend of Elizabeth's; he had played with his boys before her in 1551.[1] Yet that hardly enables us to understand why Westcote's company was so much more acceptable than the Chapel.

We get no notice of plays in the *Declared Accounts* till 1568, yet the Chapel played long before that. Under Bower they acted at the second Christmas season, of 1559-60, for an inventory in the *Revels Accounts*[2] tells us that they were furnished with garments while Sir Thomas Benger was master, i.e., since August 25, 1559, when Sir Thomas Cawarden died, and before the spring of 1560, when the present inventory was taken. There appears in the inventory an item of five yards of white sarsenet used "in ffurnisshinge of a pley by the children of the Chapel." If Wallace is correct[3] in stating that only one play was acted this Christmas season, then this Chapel play seems to be identified with the play of New Year's eve, 1559, which Machyn tells us was stopped in the middle by the orders of the queen.[4]

This was the last play we hear of under Richard Bower's régime. Bower died July 26, 1561,[5] and was succeeded by a man of genius,

[1] Cf. p. 116.

[2] Feuillerat, *The Revels of Queen Elizabeth*, p. 34.

[3] *Evolution*, p. 106. He is probably wrong, for the *Revels Accounts* tells us that there were "playes and other pastymes" set forth at this season.

[4] *Machyn's Diary*, ed. J. G. Nichols, 1848, p. 221; under date December 31, 1559-1560. "The sam day at nyght at the quen('s) court ther was a play a-for her grace, the wyche the plaers plad shuche matter that they wher commondyd to leyff off, and contenent the maske cam in dansyng."

[5] The date on his gravestone.

possibly the most gifted of all the Chapel masters—Richard Edwards, whose patent bears the date October 27, 1561.[6] Edwards was a versatile man, in his day a noted poet and dramatist.[7] The greater part of his poems appeared in 1576 in *The Paradise of Dainty Devices*, to which Edwards was the most important contributor;[8] one of his poems has been reprinted from manuscript in Park's *Nugae Antiquae*[9] His fame was sounded in unmeasured terms by the writers of his own day;[10] and indeed when we compare his products with the average lucubrations of the period, we must admit that in him there was something of the genius which recreates and gives a new impulse and direction to literature. That he did not exercise the influence which was his due must be laid to the door of his premature death. His songs—for songs they truly are, set to music in many cases by himself—have the qualities of grace, an unwonted sureness of rhythm, and tenderness of sentiment. His meter is nearly always the same, yet is characterized by elasticity and real elegance, to an extent hitherto unknown. His most praised poems are the song to May and the truly beautiful elaboration of the motto *Amantium irae amoris redintegratio est*;[11] yet his other poems are tasteful and worthy of reading.

[6] *Patent Rolls*, 3 Eliz., Pt. 6, m. 33.

[7] To the familiar facts of his life I have only one thing to add: that on November 28, 1565, the queen bestowed on him the lease of various parcels of land in Wyrrall, in the parish of West Kyrkeby, Chester, and in Repingdon, Derbyshire, to hold them for twenty-one years at the total rent of £12-3-2. *Patent Rolls*, 8 Eliz., No. 1019. For the facts of Edwards's life, so far as they are known, and for critical estimates of his work, cf. *D. N. B.*, Sir Egerton Brydges' introduction to the 1810 reprint of *The Paradise of Dainty Devices*, Mrs. Stopes's *William Hunnis*, Wallace's *Evolution of the English Drama*, and two corrective articles by W. Y. Durand: "Some Errors Concerning Richard Edwards," in *Mod. Lang. Notes*, XXIII, 128, and "Notes on Richard Edwards," in *Jour. of Germ. Philol.*, IV, 348.

[8] Important in rank of merit, for in actual numbers his songs are not prominent. The title page of the 1576 edition reads: "The Paradyse of daynty deuises, aptly furnished with sundry pithie and learned inuentions: deuised and written for the most part by M. Edwards, sometimes of her Maiesties Chappel; the rest by sundry learned Gentlemen, both of honor, and woorshippe. . . . ." etc. It has been reprinted in 1810 with a biographical and critical introduction by Sir Egerton Brydges.

[9] II, p. 392, ed. 1804.

[10] Cf. e.g. Googe's eulogy, p. 82, and the praises of Turberville and Twine.

[11] This ballad is of a kind familiar to the period, built up about a proverb or motto which recurs at the end of each stanza. It exhibits Edwards's versification and sentiment at their best. Sir Egerton Brydges, in his preface to the 1810 edition of the *Paradise*, calls it with somewhat excessive partiality one of "the most beautiful morceaux of our language."

The dramatic work of Edwards, and his activities at court during his brief mastership, have been frequently and fully gone into,[12] so that there is no need to repeat in detail a familiar history to which I can add nothing new. Suffice it to say that of Edwards's three known plays we possess but one, *Damon and Pythias*, which has undergone various reprintings.[13] The prologue of that play refers to a preceding one, apparently immediately preceding, which offended because of the excessive freedom, in one direction or another, of the sentiments therein set forth.[14] It is plain that the former play was a comedy, and that comedy was the form of drama natural to Edwards's genius, since in turning from it he wrote "against his kinde"; and it would seem that the cause of the offense was licentiousness. A good deal of wild speculation has been put forth about this comedy.

The third known dramatic product of Edwards's pen was the well known *Palemon and Arcite*, in two parts, played before the Queen at Christ Church, Oxford, by the scholars there, on the nights of September 2 and 4, 1566. This play, which has been sufficiently written about,[15] is famous for the cry of hounds which was counterfeited off stage, the quips and praises of the queen concerning it, the falling of a stage at the beginning and the consequent death of some persons, the beauty of the lad who played Emilia, and the admiration of the beholders.[16] Though there is no relying on the unsupported opinions of contemporaries for our judgments of plays

[12] Cf. particularly Mrs. C. C. Stopes's *William Hunnis*, 146-149, and *passim*, and C. W. Wallace's *Evolution of the English Drama*, 106 ff.

[13] In Dodsley, e.g. Facsimile reproduction among the *Tudor Text Facsimiles*.

[14] Here are the lines in question, addressed to the audience (as modernized in Hazlitt-Dodsley):

. . . .But if your eager looks do long such toys to see,
As heretofore in comical wise were wont abroad to be,
Your lust is lost, and all the pleasures that you sought,
Is frustrate quite of toying plays. A sudden change is wrought:
For lo, our author's muse, that masked in delight,
Hath forc'd his pen against his kind no more such sports to write.
Muse he that lust (right worshipful), for chance hath made this change,
For that to some he seemed too much in young desires to range:
In which, right glad to please, seeing that he did offend,
Of all he humbly pardon craves: his pen that shall amend.

[15] For the original material from which most of the subsequent accounts have been taken, cf. Nichols, *Progresses of Queen Eliazbeth*, I, pp. 210, 212, 236; *Elizabethan Oxford*, ed. C. Plummer, 1886, pp. 128-9, 138-9, 179-80, 185; Wood's *Athenæ Oxonienses*, under the author's name.

[16] Wood relates it was said of Edwards that he would run mad if he made more plays before his death.

of this day, it must be, taking all the extravagant praises into consideration, that these plays of Chaucerian inspiration were really Edwards's *chefs d'oeuvre*.

The one existing play, *Damon and Pythias*, presents certain problems, if we are to take it as a good specimen of Edwards's genius. It is generally said to have been produced at court in Christmas, 1564, there existing in the *Revels Accounts* for that date specifications for a play by the children of the Chapel called, marginally, "Edwardes tragedy."[17] It was licensed in 1566, and printed in 1571, with the notable comment on the title page that it was printed as it was shown before the queen by the children of the Chapel, "except the Prologue, that is somewhat altered for the proper vse of them that hereafter shall haue occasion to plaie it, either in Priuate, or open Audience." The play was received with the usual enthusiasm which was aroused by everything which Edwards wrote.[18] Yet one wonders to hear it so praised. Ward has justly called it a clumsy play. The opening scenes, with their slow exposition and the purposeless enterings and exits of characters, are particularly feeble. To be sure the play warms up later on: there are good playing parts, in which the author has not spared to lay on the color after his own theories—in the depth of Dionysius's tyrannical cowardice, the goodness of Eubolus, the shifty timeserving of Carisophus. The scenes of the condemnation of Damon, the substitution of Pythias as his pledge, and the return of Damon in the nick of time, have many excellent passages of a really tragic cast, and the return of Damon especially must have thrilled the onlookers. But what doubtless made the success of the play was the comedy scenes—the fooling of Jack and Will, the beating of Carisophus, but most of all the scenes with Grim the Collier, which are excellent in a broad manner. There is much in the play that is tedious, and some scenes that are good; it is clear that, at the time this play was written, at

---

[17] Inaccurately described, since the play is a comedy at base with tragical moments. But the writers of the *Revels Accounts* were not scrupulously accurate, and the word *tragedy* had in those days enough elasticity of meaning to comprehend this play. W. Y. Durand, in *Journ. of Germ. Philol.*, IV, p. 348, takes pains to verify this dating of the play.

[18] Cf. the lines of Thomas Twine on Edwards, printed in Turberville's *Epitaphes, Epigrams, Songs and Sonnets*, 1567.

" . . . .Thy Damon and his friend, Arcyte and Palemon
With moe full fit for princes eares, though thou from earth art gone,
Shall still remain in fame, and lyke so long to bide
As earthly things shall live, and God this mortall globe shall guide."

least, Edwards possessed more skill in the individual scenes than in weaving them together, and the play bears out his admission in the prologue that comedy was his *forte*.

But many things about this play are more interesting than the play *per se*. The guarded allusions to the previous play which displeased pique our curiosity. The references in the prologue have already been quoted, as seeming to show that the comedy offended in morals, for so I understand the line "For that to some he seemed too much in yonge desires to range." The pains the prologue further takes[19] to insist that no covert satire on the court is meant hints that such was a fault of the earlier play. Mr. Fleay[20] believed that there are references in the text to the interrupted play of 1559. This play he identified with *Like Will to Like, quoth the Devil to the Collier*,[21] his main evidences being a connection of the line of Newfangle's "Thou are Hance the hangman of Calais town" with the execution on December 20, 1559, of Hurlestone and Chamberlain for neglience in not keeping the hold and castle of Calais; and the fact that the play was given at Christmas, as shown by the Vice entering with a Knave of Clubs in his hand. The play is gross in parts, though highly moral in sum, and satirizes rather keenly the newfangled fashions in clothes. It is not necessary to follow all of Fleay's textual analogies, one example will do. Newfangle in *Like Will to Like* says that Lucifer taught him to make among other oddities of dress,

"Especially breeches as big as good barrels."

This, says Fleay, was alluded to by Edwards in the conversation of Grim with Will and Jack, in which Grim comments on the size of their breeches, which make them "seem a great bug." Certain difficulties present themselves in the way of Fleay's theory, which furthermore includes the assumption that the performance of 1559 caused the inhibition of the Chapel company for four years, and that their rehabilitation is glanced at in the line of Cristippus to Will.

"For thy good service thou shalt go in thine old coat at Christmas."

Now *Like Will to Like* is printed as written by one Ulpian Fulwell;

[19] The lines are:
    "Wherein talking of courtly toys, we do protest this flat,
    We talk of Dionysius court, we mean no court but that."

[20] *Queen Elizabeth, Croydon, and the Drama*, a paper read before the Balham Antiquarian and Natural History Society, London, 1898. This presents an opinion later than the one he expresses in his *History of the Stage*, pp. 59, 60, where he picks *Misogonus* as the earlier play and ascribes it to Edwards.

[21] Reprinted in Hazlitt's Dodsley.

yet the prologue to *Damon and Pythias* declares unmistakably that it was preceded by a play of *Edwards* which won the displeasure of its hearers. That it was played, at least in part, is obvious, else it could not draw down censure, and that it was played at court and by the Chapel children is assured by Edwards's situation. Moreover, Fleay in assuming the inhibition of the children acted without sufficient evidence; in fact evidence makes us sure that they did act between 1559 and 1564.[22] Still further, is it not rather unreasonable to hold that fashions in breeches which were new enough in 1559 to deserve rallying were still subjects of remark in 1564?

We should remember all along, however, that we are dealing with hypothetical matter. The date 1564, for instance, assigned to *Damon* has a pretty slight foundation, and all conjecture about the play of 1559 is very unsubstantial.

Yet even disregarding the external evidence against Mr. Fleay's coupling *Like Will to Like* and *Damon and Pythias*, the textual evidences are all against it, baffling as they are. The vague hints contained in the text of *Damon*—all of them, by the way, from the mouth of Grim—are provoking. Here is the passage[23] in which these references occur, the italics being my own.

Grim. Are ye servants then?

Will. Yea, sir; are we not pretty men?

Grim. Pretty men, quoth you? nay, you are strong men, else you could not bear these breeches.

Will. Are these such great hose? in faith, goodman collier, you see with your nose:
By mine honesty, I have but one lining in one hose, but seven ells of rug.

Grim. That is but little, yet it makes thee seem a great bug.

Jack. How say you, goodman collier, can you find any fault here?

Grim. Nay, you should find fau't, marry here's trim gear:
Alas, little knave, dost not sweat? thou goest with great pain,
These are no hose, but water-bougets, I tell thee plain;
Good for none but such as have no buttocks.
Did you ever see two such little Robin ruddocks
So laden with breeches? *chill say no more, lest I offend.*

[22] Cf. e.g. Barnaby Googe's well-known eulogy of Edwards, printed in 1563, in which he speaks of his excellent comedies.

[23] In Hazlitt's Dodsley, 1874, Vol. IV, pp. 71 ff.

Who invented these monsters first, did it to a ghostly end,
To have a mail ready to put in other folks' stuff,
We see this evident by daily proof.
One preached of late not far hence in no pulpit, but in a
wain-cart.
That spake enough of this; but for my part,
Chill say no more: your own necessity
In the end will force you to find some remedy.

Will. Go thy way, father Grim, gaily well do you say,
It is but young men's folly, that list to play,
And mask awhile in the net of their own devise;
When they come to your age, they will be wise.

Grim. Bum troth, but few such roisters come to my years at this
day;
They be cut off betimes, ere they have gone half their
journey;
I will not tell why: let them guesse that can, I mean somewhat
thereby.

It is perfectly clear that here are veiled hints in plenty and of no
dubious signification if we but had the key. Fleay thought he had
the key, because the first hint points to some offense given somewhere in saying too much about the new and extravagant style of
bumbasted breeches, and because *Like Will to Like* contains some
incidental satire on clothes. But aside from the difficulties arising
from Fleay's dating of the two plays—which would make a play of
1564 refer back five years to one of 1559, skipping over the plays in
between, it is apparent from a reading of *Like Will to Like* that the
satire on clothes is purely incidental, and not of a nature to offend
beyond endurance. The play is a modified morality, and the plot is
the familiar one of the seduction and damnation of the weak and
vicious and the glorification of the virtuous. Fleay himself supposes
that the scene which caused the suppression of the performance was
the one in which Hance is drunk to the point of indecency, but where
there is no talk of clothes. All this does not jibe with the hints of
Grim. I know not how to take the reference to the sermon from the
wain cart unless Fleay is right in supposing it to refer to the performance of a play from a movable stage; and yet that smacks of
public performance, whereas we should look rather for allusions to
court performances, since only in them would it be dangerous to displease. The last hint, as to the roisterers who are cut off betimes, I

can make nothing of. At any rate I see no excuse for interpreting it
with Fleay as referring to an inhibition of the Chapel.

On all accounts I believe that *Like Will to Like* is to be rejected
as the subject of Grim's hints. Moreover, it seems very clear to me
that these reflections are to be taken in connection with the prologue, and that Edwards in both places had the same play in mind.
That appears to me as natural as can be; in each case a play is
referred to which has given offense—surely it is one and the same
play. Then we have to understand that not long before the production of *Damon*—for *Damon* was the result of the check which
drew him "against his kind" away from comedy—Edwards wrote a
comedy which was too free in its criticisms of court and dress, and
smacked too much of libertinage. The play has not come down to
us—was probably never sent to the printer. We must enroll it
among the comedies rivalling Plautus and Terence which Barnaby
Googe said in 1563 had already been penned by Edwards.

Enough of this hypothetical talk, which I am afraid is dull enough.
There remains one thing to say about *Damon and Pythias* which I
regard as in many ways most important of all. This play takes
rank as the first in English embodying a formulated theory of
comedy writing; and places Edwards perforce as the first theorist
in the art of comedy of the English language. The principle is bald
enough, and smacks strongly of Latin comedy, yet it is a theory,
and a working one at that. Edwards expresses it best himself:

> And yet (worshipful audience) thus much I dare avouch,
> In comedies the greatest skill is this, rightly to touch
> All things to the quick; and eke to frame each person so,
> That by his common talk you may his nature rightly know:
> A roister ought not preach, that were too strange to hear,
> But as from virtue he doth swerve, so ought his words appear:
> The old man is sober, the young man rash, the lover triumphing in joys.
> The matron grave, the harlot wild , and full of wanton toys.
> Which all in one course they no wise do agree;
> So correspondent to their kind their speeches ought to be.
> Which speeches well-pronounc'd, with action lively framed,
> If this offend the looker on, let Horace then be blamed,
> Which hath our author taught at school, from whom he doth not swerve,
> In all such kind of exercise decorum to observe.
> Thus much for his defence (he saith), as poets earst have done
> Which heretofore in comedies the self-same race did run.

This is simply an expression of the Latin theory of decorum in art; but it is one which later evolved into Ben Jonson's theory of humors, and has been an active principle down at least through the Restoration period.

It has long been known that by 1563 Edwards had written many plays[24] of which we do not even know the name; and it has been argued by inference that so popular a dramatist as Edwards must have played oftener at court than is recorded in extant documents. I have turned up one notice which has hitherto escaped investigators. In a volume of *Wardrobe Accounts* in the *Lord Chamberlain's Office*, P. R. O.,[25] under the date of December 20, 1561, are outlined the expenses of an interlude. The items unfortunately are only for yards of cloth for which the sum total was £29-19-8½, and convey no information of value; but the last item is expressive:

> "Ric*ardo* Edwardes pro diu*ersis* p*ar*cellis Sericorum pro di*cto* Interlude et pro st*auro* apparat*o* p*ro* di*cto* Interlude Precio inde ingross*o* . . . . x^{li} ix^s 1½^d."

This interlude must have been given by Edwards, else he would not have been concerned in the furnishing of it. Inasmuch as Edwards

[24] As an example of the kind of praise that was lavished on Edwards, Barnaby Googe's well-known "sonnet" will serve. The text of Arber (*English Reprints*, 1871) is used.

Of Edwardes *of the Chappell*
Deuyne *Camenes* that with your sacred food,
Haue fed and fosterde vp from tender yeares,
A happye man, that in your fauour stoode
Edwards in Courte that can not fynde his feares
Your name be blest, that in this present age
So fyne a head, by Arte haue framed out
Whom some hereafter helpt by Poets rage,
Perchaunce maye matche, but none shall passe (no doubt)
O *Plautus* yf thou wert alyue agayne,
That Comedies so fynely dydste endyte.
Or *Terence* thou that with thy plesaunt brayne,
The hearers mynde on stage dydst much delyght.
What wold you say syrs if you should beholde,
As I haue done the doyngs of this man?
No word at all to sweare I durst be bolde,
But burne with teares, that which with myrth began,
I meane your bookes, by which you gate your name,
To be forgot, you wolde commit to flame.
Alas I wolde *Edvvards* more telle thy prayse,
But at thy name my muse amased stayes.

[25] L. C. 2/4, no pagination. The present excerpt occurs in the accounts for the year lying between the feasts of St. Michael the Archangel of 2 and 3 Eliz.

received his patent of mastership on October 27, 1561, this play, which was doubtless given in the Christmas holidays, is marked as the first one of his régime.

It is during the mastership of Edwards that we first hear of the Chapel boys playing elsewhere than at court. On February 2, 1565, they appeared with their master at Lincoln's Inn,[26] of which Edwards was already a member.[27] A year later at the same time he is again recorded as conducting a play.[28] Then on September 2 and 4, 1566, came the last plays of which we have record, the two parts of *Palemon and Arcite*. Edwards died October 31, 1566,[29] prematurely, and left behind him plays still unfinished.[30]

Edwards is more interesting now for the reputation he bore in his own day and since than for the actual merit of the one play that survives to us. As a lyric poet he surpassed most of those that had gone before him; as a dramatist, to judge at least from *Damon and Pythias*, he was easily excelled by the authors of *Ralph Roister Doister* and *Jacob and Esau*. Yet he had the faculty of hitting the public fancy, and his later plays must have been superior to *Damon*. There have been attempts to attach other plays to his name, which have not been marked by sagacity of reasoning or critical insight. The crudest of them is undoubtedly the hesitating ascription to him of *Sir Clyomon and Sir Clamydes* in Bullen's introduction to his edition of Peele,[31] on the grounds, forsooth, that the lumbering verse, the antiquated diction, and the presence of the Vice mark it as an early play "by some such person as Richard Edwards." Now though *Damon* is a clumsy play, it is also a good play in many parts, and does not deserve to qualify its author as a catch-all for bad

[26] *Black Books of Lincoln's Inn*, ed. W. P. Baildon, I, 344: (Council held February 2, 1565) . . . ."Mr. Edwards shall have in reward liiis. iiiid. for his plee, and his hussher xs., and xs. more to the children that pleed." In the margin: "Children of the Quene's Chappell."

Same, p. 348. Accounts of the Treasurer, 6 and 7 Eliz. 1564-5: " . . . .38s. 2d. for a supper for the boys of Mr Edwards of the Queen's Chapel, and for the "staff torches" and clubs (baculis), and other necessaries for the play (ludum) at the Purification last; 20s. reward to the boys."

[27] *Records of Lincoln's Inn: Admission Registers 1420-1893* (ed. 1896) I, 72. Edwards was admitted Nov. 25, 1564.

[28] *Black Books*, I, 352; Accounts of Christopher Wrey, the Treasurer, 7 and 8 Elizabeth, 1565-6: " . . . .40s. to the boys of the Queen's Chapel and their Master, for their play at the Purification."

[29] *Old Cheque Book of the Chapel Royal*, ed. Rimbault for the Camden Soc., p. 1.

[30] Wood on Edwards, in *Athenæ Oxon.*

[31] A. H. Bullen, *The Works of Peele*, London, 1887, p. xlii.

anonymous plays. Professor Kittredge,[32] with a very good show of reason, has assigned the play to Thomas Preston, author of *Cambyses*. Professor Wallace[33] has also bestowed on Edwards the authorship of *Appius and Virginia*[34] and *Misogonus*,[35] apparently, with a reversal of Bullen's principle, endeavoring to credit Edwards with everything that was good in his time. Since Wallace gives no more substantial reasons for his opinions than his conviction that the style in each case is Edwards's and could not possibly be another's, it is hardly necessary to say more than that in my own opinion the styles in neither case resemble Edwards's, nor even each other. *Misogonus* is a harsh, masculine play for the most part, though smooth in spots; the style is compressed, uneven, filled with coarse cant terms, and the comedy matches it. There is much vigor in the comic parts, but none of Edwards's elegance. Moreover, the alternate rhyming scheme is not one we find Edwards using. *Appius and Virginia*, too, uses in the comic scenes, instead of Edwards's characteristic seven foot line, a cantering four foot metre. But the prologue alone disposes of Wallace's brief. "But patiently we wish you bear with this our first attempt," it says. Wallace would date the play earlier than *Damon*, and yet in the prologue to *Damon* we are told that the author, having offended in a recent comedy, now drew away from that style of writing which pleased him best, and by inference betook himself to the present piece, which he called a tragical comedy. That is, from *Damon* we learn that heretofore Edwards has been given to writing comedy,[36] and thus *Appius* cannot have come earlier; and it certainly cannot have come after, because its own prologue tells us it was a first attempt. We are on the horns of a dilemma.

Edwards was succeeded immediately by William Hunnis, gentleman of the Chapel, musician, and playwright, who was sworn into

---

[32] "Notes on Elizabethan Plays," in *Journal of Germanic Philology*, II, 1898-99, p. 8.

[33] *Evolution*, pp. 108, 111.

[34] In Hazlitt's Dodsley.

[35] Most conveniently had in Brandl's *Quellen des weltlichen Dramas in England*. Professor Kittredge ("The Misogonus and Laurence Johnson," in *Journal of Germanic Philology*, III, No. 3, 1901), has made out a good case for assigning the authorship to one Laurence Johnson, M. A. of Cambridge in 1577. The plea is brilliantly made, but is not entirely convincing.

[36] This is borne out by the eulogy of Barnaby Googe, of 1563, in which only Edwards's comedies are spoken of as being so good that they would have made Plautus and Terence burn their plays in shame, had they been still alive.

office November 15, 1567.[37] This master has had more honor paid him by scholarship than any other, for his life has been written by Mrs. C. C. Stopes[38] with a care which has exhausted the subject and has produced a volume of respectable thickness. This man enjoyed his post for thirty years, until his death in 1597; during that time he carried on the tradition of his predecessors in directing the acting of his young troupe, yet not a line of any play which can be even plausibly connected with him has come down to us.

There is no record of his playing until Shrovetide, 1568, when he presented a "Tragidie" to the queen.[39]   This tragedy has been identified by Mrs. Stopes[40] with a "Tragedie of the kinge of Scottes" which is mentioned with seven "playes" in a requisition addressed to Sir Thomas Benger and dated June 11, 1568.[41] Since the Council's Warrant speaks of a tragedy given by this company and by none other, and since the *King of Scots* is the only tragedy mentioned in the Revels list, the putting two and two together is in this case a simple and reasonably safe process.

In the next year appeared a pamphlet of tantalizing interest to our subject, which has been often referred to from the time of Warton; I mean *The Children of the Chapel Stript and Whipt.* All we know of this polemic depends on the extracts quoted in Warton; he saw it at the Bodleian, where it was registered among the books of Bishop Tanner's Collection, but since then it has disappeared. Mrs. Stopes, as she tells us in her *Hunnis*, went to Oxford to look for it, with no success, and I made a similar effort in the spring of

---

[37] *The Old Cheque Book of the Chapel Royal*, under date 1566. His patent is dated April 22, 1567.

[38] Printed in Bang's *Materialen* series in 1910 as vol. 29.

[39] *Declared Accts. of Treas. of Chamber*, Pipe Office, Roll 541, fol. 103. "William Hunnys m^r of the children of the quenes ma^{ts} Chappell upon a warr*ant* signed by the Counsell dated at westm*inster* the iijd of Marche 1567 for pr*esentinge* a Tragidie before her ma^{tie} this Shroftide by waie of her ma^{ts} rewarde vj^{li} xiij^s iiij^d."

[40] *Athenæum*, 1900, I, 410; and *Wm. Hunnis*, p. 223.

[41] Feuillerat's *Revels*, p. 119. *Harl. MSS.* 146, fol. 15b. The Treasurer and Chamberlains of the Exchequer are required to pay Benger the amount of sums spent "vppon theis playes Tragides and Maskes following viz.: Imprimis for seven playes, the firste namede as playne as Canne be, The seconde the paynfull plillgrimage, The thirde Iacke and Iyll, the forthe sixe fooles, The fivethe callede witte and will, The sixte callede prodigallitie, The sevoenthe of Orest*es* and a Tragedie of the kinge of Scott*es*, to ye whiche belonged diu*ers* howses, for the setting forthe of the same as Stratoes howse, Gobbyns howse, Orestioes howse Rome, the Pallace of prosperitie Scotlande and a gret Castell one thothere side."

1912, with like result. Warton's extracts[42] show that the tract was a part of the Puritan revolt against the stage; it is of interest because of its early date and because it bears indirect witness to the notoriety enjoyed at this time by the Chapel company. It is doubtful if any excerpts so brief as these of Warton's could have conveyed more valuable information. We learn—what, to be sure, we already knew from other sources—that the Chapel plays were handsomely set forth. Of more interest is it to know that the boys were especially given to plays derived from classical sources, after the style made popular by Edwards. Last of all, we learn that they played on Sundays, or at least did not refrain from doing so occasionally, and used the queen's Chapel as their theatre. We are interested in knowing where they played before their occupation of Blackfriars in 1576. When they came before the queen it was of course on a specially constructed stage in the "great hall" of whatever palace the queen happened to inhabit. Their public or semi-public performances seem to have taken place in the Chapel Royal, a proceeding for which there was ample precedent in the custom of the time.[43]

[42] Ed. 1871, IV, p. 217. These are the passages quoted: "Plaies will neuer be supprest, while her maiesties unfledged minions flaunt it in silkes and sattens. They had as well be at their Popish service, in the deuils garments." And: "Even in her maiesties chappel do these pretty vpstart youthes profane the Lordes Day by the lascivious writhing of their tender limbs, and gorgeous decking of their apparell, in feigning bawdie fables gathered from the idolatrous heathen poets."

[43] Whenever there was no hall or inn-yard available for the exhibition of plays, the players were often accustomed to resort to the nearest church, where a stage was set up in the nave or choir. Old church account-books are full of references to such practice. Bewdley Chapel warden's accounts, for example, give this entry: "Paid unto the queenes plaiers in the Church, six shillings and eightpence"; and in the register of Syston, under the year 1602, we find: "Paid to Lord Morden's players because they should not play in the Church, xijd." (See T. F. Thisleton Dyer's *Old English Social Life, as told by the Parish Register*, p. 204.) When Elizabeth visited Oxford and Cambridge in 1564 and 1566, she was entertained by plays in the chapels of the respective King's Colleges. (See Nichols's *Progresses of Q. Elizabeth*, I, pp. 166, 186; and Warton's *Hist. of Eng. Poetry*, III, 306.) For the play at King's College, Oxford, on August 6, 1554 (the *Aulularia*), a great stage was erected "containing the breadth of the Church from the one side to the other, that the Chappels might serve for Houses." (Nichols, *op. cit.*, I, 166.) It can be easily understood that a church would lend itself readily to the needs of theatrical production.

Common as was the custom, it nevertheless aroused a comprehensibly bitter opposition from the more strict of both ecclesiastical parties. The censure of the established church was represented by the edict of Bishop Bonner in 1542 for the diocese of London, which directed that no manner of common plays, games, or interludes should be allowed in any church or chapter. (Cf. W. H. Frere's *Visitation Articles and Injunctions of the period of the Reformation*, 1910, II, 88.) And the

Hunnis appeared at court with his children on Twelfth Day at night, 1570, and in Shrovetide of 1571,[44] and again on Twelfth Day, 1572,[45] when a play called *Narcissus*[46] was given. All of these plays are lost. In *Narcissus* there was a noise made "off stage" like hunters and hounds pursuing a fox, "which crye was made, of purpose even as the wordes then in vtterance, & the parte then played, did Requier," and there was also a counterfeiting of thunder and lightning.[47] It appears that Hunnis was following the *Zeitgeist* and the example

---

bishop of Hereford (as we are told by the compiler of the MSS. *Collections respecting Herefordshire*, catalogued at the British Museum as *Harl. MSS.* 6726) wrote in 1548 that "whereas stage playes used to be acted in the churches, which should rather be as Christ saith a house of prayer, by which playes & other appertenances to their jests the hearts of the faithfull are drawne aside to vanityes we comand & enjoyne that forthwith all playes & interludes be forborne in churches."

The edict of Bonner was not attended with much success, for we hear of plays being given in churches well into the 17th century. It was a fit subject for the wrath of the dissenters, who have left us many warm passages belaboring the custom. We have noticed one of them, in the *Children of the Chapel Stript and Whipt*; the author of *The Third Blast of Retrait from Plays and Players* in 1580 complained that the players "are permitted to publish their mametry in every temple of God, and that throughout England"; and Thistleton Dyer (*op. cit.*, p. 205) quotes from a tract, which he does not name, published in 1572, to the effect that "(the clergyman) posteth it over as fast as he can gallop: for he either hath two places to serve, or else there are some games to be played in the afternoon, as lying the whetstone, heathenish dancing of the ring, a beare or bull to be baited, or else Jack-an-apes to ryde on horseback, or an interlude to be played, an if no place else can be gotten, it must be done in the church."

Probably the strong feeling of the Puritans in this matter was shared by many churchmen, who rightly regarded such practices as a desecration to the edifice and a discredit to the indulgent clergy. But the custom did not die out until well in the 17th century, and according to Malone (ed. *Shakespeare*, 1821, Vol. III, p. 45) it was taken notice of in one of the canons of James I, soon after 1603.

[44] *Declared Accts. T. R.*, Pipe Office, Roll 541, fol. 115.
"To Willm Hunys m^r of the children of her maiests chappell upon the counsailles warrant dated vij° Januarii 1569 by waie of her highnes rewarde for presenting of a plaie before her maiestie on Twelfe Daie at nighte laste paste. .vj^{ll} xiij^s iiij^d." Fol. 127 b. "To William Honnyes, Richard ffarante, and Sebastian Westcote m^{rs} of the children of the Q: maiests Chapple Royall, windsore, and powles upon the Counsailles warrant dated ultimo Februarii 1570, for presenting of thre plaies before her maiestie at this Shrofted last past past (sic), namelye Sondaie, Mondaie and Tuesdaie by waie of her highnes rewarde xx^{li}."

[45] *Same*, fol. 137b. Dated January 1572 from preceding entry. "William Hunnyes m^r of the Children of the Chappell for presentinge a plaie before her highnes on twelf daie at nighte last past vj^{li} xiij^s iiij^d."

[46] Feuillerat's *Revels*, p. 145. "Narcisses showen on Twelfe daye at Nighte by the children of the Chappell."

[47] Feuillerat's *Revels*, pp. 141, 142.

of his predecessors in taking his subjects from classic literature and mythology. Beyond doubt in this case he went to Ovid; possibly in Golding's translation, possibly through the Chaucerian fragments of the *Romaunt of the Rose*, which had been published among Chaucer's works by William Thynne, in 1532 and in 1542.[48]

There is no mention of Hunnis in the *Declared Accounts* of 1573 or the *Revels Books*, yet Chalmers[49] and Malone[50] both say that "among the Council Register Notes on Jan. 6, 1573" there occurs this item: "To John Honyes for the Chapel Children for a play £6-13-4." This is not to be found in the printed copy, which states that there is a gap from autumn till February; but with so many gaps in the Register, that does not prove much. "John" is surely a slip for "William." It has been suggested that the Chapel play of this year may have been *Theagenes and Cariclea* or the *Play of Fortune*, both mentioned incidentally in the *Revels Books* for 1572-3[51] without designation of the company playing them; but this is simply guess work.

On Shrove Sunday, 1575, Hunnis's company played again, seemingly twice,[52] but nothing is known of the plays, beyond a few unilluminating items in the *Revels Accounts*. At this time, when the boy-players were gaining more and more popularity on the court stage and multiplying vigorously, children were still being used at court in pageants, as they had been from the time of Henry VII. For in the *Revels Accounts* of 1576-7[53] we read that one Nicholas Newdigate, gentleman, was paid 43s. 8d. "for his paynes in hearing and trayninge of the 7 boyes that should have spoken the speeches

---

[48] Cf. Stopes, *Wm. Hunnis*, p. 229. Mrs. Stopes mentions a poem of "Narcissus" —which I have not been able to consult— by Thos. Edwards, of the Privy Chamber, published with his *Cephalus and Procris* in 1595, which refers curiously to "Narcissus in another guise and gayer clothes."

[49] *Apology* (1797), p. 360.

[50] Ed. of Shakespeare, 1821, III, 423.

[51] Feuillerat's *Revels*, pp. 175-176. The items are: "ij speares for the play of Cariclia; An Awlter for theagines: To Robert Baker for drawing of patterns for the playe of fortune & altering the same."

[52] *Declared Accts*, T. R. Pipe Office, Roll 541, fol. 178 b. "To Willm Hunys m^r of the children of her maiests chappell upon the counsells warrant dated at Richmond xvj ffebruarii 1574 by way of her maiests guifte for presentinge of a playe before her heignes upon Shrove sondaie the last past the some of xiij^{li} vj^s viij^d." The sum—just double the ordinary fee for a single play—indicates certainly that there were two plays given. The extraordinary fee for one play was always £10.

[53] Feuillerat's *Revels*, p. 268.

in the Mask,[54] and for their Charges and Cariadge back againe."
We found the children of the Chapel, and other children as well,
beginning their dramatic career as singing supernumeraries in court
shows. By this time they have advanced so far in the dramatic art
and in the affections of the theatre-loving public as to become a
regular acting company, with rivals of merit and success in their
own kind, while at the same time they continue to take part in the
performance of masques and pageants. As we have seen in another
chapter, their use was not confined by any means to court pageants,
but extended from early times to all kinds of public shows, for
which they were felt to be specially fitted.

2. *1576-1584. The First Theatre at Blackfriars.*

In this same year (1576-7), the Chapel played at court on Twelfth
Day[55] at night in a piece called *The History of Mutius Scevola*,
of which nothing is known. Yet the bare facts contained in the
entries of the *Declared Accounts* and the *Revels Books* are full of
interest. From them we learn that Richard Farrant was master of
the Chapel, at a time when Hunnis was still alive and able, so far
as we know, to fulfill the duties of his post, and that the two companies of Windsor and the Chapel acted together in combination.
These have always been puzzling mysteries, together with all the
history of the Chapel, St. Paul's and Windsor, from now till the
end of the century, and especially in the years round 1583. Much
of the mists has been blown away by the publication of the highly
interesting and valuable Loseley papers relating to the first Blackfriars theatre, which appeared first in the *Shakespeare Jahrbuch* for
1912 (Vol. 48) under the signature of Professor Feuillerat, and later
in the same year with some additions in Professor Wallace's *Evolution of the English Drama;* and finally in part in the *Malone Society*

[54] There is little said about this masque in the *Accounts*. There is an item of
"two Waggons to carie stuff for the Mask, and to carie the Children that should
have served in the Maske," and one for hire of a horse "with garmentes for a Maske
to my Lord Chamberlyn." Apparently the children were not used, or the masque
was not given.

[55] *Declared Accts. T. R.* Audit Office, 382/15, (Wallace, *Evolution*, p. 218. The
corresponding entry in the *Pipe Office Rolls* is wanting.) "To Richard ffarante m^r
of the Children of the Chappell vppon the Counsailles warraunt dated at Hampton
Cowrte xx^mo Januarii 1576 for presentinge a play before her maiestie in Xpenmas
Hallydaies last past vj^li xiij^s iiij^d & further by waie of her maiestes reward x^li in all
the some of xvj^li xiij^s iiij^d."

Feuillerat's *Revels*, p. 256 (*Revels Accounts* for 1576-7). "The historye of Mutius
Sceuola showen at Hampton Court on Twelf daie at night, enacted by the Children
of windsore and the Chappell."

Publications, Vol. II, Pt. 1, 1913, again edited by Professor Feuillerat. The story revealed by these documents is too well known to make it necessary for me to repeat it here in detail. A brief résumé of the facts will suffice.

In the year 1576, on the twenty-seventh of August, Richard Farrant presented a petition on his own behalf and through the medium of his friend Sir Henry Neville, to Sir William More, owner of the Blackfriars property, to be allowed to lease of him a house in that precinct lately held by Lord Cobham.[56] He wished to knock out one partition, throwing two rooms into one, and promised to restore the property on his removal to its former condition. Sir William was nothing loath, and drew up a lease[57] which was signed on December 20. Farrant declared that his intention was to use the premises as a school in which to teach the children of the Chapel. But what he really did was to build a stage, put in seats for spectators, in short reconstruct the place as a theatre and begin regularly to exhibit the children under his direction in plays open to the general public. This state of affairs continued to the satisfaction of Farrant and the annoyance of More until the death of Farrant on November 30, 1580.[58] He left his widow with ten children to support

---

[56] These letters are among the Loseley MSS. Cf. Wallace, p. 131. For an excellent résumé of the history of the Blackfriars property from early times to the closing of the theatres, cf. Chambers's *Elizabethan Stage*, vol. II, Chapter 17.

[57] *Loseley MSS. Deeds, Elizabeth*, Bdl. 348. Wallace, *Evolution*, p. 132. The lease thus describes the property taken by Farrant: " . . . .sixe vpper Chambers loftes lodgynges or Romes . . . . latelye amongest other in the tenure & occupacion of the right honorable Sr Willyam Brok Knyght lorde Cobham And do conteyne in length from the Northend therefo to the South ende of the same one hundred fiftye and sixe fote & a half of assice whereof two of the saide sixe vpper chambers loftes lodgynges or Romes in the Northend of the premisses together wᵗʰ the bredeth of the litle rome vnder graunted do conteyne in length ffyfty & sixe fote & a half and from the Est to the west part thereof in Bredeth Twenty & fyve fote of assice And the ffower other Chambers or Romes Residue of the saide sixe vpper Chambers do conteyne in length one hundred and tenne fote and in bredeth from the Est to the west part thereof xxii fote of Assice."

[58] *Old Cheque Book*, p. 3. Farrant's will, in *Somerset House, Prerog. Court of Cant.*, 9 Darcy, was dated the day of his death, November 30, 1580, and proved March 1, 1581; it has been printed in Wallace, *Evolution*, p. 152. Farrant is shown therein to have been one of the East Greenwich colony of gentlemen of the Chapel Royal. To his wife Anne he leaves the lease of his house in Blackfriars, and therewith the lease of his house in Greenwich, until his son Richard shall come of age; also the little house "in the Gardeyne ende at Grenewich" and all his other goods. She is to provide for their children as she thinks best.

This sounds like the will of a man in reasonably comfortable circumstances, yet Anne Farrant complained later that she was in great straits to maintain her

and little means of doing so. This woman, it will be remembered, was before her marriage Anne or Annis Bower, daughter of Richard Bower. In her distress, and wishing to put the theatre to some lucrative use, she sublet it to William Hunnis, who intended to continue playing there with the Chapel boys as Farrant had done, and persuaded his patron, the Earl of Leicester, to intercede with Sir William More in his behalf. And so the nobleman did in the following letter.[59]

"Sr William Moore. Wheras my frend Mr Hunnys this bearer enformeth me that he hath of late bought of ffaran*tes* widdowe her lease of that house in black fryers wch you made to her husband disseased and meanes ther to practise the Queens children of the Chappell, being nowe in his chardge, in like sort as his pre*decesso*^r did for the better trayning them to do her Ma*ies*tie service. He is nowe a suyter to me to recom*m*end hym to yor good fauo^r wch I do very hartely as one that I wish right well vnto and will giue you thank*es* for any countenaunce or frendshipp you shall shewe hym for the furtheraunce of this his honest request And thus wth my hertie comenda*ci*ons I wish you right hartely well to fare. from the court this 19th of Septemb^r 1581.

Yo^r verie louing frend

R. Leycester."

Though More was not at all pleased with the way things had been going at his Blackfriars house, or with the shift by which Farrant, under color of presumably intending to teach the Chapel boys grammar and music, really taught them acting, nevertheless he did not yet take action to prevent the schemes of Hunnis and the widow Farrant. And so Hunnis reestablished his children in the theatre and took into partnership one John Newman. From then on there were troubles upon troubles, which may be read in detail in Wallace's *Evolution*. The joint lessees were backward in paying their rent, the widow Farrant was unable in consequence to meet her obligations to Sir William More and was put to extreme shifts to

---

family. Young Richard Farrant began raising money on his inheritance at once; for I have copies of a Recognizance dated August 26, 1581 (*Close Rolls*, 23 Eliz. No. 1119) and of a mortgage of £80, dated Oct. 26, 1585, (*Close Rolls*, 27 Eliz. No. 1208). Both involved all or part of the East Greenwich property, and both were rendered void by having their conditions fulfilled.

[59] In *Loseley MSS. Letters*. Wallace's *Evolution*, p. 154.

raise the rent money, and Sir William brought pressure to bear to oust altogether his undesirable tenants.   Hunnis and Newman doubled to save their interests which were committed to this venture, and about 1582-3 leased again the theatre to a young Welsh scrivener, Henry Evans, whom I have shown elsewhere to have been an intimate friend of Sebastian Wescote,[60] at this time lately dead. It was doubtless as a result of this bargain that the children of Paul's in 1583-4 joined forces with the Chapel in the performance of Lyly's *Sapho and Phao* and *Campaspe*; in spite of Hunnis's and Newman's apparent retirement, the Chapel boys continued to act for a while, but the main company at Blackfriars—the one Lyly wrote for and Lord Dudley was interested in—was Paul's.[61] Trouble now came thick and fast. More proceeded to eject his tenants by making a fictitious lease of the property to Thomas Smalpeece of Guildford and in Trinity term, 1583, bringing suit in the name of Smalpeece against Evans.[62] In this suit he was apparently successful, and went on then to oust Anne Farrant. She, in great distress and fear of ruin, brought suits in the Court of Common Pleas against Newman and Hunnis for the purpose of recovering £100 on the joint and several bond they had sealed to her on taking the lease. They in turn had recourse to the usual shift of suit in Court of Requests for relief in equity against her suits. The Court of Requests papers are printed in Wallace's *Evolution*, and contain pretty nearly a full synopsis of the vicissitudes of the theatre since the first lease to Farrant. But interesting as they are, the petty squabbles there revealed are not essential to the understanding of the main history of the Blackfriars theatre.

This suit was brought in January 1584. Meanwhile a new complication had been added to the tangle by the Earl of Oxford's buying the lease of Evans some time in 1583 and giving it to his protégé John Lyly. From now on the history of Blackfriars becomes the history of Paul's children, for whom Lyly wrote, and I have treated it in the chapters dealing with that company.[63] But the end was not far off. In Easter term, 1584,[64] More finally ob-

---

[60] Cf. p. 135.

[61] Cf. pp. 135 ff.

[62] Cf. Anne Farrant's petition to Sir Thomas Walsingham in 1583 and the Court of Requests papers in the suit Newman and Hunnis v. Farrant.

[63] Cf. pp. 132 ff.

[64] The widow Farrant said in her answer to Hunnis's and Newman's bill of complaint, dated January 27, 1584, that Sir William had "since made somme

tained judgment against Evans, and he was given possession. Thus ended the first Blackfriars theatre, coeval in its foundation with the *Theatre* itself, forerunner of a ten times more famous Blackfriars theatre, and itself worthy of high place in the history of English drama and playhouses. It failed not through lack of patronage, but through the wranglings of its owner and lessees. It served to introduce the first of the great Elizabethan school of dramatists, John Lyly.

What became of the theatre after Evans forfeited his lease does not concern us. It passed into private hands and finally became the Pipe Office.[65] It was reserved for an adjoining piece of property, the fencing school of the famous Rocco Bonetti, to become the Blackfriars theatre made famous by Shakespeare. It is time we are getting back to the plays of the Chapel Royal. We are at once puzzled by the part Richard Farrant plays in their management, when we should expect to find Hunnis exercising his duties. This fine musician was a gentleman of the Chapel in the time of Edward VI. He left it to become master of the Windsor children in 1564, and was

---

entry and a new Lease of the premisses to one who by colour thereof hath sued the said Evans." Sir William, in his memorandum of the case, says he brought action against Evans "at what time (he) was soe possessed" of the lease, and when it came to trial Evans demurred and this was in Trinity term; he may have brought action much earlier. More was not awarded judgment till Easter term the year later. Since the case was going on in January, 1584, as widow Farrant testifies, he may have begun just before then, in which case he obtained judgment in Easter, 1585; or a year ago, in which case judgment was awarded in Easter, 1584. But another circumstance makes it almost certain that the theatre was vacated in 1584. In July of the year Peregrin Willoughby wrote to Sir W. More in behalf of Rocco Bonetti, the fencing master, who had taken over a lease from Lyly of a house of Sir William's in Blackfriars, and was spending large sums in repairing it. (*Loseley MSS., Letters*, 1581-1600.) On April 22, 1586, Lord Hunsdon wrote angrily to More regarding a request for rent (*Loseley MSS.*, Vol. VIII of bound correspondence, letter 58). He says: "And for the leases which I bought of Lyllye, sens you meane to make no longer state of them, I must be content with those yeres I have alreddie paid for. . . . ." "Those years" would hardly be an applicable expression if the lease had only been acquired a year ago. So it seems that Lyly was unburdening himself of his Blackfriars property in 1584, and the natural inference is that the moving cause was the loss of the theatre. Still further evidence is furnished by the publication in that year of the two plays of Lyly's acted by his company—*Campaspe* and *Sapho and Phao*. *Sapho and Phao* was entered April 6, 1584, in *S. R.*, at a time, according to my theory, when it was evident that More was going to have judgment awarded him. The publication of plays nearly always indicates that they have been put out of dramatic circulation.

[65] For a minute discussion of the fate of Farrant's theatre and the identification, site, and arrangement of Shakespeare's, cf. Wallace's *Evolution*.

readmitted as gentleman in 1569.[66] That he really held simultaneously from 1569 till 1576 and later the positions of gentleman of the Chapel and master of the Windsor children is upheld by the repeated payments to him as master of the children, and by the *Cheque Book* entry of 1569 and his calling himself in his will "gentleman of the Chapel." As soon as he became settled at Windsor he organized the choristers there into a company such as Hunnis presided over, which found success on the stage and played with a regularity at court that attested to their popularity. Their first appearance before the queen was in Shrovetide, 1567, and from then on until St. John's Day, 1575, they played at court almost yearly.[67] In this time Farrant presented *Ajax and Ulysses* in 1571-2, *Quintus Fabius* in 1573-4, and a play about King Xerxes in 1574-5; none is extant or in any way known to us. Then on Twelfth Day 1577 the two companies of the Chapel and Windsor played together under Farrant's direction in *Mutius Scevola*, as has been noticed, and Farrant was entered in the *Declared Accounts* as master of the Chapel. From then till his death in 1580 Farrant is called in the records of payment "master of the Chapel," and neither the children of Windsor nor Hunnis are any longer heard of. This is strange and curious. It means that for that time Farrant was in name and fact "master of the Chapel" during a temporary retirement of Hunnis. We cannot avoid any other conclusion. Professor Wallace would have it that Farrant and Hunnis were in partnership, and that the two companies were worked as one under Farrant's direction. As to such joint operation there is no evidence, beyond the fact that both companies played on Twelfth Night, 1577. But the *Revels Books*, which afford us this information, name only the Chapel boys in all subsequent entries, and the conclusion is convincing that only the Chapel played. There is no evidence at all that Hunnis retained any interest either open or silent in the management of the Chapel company from 1576 till 1580. It has been adduced that Farrant is

---

[66] Cf. *Cheque Book of Chapel Royal* under these dates. Whether or not it was at this time customary for a singing man to belong to two choirs at once, it became common enough later. In Archbishop Laud's injunctions to St. Paul's following his visitation of 1636 (*Lambeth MSS.* 943, p. 463), he thus commands: "3. Item that speciall notice be taken, that none of your Quire, whoe doe alsoe belonge to his Maiesties Chappell, doe escape without condigne punishment, if att any time they neglect performance of their service in both places."

[67] Cf. extracts from *Declared Accounts, passim* in these years; e.g. in Wallace's *Evolution*, pp. 213 ff.

given the title of master of the Chapel in the records of payment.
There is other and stronger evidence.　The well known petition of
Hunnis in 1583 for an increase of fee[68] includes Farrant in a citation
of the masters given in chronological order from the accession of
Elizabeth.　Says he: "The burden heereof hath from tyme to tyme
so hindred the M^rs of the children viz m^r Bower, m^r Edwardes,
mysellf and m^r ffarrant . . . . ." I wish to call attention to the fact
that the names are given here in the order of their succession, and
that Farrant *succeeded* Hunnis.　Moreover, the letter with which the
Earl of Leicester forwarded Hunnis's suit to More to take over Farrant's lease,[69] said that Hunnis meant to practise the children in
plays "in like sort as his predecessor did for the better trayning
them to do her Maiestie service."　That is, Hunnis in 1581 by
resuming his duties in the Chapel had become Farrant's successor.
We cannot avoid the conclusion that there was a hiatus in Hunnis's
mastership from 1576 to 1580 which was filled by Richard Farrant,
who dropped the Windsor boys so far as play-acting was concerned[70]
and devoted himself to the Chapel.　In all the letters, petitions,
suits, and notes, to which the occupation of Blackfriars gave rise,
the Windsor children are never mentioned; it is always the Chapel
boys who are connected with Farrant's name.　And who indeed
could believe it practicable for two bodies of actors so far apart to
unite daily or even weekly to rehearse the plays which were given
in the theatre, and that the Windsor boys could be perpetually
posting into London?

　　These facts seem to me to be entirely obvious, but I cannot offer
an explanation of them.　Why Hunnis at some time between Shrove
Sunday, 1575,[71] and Twelfth Night, 1577, relinquished his post to

[68] Cf. p. 102. for the document in full.

[69] For this letter cf. *supra*, p. 91.

[70] He still retained the mastership and doubtless fulfilled his ordinary duties.
This is proved by an entry on *Pipe Office Roll* 541, of the *Declared Accounts of the
Treasurer of the Chamber*, fol. 210: "Richarde ffarant m^r of the children of her
maiests chappell at of winsore viz for the chardges of xv of the singinge men of the
said chappell and sixe of the children repayringe thither to Readinge at her maiests
laste beinge there by her maiests comaundment by the space of iiij^re daies beinge
xxj^tie in nombre at iij^s iiij^d apece *per* diem by vertue of the counsells warrant dated
at windsoure septimo die Novembris 1577 amountinge in the whole for their
chardges the same tyme to the some of xiiij^li." So far as I know it was unusual for
any other choir than that of the Chapel Royal so to attend the queen on her re-
movings from London.

[71] The date of the last performance for which he was paid as master of the children of the Chapel.

Farrant is almost beyond conjecture, nor is it profitable in our present lack of information to lose ourselves in hypotheses. In all probability Farrant was at most a substitute master, for we have no record of any formal appointment granted him or of any resignation or dismissal of Hunnis. Farrant, as gentleman of the Chapel and an experienced producer of plays, was exceptionally fit for the post. That Hunnis was not ill at the time is shown by his taking part in the great festivities at Kenilworth in 1575.[72] There is something strangely significant in the coincidence of the accession of Farrant to the mastership of the Chapel and his embarcation on the Black-friars venture which piques the curiosity strongly. I am sure there is something in it. Perhaps we shall know some day.

One more question is raised by this Blackfriars theatre discovery, which seems not to have occurred to Wallace or to Feuillerat or to Chambers, yet which is a most natural and obvious one: why did Farrant lease More's house for a theatre? The Chapel children had been playing in some place to more or less miscellaneous audiences long before this, just as the boys of Paul's were doing, and if we are to accept the word of the writer of *The Children of the Chapel Stript and Whipt*, that place was the Royal Chapel itself. Why then were new quarters so urgently needed? It is vaguely implied in documents of the More-Farrant-Hunnis-Evans-Lyly quarrel that Farrant wanted a place which would be better fitted for rehearsing the children in plays which were to be shown before the queen. But that seems a slight motive for so radical a step. Since the Black-friars theatre was constructed almost simultaneously with the *Theatre*, the playhouse of Burbage could hardly have been an in-spiration to Farrant. I prefer an hypothesis which is eminently reasonable, and which has the advantage of settling very satis-factorily another vexed question. My theory is that in or about 1576 the usual acting place of the Chapel was barred to them. If it was the Royal Chapel, as seems most probable, the cause is readily to be comprehended in a feeling the queen might naturally have of indignity done to a sacred edifice, and the long-continued op-position of the bishops to any acting at all in churches. However that may be—and whether or not the closing of the Chapel and the temporary retirement of Hunnis were related—when the Chapel was closed it was necessary to find other quarters if the children were to be continued as players; for by this time we must believe that

[72] Cf. Mrs. Stopes's *Wm. Hunnis*, Chap. 19.

the children's companies were thoroughly committed to the publication of their art and would not feel repaid, as earlier they may have
done, to prepare one or two plays a year for court consumption. So
Farrant looked about for a new playing-place, and thought none so
suitable as the old Blackfriars monastery, which was hallowed with
theatrical traditions by long association with the Revels Office. He
may have been spurred in his schemes by news of James Burbage's
daring operations in building the *Theatre*. I repeat, we must look
for some really potent reason for the Chapel children's abandoning
their former hunting ground and seeking new. My hypothesis
further assumes what follows readily on the preceding, that the
right to act in their former theatre was denied the Chapel boys
forever, and that consequently when the Blackfriars theatre was
closed in 1583 or 1584, they were necessarily compelled to stop
playing entirely. So it is that we find no trace of them acting publicly
in London from 1583 until the appointment of a new master and the
acquisition of a new theatre in 1600. The gap in the operations of
the Chapel children fits so exactly the time elapsed from the closing
of Blackfriars theatre No. 1 to the opening of Blackfriars No. 2
that I feel there must be a relation of cause and effect. Thus a
troublesome question on which much ink has been spilled is easily
and naturally answered, without recourse to such dubious matter as
royal displeasure, inhibitions, and the like. Of course, the coincidence of the reopening of Blackfriars not coming until after Hunnis's death seems significant, but we must remember also that the
new theatre did not become available till then. My hypothesis also
would bring into line the petition of Hunnis in 1583, by explaining
that it was submitted either upon the final withdrawal of the income
supplied by his boys' public performances, subsequent to the closing
of their theatre, or in anticipation of such withdrawal.

The literary history of the Blackfriars under Farrant may be
speedily summed up, for of all the plays which may have been
brought out there, none has come down to us even at second hand.
The next performance at Court after the one of doubled forces on
Twelfth Night, 1577, came on St. John's day[73] of the Christmas
holidays at the end of the year; then another again on St. John's

---

[73] *Declared Accounts, Treas. of Chamb.* Pipe Office Roll 541, fol. 211. "Richard
ffarant m^r of the children of her ma*ie*sts chappell uppon the counsells warrante
dated at Hampton courte xx^{mo} Januarii 1577 for presenting a playe before her
ma*ie*stie uppon St. John's daye at nighte in the Christmas hollydaies 1577 wth
lxvj^s viii^d by waie of her ma*ie*sts speciall rewarde x^{li}."

Day, 1578.[74] This last is recorded in the *Revels Accounts*[75] as "The historie of .... shewen at Richmond on St. Iohns daie at night enacted by the children of the Quenes ma*iesties* chappell furnished in this office with verie manie thing*es* aptly fitted for the same." More information there is not. The next performance was a little later in 1579, when "The history of Loyaltie and bewtie shewen at Whitehall on Shrove monday at night" was "enacted by the children of the Quenes ma*iesties* chappell furnished in this office with verie manie Riche garm*entes* and prop*er*ties aptly fitted for the same."[76] From an item later in the *Revels Accounts* of "A garland of grapes and Leaves for Baccus and other of roses for .... vsed in the play of Loyaltie and Bewtie," it appears that the Chapel was clinging to its old tradition of drawing upon classical mythology and history for the sources of its plays. On St. John's Day, 1579,[77] the Chapel played for the last time under Richard Farrant. They then acted "A history of Alucius. shewed at white hall on S*t* Iohns daie at nighte enacte̍d by the Children of her Ma*ies*ties Chapell wholly furnyshed in this offyce with many garm*entes* newe made manye altered and translated whereon was Imployed for head Attyers sleeves Canyons Cases for hoase Skarfes garters and other rep*ar*acions tenne Ells of Saracenett a Cittie a Battlement and xviij paire of gloves."[78] Shortly before his death Farrant played at Lincoln's Inn,[79] just as Edwards had done before him. This was probably the last performance in his lifetime.

[74] *Same*, fol. 222b. "To M[r] fferraunte m[r] of the children of hir Ma*iests* chappel upon y[e] counsells warraunte dated xvj [to] die Januarii 1578 for pr*e*senting a play before hir Ma*ie*stie on twelf daie at night vj[li] xiij[s] iiij[d] and by waie of hir Ma*iests* speciall rewarde lxvj[s] viij[d] in all x[li]." The date of the *Revels Accounts*—St. John's instead of Twelfth Day—is probably the right one. Another company was down for Twelfth Day. The *Revels Accts.* are to be preferred for accuracy in details over the *Declared Accts.* in all cases.

[75] Ed. Feuillerat, p. 286.

[76] *Revels Accts.*, p. 303. The entry in the *Delcared Accts.*, same reference as last, runs: "To Richarde ferrante M[r] of y[e] children of hir grace chapell upon y[e] counsells warraunte dated xij[mo] Martii 1578 for pr*e*senting a playe before her Ma*ie*stie on Shrove mondaye vj[li] xiij[s] iiij[d] and of hir speciall reward lxvj[s] viij[d] in al x[li]."

[77] *Declared Accts.* Pipe Office Roll 542, fol. 8. "To Richard ffarant m[r] of the children of her ma*iests* chappell in consideracon of one playe by them pr*e*sented before her Ma*ie*stie upon S[t] Johns daye laste paste the some of vj[li] xiij[s] iiij[d] and nowe by waye of rewarde lxvj[s] viij[d] as by a warr*ant* signed by her ma*iests* pryvie Counsell dated at Whitehall xxv [to] Januarii 1579 dothe appeare x[li]."

[78] Feuillerat's *Revels*, p. 320.

[79] *Records of the Society of Lincoln's Inn* (*Black Books*, ed. W. P. Baildon, 1897), I, 418. Accounts of Thomas Wykes, Treasurer of Lincoln's Inn, 21 and 22 Elizabeth

Upon the death of Farrant, November 30, 1580, Hunnis took up the work at once. On Shrove Sunday, 1581,[80] the Chapel played in a piece described in the *Revels Books*[81] as "A Storie of .... enacted on shrovesondaie night whereon was ymployed .xvij. newe sutes of apparell.ii. newe hat*es* of velvet xx*tie* Ells of single sarcenet for facing*es* band*es* scarfes and girdles one citty, one pallace and xviij. paire of gloves." On New Year's eve, 1581, and Shrove Tuesday, 1582, they played again.[82] In December, 1582, they acted: "A Comodie or Morrall devised on A game of Card*es* shewed on St. Stephens daie at night before her ma*ies*tie at Wyndesor Enacted by the Children of her ma*iesties* Chapple, furnished w*i*th many thing*es* w*i*thin this Office, whereof some were translated, and some newe made, and Imploied therein viz. Twoe clothes of canvas xx*tie* Ells of saracenet for iiij*or* pavilions and girdles for the Boyes and viij. paire of gloves."[83] It seems to be this play that Sir John Harrington referred to when he wrote in 1591:[84] "Then for comedies, to speake of a London Comedie, how much matter, yea, and matter of state, is there in that Comedie cald the Play of the Cards in which it is shewed how foure Parasiticall Knaves robbe the foure principall vocations of the realme, videlicet the vocation of Souldiours, Schollers, Marchants, and Husbandmen. Of which Comedie I cannot forget the saying of a notable wise Counsellor that is now dead (Sir Fraunces Walsingham) who, when some (to sing Placebo), advised that it should be forbidden, because it was somewhat too plaine, and indeed, as the old saying is, (Sooth boord is no boord) yet he would have it alloued, adding, it was fit, that they which do that they should not, should heare that they would not." Mrs. Stopes, working on

---

(17 November, 1579, to 17 November, 1580): Payments: "£3 6s. 8d. to Mr Ferrand, one of the Queen's Chaplains, for a Comedy (*pro commedia*), shown by warrant of the Governors, dated February 9th."

[80] *Declared Accts.*, Pipe Office Roll 542, fol. 21. "To the M^r of the Children of the Chappell uppon the counsells warr*ant* dated at Whitehaule xiiij^{to} ffebruar*ii* 1580 for presentinge a playe before her ma*ies*tie at Whitehaule uppon Shrove sunday at nighte last past vj^{li} xiij^s iiij^d and by way of rewarde for there Attendaunce otherwise lxvj^s viij^d in all x^{li}."

[81] Ed. Feuillerat, p. 336.

[82] *Declared Accts.* Roll. 542, fol. 33.

"To the m^r of the children of her Ma*ies*ts Chappell uppon the counsells warr*ant* dated at Grenwich primo Aprilis 1582 for two plaies presented before her ma*ies*tie one the laste daie of decembr and Shrove tuesdaie xx^{li}."

[83] *Revels Accounts*, p. 349. The payment was made to Hunnis (*Declared Accounts*).

[84] *A briefe Apology for Poetrie*, 1591.

the old theory of disgrace and disfavor cast upon the Chapel company, conceives[85] that it was this play which brought Hunnis down. But that theory, if not quite broken, is now at least very fragile. And the testimony of Harrington if it does anything goes to show that the play did *not* give serious offence. Walsingham praised it, and so does Harrington, who would surely not have failed to comment had the play met with disaster. The interesting thing about this notice, provided it really refers to Hunnis's play, is the evidence it gives that Hunnis was a solid man in his craft, who could pen a comedy of so "much good matter" as to draw forth the admiration of a literary critic nine years later. It is the one bit of evidence we have, aside from the mute but expressive testimony of the popularity of his company, of the worth and appealing qualities of Hunnis's work as a dramatist.

The Chapel played next on Twelfth Day and Candlemas Day, 1584.[86] This is the year which brought forward the mysterious company patronized by the Earl of Oxford and directed by John Lyly. They played on New Year's and Shrove Tuesday. That this company was the same as that which played at Blackfriars under the patronage and direction of the same gentlemen in 1583-4, and the same that played *Campaspe* on a New Year's day and *Sapho and Phao* on a Shrove Tuesday, and was in effect a combination of the forces of the Chapel and St. Paul's—all this is hardly to be rejected as the right conclusion from good circumstantial evidence, and will be found treated more elaborately in another part of this work.[87] There, too, I have given my reasons for believing that the company specially favored by Oxford and Lyly was the St. Paul's company, and that the Chapel was called in temporarily to a partnership. This very partnership is unique and hence worthy of notice. It is the only case known to us of such cooperation on the part of

---

[85] *Wm. Hunnis*, p. 250.

[86] *Declared Accts.*, Pipe Office Roll 542, fol. 57.

"To diverse plaiers upon the counsells warr*ant* dated at westm*inster* xij^mo Martij 1583 for presentinge sonderie plaies before her ma*ies*tie viz to her ma*ies*ts servants ix Maij 1584 for three plaies one upon St. Stevens daie at nighte another upon the sondaie followinge, and the third on shrove tuesdaie xx^li. To the master of the children of her ma*ies*ts chapell for two plaies one upon twelfdaie at nighte, and the other on Candlemas daie at nighte xx^li. paid xxix° Martij 1584. And to the Erle of Oxforde his servaunts for two playes one upon Newyeres daie at night, thother on shrove tuesdaie at nighte, paid to Johon Lilie xxv^to Novembr*is* 1584 xx^li in all lx^li."

[87] Cf. pp. 134ff.

these two companies. The union of two of the royal chapels—like Windsor and the Chapel—seems not surprising, especially considering that the Windsor master was brought up in the Chapel. But between the Chapel and Paul's there were no such affiliations— rather, so we should expect, rivalry of long standing; and the combination of 1583 becomes therefore the more interesting. It was brought about by an extraordinary course of circumstances, which temporarily threw the children's companies out of the normal tenor of their managements into the commercial hands of outsiders, who attempted to exploit them as out-and-out professionals.

It was not Oxford's boys, but the Chapel company under Hunnis that produced Peele's *Arraignment of Paris* some time in or before 1584,[88] probably on either Twelfth Day or Candlemas Day (February 2), 1584.[89] At least that is to be inferred from the title-page, which mentions only the Chapel company. Whether or not they played it at Blackfriars is simply a matter for conjecture.

Of the dozen or more[90] plays recorded as having been presented by the lessees of Blackfriars from 1576 to 1584, most of them undoubtedly were written by the masters, especially Hunnis and Farrant. Hunnis we know to have written plays;[91] we surmise confidently that Farrant did too because it had been customary from earliest times, as records show, for Chapel masters to supply in part or in whole the plays their children set forth. It looks, too, as if Stephen Gosson had Farrant and Hunnis in mind when he wrote:[92] "Neede and flatterie are two brothers, and the eldest seruitors in the Court: they were both scholars vnto Aristippus, and learned both of them to applie themselues to the time, & their matter to the disposition." Aristippus was a prominent character in Edwards's *Damon and Pythias*, and has been taken as a sketch of the author himself; and of all the men at court Farrant and Hunnis could best be described as his disciples. It is unfortunate that

[88] The title page runs: "The Araygnement of Paris A Pastorall. Presented before the Queenes Maiestie, by the Children of her Chappell. Imprinted at London by Henrie Marsh. Anno 1584." There is no *S. R.* entry.

[89] When the Chapel alone played at court.

[90] We have record only of plays given at court. Undoubtedly many more were put on simply for public consumption.

[91] Thomas Newton, in a prefatory poem to *The Hive Full of Honey* of 1578 praises "Thy Enterludes, thy gallant layes," etc.

[92] *A Second and Third Blast of Retrait from Plaies and Theatres,* 1580 (ed. Hazlitt, *Eng. Drama and Stage, Roxburghe Library,* p. 147.)

no plays by either of these two men have come down to us. There have been attempts[93] to fasten the name of Hunnis to various anonymous plays of the period, but the evidence has been too slight. Other men—among them Lyly and Peele—contributed plays for Blackfriars, and doubtless many of them. It is more than probable that the Earl of Oxford himself was of their number; he was a famous playwright in his day,[94] and would hardly have refused the chance his ownership of Blackfriars gave him to put his work before the public.

It was some time in 1584 that the lease of Blackfriars reverted to Sir William More, and the theatre ceased to exist. I believe it was the worries attending the final year or two of its existence and especially the enforced sale of his lease to Evans in 1582-3 that produced Hunnis's well-known petition to the queen. The petition is dated November, 1583, about midway between the leasing to Evans and the permanent closing of the theatre, at a time when, if I am correct, the business at Blackfriars had passed from the hands of the Chapel to those of St. Paul's, and the suits of More threatened the extinction of the profitable revenues from the theatre. Since the public exhibition of the Chapel children in plays was never more than tolerated by the queen as a means of preparing the plays to be presented at court,[95] and had never become in the least a prerogative of their master, he could not directly seek redress for the loss of something he was not entitled officially to have; hence he directed the royal attention to lapses in his regular perquisites. Although the petition has been frequently printed,[96] it is sufficiently singular to demand a place here. The document[97] is endorsed

"1583 Novembr   The humble peticion of the M^r of the Child*ren* of hir highnes Chappell," and in a different hand "To haue farther allowa*n*ces for

<hr/>

[93] Cf. especially Mrs. Stopes's *Wm. Hunnis*, Chapter 21.

[94] Puttenham, in his *Arte of English Poesie*, 1589, (ed. Arber, *English Reprints*, 1869, p. 77) says that "the hyest price" should go to "Th' Earle of Oxford and Maister Edwardes of her Maiesties Chappell for Comedy and Enterlude."

[95] Dasent's *Acts of the Privy Council*, under date Dec. 24, 1578, records a letter to the Lord Mayor requiring him to suffer the children of the Chapel, the children of Paul's, and the servants of the Lord Chamberlain, the Earl of Warwick, the Earl of Leicester, and the Earl of Essex, and no others to exercise playing within the City; these were allowed because they had been appointed to play at Christmas before the queen.

[96] Cf. Introd. to G. P. Baker's *Endimion*, Mrs. Stopes's *Wm. Hunnis*, Wallace's *Evolution of the English Drama*, and Chambers's *Elizabethan Stage*, Chap. 12.

[97] *S. P. Dom. Eliz.* CLXIII, No. 88.

the finding of the children for causes within mentioned." The petition itself runs as follows:

Maye it please yor honores william Hunnys M^r of the Children of hir highnes Chappell, moste humble beseecheth to consid^r of these fewe lynes.

ffirst hir Maiestie alloweth for the dyett of xij children of sayd Chappell daylie vj^d a peece by the daye, and xl^{li} by the yeare for theyre aparrell and all other furneture.

Agayne there is no ffee allowed neyther for the m^r of the sayd children nor for his vssher, and yet neuertheless is he constrayned, over and besydes the vssher still to kepe bothe a man servant to attend vpon them and lykewyse a woman seruant to wash and kepe them cleane.

Also there is no allowance for the lodginge of the sayd children, such tyme as they attend vppon the Courte, but the m^r to his greate charge is dryuen to hyer chambers both for him self, his vssher Chilldren and servantes.

Also theare is no allowaunce for ryding Jornies when occasion serueth the m^r to trauell or send into sundrie partes within this Realme, to take vpp and bring such children as be thought meete to be trayned for the service of hir maiestie.

Also there is no allowaunce ne other consideracion for those children whose voyces be chaunged, whoe onelye do depend vpon the charge of the sayd M^r vntil such tyme as he may preferr the same with cloathing and other furniture, vnto his no smalle charge.

And although it may be obiected that hir Maiestes allowaunce is no whitt less than hir Maiestes ffather of famous memorie therefore allowed: yet considering the pryces of thinges present to the tyme past and what annuities the m^r then hadd out of sundrie abbies within this Realme, besydes sondrie giftes from the kinge, and dyuers perticuler ffees besydes, for the better mayntenaunce of the sayd children and office: and besides also there hath ben withdrawne from the sayd children synce her Maiestes comming to the Crowne xij^d by the daye which was allowed for theyr breakefastes as may apeare by the Treasorer of the Chamber his accompt, for the tyme beinge, with other allowaunces incident to the office, which I heere omytt.

The burden heereof hath from tyme to tyme so hindered the M^{rs} of the children viz m^r Bower m^r Edwardes, my sellf and m^r ffarant: that notwithstanding some good helpes otherwyse some of them dyed in so poore case, and so deepelie indebted that they haue not left scarcelye wherewith to burye them.

In tender consideracion whereof, might it please yor honors that the sayde allowaunce of vj^d a daye apeece for the Childrens dyet might be reserued in hir Maiestes coffers during the tyme of theyr attendaunce. And in Liew thereof they to be allowed meate and drinke within this honorable householde for that I am not able vppon so small allowaunce eny longer to beare so heauie a burden.   Or otherwyse to be consydred as shall seeme best vnto yor honorable wysdomes.[98]

3. *1584-1592. Occasional Performances.*

Though the Chapel disappears from records of performances in London after 1584, it seems not to have expired altogether, but to have flitted in a shadowy way across the provinces. It played at Norwich in 1586-7 and at Ipswich in May of the same year;[99] and apparently also at Leicester in August, 1590-1.[100] It may be that in one or more of these cases another company was appropriating the Chapel children's name, but such an hypothesis is unnecessary. It seems that we must consider the Chapel in the years following 1584 as maintaining a desultory existence in the provinces, playing seldom and at long intervals. Nevertheless, considering the nature of the company and the duties and dependence of the boys who composed it, one is curious and a little puzzled over these unexplained peregrinations.

It has been argued[101] that the Chapel acted Nash's *Summer's Last Will and Testament* as a private performance in 1592 at Croydon; but I hold with Professor Baker[102] that St. Paul's was the company which gave this play, for reasons which I shall exhibit in discussing that company.[103] Then we must consider August, 1591, to be the last known date of performance by the Chapel boys before their resurrection in 1600 by Henry Evans and Nathaniel Gyles.

[98] It does not appear that Hunnis's petition bore fruit. The fees of the Chapel were generally increased by King James in 1604, when the children's daily allowance was raised from 6d. to 10d. The Chapel record of this augmentation says that "the Chappel was not augmented of manye yeares by any his Majesties progenitors." Cf. Rimbault, *Old Cheque Book*, p. 61.

[99] Murray, *Eng. Dram. Companies*, II, 366; *Chamberlain's Accts. of Norwich*, (28-29 Eliz. 1586-7): "Itm to the Children of the Q Chapell by like (i.e. Mayor's) comaundement"—20s.

Same, p. 292; *Ipswich Chamberlain's Accts.*, 1586-7, May 26: "Item, paid to the quenes players being the childoren"—20s.

[100] *Same*, p. 305; *Leicester Records*, 1590-1, Aug. 11: "Itm geven to the Queens Maiests Playors, being another companye, called the Children of the Chappell, by the appoyntment of Mr Mayor and his bretherne"—26s. 8d.

[101] Fleay, *Hist. of Stage*, p. 79; Murray, *English Dram. Comp.*, I, 337.

[102] Ed. of *Endimion*, p. clxiv ff.

[103] Cf. p. 148n.

CHAPTER IV

THE CHILDREN OF PAUL'S: CHOIR SCHOOL
AND SCHOOLHOUSE

1. *The School.*

In writing the history of the second great children's company—
the company of the choir boys of St. Paul's cathedral, London—
we are confronted with a far more difficult task than faced us in the
case of the Chapel Royal. This is the result simply of scarcity of
material; for various reasons the documentary evidences which
concern the Chapel greatly outnumber those which concern Paul's.
In the first place, there is naturally no great mass of household
records and account-books, such as the royal establishment gave
rise to. In the second place, the records now preserved in the library
of the cathedral are only a fraction of their former number, so
depleted have they been by fires and various accidents. And last
of all, there have been discovered for some reason a greater number
of legal documents respecting the Chapel company than bearing on
Paul's. The effect is that the historian is confronted by a meager
array of evidence, which has not been materially added to since
the time of John Payne Collier. There still remain lacunae in the
known history of this company which can be filled only by the
discovery of new and informative documents.

It is essential in connection with the boys of St. Paul's to keep the
choir school separate from the grammar school. The latter was the
"scoles," the school *par excellence*; it was founded in the time of
Henry I by the gift of a habitation and a library to canon Durandus,[1]
and became merged finally into the new school instituted by Dean

[1] *Vide* Dugdale, *History of St. Paul's*, ed. 1818, p. 6; also Maria Hackett, *Documents and Authorities Respecting the Ancient Foundation for the Education of The St. Paul's Choristers*, etc. (London, 1812?) p. ii. Miss Hackett worked long and zealously for the restitution of the fees, obits, and rights to education of the St. Paul's choristers, who by the 19th century had lost nearly all their perquisites; but she unfortunately confused the song and grammar schools, so that her exposition needs a great deal of sifting and excision. The best treatment, and indeed the only good one, of the history of the pre-Coletian grammar school, and to a less degree of the song school too, is A. F. Leach's article on "St. Paul's School before Colet" in *Archæologia*, LXII (Second Series, Vol. XII) Pt. 1, 1910, p. 191. To this scholarly treatment of the subject I am greatly indebted in my summary.

Colet. When Colet in 1512 petitioned the pope to annul the traditional powers exercised by the chancellor of St. Paul's over the
schools of London, he described his school as being built "loco
quidem precipuo ac celebri, et quasi inter ipsos oculos civitatis, ubi
aliter fuit quedem Scola nullius plane momenti."[2]

But the charity boys of the almonry—the *pueri eleemosynarii*—
who at Paul's as elsewhere served in the choir, were taught by their
master, the almoner; and their school, when alluded to at all, was
called the song school to distinguish it from the grammar school.
These relations were much confused by Miss Hackett, who worked
so hard in the early years of the nineteenth century to restore to the
almonry boys their dues of education. She demanded for them not
only their proper endowments and the due oversight of the almoner,
but also the funds attached to the chancellorship, which never
belonged to them. Mr. Carleton Browne, in his Harvard thesis of
1903 on English grammar schools, has taken the stand that the
grammar schools grew up in monasteries and churches primarily
for the benefit of the almonry boys. This is open to grave question.
Undoubtedly there was much interrelation between the song and
grammar schools—how much we can hardly tell; but there are
sometimes clear evidences that a distinction existed. Thus at
Beverley, in 1312, when the grammar schoolmaster wished to make
all choristers beyond seven, the original number who attended the
grammar school, pay fees, the succentor, who was the master of
song, contended that he was bound to teach them all free.[3] While
this indicates that the education of the choristers in grammar
naturally devolved upon the grammar school, it shows that a feeling
of difference existed strong enough to make argument. At any rate,
by 1345 the choir and grammar schools at St. Paul's had become
separated. In the "Registry of the Almonry of St. Paul's,"[4] a
volume which belongs to that year, we are told that "if the almoner
does not keep a clerk to teach the choristers grammar, the schoolmaster of St. Paul's claims 5s. a year for teaching them, though he
ought to demand nothing for them, because he keeps a school for
them, as the treasurer of St. Paul's once alleged before the dean and
chapter is to be found in ancient statements." Whatever the early

---

[2] Leach in *Archæolgia*, LXII, Pt. 1, p. 237. From the *Book of Evidences* of the
Mercer's Company, fol. 29.

[3] *Same* p. 198.

[4] *Same*, from *Harl. MSS.* 1080.

purposes of the grammar school, then, it had by this time drifted away from the song school.

Yet doubtless the relations between the choir and grammar schools were always close. Even so late as 1584 we find the school of Dean Colet taking over the grammatical education of the choir boys. At the same time, the very statutes which made this provision show how clear with the distinction between the two schools. They are thus reviewed in Churton's *Nowell:*[5]

When he (Nowell) with the Chapter of St. Paul's, appointed their almoner Thomas Gyles "Master of the Quiristers," it was covenanted with him that he should instruct them "in the principles and grounds of the Christian Religion, contained in *the little Catechism* set out by public authority, and after, when they shall be elder, in the *middle* Catechism; and in writing and music—; and then suffer them to resort to Paul's school, that they may learn the principles of grammar, and after, as they shall be forwards, learn the said Catechisms in Latin, which before they learned in English, and other good books taught in the said school."[6]

When the song school first began it is impossible to say. Probably it was nearly as old as the choir itself. The almoner, as has been said, had charge of a certain number of boys, eight according to the statutes,[7] who served in the choir, and whom he was expected to

---

[5] Ralph Churton, *Life of Alexander Nowell*, Oxford, 1809, p. 190. Cf. also Hackett, *Evidences Respecting*, etc., p. 147; and R. B. Gardiner, *Admission Registers of St. Paul's School*, 1884, p. 11.

[6] R. B. Bond, in his *Lyly*, I, 34, note 2, makes this passage the subject of a curious note. He is trying to maintain his conclusion that John Lyly was really a vice-master, or assistant master of some sort, in the cathedral school, and is further assuming that the Paul's boys were inhibited from playing about 1584. He says: "This reads as if a new arrangement, made perhaps in consequence of their inhibition, which would leave them more time for study. On the removal of that inhibition and Lyly's appointment as vice master, their attendance at Colet's school probably ceased, and their instruction devolved largely on Lyly himself." This is an unwarrantable piece of interpretation for a special purpose, of which there is too much in Bond. While there is nothing impossible in the hypothesis here put forward, there is nothing in support of it to warrant its submission. If the inhibition of the Paul's boys would give them more time for study, it would also give Westcote more time to teach. At any rate, there is no reason to assume that the directions quoted by Churton indicate an *increase* in studiousness. I shall dispose of the myth of Lyly's vice-mastership in another place (cf. p. 136).

[7] From the statutes of the cathedral as they are given in Dugdale's *St. Paul's*, pp. 347-9, I submit the section relating to the almoner.

"De Elemosynario.

Habet etiam Ecclesia Sancti Pauli Elemosynarium: is homo pius et pauperum necessitatibus compatiens sit. Ejus officium est statutis diebus Elemosinas dis-

instruct in music and letters. He was to be a pious man, compassionate to the poor, and it was his care to distribute alms on stated days, according to the wishes of the donors of the alms. Since the almoner thus was the guardian of the choir boys, he had a second office and title of "master of the choristers." The three men with whom we are concerned in this subsequent history—Sebastian Wescote, Thomas Gyles, and Edward Pierce—were all almoners and choir masters, and received pay for services rendered in both capacities.

It would seem that although provision was made in the almonry for only eight boys there were ten choristers provided for in St. Paul's by the first articles of establishment. Richard Smith, deposing in Bishop Bancroft's visitation in 1598, said: "*Item* there are ten Choristers Accordinge to the first foundac*i*on as I have hard."[8] There were ten choristers in Westcote's time (1550?-1582), as we shall see. We need not concern ourselves with the history of the choir before the time of Westcote, for with him begin the plays "by the children of Paul's," and indeed it is not until his time that we have definite information as to the state of the almonry and choir.

The same Richard Smith just quoted says a little farther on in his deposition: "I*tem* that the said Choristers m*aste*r have fyftie pownds A yere payd by the Deane And Chapter & Rec*eive* in Rents of houses belonging to the Almeno*ur* As I have hard xx*li* buy the yere."[9] There is more definite information in an interesting volume in St. Paul's library entitled "Michael Shaller's note book of such things as past in his time in the Church."[10] On fol. 76, I found this table headed "At the feast of Christmas." There is no date, but it belongs some time after 1571, the date of fol. 41b.

Also to the M*aste*r of the Almery for the Commons } vij^s vij^d
of the Querysters at vij^d the weeke................ }

---

tribuere egentibus, uti voluerint illi, qui publicam in elemosinam redditus contulerunt, et pauperes si qui sint qui juxta Ecclesiam moriuntur, in majori cimiterio gratis sepelire. Is octo pueros bonae indolis et honestae parentelae, habeat; quos alet et educet in morum disciplina; videat etiam instruantur in cantu et literatura, ut in omnibus apti ad ministerium Dei in Choro esse possunt. Caveat ne quicquam pro admissione eorum accipiat, sed gratam in Ecclesiae elemosinam admittatur redditus Elemosinae, unde et a quibus solvitur colligat et describat, detque calculum tum recepti, tum expensi."

[8] St. Paul's library; A. Box 53/17, fol. 36.

[9] According to a schedule of the revenue of the almoner printed in Miss Hackett's *Documents and Authorities*, p. xiii, the ordinary income of the almoner was £47-13-4.

[10] W. D. 32.

for v dayes dedicacione all sayntes.St.Erkenwald Con-⎫
ception of our Lady & Cristemas even to every quer-⎬xvjˢ viijᵈ
ister for everye daye iiijᵈ in all . . . .⎭

Itm to hym for the pencione of saynt pancras . . . . xvjˢ viijᵈ

Mas- It to hym for the pencione of the mannor of   powle . . xxvjˢ viijᵈ

ter Itm to hym for the pencione for the grace,(?) . . . .⎫
of the nortoy (?) . . . .⎬xxvjˢ viijᵈ

Alm- Itm for the psalme of de profundis . . . . ijˢ vjᵈ

erye Itm for the Anthem of Qua sapientia . . . . xijᵈ

Itm to hym for the Annuyte of master Restone at⎫
xxiijˢ iiijᵈ by yere . . . .⎬viijˢ iiijᵈ

Itm to hym out of the Rentes of holmes colledge at⎫
xxˢ by yere . . . .⎬vˢ

Similar lists are given for other quarter-days. In that for the Annunciation of our Lady is added: "It for the lyverye of the sayed Queristers iiijˡⁱ." These entries, which can only cover a part of the income of the master of the choir boys, show that, aside from special acquisitions resulting from the union of the offices of choir master and almoner, the routine of St. Paul's, as far as it affected the boys and their supervisor, was much like that of the Chapel Royal. There are the special payments for "de profundis" and "qua sapientia," and the weekly payment for the children's board. In addition to the incomes from the almonry, which amounted by my schedule to over £22 a year, but which Miss Hackett says were over £47 a year, the master had his salary as teacher of music and grammar. The least income we can assign him—the income that Richard Smith computes—was £70. It appears then that the office of master of Paul's was *per se* more lucrative than that of master of the Chapel.

From the *Statuta Elemosynaria*[11] it appears that the almoner was not to receive any remuneration other than the (very adequate) emoluments of his office. He was, moreover, to be so solicitous of the welfare of his charges, that he was to appoint a man of discretion to supervise their walks.

"Pro dictis vero Pueris recipiendis vel alendis nihil recipiat ex pacto ab aliquibus exteris preter stipendia constituta, nec per favorem recipiat, nec retineat Pueros aliquos nisi ydoneos ad Ecclesie Ministrum supradicte.

[11] Maria Hackett, *Documents and Authorities Respecting the Ancient Foundation for the Education of The St. Paul's Choristers*, p. xvii.

"Quociens vero dicti Pueri ad Scolas, vel spaciatum, ire debent, pariter eant et redeant sub ducatu alicujus maturi hominis ad hoc per Elemosynarium assignati, ne puerili levitate sparsim evagentur inhoneste."

The offices of almoner and schoolmaster were upheld by liberal revenues, as records still extant in fragments show. The choristers themselves had their own obits and endowments which were quite separate from the revenues of the almoner. Though the policy of the sovereigns after the dissolution of the monasteries was to protect and spare the estates from which such revenues were derived, yet the boys had on one occasion at least to fight for their rights. In 1554 (a° 1 & 2 Philip & Mary), they petitioned through the Court of Exchequer for the payment with arrears of a yearly revenue amounting to £27-2-10, granted in the second year of Edward VI. With them were associated the vicars choral, petitioning for the payment of a revenue of £19-11-0½, and the attorney for both parties was Sebastian Westcote. The suit was successful.[12] The same revenues, along with others, were confirmed by Letters Patent of Elizabeth in 1571-2.[13]

2. *The Personnel of the Choir.*

I have found five lists of names of the vicars choral and choir boys at St. Paul's, extending from 1554 to 1598. None of the names is familiar, unfortunately, but I submit the lists here none the less, for they may be of possible future use. The first is taken from the suit in the Court of Exchequer in 1554, just referred to:

Vicars choral	*Choir boys* (*Choriste*)
Sebastian Westcote	John Burde
Philip Apryce	Simon Burde
Robert Seye	Richard Hewse
Thomas Martyn	George More
John More	John Alkok
Robert Bale	Gilbert Maxsey
	Roger Stakhouse
	Richard Prynce
	John Farmer
	Robert Chofe

[12] *Exchequer K. R., Memoranda Roll*, Michaelmas, 1 & 2 Philip & Mary, r. 238 *dors.* There being nothing of interest in the suit aside from the names of the plaintiffs (given in the next section of this chapter), I have not thought it worth reprinting here.

[13] See Hackett's *Documents and Authorities*, p. xlvii, note f.

From the *Visitation Book* of Bishop Edwin Sandes, I take this list for 1574.[14]

Vicars choral	Choir boys
Thomas Sterrie	George Bowring
Thomas Woodsone	Thomas Morley
Giles (Egidius) Hawkes	Peter Phillipp
Henry Mudde	Henry Nation
John Ramsay	Robert Knight
John Meares	Thomas Brande
	Edward Pattmie (?)
	Robert Baker
	Thomas Johnson

The following list, of 1594, comes from the *Register* of Archbishop Whitgift, at Lambeth Palace library.[15]

Vicars choral	Choir boys
John Ramsay	Edward Buckeredge
John Sharpe	William Thayer
Thomas Harrolde	John Taylor
Thomas Gyles	Germaine (Germanus) Wilson
Michael Amner	Richard Badlowe
Nicholas Younge	Thomas Weste
Episteler	Giles Jennynges
Robert Brown	Humphrey Weste
	William Maycocke

The next list is dated 1598, and comes from the report of the visitation of that year by Bishop Bancroft.[16]

Vicars choral	Choir boys
John Ramsay	John Taylor
John Sharpe	William Thaire
Thomas Harrolde	Richard Brackenbury
Thomas Gyles	John Norwood[17]
Michael Amner	Robert Coles[17]
Nicholas Younge	John Thomkins
Reader of the Epistle	Samuel Marcupp
Robert Browne	Thomas Rainescrofte
Reader of the Gospel	Russell Gyrdler
Robert Gunsley	Carolus Pytcher
	Charles Pendry

[14] In the *Bishop of London's Registry.*
[15] 1583-1604, Vol. II, fol. 257 a.
[16] In the *Bishop of London's Registry.*
[17] These two boys acted in *Antonio and Mellida;* see p. 289.

In the visitation book of Bishop Thomas Ravis, also in the
Registry, we are given these names for October, 1607.

Vicars choral	*Choir boys*
John Sharpe	Henry Burnett
Nicholas Young	Richard Kenede
Thomas Harrolde	John Mansell
William Grantham	Thomas Peers
Peter Hopkins	Richard Patrick
Edward Peers "Mʳ	Nicholas Crosse
Choristar*um* sive Elemonsinarius"	Thomas Waters
"*Lector Epistolarum*"	John Dawson
George Browne	Thomas Codbolt
	Lightfoot Codbolt

3. *The Schoolhouse and the Theatre.*

When we try to fix the place in which the Paul's boys set up their
theatre, we meet everywhere with the most baffling uncertainty.
One good authority names the choristers' singing school. This
authority is Stow's *Annals* of Howe's continuation (testimony of
weight), wherein it is said[18] that among the buildings erected or
converted for theatrical purposes in the sixty years prior to the
publication of the *Annals* (1631) was St. Paul's singing school. This
ascription is easy to believe, because we might expect the choir
boys to perform on their own ground, and we know that their
singing school was a building distinct from the grammar school.
Consequently most historians of the theatre have accepted Howe's
statement,[19] and some have gone to considerable pains to identify
that building of the many crowded about the cathedral which
contained the singing school. But unfortunately it seems impossible
to make the identification with any degree of certainty. A tradition
exists that in the twelfth century the singing school was housed in
the parish church of St. Gregory,[20] and there it may have remained
until the seventeenth century, for aught we know to the contrary.
And indeed a church would lend itself excellently to the arrangements of a theatre.[21] Furthermore, St. Gregory's was being used

[18] P. 1004.

[19] Including the latest and most scholarly, Mr. E. K. Chambers, in *The Elizabethan Stage*.

[20] Chambers (*Eliz. Stage*, II, 11) cites Stow's *Survey* (II, 19) in confirmation,
but I cannot find that Stow makes any positive connection between the singing
school and St. Gregory's.

[21] As to the prevalence of acting in churches, cf. p. 86*n*.

toward the end of the sixteenth century, in such a way as to give
color to its identification with the singing school, for at the visitation
in 1598 this statement was made:[22] "Item that the schollers of one
teaching in St. Gregoryes do greatly annoy the Church by playing
crying, etc. & some other obstinate boyes have threatened & offed
to beate Us the said Bellringers." On the whole it is rather likely
that the master vaguely referred to as "one teaching" was not the
well known almoner but some outside schoolmaster, and of course
the "playing" must not be supposed to refer to acting. But the
fact is shown that in 1598 St. Gregory's was a schoolhouse. At the
same time, the evidence connecting St. Gregory's with the Paul's
theatre is exceedingly thin.

The most puzzling contribution to this exasperating question,
because the most definite and yet the most elusive, is made in
J. P. Malcolm's *Londinium Redivivum*.[23] "The house of John Gyles,"
we are told, "was partly formed by St. Paul's and was 'lately used
for a playhouse.' " This statement, made under 1598, along with
many other items about the condition of St. Paul's, is said[24] to be
"from MS. presentments on visitations at St. Paul's." It will be
noticed that the words "lately used for a playhouse" are printed by
Malcolm in quotation marks, as being taken literally from the
source. No statement could be simpler, nor seem founded on better
authority; and there does exist in St. Paul's library a single bundle
of MS. presentments at the visitation of 1598, just now referred to.
Yet I have searched that manuscript through and through, finding
many of the items corresponding to the digest in Malcolm, but not
a word on John Gyles or a playhouse. More than that, there exists
in the Bishop of London's Registry a copy of the whole proceedings
at the visitation of 1598, including in minute detail all presentments
as well as the articles—the most interesting of all official records of
visitations I have seen. Yet there is in it no mention of playhouse or
John Gyles. Where Malcolm got his information I am at a loss to
imagine: certainly not from the MSS. now at St. Paul's; and almost
as certainly not from the visitation of 1598, for this item would
have appeared on one or another of the presentments in the transcript in the Bishop of London's Registry. There is something

[22] Presentments of the visitation of 1598, in St. Paul's library, A. Box 53/17,
fol. 47 (the presentment of Robert Parker and Reginald Chunall, bellringers).
[23] Ed. 1803, III, 73.
[24] In a note on p. 71.

suspicious in the name "John Gyles," for the only Gyles I have
been able to connect with the cathedral at this time was Thomas,
the almoner and choir master; there are several references to him in
the presentments of 1598. To be sure, the "John" of Malcolm may
have been a slip for "Thomas," since in a bad script or on a hasty
reading "Jhn" might easily be misread "Thos."

All the meager bits of evidence we possess on this question can
be made to agree with fair satisfaction, if we assume that the house of
the almoner and choir master, which was used as a school for the
choristers, was also turned to account as a playhouse. The house
may have been one of those large residences in the northwest part
of the south church-yard which Stow says were once lodgings of
resident priests, and were by now (1599) "either decayed or otherwise converted."[25] I am disposed to accept the evidence of Howe
and Malcolm, perplexing as the latter is, as offering genuine weight,
and to be greatly preferred to other vague hypotheses which have
tried to find another abiding place for the Paul's company. Paul's
theatre, of course, was a private one, and so presumably small.
Blackfriars, as Farrant built it, was made out of the upper rooms
of a dwelling house; the same might easily have been done in the
case of Sebastian Westcote's house at St. Paul's.

[25] *Survey*, ed. 1603, p. 373.

"On the north west side of this Church yeard, is the Bishops pallace, ... and
also diuers large houses are on the same side builded, which yet remayne, and of
olde time were the Lodginges of Prebendaries and Residenciaries, which kepte
great Householdes, and liberall Hospitality, but now eyther decayed, or otherwise
conuerted."

Perhaps we can pin the house down more definitely. In 1315 Bishop Richard of
Newport gave to William of Tolleshunt, almoner, and to the almoner for the time
being, a house near Paul's, "for the support of one or two of the almonry boys for
two years after they have changed their voices." Cf. A. F. Leach, *Archæolgia*,
LXII, Pt. 1, p. 199. But of course by 1550 the almoner may have moved many
times.

CHAPTER V

ST. PAUL'S, 1551-1590

I. *Early Performances.*

It is impossible to assign a precise date to the first appearance of the choristers of St. Paul's as players. The incident of their petitioning[1] in 1378 to prevent the theft of their miracle play on the Old Testament offers too little evidence upon which to judge the extent of their acting during the middle ages. But in the sixteenth century the boys of St. Paul's presented to the contemplation of London an organized body of stage players, whose activity lasted from about 1550 well into the first decade of the seventeenth century, and who played in that period, aside from some interruptions, with great assiduity. Certainly the history of this company begins in the sixteenth century, and any previous theatrical exhibitions of the choir boys cannot be shown to have influenced the outbreak of dramatic activity which attended and preceded the reign of Elizabeth; except that, as I have tried to show, the persistent use of children in public exhibitions of a dramatic nature, whether in the ceremonies of the *Episcopus Puerorum* or in miracle plays, tended to accustom the general mind to such uses, and doubtless paved the way to a more ready acceptance of the child-companies of the sixteenth century.

For immediate causes we must look elsewhere, and we have not far to go; the Chapel Royal presents itself to our consideration at once. The enthusiasm with which this organization had pursued the comic muse, and their great success in private court theatricals, must have made a considerable impression on similar institutions in London. Particularly attractive must have seemed the opportunity to approach royalty and take part in the gaiety of court affairs. Now of all bodies of choristers about London, the children of Paul's could claim through the exalted station of their church a right second only to that of the Chapel in waiting on majesty. Rivalry is easily kindled when two parties are far above their fellows and close to each other in their daily life. It would. be hard for Paul's boys to watch the success of the Chapel in a comparatively

[1] Cf. p. 10.

new and fascinating field with anything but jealous eyes. Their anxiety to enter the field is easy to understand. Then, too, we should not forget the example of the scholars of St. Paul's school of Colet's foundation. These boys, like the pupils of grammar schools generally, were in the habit of preparing occasional plays, probably always in Latin. As we have seen, they had given an interlude at court in 1527[2] on an important occasion, and were accustomed much later to play from time to time at Mercer's Hall.[3] The example of these boys, with whom the choir boys came in some measure of contact, backed by the general custom on the part of grammar school scholars of giving Latin and even colloquial plays, may have had some influence on Paul's choir boys.

That this is all hypothesis, and that we have no evidence in black and white of the why and wherefor of the entry of Paul's children into the dramatic ring, is of no importance. Enter they did, and that is sufficient for us. Perhaps of all possible general causes, the country-wide awakening to interest in drama and players was as potent as anything.

The beginnings of the theatrical industry of the Paul's boys are shrouded in obscurity. We cannot follow these lads as we can the Chapel children, through a definite course of development from dabbling in court masques to full-fledged acting. The first notice I can find of them seems to present them as already organized into a company of actors. In the *Household Accounts* of the Princess Elizabeth[4] of the year 1551-2 stands this item:

Paid in rewarde to the Kinges Maiesties drommer and phiphe, the xiij.[th] of Februarye, xx. s.; Mr. Heywoode, xxx. s.; and to Sebastian, towardes the charge of the children with the carriage of the plaiers garmentes, iiij. li xix. s.

The payment to Heywood may have been independent of the item concerning Paul's boys and the plays, but it sounds as though it were intended for the same service; Heywood was at that time a player of the virginals, among the musicians of the court, and also a kind of court entertainer of a superior order.[5] Nevertheless, the operations of this interesting and puzzling figure extended as well to the presentation of interludes and plays; whether directing the

---

[2] Cf. p. 16.
[3] Cf. R. B. Gardiner, *Admission Registers of St. Paul's School*, pp. 12, 13.
[4] *Camden Miscellany*, II, 37.
[5] Cf. p. 67.

six singing children among the musicians, as I have tentatively proposed,[6] or acting indiscriminately with the companies of the Chapel and St. Paul's, is hard to determine. The latter conclusion has, I think, most basis. It is almost certain that the children with whom his name is connected in household accounts were sometimes the children of the Chapel, and one entry at least links him indubitably with the Paul's boys. We learn from Machyn's *Diary*[7] that at Nonsuch on the Monday after August 5, 1559, there was "a play of the chylderyn of Powlles and ther master Se(bastian), master Phelypes,[8] and master Haywod, and after a grett bankett." This suggests what I have strongly suspected, that in many cases at least adult actors took prominent parts in plays supposedly given only by children. The principal and more difficult parts, or the parts of old men, may have been taken by these mature assistants. It will be remembered that Crane, Cornish, and other gentlemen of the Chapel were often accustomed to appear in the interludes designated as given by the children.

2. *Sebastian Westcote.*

It is significant, I think, that the man who appears as payee for the children in 1551 was Sebastian Westcote.[9] This man, vague as

---

[6] Cf. *Appendix I.*

[7] Ed. J. G. Nichols, 1848, p. 206.

[8] This was doubtless the Phillips who was organist at Paul's at this time. It has been suggested that he was the John Phillips who wrote *Patient Grissell*, but this is merely a guess. Cf. Chambers, *Elizabethan Stage*, II, 13.

[9] The evidence that there were plays given at St. Paul's by the almonry boys before the time of Westcote is so slight as hardly to justify consideration; and indeed we know little enough about masters of the choir before Westcote. Some vague lists have been put together of masters in the Tudor-Stuart period, but they are highly unsatisfactory. Sparrow-Simpson (in his *Gleanings from Old St. Paul's*, p. 106) presents an erratic list mostly made up from Cunningham's *Revels* and Collier. He calls Thomas Mulliner, organist and author of a *Boke for ye Organe or Virginalls*, a master preceding Westcote, but gives no authority. Since he also includes Edward Kirkham as master in 1596, his evidence is of no great value. Maria Hackett, who should have known, if any one did, is vague on this subject, as she is on many others. She does say that John Rogers was Almoner in 1519; Thomas Hickman was Minor Canon and Almoner in 1521; and John Redford was Music Master and Organist between 1530 and 1540. But she also gives no evidences. Redford is now chiefly famous to students of drama, aside from his name as a musician of excellence, as the subject of Tusser's quaint and well known poem. (Often reprinted. Cf. Sparrow-Simpson, *Gleanings from Old St. Paul's*, p. 190, and Hawkins, *History of Music*, edit. Novello, p. 537.) Tusser was impressed as a lad for service in various choirs and finally came to Paul's, to remain a while
"With Redford there, the like no where
For cunning such and vertue much

he is to us, yet looms big in the dramatic history of the middle sixteenth century. From this date, 1551, till his death in 1582 he presented an almost unbroken string of plays at the court and in his playhouse. We know almost nothing about his plays or his means of producing them, and very little about the man. Yet from the length of his service as producer of plays, and the apparent popularity of his company at court, and from the mysteries attending the fate of his company after his death, he is worthy to be considered of importance. There is no question about the interest he inspires, if only for the baffling vapors that hang round him.[10]

He first appears at court, where he held the office of one of the Yeomen of the King's Chamber, in 1545; his name is given among the quarterly payments, for Christmas, a° 37[11], and from the way his item is worded,[12] it looks as if this were the first assignment to him in this capacity. There is significance in the fact that the future master of Paul's boys had his beginnings at the court. It meant that he came into contact with the life of the court, with its revels, masquings, and interludes, and may readily have been inspired with a lasting interest in dramatic affairs, an interest which caused him to put his knowledge into practice as soon as he was established as almoner and master at St. Paul's. If our scanty records do not hide vital facts from us, and if the first appearance of St. Paul's children as actors *was* under Westcote in or near 1551, then there is one more influential reason for thinking that the Chapel company and the court revels were a moving cause for the establishment of Paul's company.

By whom some part of musicke art
So did I gaine."
An attempt has been made (*Shakespeare Society Papers*, II, 76) to prove that the *The Marriage of Wit and Science* was written by Redford and hence given at Paul's; but the evidence is too slight to warrant serious consideration. And even if the interlude were the work of Redford, it does not follow that Paul's boys were then an acting company and played it. However, Mr. A. W. Reed is of the belief, not only that Redford was a dramatist and used his children as actors, but also that John Heywood was occasionally associated with him. (See "John Heywood and his Friends," *Library*, 1917, Ser. 3, Vol. VIII, p. 294.)

[10] I have summarized the biographical facts contained in the following pages and proposed the likelihood of Westcote's having written *The Contention between Liberality and Prodigality* in an article published in the *Journal of English and Germanic Philology* for October, 1915.

[11] Brewer and Gairdner, *Letters and Papers*, Vol. XX, Pt. 2, §1035.

[12] "To pay this quarter and so to continue quarterly to Sebastian Wescote, at Mr. Pers' assignment."

From his will[13] we learn that Westcote was born in the parish of Chimley[13a] in Devon, but when I do not know. Our next information is the payment to him as Yeoman of the Chamber in 1545. Between 1545 and 1551, when he first appears as master of Paul's children, he must have secured the appointment to St. Paul's as almoner and schoolmaster.[14] From 1551 to 1582 he appears with great regularity in the court account books as master of the company of players known as "the children of Paul's," and as producer of plays. In this business, or in the various businesses in which he may have engaged, he made a fortune; the extent of his possessions, as made known by his will, and the liberality of his legacies show him to have died possessed of what passed in those days for considerable wealth. The unusual number of his household goods was in part due to his keeping a sort of hostelry for the almonry children. Yet they were his own, and not the possessions of the office, for he bequeaths them to the "use of the same Almenrye howse," in the care of the Dean and Chapter. His gifts of money, moreover, show him to have been a well-to-do man.

From his will, too, we learn that his family was a large one, though he himself seems not to have married, from there being no mention of wife or children. He names a brother George and his children; a brother William then dead; a sister-in-law Elizabeth Westcote, widow, whom I suppose to have been the relict of William; three sons of William—Roger, Sebastian, and Francis; a brother Robert and his son Andrew; his sister Jaquet Goodmowe and four daughters; his sister's daughter—whether Jaquet's or not he does not say—and her two children; Margaret Riche, sister-in-law; and "Westcote that is blind." To all these people he leaves generous legacies; the fact of his dispersing all his possessions among them and others not his kin proves almost beyond question that he had no personal family.

From the fact of his giving small legacies to the poor of Taunton in Somerset, Kingston near Taunton, and Kyrton in Devon, just

---

[13] Hitherto unpublished. Cf. *Appendix*, p. 327. An abstract of it has been published by Flood, in a note on Westcote in *Musical Antiquary*, IV, 187. From the will also I adopt the spelling *Westcote*, in preference to *Wescote* or the modernized *Westcott*.

[13a] A correspondent in *Musical Antiquary*, IV, 187, suggests that this may be Chulmleigh.

[14] In 1560 he was made Head of the College of Minor Canons, or Subdean. Chambers, *Eliz. Stage*, II, 14.

as he did to the poor of Chimley and St. Gregory's near Paul's, I judge he had at some time in his early life lived in these places. To his sister-in-law Elizabeth Westcote,[15] who seems to have been closer to him than the rest, he left the lease of an unidentified estate called Westgreen.

That Westcote fattened and grew rich while holding the position of dramatic impresario and ruling a company of children, whether his fortune came from that source alone or not, is extremely interesting. We know, however, that his life was not uninterrupted by crosses. In fact he got into grave difficulty over his religious tenets, being suspected at various times with apparent good ground of harboring popish beliefs. The seriousness of a charge of recusancy is familiar to one who knows anything at all of the sixteenth century. Strype[16] says that on the visitation of St. Paul's by Grindal, then bishop of London, in April, 1561, Sebastian Westcote, a vicar choral, was presented for refusing the communion, and for being suspected of adhering to popish principles. But the bishop had mercy, expecting his submission, until July, 1563, when he finally pronounced excommunication.[17] Sir Robert Dudley, Earl of Leicester, at that time seemingly patron of Westcote, wrote in his behalf to the bishop; to whom the bishop replied with a long and detailed explanation, almost apology, which is preserved fortunately enough in Strype.[18] The letter is interesting enough in itself and valuable enough in the light it casts on Westcote to reprint *in toto*.

Please it your good Lordship. Being at *Farnham* with my Lord of *Winton*, I received your Lordship's letters for *Sebastian*, who at this present standeth Excommunicate. I will open to your Lordship some Circumstances of the Matter, and then I doubt not, but your Lordship will well approve my Doings therein.

[15] He charges Henry Evans, whom he names overseer, "to be carefull for my sister Elizabeth Westcote widow in her affayres and busynes as tyme shall serve."
[16] John Strype, *Life of Grindal*, ed. 1710, pp. 59, 76-78.
[17] The note of this excommunication is enrolled among the records of the Consistory Court of London, in the Principal Probate Registry, in Somerset House, London. The reference is *Libri Vicarii Generalis, Huick, 1561-1574*, Vol. 3, fol. 77.
[18] P. 77. The letter of Dudley to Grindal seems not now to be extant; but there is preserved in *Lansdowne MSS.* 6, no. 69, a letter from Grindal to Sir William Cecil, dated August 12, 1563, which refers incidentally to Dudley's letter and his own reply, quoted at length above. "My L. Rob. wrote to me earnestly for Sebastiane to whom I haue written a longe letter moche lyke an Apologie, the copy whereoff I sende you herwith."

Sebastian was complained of in my Visitation, now more than Two Years past: And that not by One or Two, but by a good Number of the best Learned of my Church, That he utterly abstained from the Communion. The said *Sebastian* being Examined by me, confessed the same, but chiefly, that he was not in Charity, because of certain Actions of Debt and Suretiship between him and Sir *William Garret*, &c. I answered, that the latter Allegation was meerly Frivolous, as it was indeed. The first was worthy of Consideration. And therefore I gave him a good long Day for the better instructing of his Conscience: Willing him in the mean Space to frequent Sermons, and to confer with Mr. *Dean*, and others of the Church, offering also mine own Labour therein.

When his Day appointed came, I found him as far off as at the first. That notwithstanding, I gave him a longer day: And so from Day to Day till *July* last past. I also one Day conferred with him my self: And perceiving that he sticked much at the Matter of Transubstantiation, I shew'd him Testimonies not only of the Scriptures, but also of the Old Fathers, most evidently against that Error; and gave him then Time to think upon the Matter. But all in vain. And therefore I was at length compelled to pronounce him Excommunicate, who afore in Doings had Excommunicated himself. And these were the Causes that moved me so to do:

First, The Discharge of mine own Duty and Offices, to whom not only the Word of Exhortation, but also the Sword of Excommunication is committed. Whereof neither can be omitted in his Time and Place, without Offence against God.

Secondly, I seek herein his Reformation. For Excomunication in such Disobedient Persons, is the ordinary Mean taught by the Holy Ghost, to reduce Men to God. Therefore saith S. *Paul, Tradatur Sathanae ad interitum Carnis ut Spiritus Salvus sit in die Domini Jesu.*

Thirdly, He hath been of long time very Offensive, not only to the Godly of my Church, but also to all other well-affected Persons, frequenting Common Prayer there; seeing such an one joined with us in Common Prayer, which refused to join with us in the Lord's Supper, as one accounting our Form of Administration Heretical and Schismatical. Whereas Communion of Prayer and Sacraments ought to be one, saith *Chrysostom.*

Fourthly, (Which is a matter of great Moment) there is committed unto him the Education of the Choristers, or Singing Children; he remaining therefore in the Mind he doth, with what Conscience can I commit Youth to his Instruction?

Your Lordship thinketh him to be Obstinate: But I pray you remember that Obstinacy is better known by Doings than by Sayings. Ye think also he doth it of Zeal. Admit it be so, he is not therefore Excusable especially after so long Toleration. Tho' not Communicating with God's

Church in Christ's Institution, ceaseth not to be a grievous Sin against God, altho' it do proceed from an erronous Zeal.   And yet I assure your Lordship, I doubt much of his Zeal.   For now after so long Trial, and good Observation of his Proceedings herein, I begin to fear, lest his Humility in Words be a counterfeit Humility, and his Tears, Crocodile Tears, altho' I my self was much moved with them at the first.

Last of all, where your Lordship thinketh, that Haste in such Cases might be hurtful, and time might win him, it may please your Lordship to undesrtand what Time he hath had already, and how long I have born with him.   Which is no less than all the time since my first Entry, being now almost Four Years.   And therefore I am afraid I have rather been too slow than too hasty; and that I have an Account to give to God for all those corrupt Lessons of false Religion, which he the space of Two or Three Years hath instilled into the Ears and Minds of those Children commited unto him.   Wherein, no doubt, he hath been too diligent, as hath appeared by his fruits.

If *Sebastian* will acknowledge his Faults and amend, I am ready most willingly to receive him.   If no, I dare not absolve an impenitent Sinner.   For that were to loose him whom God bindeth, and to abuse the Keys of the Church.   I am content, because your Lordship writeth so earnestly for him, to forbear prosecuting the Penalties of the Laws against till after *Michaelmas*, or *Hallowentide*: That he may yet have more Time to Search and to understand, praying God in the mean time to open his Eyes. Thus being bold to trouble your Lordship with a long Letter, because I wish your Lordship should be fully satisfyed in this Matter, I commit the same, &c.

This letter is of considerable value for the information it gives about Westcote—his character and life.   It brings out the fact that he had managed to put himself under the protection of the powerful Earl of Leicester; how or when we have no means of knowing.   It shows that he was certainly not a man of little character, for to stand out so long against the power of the bishop and the dignitaries of his own church argues courage and persistence of no mean sort. Indeed, I cannot help suspecting that the wording of the writ of excommunication was not in this case a mere form and that Sebastian was fitly called "contumacious" and obstinate.   I should like to know what the reverend bishop meant when he deplored the popish influences of Westcote on his charges, "wherein, no doubt, he hath been too diligent, *as hath appeared by his Fruits.*"

The intervention of the Earl of Leicester seems not to have availed the recusant schoolmaster, for I find among the records kept at St.

Paul's a bond[19] dated November 8, a° 6 Elizabeth (1564), between Westcote and Grindal for the sum of one hundred marks, by the terms of which Westcote must frame his conscience to the required standard by Easter next, or if that is impossible, resign his offices in St. Paul's; otherwise the bond is forfeit.

Evidently Sebastian submitted to the inevitable, and like a sensible man forfeited neither his bond nor his emoluments, for he remained in the enjoyment of his offices until his death. But the year 1564 did not hear the last of his troubles as a suspected recusant. He is again referred to at a much later date, and by a different authority—this time the Common Council of the City of London. The passage cited occurs in the *Repertories of the Court of Common Council*[20] under the date December 8, a° 18 Elizabeth (1575) and runs as follows:

...........And also for asmoche as this Courte ys enformed that one Sebastian that wyll not commvnycate with the Church of England kepethe playes and resorte of the people to great gaine (?) and peryll of the Coruptinge of the Chyldren with papistrie

master Morton to goe vnto the Deane of Powles

And therefore master Morton ys appoynted to goe to the Deane of Powles and to gyve him notyce of that dysorder, and to praye him to gyve suche remeadye

therein, within his iurysdyccion, as he shall see meete, for Christian Relygion and good order.

What became of this resolution, or of the visit of Master Morton to Dean Nowell, does not appear from any further notice in the records of the city of London. But from the *State Papers Domestic*, we learn that he was committed to prison "for papistry" on December 21, 1577, and was released on March 19, 1578.[21] Truly he was an "obstinate heretic."

Just before the investigation instigated by the city fathers, a curious accident had happened to Sebastian. In 1575, sometime not long before December, one of his boys, a player of importance, was kidnapped. Thus much we learn from an order of the Privy

[19] *Vide Appendix*, p. 326.
[20] *Rep.* 19, fol. 18.
[21] See *Catholic Record Society*, I, 70, cited by Chambers, *Eliz. Stage*, II, 15.

Council[22] directing an inquiry into the matter and an examination of suspected persons. More than that bare fact we do not possess and what the meaning and result of this affair were we have not even a means of guessing. Whether the boy was kidnapped for reasons connected with theatrical affairs, or whether he was impressed for choir service in the Chapel Royal in defiance of the right of exemption belonging to St. Paul's, cannot be known until more illuminating information turns up.

3. 1551-1582.

I have said that the first definitely recorded performance by the children of Paul's was in 1551-2 before the Princess Elizabeth. A vague seeming reference to these boys exists in the records of Hedon in Yorkshire,[23] which notes, with no more exactitude than that it is after Edward VI, an item of two shillings "payd to the .... pawlle players." That this really means Westcote's company I do not at all believe. The possibility of error in transcription, the blank before the "pawlle," the unnaturalness of the expression itself if it applies to the players of St. Paul's, but more than anything the unlikelihood that this company would be found apparently touring so far from home at so early a date in its history—all these reasons seem to me sufficient to reject the implication of the record.

Certainly the only authentic[24] reference to Sebastian's boys after 1551 does not occur till 1559, after the accession of Elizabeth, when on the night of August 7 a play was given "by the children of Paul's and their master Sebastian."[25] The occasion was the entertainment of Elizabeth at Nonsuch House in Surrey by Lord Arundel, the queen's superintendent at that place.

[22] Contained in the *Privy Council Registers*, Elizabeth, Vol. II, p. 408.
> "At Windsor the iii^de of December, 1575,
> Subscribed As before addinge Thearle
> of Warwicke & Thearle of Bedford.

A Lettre to the master of the Rolles and master wilson that wheare one of Sebastianes boyes being one of his principall plaiers is lately stolen and conveyed from him They be required to examine such persons as Sebastian holdeth suspected and to proceade with such as be found faultie according to Lawe and thorder of this Realme."

[23] Murray, *English Dramatic Companies*, II, 286.

[24] Warton (*Hist. of Poetry*, 1871, III, 312) tells that in 1554, while Elizabeth was at Hatfield, she was visited by Mary, and that after supper one evening a play was presented by the children of Paul's. But grave doubt has been cast on the authenticity of this anecdote by Herbert E. D. Blakiston in an article on "Thomas Warton and Machyn's Diary," in the *English Historical Review*, Vol. XI, April, 1896.

[25] Cf. p. 117.

F. G. Fleay,[26] with his usual decisive vision, has perceived that the play given on this occasion was the well known interlude *The Nice Wanton*. His reasons are these. On June 10, 1560, *The Nice Wanton* and *Impatient Poverty* were licensed for printing and the former was published in the same year. Of these, *The Nice Wanton* had been performed before the queen, because at the end is a prayer for her, an infallible sign according to Fleay. The only court performances before this date were the one at Nonsuch on August 5, 1559, and one on New Year's Eve, which gave offence and was stopped in the midst.[27] It is hard to see how *The Nice Wanton* could have given offence, in any possible way; this leaves the one date open. "It is therefore," concludes Fleay absolutely, "the play acted at Nonsuch." Though the performance in 1559 is thus settled, the play nevertheless was written earlier, during the reign of Edward VI, for the rhymes of the final prayer indicate that it had been originally addressed to a king:

"Now for the Quenes Royal Maiestie let vs pray,

*   *   *   *   *   *

That Her Grace may long raign and prosper in all things
In Gods word and iustice may giue light to al quenes."[28]

Here it is evident that *things* originally rhymed with *kings*.

So much for Fleay's evidence; what is there against it? In the first place, we are not justified in concluding that these two occasions were the only ones in 1558-9 on which plays were given. It is noteworthy that neither performance is mentioned in any official record of payment, either in the accounts of the Treasurer of the Chamber, or in the Acts of the Privy Council. Their preservation is fortuitous, and we may justly feel doubt that there were not other performances of 1558-9 which have not come down to us. The Revels books are not enlightening; all the information the accounts for 1558-9 give us is that there were "playes and other pastymes sett forth and shewen in her Maiesties presence."[29] Fleay's assertion that "the only Court performances anterior to its publication were that at Nonsuch and one on New Year's Eve," is thus seen to be dogmatic and untenable.

---

[26] *Queen Elizabeth, Croydon, and the Drama*, A paper read before the Balham Antiquarian and Natural History Society, January 24, 1898.

[27] Cf. p. 74.

[28] J. M. Manly, *Specimens of Pre-Shakesperean Drama*, I, 479.

[29] Feuillerat, *Documents relating to the Office of the Revels in the Time of Queen Elizabeth*, p. 79.

But granting the two performances of plays in 1559, a confusing complication is introduced by Fleay himself in showing that the play was composed during the time of Edward VI, at least six years earlier than the date in question, and hence not for the occasion, as was, I believe, generally customary. If the play was performed before Edward VI, and later published after the accession of Elizabeth, a sufficient reason for substituting the queen for the king in all such references could be found in the natural impropriety of printing a play addressed to a defunct prince during the reign of a living one. There might have been, moreover, the incentive to make the play appear up to date. Last of all, is it certain that the queen for whom the play may have been revised was not Mary, instead of Elizabeth? Its moral tone would suit the taste of the Catholic princess.

The only safe conclusion, then, which develops out of a consideration of Fleay's theory, if so gentle a description may be given to so vigorous a belief, is that *The Nice Wanton* was written and performed during the reign of Edward VI, if indeed, not earlier, in Henry VIII's time. Yet the play seems a well developed, late form of morality,[30] and common consent has united to place it in the time of Edward, where I am content to leave it. Moreover, it was certainly composed for a company of child-actors, or the Latin motto on the title page means nothing to me:

"Et magnum magnos, pueros puerilia decus."

To assign the play definitely to any one of the several performances by boys before Edward would be to ape the rashness of Fleay. It is just, however, to note one remote possibility of reconciling his theory with the early composition of the play. We may assume that this was the play presented before Elizabeth, and, for all we know, the king in 1551-2[31] by the children of Paul's; it was kept in the possession of its owner, Westcote, possibly too the author, until it seemed advisable to use it—because he had nothing new in emergency, or by command of the queen in memory of a pleasant diversion—at the revels in 1559. Granting the performance of the play in 1559, I can construct no other theory which will explain how a

---

[30] Note, for example, the appearance of such figures of realism as Barnabas, Ismael, Dalila, and Xantippe, indicative of the newer school of *Grammer Gurton's Needle* and *Ralph Roister Doister*, along with the old abstractions, Iniquity (the Vice) and Worldly Shame. The excessively moral, not to say preachy, tone of the interlude would suit better the court of the boy king or Mary than that of King Hal.

[31] Cf. p. 116.

play already used once was revived at the first performance after the accession of a new ruler.

During the early reign of Elizabeth the children of Paul's were one of the most used companies playing at court—really the most popular, to judge from the frequency of their appearance. They next played at Christmas, 1560, one interlude, along with the players of Sir Robert Dudley, for which they received the usual sum of £6-13-4. The Revels accounts offer no information of value for this year nor for the succeeding appearances of Paul's boys at Christmas, 1561, Shrovetide (probably), 1562, Christmas, 1562, Christmas, 1564, Candlemas (February 2), 1565, Christmas, 1565, (2 plays) and one other probably in the same season "at the Ladye Cicilias lodging at the Savoye," and Christmas, 1566 (2 plays).[32] It is worth noting that in three of the entries in the *Declared Accounts* —those for Christmas tide in 1560, 1561, and 1562—Westcote's boys are coupled with the players of Lord Robert Dudley, each presenting one play; after 1562 Dudley's players no longer appear. It will be remembered that just at this time Dudley was Westcote's patron, and protested in 1563 to Bishop Grindal against Sebastian's excommunication. Significance may lie in the fact that Dudley was likewise interested in the drama, to the extent of keeping a company of his own. It may be that the bond between him and Westcote was one of mutual theatrical association, and Dudley may even have had an active interest in the venture of Paul's.

During this period from 1558 to 1566 the only children's companies, so far as records tell us, to appear at court, with one exception,[33] were those of Paul's and the Chapel, and the Paul's boys were well in the lead. Beginning with Shrovetide, 1567, a new boys' company appeared on the field in the Children of Windsor, under their master Richard Farrant. These lads played fairly often, and the Westminster company occasionally, for some time thereafter. The popularity of children's plays at court seems to have fired the zeal of other schools of young talent.

In the Christmas-Shrovetide season of 1567-8, seven performances are recorded, thus distributed: Children of Westminster, one;

---

[32] All taken from the *Declared Accounts of the Treasurer of the Chamber*. For a convenient list of such entries as concern players, see Wallace, *Evolution*, pp. 210 ff.

[33] The boys of the "gramar skolle of westmynster" played twice at court in 1565, presenting Terence's *Heautontimoroumenos* and Plautus' *Miles Gloriosus*. Cf. *S. P. Dom. Eliz.* XXXVI, No. 22; *Revels Accounts Eliz.*, edit. Feuillerat, p. 117; Dr. Scott, *Westminster Records*, in *Athenæum*, Feb. 14, 1903, p. 220.

Children of the Chapel, one, a tragedy; Lord Riche's players, two; Children of Windsor, one; Children of Paul's two. The names of the plays are given in the Revels Accounts for that year.[34] They are: *As Plain as Can Be*, *The Painful Pilgrimage*, *Jack and Jill*, *Six Fools*, *Wit and Will*, *Prodigality*, "and the sevoenthe of Orestes and a Tragedie of the kinge of Scottes." Though the *Revels Accounts* speak of "seven plays," and there are only seven performances recorded, I am much inclined to believe that there are eight plays in the list—"seven playes" and "a Tragedie." There is no conceivable connection between Orestes and the King of Scots, and the wording of the entry implies distinctly two plays. I believe the scribe intended a distinction between "plays" and "tragedies," meaning by the former term what a play usually was in those days— a form of comedy. The mention in the *Declared Accounts* that the Chapel children's play was a tragedy, gives good reason for supposing that their play was the "Tragedie of the kinge of Scottes," and Mrs. C. C. Stopes has accepted it as fact.[35] Two of the remaining plays, then, should be assigned to the Paul's boys, and one of these, I believe, can be identified with an extant play.

Several years ago[36] I put forward the theory that the *Prodigality* listed among the plays of 1567-8 was an older version of *The Contention between Liberality and Prodigality*.[37] To be sure, Fleay had already called attention to the possibility,[38] but without adducing evidence other than the similarity of names. The reasons—perhaps they should be better called coincidences—upon which I base my argument are slight, but as arguments of this kind go they have some force. I shall summarize them as briefly as may be.

The Contention was first printed in 1602, without, seemingly, having been entered in the *Stationers' Register*. It is a mixed morality of a type which was then no longer in style, but it had been rewritten so as to give some air of modernity. Thus toward the end the Clerk is made to say:

"Thou art indicted by the name of Prodigality,
For that thou, the fourth day of February,

---

[34] Feuillerat, p. 109.
[35] Cf. p. 85.
[36] In an article on "Sebastian Westcote, Dramatist and Master of the Children of Paul's," in *Journ. of Eng. and Germ. Philol.*, Vol. XIV, October, 1915.
[37] A quarto was published in 1602. It is reprinted in Hazlitt's Dodsley, Vol. VIII.
[38] *Biog. Chron. of the Eng. Drama*, II, 323.

In the three and forty year of the prosperous reign
Of Elizabeth, our dread sovereign . . . .."

That is to say, in 1601.

It is certainly a play for children because the Prologue announces
that:

"As for the quirks of sage Philosophy
Or points of squirriliting scurrility,
The one we shun, for childish years too rare,
Th' other unfit for such as present are."

Now a children's play in 1601 means either Paul's or the Chapel,
and if either company was in that year putting on oldfashioned
plays we should suspect that they came out of its own library. Both
companies, to be sure, were playing at court in 1567-8, but we know,
on pretty good evidence, that the Chapel play then was a tragedy
of *The King of Scots*. So the Chapel must be ruled out.

The Revels lists for this season yield no clue which might more
firmly associate *Prodigality* with Paul's boys. But this company
played again at court on February 2, 1575, and the Revels accounts
make interesting note of certain properties. The most significant
is the following.[39]

"The ffethermaker A Cote, A hatt, & Buskins all ou*er*
covered with ffethers of cvllers for vanytie in
sabastians playe . . . ."

If we turn now to the *Contention* we find that the first stage direction
reads: "Enter *Vanity* solus, all in feathers." The coincidence is
striking. I cannot recall any other play in which Vanity, in a cloak
of feathers, is a participant.

The only other direct reference to Westcote's play neither helps
much nor hinders. It is this:[40]

"skynnes to furr the hoode in sabastians playe . . . . ij^s.
ffor making of ij sarcenet hood*des* for Cyttyzens in
the same playe . . . . ij^s."

There are citizens in the *Contention*, but so were there in many
another play. But another item, though not connected with any
company, has corroborative value:

"A ffelt y^t was covered w*ith* mony . . . . vj^d."

[39] Feuillerat, p. 241.
[40] This and the two following entries occur on page 244 of Feuillerat's *Revels*.

For among the *dramatis personæ* of the *Contention*, and a very important member, is Money, son to Dame Fortune. The "felt covered with money" may well have been a characterizing part of his costume.

The only other item among the Revels accounts that can be applied to the *Contention* is this:

"Cownters to cast awaye by players—iij^s."

There is much talk in the play of money and the squandering of it, and the flinging away of coins may have been a part of the stage business.

This is the sum total of evidence. I can hardly say that it raises more than a likelihood, yet I think it is a good likelihood. If we accept it, we must suppose that when *Prodigalaty* was first produced at court during the Christmas festivities of 1567-8, it was a popular play, so popular that Paul's again played it on Candlemas of 1575, and revived it, with alterations, in 1601. As to the last revival, we know that when the Paul's boys reopened their theatre in 1599-1600 after nearly a decade of silence, they put forth some of their old repertory and were severely criticised for so doing.[41] It has been supposed that the *Wisdom of Doctor Doddipole* and *Maid's Metamorphosis* were two such plays; I believe that the *Contention* was a third. We have no record of a performance at court by the Paul's boys (or by the Chapel boys either, for that matter) on February 4, 1601; Paul's did play there on January 1. But that proves nothing.

I should be very glad to think that in the *Contention Between Liberality and Prodigality* we have a specimen of Westcote's talents. Even granting, however, the identification of this play with the old *Prodigality*, we must bear in mind that it has been rewritten, so that the task of estimating Westcote's qualities as a playwright is difficult. But probably the main outlines were not much changed. The plot is woven of three strands: one of the adventures of Prodigality and Tenacity, Money, Vanity, Fortune, Tom Toss, and Dick Dicer; one of the befriending of Captain Well-Done by Liberality; and one of the contention between Virtue and Fortune, this last being suggested rather than actually carried out. The interweaving of these strands is very slight. Of them all, by far the most dramatic,

---

[41] Cf. the oft-quoted lines in *Jcak Drum's Entertainment*, Act V, lines 111 ff.
  "But they (the boys of Paul's) produce
  Such mustie fopperies of antiquity,
  And do not sute the humorous ages backs
  With clothes in fashion."

vivid, and amusing is that which concerns Prodagility, Tenacity, and Money. Their scenes, which fill most of the play, are written with flavor and dash. Tenacity, despite his name, is a thick witted country lout, with a dialect full of v's and ch's, like that which was so popular in comedies of the 60's and which is represented in the person of Grim in Edwards's *Damon and Pythias*. The character and dialect of Tenacity in themselves raise a presumption that the play was first composed about the time of *Like Will to Like, Gammer Gurton's Needle*, and *Damon and Pythias*.

As I have said, since we cannot tell how much alteration the play has undergone in the vicissitudes of years, we are at a loss as to just how much credit we ought to give Westcote for his work herein. Beyond question, I think, the moralizing passages which engage Virtue, Equity, and Liberality come from the older play, but what of the remaining scenes of real life? Are they the additions of a later age? I do not believe they were entirely so, for that would mean that the old play was cut to pieces, and a new play could have been quite as easily written. Then, too, the popularity of the play surely depended upon these realistic scenes; they must have been in the original in some form, or else we are puzzled to account for the revivals of the play. As they stand now, these scenes have a continuity of treatment and theme which defies the efforts of the investigator to find any differences in the manner of handling them. Of course, the old scenes may have been pruned and polished to some extent, but I see no reason to think that revision went further than this. The character of Money comes beyond doubt from the original play, and reflects a dramatic fad of the times. We are pretty safe in taking him as an example of Westcote's best work, and that is really good.

Plays were again given at court by the children of Paul's on New Year's night, 1569, on Innocents' Day, 1570, in Shrovetide, 1571, and on Innocents' Day again, 1571. The play for this last occasion, so the *Revels Accounts*[42] inform us, was one called *Effiginia*, and was a tragedy; but we know nothing more of it.[43] Paul's boys playe again some time during the Christmas season of 1572-3 (Christmas to Twelfth Day, January 6), perhaps on the night of Twelfth Day; the warrant is dated January 7, and the day of performance is not

---

[42] Feuillerat, p. 145.
[43] Wallace, *Evolution*, p. 104, suggests that this may have been the comedy called *The Bugbears*; Chambers, *Eliz. Stage*, II, 14, thinks that it may have been Lady Lumley's translation of the Greek play.

specified. During the revels at this season, at which nine plays were offered and four children's companies assisted—Paul's, the Chapel's, Eton's, and Merchant Taylors'—a play called "Cariclia" and a "playe of fortune" were given.[44] The only reference in the *Revels Accounts* which concerns Paul's play does not help us much: "ii Squir*tes* for the playe of the children of powles—viii⁸." The Paul's boys again played at court on St. John's night, December 27, 1573, presenting a play called "Alkmeon."[45] Other performances were on Candlemas Day (February 2), 1575, when, if I am right, *Prodigality* was repeated, Twelfth Night, 1576, and January 1 and Shrove Tuesday[46] (February 19), 1577. On the former occasion, they acted "The historie of Error" and on the latter "The historye of Titus and Gisippus."[47] For "Titus" one set of properties is given in the *Revels Accounts*—"two formes for the Senatours." The boys played again on December 29, 1577. On January 1, 1579, they gave "A Morrall of the marryage of Mynde and Measure,"[48] and on Sunday, January 3, 1580, "The history of Cipio Africanus."[49] On Twelfth Night, 1581, they acted "A storie of Pompey . . . . Whereon was ymploied newe one great citty, A senate howse and eight ells of dobble sarcenet for curtens and .xviii. paire of gloves";[50] and again performed that year on St. Stephen's Day, December 26.[51]

4. *1582-1587.   St. Paul's and Blackfriars.*

During this period of over twenty years the children of Paul's had appeared at court almost once a year, that is to say, with a regularity which showed the esteem in which they were held. But from now until February 27, 1587, they disappeared under their familiar name from court. We may talk of inhibition, of tl eir giving offense at court through one of their plays, of various possible circumstances which could have stopped them for a time; it is all useless speculation. Rather let us be sure that they *did* cease.

[44] Feuillerat, *Revels*, pp. 175-176.
[45] *Same*, p. 193.
[46] As in the *Revels Accounts*, p. 270. The *Declared Accounts* say Shrove Sunday, but this is hardly right, for the Earl of Warwick's men played on Shrove Sunday, while on Shrove Tuesday there was only a masque.
[47] *Revels Accounts*, pp. 256, 270.
[48] *Same*, p. 286.
[49] *Same*, p. 321.
[50] *Same*, p. 336.
[51] Chambers suggests (*Eliz. Stage*, II, 15) that this may have been the *Cupid and Psyche* mentioned by Gosson as played at Paul's presumably not long before 1582, when he published *Plays Confuted*.

In that hurly-burly time between 1580 and 1584, during the quarrels and cross suits over the widow Farrant's Blackfriars theatre much confusion still awaits clarification, particularly in respect to the meteoric company known as the Earl of Oxford's children or servants. They first appear in the *Declared Accounts* on January 1, 1584, and played again on March 3 (Shrove Tuesday) and December 27 (St. John's Day), 1584. Possibly the "servants" of the Earl who played on January 1, 1585, were the same company; perhaps they were adults. Was this company, as has been argued,[52] made up of members both of the Chapel and Paul's?

The documents unearthed from the *Losely MSS.* by Wallace and Feuillerat reveal, it will be remembered, that Richard Farrant took over in 1576 some rooms in the precinct of the dissolved monastery of Blackfriars in London, turned them into a playhouse, and exercised the Children of the Chapel there as a regular playing company until his death in 1580. The building was afterwards leased by the widow to William Hunnis and John Newman, who attempted to carry on the business. But trouble was brewed by Sir William More, who had all along objected to having a playhouse in his property, and who was now plagued with arrears in rent. He began to make efforts to recover the lease, and apparently to escape their obligations and the prospects of a lawsuit, Hunnis and Newman made over their lease to Henry Evans, a young scrivener of London. The prosecutions of More continuing, Evans sold the lease to the Earl of Oxford, about June, 1583;[53] and Oxford later gave it to John Lyly, the dramatist and author of *Euphues*. These shifts and jugglings with the lease, in an effort to escape the wrath of More, are significant only in that they show an understanding, a kind of partnership, between three at least of the men involved—Evans, Oxford, and Lyly. Both Evans and Lyly, it will be remembered, appeared in 1584 as payees for Oxford's boys. I am not quite so sure that Hunnis was one of the partnership. In the first place,

---

[52] Wallace, *Evolution*, p. 171; Chambers in his *Eliz. Stage*, thinks the company that played in 1584 was made up of Paul's, the Chapel, and Oxford's own boys.

[53] The widow Farrant in her answer to the Bill of Complaint in the case Newman and Hunnis vs. Farrant, dated January 27, 1584 says, "Besides that the saide Sir william moore hath since made somme entry and a new Lease of the premisses to one who by colour thereof hath sued the said Evans." (Cf. Wallace, *Evolution*, p. 165.). In an undated petition to Sir Francis Walsingham she refers to this proceeding as taking place in "this laste Hilliary Terme." It was probably on account of this action that Evans sold out to the Earl of Oxford.

there is his urgent petition to the Queen in November, 1583,[54] in which he represents himself as on the verge of ruin through the inadequate income now pertaining to the office of master of the Chapel boys. This looks as though a quietus had been put on his theatrical business. It may well be that this resulted after More's prosecutions forced him to sell his lease to Evans. In the second place, Hunnis appeared with the children of the Chapel[55] on Twelfth and Candlemas days, 1584, at the time Oxford's company was playing.

To recapitulate, the year 1584 saw at court a new company called the servants of the Earl of Oxford, which was controlled by the three men—Oxford, Evans, and Lyly—who were engaged in bandying the lease of the Blackfriars theatre among them. Most certainly this company appeared at the Blackfriars. Moreover, it is significant that Lyly's *Campaspe* and *Sapho and Phao* were published in this year as acted at court by both the children of Paul's and the Chapel on the very dates when Oxford's company was said in the *Declared Accounts* to have played before the Queen[56]. Was Oxford's company a combination of the two main children's companies acting together, the Chapel children keeping up their playing unaffected by the legal jugglery of the theatre lease, and calling in the Paul's boys to their aid when necessary? Or were Paul's boys the incumbents at Blackfriars after Hunnis surrendered his lease, and the Chapel boys the visitors? Dr. Wallace[57] proposes the first view; I incline to the second, with more reason, as it seems to me.

This is my construction of the events which succeeded the last recorded appearance of Paul's boys at court on St. Stephen's Day, 1581. The prosperous course of this company was interrupted by the death of its master in April, 1582.[58] Probably Thomas Gyles

[54] Cf. p. 102.
[55] *Declared Accounts.* Cf. p. 100.
[56] Title pages:
"A moste excellent Comedie of Alexander, Campaspe, and Diogenes, Played beefore the Queenes Maiestie on twelfe day at night by her Maiesties children, and the children of Poules. Imprinted at London for Thomas Cadman. 1584." So one 4[to] of 1584; but the other two have "newyeares day at night." which harmonizes with the *Declared Accounts.*
"Sapho and Phao, Played beefore the Queenes Maiestie on Shroue-tewsday, by her Maiesties Children, and the Boyes of Paules."
Imprinted at London for Thomas Cadman, 1584."
[57] *Evolution*, pp. 170, 171.
[58] His will was drawn up April 3 and proved April 14.

succeeded him at once as almoner and master of the boys, though
we first hear of him in 1584,[59] when he is directed to send his pupils
to Colet's school to learn the principles of grammar. For some
reason he did not take up at once the business of producing plays,
for we do not hear of him in that capacity at court until Shrove
Sunday, 1587. Now the man about whom subsequent events
developed was Henry Evans. He had been Westcote's "deere
friende";[60] he had watched with interest the success of Westcote as
theatrical impresario, and he was fired with the desire to carry on
the lucrative business after his friend's death, seeing that Thomas
Gyles was not eager to do so. And so at an opportune time[61] he
took over Hunnis's lease; either on his own initiative or else, as
seems more likely, in cooperation with Oxford and his protégé Lyly.
Then began the partnership which resulted in the production of at
least two plays of Lyly's, and doubtless many more that never got to
court. For such plays as demanded larger casts, the Chapel boys
were called upon too, and hence we have the title pages of *Campaspe*
and *Sapho and Phao*; or else Hunnis was likewise in the bargain, and
the two companies acted more or less regularly together. But I do
not believe this, from the fact that Hunnis acted independently in
the early part of 1584. The resuscitated Paul's company was called
after the Earl of Oxford, the patron of the enterprise. It did not
act at the regular playing-place at St. Paul's for the same reasons
that kept its regular master Thomas Gyles from directing them. The
theatre remained somewhat over a year in these hands, until in
Easter term, 1584, the lease was given by judgment again into the
hands of Sir William More.

Now what advantage does this hypothesis that Paul's boys were
the company known as the Earl of Oxford's boys give us over the
hypothesis that the Chapel company played on after Hunnis lost
his lease of the theatre? In the first place, it permits us to understand how Henry Evans became involved in the enterprise; next,
it explains as well as the other theory how the Chapel and Paul's
boys came to be playing together in certain plays; thirdly, it explains
why the Chapel should be playing in their own name at court when
Paul's were not; and lastly, it enables us to understand what has
proved a stumbling block and subject of speculation to all who have

[59] R. B. Gardiner, *Admission Registers of St. Paul's School*, p. 11.
[60] So called in Westcote's will.
[61] Probably before November, 1583.

discussed this knotty period in the history of Paul's—namely, why
Gabriel Harvey said of Lyly:[62] "He hath not played the Vicemaster
of Poules, and the Foolemaster of the Theatre for naughtes." Now
it is absurd to take this ironical dig seriously and suppose, as does
R. W. Bond in his construction of Lyly's life, that Lyly really held
some such post as vice- or assistant-master of Paul's. There was no
such post, any more than there was in the Chapel. Thomas Gyles
was master, and his duties did not require the aid of a subordinate.
Nor do the records of St. Paul's Cathedral give any hint of the
existence of such an officer. But Lyly, for having served a few times
as manager of the company acting as Oxford's boys and well known
to be the children of Paul's under a different name, might have
made the thrust possible.

Oxford's boys again appeared at court on St. John's Day (December 27), 1584, when they acted "The history of Agamemnon &
Ulisses."[63]   Evidently the loss of a theatre had not ended their
career; yet from the fact that the payment in the *Declared Accounts*
is to Henry Evans and not Lyly and that Lyly's two plays had been
published in that year, it looks as though Lyly had severed connections with the company. This is the last notice of Oxford's boys.[64]

[62] *Works*, edit. Grosart, II, 212.

[63] *Revels Accounts*, p. 365.

[64] The obscurity which hangs about the Earl of Oxford's theatrical ventures is
deep and vexing. We have no concern, of course, with that early company which
bore his name and disappeared about 1563. But by 1579 or 1580, he was supporting
a troupe of men players, who appear in the records for several years thereafter.
Did he also have a company of boys? It would seem to be so, for in September of
1581 a company calling themselves the "Lord Oxford's players" and composed of
nine boys and a man acted at Bristol (Murray, *Eng. Dram Companies*, II, 215).
They also played at Norwich in 1580-1 (where they were described as "the Earle of
Oxenfordes lads"). This may have been the same company that acted *Agamemnon
and Ulysses* at court on December 27, 1584, and were described as "the Earle of
Oxenford his boyes." Who were these boys? Mr. Chambers thinks that they were
members of the Earl's domestic chapel, who travelled either independently or as
an adjunct to his adult company (*Eliz. Stage*, II, 100-101). That may have been so.

At any rate, as I have pointed out above, the company called the "Erle of
Oxford his servantes" which played *Campaspe* and *Sapho and Phao* on New Year's
and Shrove Tuesday of 1584, was neither the Earl's adult company, nor his company of children, but seems to have been composed of the combined companies of
Paul's and the Chapel. Mr. Chambers believes that Oxford's own boy troupe was
also part of it, but I cannot see what need there was of *three* companies to do these
plays. It is all very puzzling.

The confusion would be lessened if we were to suppose that this boy company of
Oxford's which first appears in 1580-81 was really the company at Paul's, which
put itself under the Earl's protection while touring the provinces. One might

From St. John's Day, 1584, till Shrove Sunday, 1587, there is no record of any performance at court which can in any way be linked with the children of Paul's. The reason for this gap it is useless to inquire. We may suppose they were in disfavor and inhibited from court, we may suppose this disfavor arose from a play of Lyly's— we may suppose any number of such things, without even the shadow of ground. We cannot be too careful about using the excuse of inhibition to explain the non-appearance of a company at court. We are only sure of one instance—when the Paul's boys were "put down" round about 1590 for thrusting into the Marprelate controversy—and there is no evidence that the court was especially touchy and ready to withdraw the favor of its countenance. Of course, when a long and seemingly prosperous course in interrupted, there must be reasons, and occasionally in sheer desperation we fall back on the explanation "royal disfavor." But the cause is just as likely to lie within the personal affairs of the company itself, and be due to lack of money, or other complications. Then, too, it must be remembered that absence from court does not necessarily mean stoppage of playing in any capacity, though in a company long accustomed to be in court favor that conclusion is in a measure justifiable. The tenor of these remarks is that Paul's boys may have been playing publicly between 1584 and 1587, though not appearing at court.

5. *1587-1590 ('91). Lyly's Plays.*

When they did return, on Shrove Sunday, 1587, it was under a new manager. Thomas Gyles, though he had followed Westcote in the place of almoner and choir master[65] at St. Paul's, had not appeared before this time in connection with the drama at court. This man is a much vaguer entity than Sebastian Westcote. We really know nothing about him, aside from a few facts relating to the execution of his duties. Whether or not he was connected with the Thomas Giles, haberdasher, who supplied the Revels Office with

---

suppose that choir boys would not be allowed to roam so far afield, but in fact a company calling itself the "Children of powles" is known to have played in Gloucester in 1590-91 (Murray. *op. cit.*, II, 284). I must admit that I have no proof to support this hypothesis, but I may point out in self defense that it paves the way to a clearer understanding of what happened at Blackfriars in the vexing years 1583 and 1584.

[65] He became choir master on May 22, 1584. Cf. Chambers, *Eliz. Stage*, II, 17.

vizards[66] from about 1570 to 1576, is impossible to say; it is conceivable. The name is too common to make identification sure unless there is other confirming evidence. Thus I cannot be certain that a Thomas Gyles appointed in 1606 to be music master to the Prince Henry[67] was or was not this man. He may well have been, for we have no record of his death at Paul's—only that he was succeeded in 1601 by Edward Pierce of Pearce; and his experience as music master of the choir would fit him admirably for the post.[68] The Thomas Giles of St. Paul's was granted on April 27, 1585, a writ of impressment permitting him to take up "in anye Cathedral or Collegiate Church or Churches, and in every other place or places of this our Realm of England and Wales, such child and children as he . . . . shall find and like of."[69] This was a writ of the kind issued frequently before and after this instance to masters of the choirs connected with the court by means of which they were to replenish their choirs, when the voluntary increase was insufficient. There is no provable connection between this grant and the dramatic history of the Paul's boys, nor between any other such grant and the dramatic history of any company whatsoever.

Under this master Thomas Gyles, the Paul's boys returned to court in 1587, when they played on Shrove Sunday, February 26;[70] and again on the following dates: January 1, 1588, February 2, 1588, St. John's Day (December 27), 1588, January 1, 1589, Sunday after 12th Day, 1589, December 28, 1589, January 1, 1590, January 6, 1590. From then on they mysteriously disappear from court until 1601. During this 1587-1590 period many of Lyly's plays were given; that much we are sure of, but it is quite a different matter to try to date them.

---

[66] Cf. *Revels Accounts*, pp. 141, 158, 184, 268, 409.

[67] *Privy Signet Bills, Treas. of Receipt*, Dec. 3 Jas. I, no. 36.

[68] The music master Giles appears rather often in court accounts after his appointment, either in connection with an increase in fees or with the festivities at court. Thus for the "Prince's Masque" of 1611 Giles devised three dances, for which he received £40 (cf. Fred. Devon, *Issues of the Exchequer*, p. 136); and in the accounts of a masque of 1613 his name is listed opposite a payment of £30 (cf. Devon, *Pell Records*, p. 164).

[69] Frequently reprinted. Cf. Collier, *Annals of the Stage*, I, 258; and *The English Drama and Stage*, edit. Hazlitt for the Roxburghe Library.

[70] *Declared Accounts*.

Galathea[71] would not at first seem to be one of them, for it was licensed in the *Stationers' Register* on April 1, 1585,[72] though not printed until 1592; and so far as we can judge, no play was presented before the queen *after* it was licensed. The licensing and printing seem to have come when there was no longer a market on the stage for the play. Yet in this case the holding-off of the printing so long after the licensing looks as though the mind of the owner had changed suddenly; perceiving, shall we say, an opportunity, by the reinstatement of a company temporarily disbanded, to have the play run longer. That is, I surmise that shortly after the licensing of *Galathea*, it was feasible for the Paul's company and its master Gyles to begin playing anew; and the publication of this play was held up on that account.

I am sensible that this theory does not explain why *Galathea* was not licensed and published at the same time with *Campaspe* and *Sapho and Phao*, with which it would have been in the same boat. But that can be explained. It is easily possible that at the time when the Paul's company, or the Earl of Oxford's boys, was temporarily checked by losing its theatre in Easter term, 1584, Lyly had some acted plays on hand and had one or two more under way. He unloaded his acted plays, and finished another, *Galathea*, possibly hoping to dispose of it. Not seeing an opportunity for having it played, he decided to publish, and had accomplished the preliminaries when the desired opportunity hove in sight. By this hypothesis, which it is quite impossible to prove, the performances of this play would all fall after the date of its licensing, April 1, 1585. This hypothesis is borne out by the internal evidence of the play itself.[73] Lyly used Reginald Scot's *Discouverie of Witchcraft*, published in 1584; in Act V, Sc. 3 Venus says to Cupid: "Sir boy, where have you been? Always taken, first by Sapho, now by Diana." These evidences indicate that the play was written after *Sapho and Phao* and after the date in 1584 when Scot's *Discouverie* was printed. Raffe's remark (I, 4): "Come, let us to the woods, and see what fortune we may have before they be made ships"—points to the

---

[71] "Gallathea As it was playde before the Queenes Maiestie at Greenewiche, on Newyeares day at night. By the Children of Paules. At London. Printed by Iohn Charlwoode for the Widdow Broome. 1592."

[72] "1. Aprilis 1585 Gabriel Cawood Receaued of him for printinge A Commoedie of Titirus and Galathea." (No sum given.) *S. R.*, edit. Arber, II, 440.

[73] Cf. Bond, *Lyly*, II, 424; Baker, *Endimion*, introd.; Feuillerat, *Lyly*, p. 575.

shipbuilding plans of 1584. If the play was not presented at court before licensing in 1585, it may be assigned to January 1, 1588, when Paul's boys played at court and the queen was at Greenwich, both circumstances in accord with the title page of the 1592 edition.

The date of *Love's Metamorphosis*[74] is even more difficult to fix than that of *Galathea*. The fact that it had, by 1601, been played first by the Children of Paul's, and "now" by the Children of the Chapel, indicates that it was brought out before 1591 by Paul's company. This is made more likely by many references to *Galathea*, which point to a closely following date of composition and performance. Such is Professor Baker's reasoning.[75] Bond[76] reasons in just the opposite way, maintaining that the great number of allusions argues against composition directly after *Galathea*, since Lyly was too proud of his invention to risk the appearance of repeating himself. This is extraordinary psychology. If there is to be any sense and value in allusions, if they are to be used at all, they must have point; and the point of an allusion decreases directly in proportion to its distance in time from its subject. Why, if Lyly was proud of his invention, did he repeat himself at all? Why on earth, if he must repeat himself, should he do it in allusions to a play too old to be any longer in the minds of the audience?

If *Galathea* was produced on January 1, 1588, as I think seems likely, we may choose almost any subsequent date for *Love's Metamorphosis*.

As to *Endimion*,[77] that puzzling play, the dating follows the view you hold of the allegory, and at present it seems that a satisfactory

---

[74] "Loves Metamorphosis. A Wittie and Courtly Pastorall, Written by Mr. Iohn Lyllie. First playd by the Children of Paules, and now by the Children of the Chappell. London Printed for William Wood, dwelling at the West end of Paules, at the signe of Time. 1601."

The *S. R.* entry (edit. Arber III, 176) runs: "43 Regine. 25 Novembris 1600 william wood Entred for his Copie vnder the handes of Master Pasfeild and the wardens A booke Called Loves metamorphesis wrytten by master John Lylly and playd by the Children of Paules . . . . vjd."

[75] *Endimion*, p. xcvi.

[76] *Lyly*, III, 295.

[77] "Endimion The Man in the Moone. Played before the Queenes Maiestie at Greenewich on Candlemas day at night, by the Chyldren of Paules. At London, Printed by I. Charlewood, for the widdowe Broome. 1591."

S. R. entry (Arber, II, 596) runs: "4ᵗᵒ Octobris 1591 mystres Broome Wydowe Late Wyfe of William Broome Entred for her copies vnder the hand of the Bishop of London: Three Comedies plaied before her maiestie by the Children of Paules th one Called Endimion. Th other. Galathea and th other, Midas . . . . xviijd."

interpretation is an impossibility. I shall therefore confine myself
to some considerations outside the play itself. Bond[78] dates the
performance of the play Candlemas day (February 2), 1586, and
Feuillerat[79] agrees. But there is no record of a performance by
Paul's on that date, and while that may not be absolutely final, it
ought decidedly to make us hesitate. As to its being written before
1585, there is only Professor Baker's hypothesis of the allegory to
bear that surmise out; and this both Bond and Feuillerat have
shown to be unlikely and difficult to prove. Both these gentlemen,
for different reasons, favor 1585-6. Is there not another bit of
evidence in the entries of the *Stationers' Register*? Is it not significant that the license to the widow Broome for *Endimion* groups
with it *Galathea* and *Midas*, both of which were undoubtedly
written in or after 1584, and the license for *Campaspe* and *Sapho
and Phao* stands separate? That is, had *Endimion* been written
and acted by 1584, why did it not pass over to William Broome
with the other two? Why, indeed, was it not published then? It
looks as though the two sets of plays had been acquired at different
times, and discounting *Endimion*, the dates of the two sets are seen
to lie on either side of 1584. Was it chance that put *Endimion* with
the later set? Or did it go there because it belonged there?

A date is open to *Endimion*—that it is the right one I do not
venture to aver—in February 2, 1588. That was Candlemas Day,
the queen was at Greenwich, and Paul's boys played before her.[80]

As to the date of *Midas*,[81] I have nothing to add to the arguments
of Bond,[82] which I am inclined to join with Feuillerat in accepting.
The play would seem to have been composed between May and
November of 1589, and may have been played at court on Twelfth
Day, 1590. Nor have I anything to contribute to the discussion of
Mother Bombie.[83] Certainly, in style and workmanship, it is a late

[78] *Lyly*, III, 10.
[79] *Lyly*, p. 576.
[80] *Revels Accounts*, ed. Feuillerat, p. 388; *Declared Accounts*.
[81] "Midas. Plaied before the Queenes Maiestie upon Twelfe Day at night, By
the Children of Paules. London Printed by Thomas Scarlet for I. B. and are to be
sold in Paules Churchyard at the signe of the Bible. 1592."
The *S. R.* entry is dated Oct. 4, 1591. Cf. note under discussion of *Galathea*.
[82] *Lyly*, III, 110.
[83] "Mother Bombie. As it was sundrie times plaied by the Children of Powles.
London, Imprinted by Thomas Scarlet for Cuthbert Burby. 1594."
The *S. R.* entry (Arber, II, 654) runs: "xviij Junii 1594 Cuthbert Burby. Entred
for his copie vnder th and of master warden Cawood a booke intituled mother
Bumbye beinge an enterlude . . . . vjd. C."

play, and may well have come after *Midas*, even though we give *Midas* the last recorded performance at court, for *Bombie* is not recorded as having been presented at court.

I omit discussion of *The Woman in the Moone* because there is no good evidence of its having been given by a children's company,[84] and postpone consideration of *The Maydes Metamorphosis* until a later time.[85] The schedule of performances of Lyly's plays I have submitted is extremely provisional, as I am ready to admit. I have merely attempted to show that it is really possible to fit many of the plays pretty satisfactorily with dates from the *Declared Accounts*. I have no strong conviction of the accuracy of the assignments, nor, as a matter of fact, do I much care. What seems more important to me is the larger and well established fact that from Shrove Sunday 1587, till Twelfth Day, 1590, the Children of Paul's played at court with greater frequency than ever before, and that during the same period many of Lyly's plays were produced. There may have been various reasons why he thus exclusively patronized this company. It is virtually certain that the Chapel boys were not playing at this time. If Lyly had begun by writing *Campaspe* and *Sapho and Phao* for them, he must have of necessity gone over to the other company at this time, since his plays were designed for the talents of child actors. But if, as I have supposed, he began by writing for Paul's, when it played under the patronage of the Earl of Oxford, then his continuance in harness with them is in the natural course of things.

That the company of Paul's boys was inhibited, ceased for lack of money or for some other hitch, became dissolved and played no more publicly or at court in or about 1590, is indubitably borne out in contemporary evidence. The notice of the printer to the reader in the 1591 quarto of *Endimion* says so.[86] This notice limits the date of closing to the period between the last appearance of Paul's boys at court, on January 6, 1590, and the licensing of the play, October 4, 1591. The question is complicated by the fact that

[84] But see p. 288.

[85] Cf. p. 293.

[86] "Since the Plaies in Paules were dissolued, there are certaine Commedies come to my handes by chaunce, which were presented before her Maiestie at seuerall times by the children of Paules. This is the first, and if in any place it shall dysplease, I will take more paines to perfect the next. I referre it to thy indifferent iudgement to peruse, whome I woulde willinglie please. And if this may passe with thy good lyking, I will then goe forwarde to publish the rest. In the meane time, let this haue thy good worde for my better encouragement."

this company seems to have played in the provinces some time after January 6, 1590; for in the Chamberlain's Accounts[87] of Gloucester, under the not very definite date of September 29, 32 Eliz. (1590), to September 29, 33 Eliz. (1591), occurs this payment: "to the Children of powles xx⁹." The question is whether the dissolution spoken of in *Endimion* debarred the company from playing anywhere, or only in London; in the latter case they could take refuge in travelling. I am inclined to take the dissolution as absolute, from the very use of the term "dissolved," which implies breaking up, and not simply restriction. In that case, we have the limits of disbandment narrowed to the period between October, 1590, and October 4, 1591. Some time must be allowed for the manuscript of the plays to get to the printer; the owners would not publish until the chances of reopening were seen to be entirely hopeless. We can hardly put the closing of Paul's later than the summer of 1591.

They were still disorganized in 1596. Nash, in *Have with you to Saffron Waldon*, published in that year, says:[88] "We neede neuer wish the Playes at *Powles* vp againe, but if we were wearie with walking, and loth to goe too farre to seeke sport, into the Arches we might step, and heare him (i.e., Gabriel Harvey) plead; which would bee a merier Comedie than euer was old Mother *Bomby*." We cannot be sure the boys came up again, as a company performing publicly, until 1600.

6. *The Dissolution of Paul's.*

And why were the Paul's boys dissolved in 1590? The reason now generally accepted, than which no better presents itself, is that they were put down for mingling in the Marprelate controversy. Fleay, to be sure, thought it was a royal inhibition, brought on by displeasure at the satire of Elizabeth contained in *The Woman in the Moon* and at intermeddling with state affairs in *Midas*. But only on the flimsiest of evidence can *The Woman in the Moon* be assigned to a period before 1590, and Baker, Bond, and Feuillerat unite in placing it after the dissolution. As for *Midas*, it may well have been one of the Martinist plays to judge from glancing allusions in pamphlets of the time. Thus in *An Almond for a Parrot* (1590) we read: "A man cannot . . . . write *Midas habet aures asininas* in great

[87] Murray, *Eng. Dram. Companies*, II, 284.
[88] *Works*, ed. McKerrow, III, 46.

Roman letters but he shall be in danger of further displeasure."
And the author of *The Admonition to the People of England*, printed
in 1589, describes Martin Marprelate thus:[89] "Hee was like Mydas
that couetous King: for hee had long eares like an Asse." But no
certainties can be drawn from these hints, and whatever plays took
part in the war either were drastically revised for publication or
were never printed at all. Which is a matter of regret for the historian of the stage.

No doubt, however, exists that the theatres did take part in the
war.[90] The first gun of satire was fired about October of 1588, when
appeared the first tract to bear the title of Martin Marprelate
(known for short as *The Epistle*). Then followed a bombardment
of jocular, scandalous pamphlets to which the bishops at first
replied with dignity, but which soon drew them to fight fire with
fire, and to summon to their aid the sharp pens of such wits as Lyly
and Nash. The Martinist press even accused them of suborning
the stage. Thus *The Protestacyon of Martin Marprelate* (1589):[91]
"Then among al the rimers and stage plaiers, which my Ll. of the
cleargy had suborned against me I remember Mar-Martin," etc.
And the same charge is made in *The Just Censure and Reproof*
(July, 1589):[92] "Thou sawest well enough that Martins doings were
almost forgot and husht. And the men of sin themselves, I mean the
Canterbury Caiaphas and the rest of his antichristian beasts, who
bear his abominable mark, were content, in a manner, to turn his
purposes from a serious matter to a point of jesting; wherewith they
would have only rhymers and stage-players (that is plain rogues,
as thou hast well noted) to deal."

Yet I do not believe that the theatres came to the defense of the
bishops at any call from them. The Martinist asseverations on this
point are of little weight because in such a bitter war as this no
scruples of truth would stand in the way of a taunt, nor were the
Martinists likely to inquire as to whether the bishops were or were

---

[89] P. 94.

[90] The chief books of reference for the Marprelate controversy are Edward
Arber's *Introductory Sketch to the Martin Marprelate Controversy*, London, 1879;
William Pierce's *An Historical Introduction to the Marprelate Tracts*. London, 1908;
the same author's *The Marprelate Tracts*, London, 1911 (a collection of the chief
pamphlets); and G. Bonnard's *La Controverse de Martin Marprelate*, Paris, 1916.
J. D. Wilson's chapter on the subject in the *Cambridge Hist. of Eng. Lit.* (Vol. III)
is also useful.

[91] Cf. Chambers, *Eliz. Stage*, IV, 231.

[92] Cf. Wm. Pierce, *Marprelate Tracts*, p. 352.

not guilty of every hostile act. That they were guilty was taken for granted. As to the reasons for which the theatres entered the quarrel we have not far to seek. Their dislike of the Puritans was one, and their liking for satire was another. Such a chance was not to be missed. So we find them, early in 1589, engaging in the fray, mainly on the side of the church party. I say mainly on that side, for I strongly suspect that they dealt more than a few blows on the ribs of friends as well as of foes. Otherwise I am at a loss to understand the deep displeasure which fell upon them.

This is broadly hinted at in *Pasquill's Return* (1589):[93] "Me thought *Vetus Comedia* beganne to pricke him at London in the right vaine when shee brought foorth *Diuinitie* wyth a scratcht face holding of her hart as if she were sicke, because *Martin* would have forced her, but myssing of his purpose, he left the print of his nails vppon her cheekes, and poysoned her with a vomit which he ministerd vnto her, to make her cast vppe her dignities and promotions." If this is a description of an actual play, as it would seem to be, one can see that whatever the playwright's anti-Martinistic bias might be, he had treated the church in a dangerously jocular manner. The stage of that day was neither godly nor reverent, and though one can hardly suppose that it was anywhere pro-Martinist, one can easily believe that its defense of the church had a double edge. At any rate, the offense which it caused the authorities did not arise, we may be sure, from satire directed against the Marprelate party.

The companies implicated by name in this controversy were those playing at the *Theatre*, the *Curtain*, and St. Paul's. As to the latter, our chief information comes from Lyly's *Pap with an Hatchet*:

Would it not bee a fine Tragedie, when Mardocheus shall play a Bishoppe in a Play, and *Martin* Hamman, and that hee that seekes to pull downe those that are set in authoritie aboue him should be hoysted vp on a tree aboue all other.   If it be shewed at Paules, it will cost you fourepence: at Sainct Thomas a Watrings[94] nothing.

A passage in *Martin's Month's Mind*, though by no means so precise, seems also to implicate the Paul's company. Martin is here

[93] Cf. Chambers, *Eliz. Stage*, IV, 231-2; Nash's *Works*, ed. R. B. McKerrow, I, 92.
[94] A place of execution.

imagined by the satirist as telling the causes of his death, first among which are his apish demeanor. "The wooden dagger may not bee worne at the backe, where *S. Paules* sword, hangs by the side: neither can he well find a fault with the *corner cap*; that weareth the surd night cappe on his head, as I did. These gambols (my sonnes) are implements for the Stage, and beseeme Iesters, and Plaiers, but are not fit for Church plotters . . . . such as we are." The wooden dagger, of course, was the sign of the vice or fool, and was carried by the comedian playing that part.

As to the manner of the stage satires on Martin, the tracts tell us something. In *Pap with an Hatchet* we read:

"Sed bene tu, dic sodes, will they (i.e. Martinists) not bee discouraged for the common players? Would those Comedies might be allowed to be plaid that are pend, and then I am sure he would be decyphered, and so perhaps discouraged.

"He shall not be brought in as whilom he was, and yet verie well, with a cocks combe, an apes face, a wolfs belly, catts claws, &c. but in a cap'de cloake, and all the best apparell he ware the highest day in the yeare, thats neither on Christmas day, Good Friday, Easter day, Ascension, nor Trinitie sunday (for that were popish) but on some rainie weeke-daie, when the brothers and sisters had appointed a match for particular praiers, a thing as badd at the least as Auricular confession." *An Almond for a Parrot*[95] says Martin was "attired like an Ape on yᵉ stage." The reason for this particular form of ridicule is explained in *A Whip for an Ape*:

"Who knoweth not that Apes men Martin call;
Which beast this baggage seemes as t'were himselfe."
and this pun on Martin's name was doubtless enhanced in the minds of the defenders of the faith by the apish quirks of Martin's humor.

The theatres were active in the Martinist war during 1589. Then in November of that year the Privy Council, on the application of Tilney, Master of the Revels and licenser of plays, directed the Mayor of London to stop all players then acting in the city.[96] Immediately thereafter the Council appointed a commission of three men to inquire into the abuses of the London theatres. One was to be the Revels Master Tilney, another was to be appointed by the

---

[95] Nash's *Works*, ed. McKerrow, III, 354.

[96] For the documents in this action cf. Dasent, *Acts of the Privy Council*; Collier, *Annals of the Stage* (1879) I, 265, 268. The three letters of the Privy Council appointing the licensing commision were first printed by Chalmers, in his *Apology*, p. 483.

Archbishop of Canterbury, and the third was to be appointed by the Mayor of London. The instructions to Tilney, who was to be chairman, were to call before the commission "the severall companies of players (whose servaunts soever they be) and to require them by authorytie hereof to deliver unto them their books, that they may consider of the matters of their Comedyes and Tragedyes, and thereuppon to stryke out or reforme such parte and matters, as they shall fynd unfytt and undecent to be handled in playes both for Divinitie and State: commanding the said Companies of players in her Majesties name, that they forbear to present and play publickly any Comedy or Tragedy, other than such as they shall have seen and allowed: which if they shall not observe, they shall lett them know from their Lordships that they shalbe not onely severely punished, but made (in)capable of the exercise of their professions for ever hereafter."

It appears then that the theatres were guilty of meddling with the two forbidden subjects—Divinity and State. And it appears furthermore, from all the circumstances, that their guilt was deemed to be of extraordinary moment. This is a reasonable deduction from the extraordinary nature of the licensing board. Heretofore, ever since the government had begun to pass licensing acts for the control of the stage, the principle was observed of making each community responsible for its own licensing. Thus the plays which appeared in London were subject to the approval of the Master of the Revels. But the commission set up in November, 1589, was a special body, designed to meet a special emergency, and the importance of its duties and the extent of its authority can be estimated from the three powers represented—the court, the church, and the city of London. No previous licensing officer or body had been given such stringent powers of rendering the guilty players "incapable of the exercise of their profession for ever hereafter."

It was a grave offense, then, this meddling with the affairs of Divinity and State, with which the players were charged. I think there can be no doubt that their sin was taking part in the Marprelate controversy; it was an affair of Divinity and State, and it was the only scrape which the players could get into, so far as we can see back into the period, that was serious enough to justify appointing a commission of inquiry such as that directed by the Privy Council. Again, there seems to be a direct allusion to distresses suffered by the stage in connection with the controversy in one of the tracts themselves, *Pasquill's Return*,[97] which was published in 1589.

"(Pasquill), But who cometh yonder *Marforius*, can you tell me?

Mar. By her gate and her Garland I knowe her well, it is *Vetus Comædia*. She hath been so long in the Country, that she is somewhat altred: this is she that called in a counsell of Phisitians about *Martin*, and found by the sharpnes of his humour, when they had opened the vaine that feedes his head, that hee would spit out his lunges within one yere. . . . .

Pas. I haue a tale to tell her in her eare, of the sly practise that was vsed in restraining of her."

By "she hath been so long in the Country" Marforius doubtless meant that the players referred to had taken to the provinces, as the result of being inhibited in London, and had just returned.

If one or two or even more of the London companies had got into trouble over a too zealous opposition to Martin Marprelate and had therefore been made to feel the displeasure of the powers that were, and if Paul's boys took part in the same controversy, as they certainly did, then here is a sufficient excuse for their inhibition in 1590; and this excuse I am inclined to accept. At the same time it must be remarked that whereas the other companies involved— Lord Strange's, the Lord Admiral's, and possibly the Queen's own men—suffered lightly or not at all, and are found playing again at court in succeeding years, the Children of Paul's were quite "put down," and did not appear at court from January 6, 1590, to January 1, 1603. They cannot with certainty be traced as playing in London[98] between some time within the year following September

---

[97] Cf. Chambers, *Eliz. Stage*, IV, 231-2.

[98] *Summer's Last Will and Testament*, a play by Thomas Nash, was acted at Croydon in August or September, 1592, as common consent has interpreted the allusions in the text. (Cf. Baker's ed. of *Endimion*, p. cxxix.) Fleay (*Drama*, II, 148) and Murray (*Eng. Dramatic Companies*, I, 337) believe the play was given by the Chapel, but Professor Baker assigns it, and rightly, I am convinced, to Paul's. That it was played partly by children is evident from the text, but it seems certain as well that one or two of the main characters—Will Summer at least—were adults. Thus Will speaks of two of the actors as "a couple of pretty boyes, if they would wash their faces, and were well breecht an houre or two," and takes the diminutive Epilogue upon his knee with the banterings of a grown man encouraging a small boy. This was all in accordance, as I believe, with the custom in the production of plays by the children's companies of this time, for unless I am mistaken, the master and perhaps one or two other grown men of the choir acted with the youngsters, and their parts can often be pretty accurately distinguished in the plays they gave. But to come back to the play. My reasons for believing the play

28, 1590, and 1599. To surmise that they were dissolved in 1590 because of their Marprelate interferences is one thing; to explain why they should have suffered thus heavily is another.

And yet one does not have to go far to find adequate hypotheses. It is clear that among several companies sinning against Divinity and State, that company would be most liable to censure which was itself part of an ecclesiastical institution; part indeed of the very church whose bishop was singled out by the Martinists for attack.

---

given by Paul's generally agree with Professor Baker's in his introduction to *Endimion* (p. cxxix), with this strengthening. In the days when that essay was written, the theory of the disgrace of the Chapel about 1583 was as firmly accepted as that of the suppression of Paul's in 1590-91. Now I am confident that what has since turned up regarding the ventures centering in the Blackfriars theatre, which closed in 1584, and especially what I have deduced in this connection from those facts, has weakened that theory—never very strong— to the vanishing point. We are not entitled to believe the Chapel company was ever formally banned or suppressed. On the other hand, we know that Paul's was suppressed in 1590 or by the middle of 1591. The conclusion is that the strong hints in the play at reversee not long since sustained by the company can only point to Paul's boys. The passages from tne prologue which contain these hints run as follows:

"At a solemne feast of the *Triumuiri* in Rome, it was seene and obserued that the birds ceased to sing, & sate solitarie on the house tops, by reason of the sight of a paynted Serpent set openly to view. So fares it with vs nouices, that here betray our imperfections: we, afraid to looke on the imaginary serpent of Enuy, paynted in mens affections, haue ceased to tune any musike of mirth to your eares this tweluemonth, thinking that, as it is the nature of the serpent to hisse, so childhood and ignorance would play the goslings, contemning and condemning what they vnderstood not. Their censures we wey not, whose sences are not yet vnswadled . . . . Such like foolish beasts are we, who, whilest we are cut, mocked, & flowted at, in euery mans common talke, will notwithstanding proceed to shame our selues, to make sport . . . . Moralizers, you that wrest a neuer meant meaning out of every thing, applying all things to the present time, keepe your attention for the common Stage: for here are no quips in Characters for you to reade. Vayne glozers, gather what you will. Spite, spell backwards what thou canst. As the *Parthians* fight, flying away, so will wee prate and talke, but stand to nothing that we say."

This is all perfectly intelligible if we understand that the play was acted by Paul's boys, who, a year or more before, had been forbidden to play publicly for mixing into the Marprelate dispute, along with certain adult companies. It is quite without meaning if it applies to the Chapel. That the Paul's company could play at all was due to the performance being a private one, in the house of a nobleman.

As I have shown, the performance by Paul's children noted in Gloucester in 1590-91 may have come before the inhibition. If that is true, then the play at Croydon in 1592 is the only instance known to us of this company's acting after the inhibition.

It was more imprudent for the Paul's boys to enter this controversy, because of their youth and their quasi-ecclesiastical character, than for the adult companies. Moreover, they had no strong patrons to temper the winds of official wrath; they were but children, to be summarily chidden and stood in a corner. It is quite possible, too, that their dissolution may have been as much an act from within St. Paul's cathedral as from the licensing board. There is no reason to suppose that the company enjoyed any special favor from the dean and chapter.

CHAPTER VI

THE RENASCENCE AT BLACKFRIARS IN 1600

1. *The Date of Opening.*

The period we are approaching now in our history of the Chapel company is one crowded with incident and obscured, almost as often as illuminated, by a multiplicity of documents. The first scholar to make a thorough study of this subject was Mr. C. W. Wallace, who in 1908 published a monograph on *The Children of the Chapel at Blackfriars*.[1] His book, though based on many carefully chosen and authenticated documents, succeeded in throwing darkness as well as light, through the pursuit of a number of not well considered theories. Much of my attention must necessarily be given to brushing away these cobwebs. Fortunately I have sterling support in two studies by Mr. E. K. Chambers, the first an article on *Court Performances under James I* which appeared in the *Modern Language Review* for 1908-9,[2] and the second his chapter on the Chapel Royal companies in his recent, admirable *Eliazbethan Stage*. The treatment accorded the Children of the Chapel at Blackfriars by Mr. J. T. Murray, in his *English Dramatic Companies* (1910), is negligible, being little more than a compilation of Collier and Fleay.

It has long been known that by 1601, when the children of the Chapel played at court for the first time in seventeen years, they had reestablished themselves as a playing company, and were using for their acting place a theatre constructed in Blackfriars by James Burbage. The first moot point is the date of their resumption of the sock and buskin; it is a matter which has been long misrepresented and has been the subject of much debate, and yet it is clear enough, after all. It has usually been said that the Chapel boys began playing about 1597, after the theatre in Blackfriars had been built, and after Nathaniel Gyles had succeeded to the mastership of the Chapel, and that Jonson's *The Case is Altered* was played by them in 1597 or 1598. Now as a matter of fact, the boys did not begin until 1600.

It will be remembered that on February 4, 1596, James Burbage, actor and builder of the *Theatre* in 1576, puchased for £600 from

[1] Nebraska University Studies, Vol. VIII, Nos. 2, 3; April-July, 1908.
[2] Vol. IV, p. 153.

Sir William More, the principal heritor of the old Blackfriars monastery estates, certain rooms in a house in Blackfriars which he straightway set about turning into a playhouse.[3] For various reasons which we shall consider later, the theatre was not used by the builder, and was not let to the managers of the Chapel company until September 2, 1600. The evidence that the Chapel did not acquire the property before that date is conclusive, and the objections weak. The petitioning Burbages, in the Blackfriars-Globe sharepaper suit of 1635,[4] thus chronicle the event. "Now for the Blackfriers, that is our inheritance; our father purchased it at extreme rates, and made it into a playhouse with great charge and troble; which after was leased out to one Evans that first sett up the boyes commonly called the Queenes Majesties Children of the Chappell." The date of the entry is made indubitably clear in the following quotations from an unpublished King's Bench suit of William Rastell and Edward Kirkham v. Alexander Hawkins in 1609,[5] one of the many suits which resulted from the partnership of Rastell, Kirkham, and Kendall in managing the Chapel boys. Richard Burbage's lease of Blackfriars to Evans is thus described:

"The Condicion of this obligacion is such That whereas Richard Burbage of the parishe of S[t] leonardes in Shorditch in the Countie of Midd gent by his Indentures of lease bearinge date the second day of September in the two and fortith yere of the raigne of our Soueraigne ladye Elizabeth the Queenes Maiestie that now is hath leased and to farme letten vnto the within bounden henrie Evans all that great hall or Roome with the roomes ouer the same in the said indenture mencioned scituate within the precincte of the blackfriars london to hold vnto the said henrye Evans his executors and Assignes from the feast of S[t] Michaell Tharkangell next ensuinge after the date of the said Indenture vnto the ende of twentie yeares from thence next ensuinge," etc. The yearly rent was to be £40.

Then in his commentary on the events supporting his case, which follows the citation of the indenture, Hawkins says that Evans further agreed with Burbage to make all needful reparations in the premises so often as it should be necessary, and then *immediately*

---

[3] Halliwell-Phillips, *Outlines of the Life of Shakespeare*, 9th ed., Vol. I, pp. 299 ff.

[4] *Same*, p. 317.

[5] *Coram Rege Rolls*, Easter, 7 Jas. I, m. 456. For a full summary cf. pp. 180 ff. For references to the lease of 1600 see also the Evans-Kirkham and Kirkham-Painton suits in Fleay, *Hist. of the Stage*.

after the feast of St. Michael, named in the bond as the beginning of
the tenure, *entered into the property and took possession.*[6] Nothing
could be more definite. Hawkins, in his review of the history of the
Chapel management, makes no mention of any lease prior to 1600,
nor in any of the voluminous papers connected with the various
lawsuits, nor in fact anywhere at all, is such a lease spoken of.
The conclusion is perfectly clear that Evans had had no lease of the
Blackfriars property prior to 1600; and the sharepapers of 1635
tell us that Evans was the first to "sett up the boyes commonly
called the Queenes Majesties Children of the Chappel."

In opposition to these plain matters of fact, the arguments for a
prior tenancy of Blackfriars by Evans will be seen to be weak indeed.
In his Bill of Complaint against Kirkham, dated May 5, 1612,
Evans in connection with the lease of 1600 speaks of the Blackfriars as "Then or late in the tenure or occupation of your said
orator."[7] But any one who has read at all in legal documents—
particularly leases and indentures—knows what meaning attaches
to the phrase "then or late" in such a context as this; it was simply
a legal redundancy and was used indiscriminately as a synonym
for "at that time." So much for the first point. Then Burbage, in
explaining why he exacted a bond of £400 security for the payment
of the lease, said that "except the said Evans could erect & keepe a
companye of Playinge boyes or others to playe playes & interludes
in the said Playhouse in such sort as before tyme had bene there
vsed, that he was lykelye to be beh(ind with) the said rent of fortie
pounds."[8] Since the publication of these arguments of Mr. Wallace
his own researches and those of M. Feuillerat have revealed the
facts of the early tenancy of Blackfriars by the children of the Chapel
and make the reference in this passage quite intelligible. Yet for
many years, at least since the days of Malone, it has been known
that there were performances in Blackfriars in the 1580's, and the
very wording of Burbage, "as before tyme had bene there vsed,"
should have made it plain enough that Burbage was speaking of a
state of affairs not in the immediate past, but at a more distant date.

---

[6] " . . . . virtute cuius quidem dimissionis idem henricus Evans in predictam
aulam & tenementa predicta cum pertinentibus sibi in forma predicta dimissa immediate post predictum festum sancti Michaelis Archangeli proximum venendum
post datum Indenture predicte inter alia intrauit Et fuit inde possessionatus . . . ."
[7] *Evans v. Kirkham*; cf. documents in Fleay, *Hist. of the Stage*, p. 211.
[8] Suit *Kirkham v. Painter*; cf. Fleay, *op. cit.*, p. 234.

There remains one further piece of evidence for the earlier tenancy of Blackfriars, which chances to be more deserving of consideration than the two we have just passed over. Jonson's early play *The Case is Altered* was published in 1609 as acted by the "Children of the Blacke-friers"; and is mentioned in Nash's *Lenten Stuff*, which was entered *S. R.* on January 11, 1599. But this evidence, while it looks fairly strong, is not sufficient to counterbalance the plain meaning of the documents I have quoted. *The Case is Altered* was not printed till 1609, and then in a form which had seemingly undergone revision;[9] and of course it may originally have been written for some other company and then passed to the children. Such was the history of Chapman's *All Fools*, which was written for the Lord Admiral's company in 1599 and appeared in print in 1605 as "presented at the Black Fryers."[10] While this explanation is purely hypothetical, it is eminently reasonable, and sufficiently undermines the last and only worthy argument of those who believe that Evans and the Chapel children occupied Blackfriars before 1600. The plain facts of my documents have been found to endure a very feeble attack. We shall observe, as we go on, further evidences which bear out the conclusion that the lease of 1600 was the first one.

The question naturally arises in the mind of the reader: Why, then, did the theatre remain unoccupied from 1596 to 1600? In the first place, let me say that I am not sure beyond a doubt that it *did* stand vacant. Possibly some kind of tenant was found for it; it may have been used for a fencing school or even a theatre. But that is a hypothesis in which I have little faith; and the explanation I propose of why the theatre passed to the Chapel boys also explains to my satisfaction why it stood vacant—depends, indeed, upon this very fact of vacancy.

My solution of the question is in no wise new, and brings into play a set of documents which have long been a source of discussion.[11] I accept the facts as they were set forth in the petition of the Blackfriars inhabitants to the Privy Council in 1619, the gist of which is given us in the order of the City fathers suppressing the Blackfriars theatre in that year.[12]

---

[9] *Vide* E. K. Chambers, *Mod. Lang. Rev.*, IV, 1908-9, p. 156.

[10] *Same*; also *Henslowe's Diary*, ed. Greg, II, 203.

[11] The documents concerning the suppression of Blackfriars in 1619 and the previous attempt in 1596, contained in *S. P. Dom. Jas. I*, Vol. 205, No. 32 (i-iv), and Vol. 260, No. 116.

[12] *S. P. Dom. Jas. I*, Vol. 205, No. 32 (iv). It is headed "Jovis xxi° die Januarij 1618, Annoque Regis Jacobi Anglie &c decimo sexto."

"Item this day was exhibited to this Court a peticion by the Constables and other officers and inhabitants within the Precinct of Blackffryers London therein declaring that in November 1596 divers honorable persons and others then inhabiting the said Precinct made knowne to the Lords and others of the privey Councell what inconveniences were likely to fall uppon them by a Comon play-house then preparing to be erected there, and that there uppon their honours then forbad the use of the said house for playes, And in June 1600 made certaine orders by which for many weighty reasons therein expressed it is limited, ther should only be two playhouses tollerated, wherof the one to be on the Bankeside, and the other in or neere Gouldinge lane, exempting thereby the Blackffriers, And that a lettre was then derected from their Lordships to the Lord Maior and Justices streitly requiring of them to see those orders put in execution, and so to be continued, And now for as the said Inhabitants of the Blackffriers haue in the said peticion complained to this Court, that contrary to the said Lords orders, the owner of the said Playhouse within the Blackfriers, under the name of a privat house, hath converted the same to a publique playhouse, unto which there is dayly so great resort of people and so great multitude of Coaches, ... that sometymes all their Streets cannot conteyne them," etc.

The main points here brought out are that in 1596 the inhabitants of Blackfriars protested against the building of the theatre there by Burbage, and as a result the Privy Council forbade the use of the house for plays; that in June of 1600 a general order was issued suppressing all playhouses about London save the *Globe* and *Fortune* and that notwithstanding the lessees of Blackfriars had carried out their original plan under cover of calling the theatre a private one. This plain statement of facts has for some reason not met with proper consideration from many historians of the English theatre, chiefly, I imagine, because it does not happen to jibe with their theories as to the opening of the house. But we must have stronger reason than that for doubting the evidence of a document, especially one so well supported as this. I take it that if a document presents a series of facts of which some can be substantiated and the others are not more likely to be false, we can agree that a strong probability of truth exists in favor of the unsubstantiated facts. In the case of this document, out of the cardinal points there given, we can corroborate two by the evidence of other documents; for the appeal of the Blackfriars citizens in 1596 and the general suppressing order of June 22, 1600, exist among the public records in London.[13] The order for the restraint of Blackfriars in 1596 has not been found, it is true, but there are so many hiatuses in English public documents that this is not astonishing. The matter of the subterfuge by which the theatre was put into use is beyond the operation of documentary proof. We have, then, in the order of 1619 two statements corroborated, and no valid reason for doubting the truth of the others. For it is hard to see how any ulterior motive in a plain statement of facts and conditions would lead the petitioners of 1619 to lie in explaining how the Blackfriars theatre had evaded the previous restricting orders. It is difficult, in short, to imagine why they should have told anything but the strict truth; and the truth they must have known, living as they did at the seat of trouble.

The conclusions it leads us to, taken in combination with the ease of September, 1600, are thoroughly satisfactory. Our reconstruction of events gives us this result. In 1596 James Burbage aroused the opposition of the gentry then residing in Blackfriars[14] by preparing to turn one of the buildings of the old monastery into a common playhouse for the Lord Chamberlain's company. They protested to the Lords of the Privy Council, who issued an order forbidding the establishment of a public theatre in that precinct. What bickerings, threats, and negotiations went on in the next four years, we have no means of knowing; nor whether the theatre stood quite empty or was put to occasional uses. At any rate, the matter was clinched for the Burbages in June of 1600 by the issuing of a general order repressing all theatres but the *Globe* and *Fortune*. Their one thought now was to recover their investments in Blackfriars, and to some one came the idea of turning it into a private house and installing there a company of lads recruited from the Chapel Royal —perhaps in memory of their past successes in the same place in the 1580's, perhaps in direct imitation of their traditional rivals of St. Paul's, reinstituted some months earlier. A close corporation consisting of Henry Evans and the Chapel master Nathaniel Gyles was found to finance the new enterprise, and on September 2, 1600, a lease of twenty-one years was signed making over the property to

[13] They are to be found, respectively, in *S. P. Dom. Jas. I*, Vol. 260, No. 116; and Vol. 205, No. 32 (iv).

[14] It must not be forgotten that Blackfriars was the abode of many people of fashion and birth (the appeal of 1596 was signed by the dowager Lady Russel and Lord Hunsdon); and that their protests would carry much weight with the Privy Council.

Evans, the active member of the partnership, at the huge rental of £40 the year. Sanctified by its new title of private theatre, the Blackfriars started on its career with no hindrance from the citizens its neighbors, and no other serious lets, apparently, than the inability of the shareholders to agree among themselves. It was the establishment of the company of Shakespeare, under Richard Burbage, in 1609 which is referred to in the petition of 1619 when we are told that the owner of the theatre "under the name of a privat house hath converted the same to a publique playhouse." Certainly there is no event in the history of the king's men between 1609 and 1619 which could be meant; and we are not given to understand that the petitioners had a *recent* occurrence in mind.

What was a private playhouse? That is a difficult question to answer; it might be easier if we knew precisely what a public playhouse was. We may deduce some general differences in arrangement and conduct: for instance, that private houses were smaller, were all under cover and used artificial light, were rather more expensive, drew in consequence a choicer audience, and dispensed with the summoning of people by trumpet and drum; but these hardly explain what difference of attitude should have existed in the minds of people to enable Burbage to evade a law aimed at common stages by calling his a private one. We are not called upon to explain that difference, but only to make clear that it did exist, and that the Blackfriars theatre belonged to the privileged class. These points are brought home to us most forcibly in the 1596 petition of the Blackfriars citizens.[15] There we read that "there hath not any tyme heretofore been used any comon Playhouse within the same Precinct." That is, in a petition directed against the operation of a playhouse, the existence of the first Blackfriars theatre, which flourished from 1576 to 1584 and could not have escaped the memories of men, is entirely overlooked, and it is only insisted that there had been no *common*, or *public*, theatre, implying that only such were objectionable. If no protest was raised in 1596 against a private theatre, none would be likely in 1600, and apparently none came. It is worth noting that the vigorous protest which roused the Lords to action in 1619 came after the playhouse had reverted to the hands of public players, and when its popularity threatened the safety of Blackfriars citizens.

---

[15] *S. P. Dom. Jas.* I, Vol. 260, No. 116.

2. *The Governing Board.*

Before we go on with the history of the Chapel boys at Blackfriars, it would be well to say a word about the men who were at the
head of the enterprise. Our attention is demanded first to Nathaniel
Gyles, the one most closely connected with the children, though
certainly not the moving spirit in the undertaking. This man, well
known in the history of English church music, was born in or near
Worcester about 1559.[16] He was educated at Magdalen College,
Oxford, as chorister (1567-71) and clerk in the chapel (1577), and
took his degree of Mus. Bac. on June 26, 1585. On October 1, 1595,
he was formally appointed a clerk in the chapel of St. George's,
Windsor, and also one of the organists there and master of the
choristers in succession to John Mundie and Richard Farrant.[17] But
though he was formally appointed in 1595, he seems to have been
acting master of the choristers in 1594; for in a Chancery suit of
Gyles v. Combes which I came upon in the Public Record Office,
Gyles's Bill of Complaint, dated April 9, 1594, calls the plaintiff
"Master of her Maiestyes Chyldren of the Chapell of Saynt George
within her Hyghnes Castle of new Wyndsor."[18] When William
Hunnis, master of the children of the Chapel Royal, died on June 6,
1597, Gyles was sworn in his place on the 9th;[19] his patent of office
was issued on the fourteenth of July, and on the fifteenth the privilege was confirmed to him of impressing choristers from other
institutions.[20] This writ of impressment has been forced to bear
curious meanings, along with the similar writ to Thomas Gyles in
1585; for instance, it has been urged as significant evidence of the
queen's patronage of the Blackfriars enterprise.[21] As a matter of
fact, there is no significance in the writ at all. It is enough to say
here that the commission to Nathaniel Gyles was granted in the

[16] *Vide* Wood's *Fasti* (ed. Bliss) I, 405; and for general outlines of Gyles's life
cf. *D. N. B.* and *The Old Cheque Book of the Chapel Royal*, ed. Rimbault for the
Camden Soc., p. 198.

[17] For the terms of the appointment see *Ashmolean MSS.* 1125/33, and *The Old
Cheque Book*, p. 198.

[18] The suit (*Chanc. Proceedings, Ser. II*, Bdl. 240, No. 91) is amusing, but not
particularly instructive; it can be consulted *in extenso* in the *Appendix*, p. 330.
Suffice it to say that one William Combes, in return for the education of his son as
chorister at St. George's for four years, and for a sum of money, undertook to buy
and pasture a mare for the use of Gyles, but defaulted in his side of the bargain.

[19] *The Old Cheque Book*, p. 5.

[20] The Privy Seals can be consulted in Wallace, *Chapel at Blackfriars*, pp. 59, 60.

[21] Particularly by Wallace, *op. cit., passim.*

usual course of such writs, that is, directly upon his accession to office, and is in no way dissimilar to the previous writs to Hunnis and Edwards. The granting of it was simply a part of the routine attending the establishment of a new master.

On the accession of Charles I, Gyles was made organist[22] of the Chapel. In 1622 he took his degree of Mus. Doc., for which, according to Wood, he had applied as early as 1607, but for which he had neglected to compose the necessary exercise. He died on January 24, 1634, when, by the testimony of his tombstone,[23] he had lived seventy-five years, and was buried in one of the aisles adjoining St. George's Chapel, Windsor. Gyles's reputation as a musician is good down to the present day, although his supersubtle *Lesson of Descant of thirtie eight Proportions of Sundrie Kindes* aroused Burney to attack him as a pedant.

Such was the man under whom the Chapel boys learned music, grammar, and the moral and speculative virtues. He was a man of culture, a university graduate, a known musician; and was through some years of apprenticeship in St. George's Chapel expert in his business. Quite a different man was Henry Evans, the commanding figure in the Blackfriars directorate. Aside from his theatrical connections, we know nothing about him save that he practised the calling of scrivener when he first came to London, and hailed presumably from Wales. He was beyond doubt the same Henry Evans who had been the close friend of Sebastian Westcote, and had played his part in the history of the first Blackfriars theatre, back in the 1580's. Apparently the taste of managership which he got then lingered in his mouth; perhaps he had actually allied himself with other companies since the dissolution of Oxford's boy company.

---

[22] *Old Cheque Book*, p. 198.

[23] This inscription, preserved in Ashmole's *Berkshire*, III, 183, runs as follows: "In memory of the worthy Doctor Nathaniel Giles, Doctor of Musique, who served Q. Elizabeth, K. James, and K. Charles. He was Master of the Children of his Free Chapell of St. George 49 years, Master of the Children of his Majesty's Chaple Royall 38 years. He married Anne, the eldest daughter of John Stayner, of the county of Worcester, Esq., with whom he lived 47 years and had issue by her four sons and five daughters, whereof two sons and three daughters are now living. He died the 24th day of January, 1633, when he had lived 75 years." Obviously these dates do not quite agree with our other evidences. On a gravestone near by is also this inscription:

"Pattern of Patience, Gravitie, Devotion,
Faithful to the end, now Heyre of Heavn's Promotion.
Pietatis ergo Nat. Gyles, Filius natu maximus, moerens posuit 2 Feb. 1634
Die cinerum versus est in cineres."

At any rate, he turns up in 1600 as the lessee of Blackfriars and the moving spirit in the new enterprise to rehabilitate the Chapel company. And it is round him that the storm of 1601 centers.

3. *The Clifton Suit.*

It will be remembered that the 21-year lease to Evans of Black-friars was signed September 2, 1600. I have shown, I think conclusively, that this date marks the commencement of the dramatic activity of the Chapel boys. Further confirmation of my argument lies in the evidence afforded by the Clifton suit in 1601, though its significance seems hitherto to have escaped notice, engrossed as historians have been in the error that Evans set up his company in 1597. It is hardly necessary to go through the course of this quarrel minutely, for it is a commonplace to students of Elizabethan stage history. But it is worth examining for the light it throws on the movements of Evans and Gyles.[24]

This suit, brought in the Star Chamber in December of 1601,[25] represents that the managers[26] of the new Chapel company were in the latter end of 1600 abusing in a reckless fashion the master's privilege of impressing boys. Having collected a number from various chapels and schools, they unluckily seized on one Thomas Clifton, son of Henry Clifton, Esq., of Toftrees, in Norfolk a member of the grammar school of Christchurch, London, carried him off to Blackfriars, and set him to learning a part. Upon the father's remonstrating, they gave him scornful answers and refused to surrender the boy; whereat the father sued to Sir John Fortescue, Chancellor of the Exchequer, for aid, and secured a warrant which set young Thomas free within twenty-four hours after his capture.

So much for a bare outline of the case. The light it gives on the workings of Gyles and Evans is most interesting and valuable. It shows, primarily, that at the time of young Clifton's arrest, there was a ferment of activity at Blackfriars in impressing and training boys for the business of acting. There is no other conclusion to be drawn from the words of Clifton. He begins by referring to the

---

[24] For the Bill of Complaint of Henry Clifton cf. Fleay, *Hist. of the Stage*, pp. 127-132. The document is in the P. R. O., London, *Star Chamber Proceedings, Eliz.*, Bdl. C 46, No. 39.

[25] Clifton's complaint was dated December 15. See Wallace, *Chapel at Black-friars*, p. 84.

[26] The defendants were Evans and Gyles, and one James Robinson, about whom we know nothing.

writ of impressment granted Gyles in 1597, and says that under
color of this patent the defendants "devysed, conspired & concluded,
for theire owne corrupte gayne and lucre, to errecte, sett vpp,
furnish and maynteyne a play house or place in the Blackfryers."
That is true enough, but we are not to assume, as most have rashly
done, that the impressments were directly subsequent to the granting of the writ. Clifton makes no such statement; he merely says
that the writ was put in use at the time when it was determined to
start the new venture. Clifton goes on to say that in order to furnish
their house with children, the defendants had impressed many
children since "your maiesties last free & generall pardon." This
refers, of course, to the last proclamation of amnesty to prisoners
or others guilty of minor offenses; such pardons were issued by
Elizabeth in the thirty-ninth and forty-third years of her reign,
that is, in 1597 and 1601 (August 7). Then Clifton was manifestly
wrong if, complaining in December of 1601, he referred to the pardon
of the previous August, because his son was kidnapped on December
13, 1600. He must either have overlooked the most recent pardon,
or have stupidly lied. At any rate, all that we learn is that the
impressing was done after the pardon of 1597 and was therefore
not exonerated by it. Clifton goes on to say that the children so
taken were in no way fit for service in the Chapel Royal, and were
not meant for it, but were used solely for supplying the playhouse.
This is a point he urges throughout the complaint. Among the
lads thus impressed Clifton names seven: John Chappell, from the
school of one Mr. Spykes near Cripplegate; John Motteram, from
Westminster grammar school; Nathan, or Nathaniel, Field, from
Richard Mulcaster's school (Field afterwards became a famous
actor); Alvery Trussell, "an apprentice to one Thomas Gyles," i.e.
one of the choristers at Paul's before Gyles ceased to be master
there in 1600; Philip Pykman and Thomas Grymes, apprentices to
Richard and George Chambers; and Salmon (Salathiel) Pavey,
kept alive in our memories by Johnson's epitaph, who was "an
apprentice to one Peerce," i.e. chorister at Paul's after Edward
Pierce had succeeded Gyles in 1600. These children, says Clifton,
were "noe way able or fitt for singing,[27] nor by anie the sayd confederates endevoured to be taught to singe, but by them the sayd

[27] That cannot have been wholly true, for the Chapel players were skilled in
song and dance. There is throughout Clifton's complaint a bitterness which leads
him into exaggeration. He is making out as black a case as he can.

confederates abusively employed, as aforesayd, only in playes &
enterludes." Though Clifton does not say it in so many words, yet
the tenor and effect of his charge is that these children were gathered
together about the same time, namely, near the date of the signing
of the lease to Evans, September 2, 1600. Salathiel Pavey, for one,
was impressed not earlier than August of 1600, when Edward
Pierce seems to have passed from the Chapel to the mastership of
Paul's;[28] while Alvery Trussell must have been taken earlier, because
he was then a chorister at Paul's under Thomas Gyles.

Now, why, if the Blackfriars theatre was started *and under way*
in 1597, as Fleay and Wallace and so many others have supposed,
should there be all this turmoil over impressed boys so late as 1600?
In order to begin playing, the company would have to be gathered;
but once brought together, it should be able to run for three years
without demanding great pains in renewing it. And yet at least one
of the lads named in Clifton's bill was taken after August of 1600
besides Thomas Clifton himself, and all the other lads must have
been seized since 1597, or else by the time of Clifton's suit their
grievances would have been either satisfied or forgotten. In plain
truth, the impartial reader, in perusing Clifton's bill and making
all allowances for its bias, receives the impression that the events
there narrated all came near together—that there was a bustle of
preparation at Blackfriars, of gathering a company, and of lick-
ing the boys (even literally) into shape. The violence with which
Thomas Clifton was seized, the threats of turning over to the constable and of whipping, the insolence of the defendants towards
his father—all these point to the rapid pushing through of an undertaking. Now all this would be perfectly in accord with the inception
of the venture in 1600, but very little in accord if the date is moved
back to 1597. In that case we ask: why this burst of offensive
activity in 1600? But in the other case we understand; it falls into
its proper place in the history, and relates itself to the deed of
September 2, 1600, by which Evans acquired the Blackfriars theatre.
The project was in the air, of course, before the deed was actually
signed, and preparations were being made. Hence we find that
impressments were made before Thomas Gyles left St. Paul's. But
the majority of impressments must be understood to range from

---

[28] *The Old Cheque Book* records that in 1600 Edward Pierce (or Pearce) yielded
his place in the Chapel for the mastership of Paul's, and that John Heathman was
sworn in his place from Westminster on August 15.

early summer to early winter of 1600. They caused heartburnings
and wrath in many fathers, but the deluge did not come until the
proprietors most unhappily seized on the son of a gentleman, a man
of some influence.

The suit did not result in serious inconvenience for the company.
The defendants, while they had clearly violated the spirit of the
writ of impressment, had not exceeded the letter, and were chiefly
to blame for their harshness in exercising their powers, and especially
for having been so tactless as to meddle with the son of a man of
quality. The result, as we shall see later, was that Evans, against
whom Clifton's attack was chiefly directed, was forbidden to
associate further in the management of the company, and even had
to leave London for a time. But the company went on playing.

4. *The Business Status of Blackfriars.*

Let us consider, before going on, the status of the company,
about which there has also been some misunderstanding and mis-
information. Here, again, Dr. Wallace has been most at fault, by
the range and vigor of his astonishing hypotheses. Let me hasten,
first, to agree with him in so far as I may. It is perfectly true that
the Chapel company was established on sound authority, namely
on the powers granted the Chapel master by the writ of impressment,
for the terms of the patent were about as general and all-embracing
as they could be. Gyles not only could take up as many children as
he wished, but could take wherever he wished. He only used in
excess a privilege which was open to every master behind him.
What Gyles really did was to abuse the clear intention of the writ
in gathering more children than he had need of for the Chapel, and
gathering them, as Clifton said, not for use in the Chapel, but for
use solely at Blackfriars. That is a just conclusion from the facts.
Moreover, the boys who played at Blackfriars cannot have been
the same twelve who sang in the Chapel, as Wallace points out.[29] In
the first place, we have the evidence of Clifton, who says that his
son was dragged away to Blackfriars and there kept under lock and
key, along with the other boys. Then from the Kirkham-Painton
suit we learn of "the dietting and ordering of the Boyes vsed about
the plaies there."[30] Furthermore, an examination of the plays acted

[29] *Chapel at Blackfriars*, Chap. IV.
[30] Cf. Fleay, *Hist. of the Stage*, p. 244.

between 1600 and 1603 shows that while in one or two cases not
more than a dozen actors are required on the stage at once, yet
most of them demand fifteen, eighteen, and even twenty.[31] And
lastly, the fact that Gyles was abusing the normal powers of his
writ is apparent from the fact that when in 1606 a new writ was
confirmed to him, it was specially directed that none of the boys so
taken should be used in stage plays, "for that it is not fitt or decent
that such as should sing the praises of God almightie should be
trayned up or imployed in such lascivious and prophane exercises."[32]
So that on the whole we can hardly avoid the conclusions that the
Blackfriars managers, while they were abusing the spirit of Gyles's
writ of impressment, were well enough within the letter to avoid
royal censure, and that two bodies of Chapel children were maintained, one at the court for the service of God, and one at Blackfriars for the service of Evans and Gyles.

Thus far I agree with Wallace. But when he wishes to demonstrate
that the Chapel had the direct support of the queen, who supplied
money and apparel through Edward Kirkham, Yeoman of the
Revels,[33] then I must fundamentally disagree. It is incomprehen-
sible to me how any one reading the many documents in which the
history of this company lies entangled, can come away from the
task feeling otherwise than that the whole venture was from start to
finish a matter of business, a private enterprise set on foot and
maintained by private capital and energy. That the queen looked
with favor on the company, is undeniable, since she permitted them
to play at court directly after their revival, and seems even to have
attended a performance at Blackfriars. But this is all that the
facts will allow.

It is not necessary to go into all of Dr. Wallace's arguments; the
main ones are sufficient, and his fabric of theory stands or falls by
them. One of them—the evidence afforded by Gyles's writ of 1597

[31] E.g. *Cynthia's Revels, Sir Giles Goosecap, Poetaster, Gentleman Usher, M. D'Olive,
May Day, The Widow's Tears* (which may not belong in this period), etc. For a
convenient analysis of requirements in the number of players, cf. Wallace, *Chapel
at Blackfriars*, p. 75.
[32] Cf. *infra*, p. 196.
[33] "Both the expenditures and the furnishing of apparel were official." (Wallace
op. cit., p. 100.) For Wallace's detailed exposition of his theories, cf. Chaps. III-X
XII.

and his use of it—we have seen to mean nothing at all. Another can be easily disposed of. This is the passage quoted so triumphantly from the diary of the Duke of Stettin-Pomerania, who visited England in 1602 and left a word regarding Blackfriars.[34] In this note he says that in order to prepare for court presentations the boys were required to play a comedy weekly, and that for this purpose the queen had built a fine theatre and had supplied it with an abundance of expensive apparel. The refutation of this statement stands within it; the queen certainly did not build Blackfriars, and if the duke was so misinformed on this point, we must hesitate before accepting his other statements. In fact, a foreigner of noble rank engaged in running over the sights of a capital is not to be taken for an exact authority on the conditions lying behind the management of a playhouse. He might easily deduce from the name of the company —"Children of her Majesty's Chapel Royal"—that the maintenance of the company was a fancy of the queen's, and how purely personal

---

[34] For Wallace's interpretation of the document cf. *Chapel at Blackfriars*, Chap. IX. The man who really kept the diary was Frederic Gershow, in the train of the duke, although he did so at his master's command. The diary now reposes in the library of Count von der Osten of Plathe, Pomerania, and has seemingly never been published. Such parts as relate to the visit to England have been printed by Dr. Gottfried von Bülow, Superintendent of the Royal Archives in Stettin, assisted by Wilfred Powell, English Consul in Stettin, in *Transactions of the Royal Historical Society*, New Series, 1892, VI, 4-67.

"18 (Sept., Samstag, 1602) . . . . Von dannen (i.e. von einer Kunstkammer) sind wir auf die Kinder-comoediam gangen, welche im Argument iudiciret eine castam viduam, war eine historia einer königlichen Wittwe aus Engellandt. Es hat aber mit dieser Kindercomoedia die Gelegenheit: die Königin hält viel junger Knaben, die sich der Singekunst mit Ernst befleissigen müssen und auf allen Instrumenten lernen, auch dabenebenst studieren. Diese Knaben haben ihre besondere praeceptores in allen Künsten,* insonderheit sehr gute musicos.

Damit sie nun höfliche Sitten anwenden, ist ihnen aufgelegt, wöchentlich eine comoedia zu agiren, wozu ihnen denn die Königin ein sonderlich theatrum erbauet und mit köstlichen Kleidern zum Ueberfluss versorget hat. Wer solcher Action zusehen will, muss so gut als unserer Münze acht sundische Schillinge** geben, und findet sich doch stets viel Volks auch viele ehrbare Frauens, weil nutze argumenta und veil schöne Lehren, als von andern berichtet, sollen tractiret werden; alle bey Lichte agiret, welches ein gross Ansehen macht. Eine ganze Stunde vorher höret man eine köstliche musicam instrumentalem von Orgeln, Lauten, Pandoren, Mandoren, Geigen und Pfeiffen, wie denn damahlen ein Knabe cum voce tremula in einer Basgeigen so lieblich gesungen, dass wo es die Nonnen zu Mailand ihnen nicht vorgethan, wir seines Gleichen auf der Reise nicht gehöret hatten."

* This is another mistake on the part of the writer. The Chapel children had only their master to teach them music and grammar.

** About 12d.

and rash his conclusions were is shown by his attributing everything
—building, equipment, and all—to her. "Die Königin ein sonderlich
theatrum erbauet," he says; and whatever ambiguity and looseness
may have attached to the English words "erect" and "set up" in
that connection, "erbauet" meant "build" and nothing else.[35]

While we must reject whatever in this diary entry smacks of
guess-work, we can accept with gratitude the sound parts of the
evidence, relating to the conditions at Blackfriars on the occasion
of the duke's visit. Thus we are interested to know that the top
price was about 12d., that a large and respectable audience attended,
that the play was preceded by an instrumental prelude of an hour's
duration, and that one of the youths sang to the music of a bass-viol
so ravishingly that his noble auditor could recall nothing so lovely
heard on all his travels, unless it were the singing of the nuns at
Milan.

Another of Wallace's arguments for the royal support of Blackfriars need not detain us long. This is the evidence that the queen
went to a play in Blackfriars on December 29, 1601. Dudley Carleton, writing to John Chamberlain under this date, thus records the
event:[36]

"The Q: dined this day priuatly at my Lord Chamberlaine; I
came euen now from the blackfriers where I saw her at the play with
all her candidae auditrices."

All that is necessary to say in this connection is that we are not sure
in the first place that the play in question was not given at Lord
Hunsdon's after the banquet,[37] and that in the second place, even
granting that the queen did visit the theatre, that argues nothing
for active support of the Blackfriars venture. It merely shows
unusual condescension in distinguishing the theatre by a visit.

One more evidence remains to be disposed of—the matter of the
payment of 8s. weekly to Evans which was arranged between Evans
and Edward Kirkham as a result of the agreement of 1602, by which
Kirkham and his friends were made partners in the enterprise. It

[35] Wallace saw the difficulty here and tried to get round it by urging that "erbauet" was used in a loose sense for "set up." He seemed to think it sufficient to
prove such a looseness in the English terms, which no one will deny. Cf. *Chapel at
Blackfriars*, p. 128, note 4.

[36] Cf. *Cal. S. P. Dom. Eliz.*, 1601-3, p. 136.

[37] *Vide* E. K. Chambers's review of Wallace's book in *Mod. Lang. Rev.*, 1910,
p. 224; and the same writer's account of the revels at court before Elizabeth in
Mod. Lang. Rev., Oct., 1906. Also his *Eliz. Stage*, II, 48.

is thus described by Evans in his answer to Kirkham in the suit
Kirkham v. Painton (1612).[38]

And touching the Eight shillings to be paid,...this defendant (Henry
Evans) saith that there was a bond of ffiftye poundes made by the said
complainant (Edward Kirkham) and his partners condicioned for paiement
of the said some of eight shillings weekely vnto this defendant because after
the said agreements made, the complainant and his said Partners would at
their direction haue the dietting and ordering of the Boyes vsed about the
plaies there, which before the said Complainant had, and for the which he
had weekely before that disbursed and allowed sommes of monie.

That means simply that Kirkham and his partners entered into an
agreement with Evans to pay him 8s. weekly—why, does not particularly concern us here—from the time when they took over the
direction of the company, and assured Evans his income by filing a
bond of £50. The puzzling feature is contained in the last lines,
which say that Kirkham, the complainant, had been directing the
company previously and had spent large sums on it. From this
Wallace concludes that Kirkham, who had held the office of Yeoman
of the Revels since 1586,[39] acted as a deputy of the queen in dis-
pensing sums from the public treasury on the boys' company and
equipped them from the office of the Revels. Certainly this is as
rash a conclusion as one could draw. In the first place, the logic and
sense of the document seem to show that "complainant" in the
phrase "the plaies there, which before the said Complainant had"
is an error for "defendant," because then the payment of 8s. weekly
would have meaning. It would then appear as a kind of interest on
all the money Evans heretofore disbursed in setting the company
going, paid him in view of his interests in Blackfriars and his withdrawal from active management. But I can see no reason in Kirkham's agreeing to pay Evans 8s. weekly because he, Kirkham, had
been at expense in maintaining the boys. That is not business. The
reductio ad absurdum becomes still plainer when we reflect that we
are asked to believe that Kirkham agreed to pay the 8s. because of
spending money which *had come from the public treasury!* And we
must further believe that all Kirkham's subsequent suits and complaints about the heavy expenses he had been put to were based on

[38] *Vide* the full document in Fleay, *Hist. of the Stage.* The date of the agreement,
as we learn from the suit *Evans v. Kendall* (cf. *infra*, p. 186), was April 20, 1602, the
the date of the admission of Kirkham, Rastell, and Kendall to partnership.

[39] For the appointment cf. *A Collection of Ancient Documents Respecting the
Office of Master of the Revels*, etc., ed. J. O. Halliwell, 1870.

this same expenditure of public funds. It is beyond belief. Kirkham was a rascal, "a base fellow," as Jonson said, but his roguery did not carry him to such extremes of impudence.

Of course Kirkham went into this venture as into a private business. What evidence we have as to the business arrangements between Evans and Kirkham all goes to show it. The £200 bond drawn up on the same day as the £50 bond stipulates that Kirkham and his associates are let in to an equal share in the profit of the house on condition that they bear half the expenses;[40] Painton, in his reply to Kirkham's bill in 1612, says "that he hath hard that about suche trashe as appertayned to plaies, interludes, and plaiers the said playntif disbursed muche money;"[41] John Hemings and Richard Burbage, in their answers in the same suit, say: " . . . .as this defendant thinketh, the said complainant & the said persons, in Playinge apparell & other Implements & properties touchinge & concerninge the furnishinge and settinge forth of Players & Playes, dyd disburse & dispend dyvers sommes of money, & were, as this defendant hath heard, therevpon to be partners or sharers of such moneys, profitts & comodities as should arise or be made by reason of the said Playes."[42] These statements came forth in response to the ridiculous plea of Kirkham that he and his friends had spent £400 on the theatre subsequent to being admitted to partnership.[43] Though this was an absolute lie on Kirkham's part, nevertheless it shows that he had not been spending public money on the company, for in that case his claim of large personal expense would bring down an avalanche on his head from those who knew where the money came from.

The theory that Kirkham acted as the official go-between of the queen in supplying the Blackfriars company with money and clothes is thus seen to have no legs to stand on. And when we reflect that such action on his part could not be carried on without documentary authority and the keeping of some form of accounts, and that, as Wallace himself admits, there is not the least vestige of such account or such authority extant, we may rightly conclude that any further consideration of his hypothesis is unnecessary.

[40] For the text of this bond cf. the suit *Rastell and Kirkham v. Hawkins, infra.* p. 180
[41] Fleay, *Hist. of the Stage*, p. 231.
[42] Fleay, *op. cit.*, pp. 234, 235.
[43] *Same.* p. 224.

This is a long and laborious analysis of a simple situation, many times as long as would be requisite if the facts were not so befogged and distorted. It is worth spending the time if I have succeeded in clearing away the clouds and restoring this portion of the Chapel company's history to its true guise, as a purely private venture from start to finish, without an atom of royal support other than the encouragement of sympathy which Elizabeth had always shown the principal children's companies. It is quite right to insist, as Wallace has done, that the sovereign had nothing to do with the disappearance of the Chapel in 1584; it is equally true that she had nothing to do with their reinstatement in 1600.

CHAPTER VII

THE CHAPEL AT BLACKFRIARS, 1600-1609

1. *Early Performances.*

Having cleared the way of impedimenta, we may now get down to the actual course of events at Blackfriars. It is not my purpose here to go at all deeply into the questions of plays, authors, and dates, for it is the business rather than the literary aspects of the Chapel company, with all the complexity of quarrels and crosses, that I wish to present now to the reader. We must understand what happened to this company before we can begin to work in earnest on their repertory; and so I shall content myself with tracing the course—uneasy enough, but still fairly clear—of events at Blackfriars, with enough discussion of the plays acted there to round out my story.

We have seen that the new company called "The Children of the Chapel at Blackfriars" began operations in or about September, 1600, when the theatre was acquired by Evans. How many boys composed the company we have no sure means of knowing—probably about twenty; we do know the names of thirteen of them. From the lists of principal actors in *Cynthia's Revels* and *Poetaster*, played in 1600-1601, printed in the First Folio of Jonson's works, we have the names of Nathaniel Field, John Underwood, Salathiel Pavey, Robert Baxter, William Ostler, Thomas Day, John Frost, Thomas Martin; and from the Clifton suit these names: John Chappell, John Motteram, Alvery Trussell, Philip Pykman, Thomas Grimes. Thomas Clifton, of course, cannot be counted, because he was released a day or more after his impressment.

With this company the managers began playing. Just when the first performance came we cannot say. We have seen that the impressments were under way by August of 1600, so that it is likely that the managers were ready to begin soon after acquiring their theatre, on September 2, 1600. Nor can we tell what was their first production. *Cynthia's Revels*, which was licensed May 23, 1601, was undoubtedly an early play; and so also was *Love's Metamorphosis*, an old play of Lyly's resurrected from the past, originally

171

(c. 1588-9) played by Paul's.[1] Other plays given between 1600 and January of 1604 were the old and famed *Jeronimo*, stolen from the king's men,[2] Chapman's *Sir Giles Goosecap* and *May Day*,[3] Jonson's *Poetaster* (licensed December 21, 1601), and Marston's *Malcontent*, *What You Will*(?), and *The Dutch Courtesan*. Dr. Wallace would identify the *Casta Vidua* which the Duke of Stettin-Pomerania saw at Blackfriars on September 18, 1602, with Chapman's *Widow's Tears*, but I think there is no doubt that Chapman's play belongs to a later date. In the first place, it was not licensed till April 17, 1612, but more than that, it is difficult to see in what way the term "chaste" can be applied to Chapman's Ephesian matron. The bitter invective against legal injustice which marks the play is much better understood in the light of Chapman's own calamaties after the illfated production of *Eastward Ho* than as a protest against the prosecution of Evans in consequence of the Clifton suit. The only grounds for Wallace's identification lie in the single word "widow," and that is slight evidence indeed.

As was to be expected upon the revival of a once popular company, the Chapel boys soon appeared at court—to be exact, upon Twelfth Night and Shrove Sunday of 1601. Then payment was made "To Nathanyell Gyles m*aste*r of the children of the chapple vppon the councills warraunte dated at whitehall iiijto Maij 1601 for a play pr*es*ented before her m*aie*stie on Shrovesunday at nighte x^{li} and for a showe with musycke and speciall songes prepared for that purpose on Twelfth day at nighte C^s—in all xv^{li}"[3a] Just what the nature of the show with music was, we can only conjecture, probably something on the order of a masque-like entertainment with a great deal of singing and doubtless dancing too. At any rate, we may be sure that it was not a play of the ordinary kind, or the common

---

[1] Cf. title page. The date of the *S. R.* entry—November 25, 1600—may indicate when the play was released for publication, and thus place *Love's Metamorphosis* as probably the earliest Blackfriars play. This likelihood is much strengthened by the play itself; the company would not be likely to make use of old plays after it had secured playwrights to work for it, but in the hurry of opening necessity may have compelled it to have recourse to plays which were ready to hand. It was probably at this time that the Chapel company stole *Jeronimo* from the king's men.

[2] *Vide* the induction to Webster's version of the *Malcontent*. In reprisal the king's men took over Martson's play, which had first been produced by the Chapel.

[3] *Sir Giles* belongs probably in 1601; *May Day* in 1601-2. Professor Parrott's discussion of the dating of these plays in his excellent edition of Chapman (1914) is thoroughly satisfactory.

[3a] *Declared Accts., Treas. of the Chamber*, Pipe Roll 543, fol. 69 b.

term "play" or "interlude" would have been used. This performance recalls to us that the Duke of Stettin-Pomerania in 1602 found the *Chaste Widow* preceded by a musical program an hour long.

The favor which the Chapel boys found at court was extended them even more signally the next year, when they played three times,[4]—on Twelfth Night, the Sunday after, and Shrove Sunday. On all occasions Nathaniel Gyles was the director of the company, as befitted his position of Chapel master. But he seems not to have been an important member of the managing board; he was never involved in the suits that were set on foot against nearly every one else concerned in the enterprise, and he soon dropped out altogether.

2. *Readjustments in the Board of Managers.*

So far the new company was going before a fair breeze under full sail, but not for long, because troubles loomed up as a result of the Clifton affair. Clifton senior did not bring suit until December, 1601, nearly a year after the event which gave rise to it; so he tells us in his complaint.[5] The decree of the court has not come down to us, but we know its tenor, nevertheless, from references to it in later suits. Kirkham, in his Replication in the suit *Kirkham v. Painton,* refers to it thus:[6]

And this replyant doth much mervell that the said Evans doeth by his Aunswere challenge any interest in the said great Hall, or of any other assureaunce concerninge the said House or playes, when that the said Evans in or about the three and ffortieth yeare of the raigne of the late Queen Elizabeth (1601)[7] was censured by the right honorable Courte of Starr-Chamber for his vnorderlie carriage and behauiour in takinge vp of gentlemens children against theire wills and to ymploy them for players, and for other misdemeanors in the said Decree conteyned, and ffurther that all assureances made to the said Evans concerninge the said house or playes or Interludes should be vtterlye voyde, and to be deliuered vpp to be cancelled as by the said Decree more at large it doth and may appeare.

[4] *Decl. Accts.*, Pipe Roll 543, fol 83: "To Nathaniel Gyles ma*st*er of the children of her ma*ie*sts Chappell upon the counsells warraunt dated at the courte at Richmount vij mo die Martij 1601 for thre severall playes or enterludes presented before her ma*ie*stie at expianmas laste paste viz on Twelfe night the Sunday night next after and uppon Shrove sunday at night after the rate of vi^{li} xiij^s iiij^d for every playe xx^{li} and to them for her ma*ie*sts rewarde for every playe lxvj^s viij^d-x^{li}. In all xxx^{li}."

[5] Clifton said: ". . they . . . about one yere last past . . . did . . . vnlawfully practize . . . vyolentlie & vnlawfully to surprise the sayd Thomas Clifton." Elsewhere he had dated his son's arrest Dec. 13, 1600.

[6] Fleay, *Hist. of the Stage*, p. 248.

[7] Not 1600, as Fleay prints it.

Evans seems to refer to the same occasion when he says:[8]

And the Complainant further for Replicacion saith, that he was, by the defendant and his said Associates vpon false informacion made to the late Lord Hunsdon, late Lord Chamberlaine, against this Complainant, comaunded by his Lordship to avoyd and leave the same (i.e. Blackfriars, seemingly), for feare of whose displeasure the Complainant was forced to leaue the Country, and lost in want of not looking to his proffitt there and Charge otherwise neere three hundred pounds.

The date of Evans's departure from London is more precisely given in his Bill of Complaint in the suit *Evans v. Kirkham*:[9]

And within one moneth or thereabouts next after then sealinge of the same obligacion (of £200, sealed April 20, 1602) your said oratour did departe into the Countrye and relinquished and left all the aforesaid demised premisses to them the said Rastell Kyrkham and Kendall onely to there vse....for a longe space and tyme to there great benefitt and profitt and the damadge of your poore oratour at the least to the value of three hundreth powndes.

These evidences are perfectly congruent. Kirkham's lawyer seems to have written with the Star Chamber decree before him, so explicit is he; and we are interested to learn that Evans's crime was impressing *gentlemen's* children, for this shows how liberally the court looked on the use to which Gyles's writ of impressment was put. If Evans was ordered near the end of 1601 to get out of the Blackfriars management, some time would be given him to set his affairs in order, and consequently we do not find him actually leaving town until May of 1602, five months after the suit was brought. Before he went, however, he made secure his interests at Blackfriars, as we shall see directly.

But even before Clifton brought his suit, seemingly, Evans had deeded over the theatre property to one Alexander Hawkins, his son-in-law, a man who had helped him in the venture from the start and had signed with him the bond of £400 by which the Burbages were assured their rent of £40 for the theatre.[10] Painton,[11] in 1612, said that the deed was made October 21, 1601.[12] It does not appear

[8] In the Replication of Henry Evans in the suit *Evans v. Kirkham*, 1612; Fleay, *Hist. of Stage*, p. 220.

[9] Fleay, *op. cit.*, pp. 212-3.

[10] So said Richard Burbage, in his reply to Kirkham (Fleay, *op. cit.*, p. 234.)

[11] He married Hawkins's widow, and so came into the embroilment as inheriting Hawkins's estate.

[12] Fleay, *op. cit.*, p. 230.

that the brewing trouble had anything to do with this action; at least Evans does not give such a hint. He explains that his purpose was to protect Hawkins in respect to the £400 bond to the Burbages,[13] and that the deed was drawn up long before he negotiated with Kirkham. His evidence is interesting and valuable along here, for he testifies that in spite of deeding all his property to Hawkins, he kept the theatre lease, and received and disposed at will of the profits therefrom. Thus by a kind of subterfuge and with the help of his son-in-law, he was able to get out of the management of Blackfriars and yet stay in it. Kirkham, in his suit years later against Painton, expressed simulated surprise that Evans still pretended interest in Blackfriars, after he had been ordered by the Star Chamber to cancel all his assurances and deeds relating to the theatre.

Having been ordered to quit Blackfriars, Evans set about finding more capital for its support and putting his affairs in such order that he could seem to obey the court's decree and still keep a guiding hand on the rein. He found the men he wanted in Edward Kirkham, Yeoman of the Revels, and two men of small individual importance, William Rastell (or Rastall) and Thomas Kendall. Whether or not Kirkham had anything to do with the theatre before the formal agreement with Evans was drawn up, seems to be a moot question. If "complainant" in Evans's animadversion on the £50 bond[14] be not an error for "defendant," then we must believe that Kirkham had a prior connection with the Chapel company, as I have already

---

[13] Fleay, op. cit., pp. 244-5. "(The defendant) confesseth that long tyme before any communicacion had betweene this defendant and Alexander Hawkins on the one partie, and the complainant, Rastall, and Kendall on the other partie, he this defendant did vpon meere trust and confidence and of intent and purpose to saue harmles the said Alexander Hawkins of & from one bond of ffower hundred powndes, which the said Alexander Hawkins, entred into vnto the said Richard Burbage as suretie for this defendant for the paiement of the said rent of ffortie pownds by the yeare reserued vpon the said Lease made by the said Richard Burbage vnto this defendant, vpon the earnest and ymportunate request of this defendants wife, graunt & convey vnto him the said Alexander Hawkins, who married this defendants daughter, all his goodes chattells and leases, implements howshold-stuff, wares, comodities, & all his goods. Notwithstanding which graunt this defendant kept the said originall Lease made by the said Richard Burbage, and hath ever since enioyed and contynued the possession as well of all his goodes, leases, implements & other the premisses, and the same howse and roomes so leased by the said Richard Burbadge, and the proffitts thereof haue ever since bene taken disposed and ordered as yt pleased this defendant vntill about Aprill last was fower yeares."

[14] Cf. p. 167.

pointed out; but on the other hand, Evans said that he made over to Hawkins the lease of Blackfriars by a deed which was dated October 21, 1601, "long tyme before any communicacion had between this def*endan*t . . . . and the compl*ainan*t, Rastall, and Kendall." Since the final agreement followed in April, 1602, it seems not likely that Kirkham had any connection with the management of Blackfriars before then.

Some time before the middle of April, 1602, Evans got into communication with Edward Kirkham, William Rastell, and Thomas Kendall with a view to forming a partnership. The result was that these three new men came in on equal terms with Evans and Hawkins,—were to pay half the theatre rent and half the expenses which should arise, and were to receive in turn half the profits. The agreement was made firm by having Evans and Hawkins enter into a bond of £200, which may be read in Evans's Answer to Kirkham (*Krikham v. Painton*).[15] This bond was sealed April 20, 1602, and on the same date other formal agreements were entered into. One was a set of "Articles of Agreement," referred to at various places in the suits, but nowhere recited in full. We gather from Evans's Answer that according to the Articles "the true meaning of the said parties was yt the compl*ainan*t and the said Rastell and Kendall should haue the benefitt and effect of the said Agreements indented as well against this def*endan*t, as the said Hawkins";[16] and that they were drawn up "because this def*endan*t was desirous to deale honestly and squarely with the compl*ainan*t."[17] The third document signed on the same day was a bond of £50, already discussed, by which Kirkham and his allies bound themselves to pay Evans 8s. weekly on Saturdays for fifteen years, "when & soe often as anye enterludes playes or showes shalbe playde vsed showed or published in the greate hall" at Blackfriars.[18]

With these three agreements, destined to breed such dire discord later on, the new joint management started forth. Evans left the city, for how long we cannot determine, and the direction of the company must have devolved on Kirkham, who next to Evans was thereafter most prominent of all who were connected with the theatre.

[15] Fleay, *Hist. of Stage*, pp. 240-1.
[16] *Same*, p. 243.
[17] *Same*, p. 245.
[18] For the text of this bond cf. the suit *Evans v. Kendall*, p. 187.

3. *Children of the Queen's Revels: the Daniel Suit.*

The new management took on a different form soon after the accession of James, for then it was deemed wise to obtain Letters Patent enrolling the children among the officially licensed companies of London. Accordingly the much cited patent of February 4, 1604,[19] was issued, bestowing on the Chapel children the title of "Children of the Revels to the Queen" and the privilege of playing at Blackfriars. The company now lost its last bond with the Chapel Royal,—its name; and it is a reasonable supposition that Blackfriars plays which are printed as having been acted by the "Children of the Queen's Revels" belong after the granting of this patent. To the familiar names of Hawkins, Kendall, and Kirkham (Rastell is not noticed) as directors, is added the name of Robert Payne. Perhaps the most interesting provision of all is the clause which vests the power to license plays given by this company in Samuel Daniel. The Revels Master, who was usually so eager in maintaining his rights as general licenser of plays, seems in this case to be deliberately set aside. It is a curious situation, for which no one has yet offered a satisfactory explanation; nor have I any solution to offer except that, as I shall show presently, the office carried with it a substantial remuneration, which Daniel may have hungered for and been influential enough to compass.

Though I cannot explain the wherefor of this arrangement between Daniel and the shareholders, I am fortunately able to throw light on its precise nature and operations, by means of a Chancery suit which has hitherto escaped investigators. It is not greatly important, in that it solves no difficulties and lights up no corners which it is essential to explore, but it does form a useful link in the chain of evidence relating to the Blackfriars management, and it tells us things we are glad to know about the circumstances attending an employment so closely connected with the Jacobean stage. It seems that on April 28, 1604, Kirkham and Kendall became bound to Daniel in the sum of £100 to pay him £10 for every year that the Revels company was maintained, provided they played their full time of six months. This point in regard to the season at Blackfriars is interesting and new. If by reason of plague, or otherwise, they should not play the full six months, then Daniel

[19] Printed in various places. E.g. Collier, *Hist. Eng. Drama. Poetry,* 1879, I, 340, and Chambers, *Eliz. Stage,* II, 49.

should be paid at the rate of 16s. 8d. a month for the time they did play. According to Kirkham's story, the payments were made promptly, with Daniel ever needy and importunate for advances, until October 25, 1605, when a new agreement was made, by which Daniel was to surrender the old bond and receive a weekly stipend of 5s. whenever and so long as the children played. For a time matters went well, and then Daniel, taking advantage of the fact that the agreement was private and personal and retaining possession of the bond, brought suit in King's Bench shortly before May of 1609 for the full forfeiture of the bond. The present suit in Chancery[20] was for the purpose of staying the suit in common law. Daniel in answer admitted the facts of the bond and the £10 salary, and declared that the payments were made satisfactorily up to April 28, 1606, when by Letters of Attorney he made over the benefits of the obligation to one John Gerrard. He admitted that there had been talk of a 5s. rate of payment, but maintained that nothing had come of it, and the subject had been dropped; and that in consequence of cessation of payments after the date of the assignment to Gerrard, Gerrard had brought suit in Daniel's name, through his Letter of Attorney. Thus the case stands, and I am unaware of the issue; the reader may consult it in full in the *Appendix*.[21]

The items in this suit which interest us are those which relate to the management of the Revels boys. Their acting season, it seems, ran six months for an ordinary maximum. During that time Daniel was paid for licensing plays as often as children should play. His first salary of £10 was excellent remuneration for a season's work, seeing that the boys played only once, or at most twice, a week. Daniel's account, with its definite references to Gerrard, has the ring of truth in it. Coupled with Kirkham's flings about his perpetual poverty, it shows clearly that Daniel disposed of this important part of his income to raise money, not improbably to settle debts. There is a pretty comedy of impoverished genius behind all this at which we can at least guess.

4. *The Events of 1604; The Rastell-Kirkham-Hawkins Suit.*

The course of the new Children of the Queen's Revels Company was as uneasy as it could well be. We are not clear even yet as to

---

[20] *Chancery Bills and Answers, Series I.* Jas. I; K 4/33.
[21] P. 334.

just where and when some of their troubles arose; but we do know
that they got into difficulty in two ways, either of which would have
brought any company to grief—through internal dissensions and
through entanglements with the censorship. With the latter we are
not much concerned, for the chronology, purpose and effect of the
satirical plays which they poured forth have been pretty thoroughly
discussed. I intend rather to trace the company's history from the
evidence which documents give us, using the evidence of plays as a
background. For this period of our history the Greenstreet-Fleay
suits of 1612 are still our most valuable source; but I have some
additions of my own to make to them.

The first troubles came immediately after the incorporation of
the new company, which received its patent on February 4, 1604,
and they came from within. The source of the difficulty, which lay
between Kirkham and Evans, was, as usual from now on, one of the
bonds sealed on April 20, 1602. In this case it was the £200 bond,
which guaranteed Kirkham and his friends an equal share in Blackfriars receipts and expenses. The suit through which this chapter of
bickering comes forth was not brought till 1609,[22] but since the
facts concerned all belong in 1604, this seems to be the proper place
to introduce it. Roughly and briefly, this is the substance of the
conflict. Hawkins maintained that Kirkham and his associates had
failed to pay their half for some reparations undergone in the
theatre in the latter half of 1604, and that consequently on December 20 of the same year he had shut them out, and deprived them
of their share in the management. This is a new and interesting
fact; the trouble is, he does not tell us how long the inhibition
lasted. Kirkham and Rastell, who brought suit, alleged that Evans
had violated the £200 bond, according to which all the theatrical
premises were to be open to them, in that he had locked up some
small rooms above a room called "The Schoolhouse," which was
itself over the theatre. I shall let the records of the suit speak for
themselves in filling in the details of this outline. The suit might
not be valuable enough in itself to quote extensively, were it not

---

[22] King's Bench, *Rastell & Kirkham v. Hawkins*. This is one of my finds. Dr.
Wallace, in the *London Times* of Sept. 12, 1906, announced that he had discovered
certain highly important documents respecting the Blackfriars theatre under the
Queen's Revels. From his very brief description it appears that they included this
suit, the one following, and possibly one or two more of my discoveries. He used
a few extracts in his *Chapel at Blackfriars*, but has never printed the suits or made
known their identity; hence I have no hesitation in revealing them here.

for the fact that it gives a remarkably clear and definite résumé of
the proceedings at Blackfriars from the time of the drawing of the
£200 indenture on April 20, 1602, until December 20, 1604, and
does in no way bear out the special contentions of Dr. Wallace.
In giving here a translation of the original Latin, I shall curtail or
omit as much as possible the purely technical and uniformative
parts of the phrasing—the parts which are customary to King's
Bench suits of this nature—and give only what bears on the case at
issue.

[23](William Rastell and Edward Kirkham in the person of Simon Har-
borne, their attorney, have in the last Michaelmas term presented a bill
in the Court of King's Bench against Alexander Hawkins, which follows in
these terms)· William Rastell of London, merchant, and Edward Kyrkham, gentleman, bring complaint against Alexander Hawkins, gentleman,...suing that he repay to them two hundred pounds of legal English
money which he owes them and unjustly withholds; on these grounds,
namely, that whereas the said Alexander on the twentieth day of April in the
forty-fourth year of the reign of the late queen Elizabeth, in London, to wit
in the parish of Marylebone in the ward of Cheap, by means of a certain
obligatory writing sealed with the seal of the said Alexander...and dated the
same day and year, Acknowledges that he is held and firmly bound to the
said William Rastell and Edward Kyrkham and one Thomas Kendall now
dead in the sum of the said £200, to be paid the same William, Edward, and
Thomas when he should be required, but the said Alexander was often (so)
required and never paid the said £200 to the said William, Edward, and
Thomas or to any one of them during the life of the same Thomas or to the
said William and Edward or either of them after the death of the same
Thomas, But wholly refused to pay them to the said William, Edward, and
Thomas during the life of the said Thomas And still refuses to pay the said
William and Edward to the damage of the said William and Edward of
£40 And hence they bring suit &c.

And on this day, namely, the next Tuesday after the eighteenth of
Easter in the same Term, until which day the said Alexander had permission
to challenge the said bill and then to make reply &c. there came before the
King at Westminister as well the said William and Edward in the person of
their said Attorney as the said Alexander in the person of Thomas Hegman,
his Attorney. (And the defendant, as usual, requested a reading of the
obligation, the indorsement of which follows in English):

The Condicion of this obligacion is such That whereas Richard Burbage
of the parishe of Saint leanardes in Shorditch in the Countie of Middlesex

---

[23] *Coram Rege Rolls*, Easter 7 Jas. I, membrane 456.

gent*leman* by his Indenture of lease bearinge date the second day of September in the two and fortith yere of the raigne of our Soue*raigne ladye Elizabeth the Queenes Ma*ies*tie that now is hath leased and to farme letten vnto the within bounden henrie Evans all that greate hall or Roome with the roomes over the same in the said indenture menc*i*oned scituate within the p*recincte of the black friers london to hold vnto the said henrye Evans his executors and Assignes from the feast of S*aint* Michaell Tharkangell next ensuinge after the date of the said Indenture vnto the ende and tearme of one and twentie yeares from thence next ensuinge fullie to be compleate and ended yealdinge and payinge therefore yearley duringe the saide terme vnto the said ·Richard Burbidge his heires and Assignes fortie pound*es* of lawfull money of England att fowre feastes or tearmes in the yeare that is to saye att the feast*es* of the birth of our lord God thanuncia c*i*on of the blessed virgyn Marie the Nativitie of S*aint* John Baptist & S*aint* Michaell tharkangell by even and equal porc*i*ons to be payd if now the within named William Rastell Edward kirkham and Thomas kendal! and eu*erie* of them their and eu*erie* of their executors and administrators and Assignes shall or may from hence forthe during the continuance of the said lease have the ioynte vse occupac*i*on and p*rofytt together with the within bounden henrye Evans & Alexander hawkyns their executors Administrators and Assignes and euerye of them of and in the said greate hall or Roome and other the p*remisses without the lett or trouble of the said henrie and Alexander their executors Administrators and Assignes or any of them or of any other p*erson or p*ersons by their or any of their meanes or p*rocurement they the said William Edward and Thomas their executors administrators and Assignes or any of them payinge vnto the said henrie and Alexander their executors or Assignes or to some or one of them from henceforth yearlie duringe the continuance of the saide lease the moyetie or one half of the said yearlie rente att the fower vsuall ffeast*es* in the yeare or within one and twentie dayes next after euerye of the said feast*es* by even porc*i*ons and also bearinge and payinge of the moyetie of such Chardges as from tyme to tyme shalbe laide out or disbursed for in or aboute the rep*aracions of the p*remisses by and accordinge to the purporte and true meaninge and limitac*i*on of the said lease And alsoe permittynge and suffringe the saide henrie & Alexander their executors and Assignes and eu*erye of them to have ioynte vse occupac*i*on and p*rofytt together with them the said William Edward and Thomas their executors Administrators and Assignes and eu*erie of them of and in the saide greate hall and p*remisses without their or any of their lett*es* troubles and interrupc*i*ons That then this p*resent obligac*i*on to be voide and of none effect or els it to stand in full force and vertue.

[24]Which being read and heard, the same Aexander declares that said William Rastell and Edward Kirkham ought not to bring or maintain their said action against him Because he says that the said Indenture mentioned in the Indorsement above was made at London in the said parish and ward on the second day of September in the forty-second year of the reign of the said late Queen Elizabeth between the said Richard Burbage named above in the said Indorsement, by the name of Richard Burbage of the parish of St. Leonard's in Shoreditch in the county of Middlesex, gentleman, on the one part, and the said Henry Evans, by the name of Henry Evans of London, gentleman, on the other part, by the means of which Indenture the said Richard Burbage for and in consideration of a yearly rent expressed in the same Indenture demised to the said Henry Evans the said great hall and other premises mentioned among other things in the said Indorsement, by the name of all that great hall or place (in English Room[25]) with places (in English rooms) above it as they were then built, adorned (in English furnished), and erected with a Theatre (in English a Stage) porticoes (in English Galleries) and seats[26] to the amount specified in the Schedule thereto joined, situate and being toward the northern end of certain places (in English Rooms) then in the tenure and occupation of one John Robbinson or his assigns within the precinct of Blackfriars, London, and being part and parcel of those houses and edifices there which were then lately bought and purchased of Sir William Moore by the late James Burbidge, father of the said Richard, and the said Richard Burbidge, containing by estimation in length from the south side to the north sixty-six feet of assize, more or less, and in breadth from the west part to the east forty-six feet of assize, more or less, to have and to hold all the said hall or place...with places... above it among other things to the said Henry Evans his executors Administrators and Assignees from the feast of St. Michael the Archangel then next following after the date of the said Indenture until the end and termination of twenty-one years then next following to be fully completed and ended, rendering and paying yearly during the said space of time to the said Richard Burbidge his heirs and Assignees £40 of legal English money at the said four feasts or terms in the year, to wit at the feasts of the Birth of our lord, of the Annunciation of the blessed virgin Mary, of the Nativity of St. John the Baptist and of St. Michael the Archangel or within twenty-eight days following each of these feasts to be paid by equal portions; And the same Alexander further declares that the said Henry Evans for himself, his heirs, executors, administrators, and Assigns among other things agreed and conceded to and with the said Richard Burbidge his heirs and Assigns

[24] Here ends the citation of the bond, and Hawkins's defense, in Latin, resumes.
[25] " . . . . loci anglice Roome cum locis anglice roomes . . . . sicut tunc erecti ornati Angelice furnished & edificati . . . . "
[26] " . . . . cum Theatro Anglice a Stadge porticibus Anglice Galleries & sedibus."

by means of the same Indenture among other things that the said Henry
Evans, his heirs, executors, administrators, or Assigns at his or their own
costs and expenditures would from time to time well and sufficiently repair, support, maintain, and mend the said great hall or place... and the
said places...above the same among other things by the same Indenture demised, by and through all and every necessary reparations (in English needful and necessary reparations) and emendations (in English amendments)[27]
whatsoever, when and so often as need should arise or demand, or within
six months next after warning in this behalf to or for him or them given or
left in writing at the said great hall during the said term of twenty-one
years as by the same Indenture among other things more fully appears;
by virtue of which demise the same Henry Evans immediately after the
said feast of St. Michael the Archangel next coming after the date of the
said Indenture entered into the said hall and tenements with their appurtenances demised in the said form And was then in possession, And he was
thus in possession until the drawing up of the said obligatory writing, And
that the said William Rastell Edward Kirkham and Thomas Kendall from
the said time of the sealing of the said obligatory writing until the twentieth day of December in the second year of our lord James now King of
England had at London, to wit in the parish of St. Anne in the Blackfriars
in the ward of Farringdon within London, the joint use (in English the
joint use) occupation and profit along with the said Henry Evans and
Alexander Hawkyns of and in the said great Hall or place (in English room)
and other premises mentioned above in the said Indorsement, without im-
pediment or disturbance (in English trouble) on the part of the said Henry
and Alexander or their Assigns or any of them or any other person or persons through the means or procurement of them or of any of them according
to the force, form, and effect of the said Indorsement; And the same Alexander further declares that after the sealing of the said obligatory writing
and before the said twentieth day of December in the said second year, to
wit on the first day of July in the abovesaid second year, the said tenements
mentioned above in the said Indorsement were then dilapidated in various
parts and unrepaired, namely in the flooring lying on the eastern side of the
same Hall and in the flooring at the eastern end of the Theatre (in English
the Stage) in the said hall and in the wall there above the steps (in English
the stairs) and in the window glass and in the wooden windows as well
above as below on each side of the premises specified above on the indorsement and in the wall at each side and end of the said Hall and in the leaden
gutters (in English gutters of lead) and in the roof of the said premises

[27] " . . . . in & per omnes & omnimodas necessarias reparacciones anglice needefull and necessarie reparaciones & emendaciones Anglice amendmentes . . . .".

specified above in the said indorsement[28]; Whereupon the said Henry Evans afterwards, to wit on the eighteenth day of December in aforesaid second year of the reign of our said present lord the King, in London, namely in the parish and ward aforesaid, laid out and expended (in English did disburse) for and about necessary reparations of the dilapidated parts (in English decays and default) the sum of £10 of legal English money; and that the said Henry Evans afterwards, to wit on the nineteenth day of December in the aforesaid second year at London in the said parish and ward then gave notice to the said Edward Kirkham and required the said Edward then and there to bear (in English bear) and pay the half of the said £10, namely £5, according to the form and effect of the said indorsement, and that the said William Rastell, Edward Kirkham, and Thomas Kendall did not at that time pay nor did any one of them pay the said Alexander and the said Henry Evans or either of them the same £5 according to the form and effect of the said Indorsement, by reason of which the said Alexander afterwards, to wit on the said twentieth day of December in the aforesaid second year of our now lord the King[29] did prevent and hinder the said William, Edward, and Thomas from having further joint use, occupation, and profit along with the said Henry Evans and Alexander Hawkyns of and in the said great hall or place...and other the said premises, as by reason of the said condition[30] is within his rights; And this he is ready to prove, whence he seeks judgment as to whether the said William and Edward ought not to bring or maintain their said action against him, &c.

And the said William Rastell and Edward Kirkham declare that they through anything alleged by the said Alexander in his plea above should not be prevented from bringing their action against the said Alexander, Because, protesting that the said tenements mentioned in the said Indorsement were not in decay as the said Alexander in his plea above alleges, and protesting that the said Henry Evans did not spend about the reparations of the decays of the said tenements £10 as the said Alexander in his plea above also has alleged, and protesting that no notice was given the said Edward Kirkham of any money laid out in reparations of the said tenements in (such) manner and form as the said Alexander in his plea above also has alleged, nevertheless for their plea the said William Rastell

---

[28] " . . . fuerunt in diversis partibus inde in decasu & minime reparata videlicet in paviamento iacente super orientali parte eiusdem Aule & in paviamento in orientali fine cuiusdam Theatri Anglice the Stadge in aula predicta & in pariete ibidem super gradus anglice the stayres & in vitrio & in fenestris ligneis tam supra quam infra in vtrisque partibus premissorum . . . & in pariete in vtrisque partibus & finibus predicte Aule & in gutturis plumbi anglice guttures of lead & in tegulacione predictorum premissorum. . . . ."

[29] 1604.

[30] I.e., the indorsement on the £200 bond.

and Edward Kyrkeham declare that at the time of the said demise to the said Henry Evans by the said Richard Burbidge made in the said form and the said time of the sealing of the said obligatory writing there was a certain Chamber called the Schoolhouse above part of the said great hall and certain other Chambers above the said Chamber called the Schoolhouse parcel of the said tenements demised to the said Henry Evans by the said obligatory writing and before the time when it is alleged that the said tenements were in decay in the said form, to wit on the last day of February in the first year of the reign of our said lord James now King of England (and) at London in the parish of St. Anne in Blackfriars in the ward of Farringdon within, the said Henry Evans shut up (in English locked up) the said Chamber above the said Chamber called the Schoolhouse and then and there expelled the said William Rastell, Edward Kirkham, and Thomas Kendall and shut out the said William Rastell, Edward Kirkham, and Thomas Kendall from the said last day of February in the aforesaid first year until the said time in which it is alleged that the said tenements were in decay in the said form; And this they are ready to prove, whence they seek judgment And that their said debt with their said damages on the ground of the detention of the debt, be awarded them, &c.

And the said Alexander declares that the said Henry Evans did not lock up the said Chamber above the said Chamber called the Schoolhouse nor shut out the said William Rastell, Edward Kirkham, and Thomas Kendall or any one of them in the manner and form as the said William and Edward in their replication above alleged, And as to this he puts himself upon his oath And the said William and Edward similarly &c.   (And the record ends with the usual abbreviated formulae of the future course of the case. It is to come to the jury on the Tuesday next after the octave of Holy Trinity.)

The outcome of the case I have not been able to find from the records of the court, but I am sure that this is the case referred to by Evans with a slight error of date in his Answer in the suit *Kirkham v. Painter* as being brought in Michaelmas term of the *ninth* year of James I (1611) instead of 1609, and as being non-suited. The course of the case as Evans's attorney describes it is precisely the same as that of our present case, and the slip of ninth year for 1609 would be easy to comprehend. This is what Evans has to say about the suit:[31]

"And this def*endan*t . . . . for further Aunswers therevnto saith, that the compl*ainan*t for righting of himself (as he supposeth) against this def*endan*t did in Michaelmas Terme in the nynth yeare of the Kinges Ma*ies*ties raigne comence

─────────

[31] Fleay, *Hist. of the Stage*, p. 242.

suyt vpon the said obligacion of twoo hundred powndes against this defendant supposing the said obligacion had bene absolutelye forfeyted meaning to take the extreamest advantage thereof, wherevnto this defendant pleaded the forenamed condicion of the said obligacion, and vpon pleading betweene the said parties the same proceeded to yssue, and triall was had therevpon in Easter Terme last past before the Lord chief Justice of England in the Guildhall London; And vpon hereinge of the proufes produced of this now defendants behalf, the said complainant did then become non-suyt vpon the said yssue so ioyned, as by the Record thereof remayning in his Maiesties Court commonly called the Kinges bench maie appeare."

One would like to know something about the "Schoolhouse" over the theatre. Was it simply the place where the boys were rehearsed in their parts? or did they receive there some kind of instruction in grammar and the moral and speculative virtues, such as the Chapel master was bound to give the boys impressed for service in the Chapel Royal? By this time (1604) Nathaniel Gyles had dropped what slender connection bound him to the Blackfriars enterprise. His name does not occur in the annals of the company after its incorporation in January-February of 1604; and on the few occasions when the lads play at court, he is not the man who leads them.

5. *The Evans-Kendall Suit.*

While we are on the matter of quarrels and suits in the King's Bench, it may be as fitting a time as any other to introduce another suit of my finding from the *Coram Rege Rolls*—this time between Kendall and Evans, with Evans the plaintiff. It was brought in the Easter term of 1608, and centered round another of the bonds drawn up on the fateful twentieth of April, 1602, namely the £50 bond by which Evans was secured in an income of 8s. weekly. This suit is alluded to by Evans in his Answer to Kirkham in the Kirkham-Painton suit.[32] After reviewing briefly the circumstances and terms of the bond, he says that the "obligacion was forfeyted, and the obligacion being put in sute and readye for triall and the arrerages being great, the said complainant and the said Kendall did by agreement take vp the Obligacion so made to this defendant and

---

[32] Fleay, *Hist. of the Stage*, p. 244.

they did enter into a new bond vnto the said Alexander Hawkins, &
he gave them therevpon a further daie for the paiement of ffiftye
& ffower pounds as this def*endan*t thincketh, and therevpon and
vpon that grownd the said Alexander Hawkins by this def*endan*ts
agreement did satisfie vnto this def*endan*t the some of ffortie and
eight powndes ten shillinges and not ffiftye & twoo powndes ten
shillinges as in the bill is alleadged."

The suit thus generally referred to, which I submit here as bearing more on the earlier history of the company than on the later, is
valuable for two reasons: first, for giving us another glimpse of the
inner workings of the Revels company such as we had in the Daniel-
Kirkham suit, and secondly, for giving us the text of the £50 bond,
thus filling in a gap in our chain. The one document still unknown
to us of the three which were signed in April of 1602 is the Articles
of Agreement, to which general reference is made in the Greenstreet-
Fleay suits. I shall condense the purely technical portions of the
present document even more than I did in the last case. Why the
action is brought against Kendall and not his more prominent partner, Kirkham, is not clear.

[33](Henry Evans in Trinity term of 1604 began suit against Thomas Kendall of London, citizen and haberdasher, for the forfeiture of a bond of £50
dated April 20, 1602. Kendall, appearing on summons, desires the usual
reading of the conditions of the bond, which follow in English):

The Condic*i*on of this obligac*i*on ys suche That yf the within bounden
William Rastell Edwarde kirkham and Thomas kendall or any of them
theire or any of theire executors, administrators or assignes everye weeke
weekly on Saturdaye duringe the space of fifteene yeres next ensuinge the
date within written when & soe often as anye enterludes playes or showes
shalbe playde vsed showed or published in the greate hall and other the
Roomes scityat in the Blackfriers london or any parte thereof menc*i*oned
to be demysed by one Richard Burbage gent to the within named henry
Evans in and by one Indenture of lease bearinge date the second daye of
September in the twoe and fortith yere of the raigne of our Souereigne
ladye Elizabeth the Queenes maiestie that now ys[34] or else where by the
Children of the queenes Maies*tes* Chappell or by any other Children which
by the consent of the sayd William Edward Thomas henrie and one Alexander hawkins gent theire executors or Administrators or any three of
them wherof the saide henrie or Alexander theire Executors or Administra-

---

[33] *Coram Rege Rolls*, Easter, 6 Jas. I (1608), m. 303. For the original Latin, see
Appendix, p. 332.
[34] 1600.

tors to be one shalbe dyeted kepte or retayned for the exercise of the saide
enterludes or playes doe and shall well & trewlie paye or cause to be paide
vnto the saide henrie Evans his Executors or assignes att or in the saide
great hall the some of eighte shillinges of lawfull money of England The
first payment thereof to begynne and to be made on Saturdaye beinge the
fower & twenteth daye next commynge of this instant moneth of Aprill
within written That then this present obligacion to be voide & of none
effect Or els to stande in full force and vertue.

These[35] having been read and heard, the said Thomas Kendall says that
the said Henry Evans ought not to maintain his said suit against him because he says that he himself after the date of the said writing, that is to say
on Saturday the twenty-fourth day of the said Month of April & thus
every week[36] on Saturday until the day of the suing of the said bill, as often
as any plays (in English interludes) games[37] or spectacles (in English shows)
were played, used, shown, or presented[38] in the said great hall and other
places....situate in the Blackfriars, London, or in any part therein mentioned
to be demised by the said Richard Burbage to the said Henry Evans by
the said Indenture specified above in the said Condition, or elsewhere by
boys or any others called by the name of boys of the royal Chapel of the
sovereign (in English children of the Queen's Majesty's Chapel) or any
other boys who by the consent of the said William, Edward, Thomas,
Henry, and Alexander or three of them should be fed (in English dieted)
served and kept (in English retained) for the exhibition of the said interlude or interludes—did well and truly pay the said Henry Evans in the
said great hall, to wit in the parish of St. Anne in the Blackfriars in the
ward of Farringdon within London, the sum of 8s. of legal money of England according to the form and effect of the said indorsement And this he
is ready to verify, whence he seeks judgment as to whether the said Henry
Evans is justified in maintaining his action against him.

And the said Henry Evans says that he ought not to be hindered by
anything alleged by the said Thomas Kendall in his plea above from bringing his action against the said Thomas because, protesting that the said
Thomas did not pay the Henry any sums of pence[39] specified above in the
said Indorsement according to the form and effect of the said Indorsement
in the manner and form as the said Thomas in his plea above alleged, the
said Henry for his plea says that after the drawing up of the said obligatory
writing & before the day of the suing of the said bill, that is, on the Saturday
being the sixteenth day of June in the second year of the reign of the lord

---

[35] Here begins the Latin.
[36] "Qualibet septimana septimanatim super diem Sabbati. . . . ."
[37] "ludi," properly "plays."
[38] "publicata."
[39] "aliquas denariorum summas."

James now king of England, a certain play (in English an interlude) was played in the said great Hall mentioned in the said Indorsement situate in the Blackfriars, in the ward of Farringdon within London by boys who by the consent of the said Edward, Henry, and Alexander were kept for the exercise of the said plays and that the said Thomas Kendall on the same Saturday, to wit, on the said sixteenth day of June in the abovesaid second year of the said lord James now King, did not pay the said Henry Evans the sum of eight shillings which he ought to have paid him on that day according to the form and effect of the said Indorsement in the manner and form as the said Thomas in his plea above has alleged And this he is ready to verify.....

And the said Thomas Kendall says that no interlude (in English interlude) was played in the said great Hall specified above in the said Indorsement on the said Saturday being the sixteenth day of June in the said second year of the reign of the said lord now King by boys who by the consent of the said Edward, Henry, and Alexander were kept for the exhibition of the said plays in the manner and form as the said Henry Evans in his reply above alleged. (And so the record ends with the usual legal formalities.)

I have not been able to find any record of judgment rendered in this case; but as I have already pointed out, Evans himself has given us the outcome in an animadversion upon it contained in a later suit. It seems that a kind of compromise was arrived at, by which Kirkham and Kendall took up the old bond to Evans and entered into a new one to Hawkins, and were given an extension of time in which to pay the £54 due Evans; and that "upon that ground" Hawkins paid Evans the sum of £48-10-0, instead of the £52-10-0 which Kirkham asserted was paid.[40]

6. The Events of 1604-6: Satire and Disgrace.

In this period of four years, the Blackfriars management had undergone a storm and stress that ought to have wrecked it. It had first withstood a sharp tilt from the irate Clifton senior, then suffered various internal shocks and conflicts,—between the old and new halves of the directorate on the one hand, and between the directorate and its officially constituted censor on the other—and was soon to undergo the severest assault of all, from the law, inter-

---

[40] Hawkins had his difficulties in getting the money from the slippery Kirkham. I have in my possession a transcript of a King's Bench suit of Easter Term, 1609 (*Coram Rege*, Easter 7 Jas. I, m. 365b), by which Hawkins endeavored to get judgment against Kirkham for forfeiting the bond he entered into for the payment of this £54. I have not thought the suit important enough for publication.

posing its arm before outraged majesty. Yet it would seem that in all this turmoil the company went on playing. They did not, apparently, play at court in 1603, but they did return there for a performance on Shrove Tuesday, 1604.[41] The official notice of this event is interesting, for it names Edward Kirkham as payee, showing that he was by now actively in charge of the company, and that Nathaniel Gyles was no longer in any way officially connected with it. Probably he had dropped out of the management at the time of the Clifton earthquake; his name, it will be remembered, did not appear on the patent granted the company in 1604.

The boys played again at court on January 1 and 3, 1605.[42] Here again the official record is of interest, for it tells us that on this occasion Henry Evans and Samuel Daniel were the payees. Probably time had exerted its accustomed effect in Evans's case, and his delinquencies and the rulings of courts four years old were now forgotten or forgiven. He had always exercised a powerful influence in the direction of the company, even when he was under disgrace and was forced to act through his son-in-law Hawkins. Now he had come fully into the light. This performance at court was the last until Christmas 1608-9, and after it troublous days fell upon the company. But before we come to that part of their history, let us pause to gather up a few threads.

On September 2, 1604, the first writ of impressment under James I was granted Nathaniel Gyles for the replenishment of the Chapel Royal. Upon the death of Elizabeth and the accession of James, a new writ had to be issued, in accordance with the invariable custom in such matters. It is a long document, significant mainly for the measures it authorizes for sending overgrown Chapel boys to the Universities, and we have already discussed it in that connection.[43] Another feature worthy of remark—especially in view of the terms

[41] *Declared Accts.*, *Treas. of the Chamber*, Pipe Roll 543, fol. 117: "To Edwarde Kircham m^r of the children of the Queenes maiests Revells uppon the Counsells warrant dated at the courte at white-hall ultimo die Aprilis 1604 for one enterlude or playe presented by the said children before his maiesty uppon Shrovetuesday laste at night x^{li}."

[42] *Decl. Accts.*, Pipe Office Roll 543, fol. 137: "To Samuel Daniell and Henrie Evans uppon the Counsells warraunte dated at thee Courte at Whitehalle xxiiij^{to} die ffebruarij 1604 for two Enterludes or plaies presented before the kinges Maiestie by the Queenes Maiests Children of the Revells the one on Newyers daie at night 1604 and the other on the third daie of Januarie followinge xiij^{li} vj^s viij^d and by the waye of his highnes rewarde vj^{li} xiij^s iiij^d in all xx^{li}."

[43] Cf. p. 43. The date of issue was Sept. 17, 1604.

of the next writ—is that no exception is taken to the misuse of the writ of 1597 in furnishing the boys for the Blackfriars theatre. This may signify, and probably does, that the previous tribulations and controversies which the theatre had undergone had bothered official circles little or not at all. The attention of James was not drawn to the abuses perpetrated under the sanction of his letters patent until the players had dared to aim their darts at his own royal person. It is difficult to believe that the sovereign—either in the case of Elizabeth or James, and particularly in the latter—ever busied himself with the vicissitudes of players or knew more of them than what he saw when they played before him at court, except in rare instances when his attention was directed to them.

It is very difficult to tell what plays were being given in this period from 1603 to the beginning of 1605. It seems probable that Marston's *Sophonisba*[44] was put on in 1602-3 and his *Parasitaster* in 1604; that his *Dutch Courtesan* was revived in 1604; that Daniel's *Philotas* and possibly Middleton's *Trick to Catch the Old One* appeared in the same year, and *Eastward Ho* of Chapman, Marston, and Jonson and Day's *Isle of Gulls* early in 1605. To the winter of 1604-5 is also to be assigned Chapman's *Monsieur D'Olive*. The three plays of *Philotas*, *Eastward Ho*, and *Isle of Gulls* with two others by Chapman, brought manifold woes upon the directors at Blackfriars. We know in a general way what happened to them, and how it came about, but our knowledge of particulars is still hazy. We know at least that a series of plays appeared in 1604-5 at Blackfriars which were taken, rightly or wrongly, by the powers of censorship to trespass upon the forbidden ground of state affairs, and to ridicule the very person of royalty. As a consequence, certain of the authors, players, and managers were locked up, as we shall see, and though they were eventually set free, they lost the Queen's patronage and suffered a reversal of fortune from which the company never entirely recovered.

The disaster is twice referred to in the Fleay-Greenstreet lawsuit papers, and each time it is made clear that the plays at Blackfriars were inhibited, and that the theatre stood empty for a long time. Henry Evans, in his Answer in the suit *Kirkham v. Painton*,[45] says:

And for that this defendant hopeth to make yt plaine and manifest to this honorable Court that the complainant and this defendant by his

---

[44] Cf. Fleay, *Drama*, under Marston.
[45] Fleay, *Stage*, p. 245.

Ma*ies*ties speciall commaundement being prohibited to vse any plaies there, and some of the boyes being committed to prison by order from his highnes, and so no proffitt made of the said howse but a contynuall rent of ffortie powndes to be paid for the same, that the same made the compl*ainan*t willing voluntarily to forgoe the same howse as this def*endan*t conceaved.

And Evans said again in regard to the same events, in his Replication in the suit *Evans v. Kirkham*:[46]

But yt is true that after the Kings most excellent Ma*ies*tie vpon some misdemeanors committed in or about the plaies there, and specially vpon the def*endan*ts (Kirkham's) Act & doings thereabout, had prohibited that no plaies should be more vsed, that vpon such prohibicion the def*endan*t and his Associates seemed to goe back: for no plaies being vsed, and little or no proffitt made of the howse,

the defendant in July of 1608 caused the apparel and properties of the company to be divided among the shareholders, and surrendered the lease to Burbage.[47]

These declarations of Evans show that such great offense had been given through the matter contained in certain plays that the theatre was peremptorily closed and some of the participants were jailed. We cannot take too seriously Evans's charge that Kirkham was chiefly to blame, because such a charge may have sprung from no other source than the animus inspired by the suit at law, and because we have no other evidence to corroborate it.

The first play which was objectionable seems to have been Daniel's *Philotas*, licensed in November of 1604 and published in 1605; it was played presumably in the autumn of 1604. This play, as everyone knows, offended from seeming to follow too closely in its fable the career of the Earl of Essex, and therefore came under the ban for meddling in affairs of state. Daniel was called to account, and had to appear in his defense before the Privy Council. He denied in a letter to the Earl of Devonshire[48] and in the excuses

---

[46] Fleay, *Stage*, p. 221.

[47] But the actual surrender, and the consequent entry of Burbage and his fellows, did not take place till a year later. Cf. p. 203.

[48] This interesting letter—interesting for the facts contained therein and for its commentary on the character of Daniel—though well enough known, has not been made very accessible in its full text (it does not occur in Collier or Fleay), and I may therefore be excused for including a transcript from the original document (*S.P. Dom. Jas. I*, Vol. XI, no. 4). It bears neither date nor superscription.
    "My Lorde
        Understanding yor ho: is displeased w^t mee, it hath more shaken my harte then I did thinke any fortune could have done in respect I have not deserved it, nor

which attend the printed play any intention of drawing the parallel charged against him, but not in the most convincing terms. In the *Apology* affixed to the 1605 edition, Daniel tells that he had conceived the subject eight years ago, written three acts six months before the Essex rebellion, and had finished and produced the play against his will under the stress of need. This may all be true, and the author may have been guiltless of any intentional misdemeanor; but he fails to inform us why he should have allowed a play containing such strong analogies to reach the stage. Just what the fate of the play was we do not know; of course it was inhibited, and probably its author was merely censured, for he still retained his laureateship. Nevertheless, the censure must have been severe enough to sting, for the address to Prince Henry and the *Apology* printed with the play in 1605 have a rueful, almost a bitter sound.

This adventure brought no serious discomfort to the coterie which was then devoting its talent to the Revels company. But there followed hard upon the heels of this misstep a calamity of a more serious nature. The source was the production of *Eastward Ho*,

---

donne or spoken anything in this matter of Philotas unworthy of yo^u or mee. And now having fully satisfyde my L. of Cranborne I crave to unburthen me of this imputation w^t yor ho: and it is the last sute I will ever make. And therefore I beseach yo^u to understand all this great erro^r I have comitted.

first I tolde the Lordes I had written 3 Act*es* of this tragedie the Christmas before my L: of Essex troubles, as divers in the cittie could witnes. I saide the maister of the Revells had per*used* it. I said I had read some parte of it to yor ho: and this I said having none els of powre to grace mee now in Corte & hoping y^t yo^u out of yor knowledge of bookes, and favor of letters & mee might answere that there was nothing in it disagreeing nor anything as I protest there is not, but out of the universall notions of ambition and envie the per*petuall argum^{ts} of bookes & tragedies. I did not say you incouraged me unto the prenting of it if I should I had bene a villayne for y^t when I shewd it to yor hono^r I was not so resolud to have had it acted, nor should it have bene had not my necessities overmaistred mee. And therefore I beseach yo^u let not now an Earle of Devonsh^r overthrow what a L. mountioy hath donne, who hath donne me good and I have donne him hono^r. the world must, & shall known myne innocencie whilst I have a pen to shew it. and for y^t I know I shall live inter historiam temporis as well as greater men, I must not be such an abiect unto my self as to neglect my reputation, and having bene known throughout all England for my virtue I will not leave a stayne of villanie uppon my name whatsoever erro^r els might scape me unfortunately thorow myne indiscreation & misunderstanding the tyme. wherein good my L. mistake not my harte that hath bene & is a syncere honorer of yo^u and seekes yo^u now for no other end but to cleare it self and to be held as I ame (though I never come nere yo^u)

yor hono^{rs}

pore follower & faithfull Servant

Samuel Danyel"

some time in the first half of 1605.[49] As every one knows, Scotchmen, the new nobility, and the king himself were scoffed at in this brilliant comedy, and in no uncertain terms. The result was that Marston, who seems (if we may believe his collaborators—not the best of authority, certainly) to have been the guilty one, escaped;[50] and Jonson and Chapman were lodged in jail, whence they wrote letters such as the unjustly accused (and not seldom the justly suspected, too) are wont to endite under such circumstances.[51] Jonson played injured innocence to the life, as he knew well how to do: "our offence a Play, so mistaken, so misconstrued, so misapplied, as I do wonder whether their Ignorance or Impudence be most, who are our adversaries." The guilty authors were pardoned and released after cooling for a time in prison.

Even this shock seems not to have affected seriously the company itself, but their turn was coming. It is indeed strange that after so many misadventures with the censorship, the directors and playwrights of the company should have taken the warnings so little to heart. Instead of drawing back from the dangerous business of satirizing public personages and events, they plunged in deeper than ever, and produced in the early part of 1606 Day's *Isle of Gulls*. This play, seemingly, swept the horizon of London in its satirical discharge, and landed some of its sponsors in Bridewell.[52] The satire is for the most part obscure to us, but it seems likely that the Duke and Duchess, originally styled King and Queen, were meant to hit off the sovereigns[53] (a most impudent deed if true), and that in the critical, bawdy, and fustian-loving spectators of the Induction are meant Jonson, Chapman, and Marston; but Fleay's identification of

[49] Jonson's petition to the Earl of Salisbury from prison must date after April 4 when the Earl was created. The play was entered *S.R.* in September.

[50] In Drummond's *Conversations* we are told that Marston was imprisoned too. But Jonson's and Chapman's letters refer only to each other as being conjointly locked up.

[51] First printed by Bertram Dobell in *Athenæum*, March 30, 1901; reprinted in the *Belles Lettres* edition of *Eastward Ho* (ed. Prof. Schelling).

[52] *Vide* Thos. Birch, *The Court and Times of James the First*, 1849, I, 60. In a letter dated March 7, 1606, Sir Edward Hoby writes thus to Sir Thomas Edmondes: "At this time (i.e. about the middle of February) was much speech of a play in the Black Friars, where, in the 'Isle of Gulls,' from the highest to the lowest, all men's parts were acted of two divers nations: as I understand sundry were committed to Bridewell." This effectively does for Fleay's dating of the play in the spring of 1605 (*Drama*, I, 109).

[53] Fleay, *Drama*, I, 109.

Samuel Daniel with Dametas has little to support it. Common
sense rejects it, in the first place, on the ground that Daniel was
still at this time licenser of plays for the company and would not be
likely to pass so vicious a caricature of himself. Moreover, Fleay
makes the mistake here, as elsewhere, of attempting to relate all
the satire to the field of drama and literature, whereas the evidence
of Sir Edward Hoby's letter and the results which followed the
appearance of the play go to prove that the satire was general and
political. It is most probable that in the person of Dametas a court
dignitary is attacked—some one who was in royal favor, controlled
suits to the king, took bribes, was greedy of money, and hated
poetry.

I do not know who were the "sundry" that were committed to
Bridewell; doubtless the author and some of the managers—possibly
even some of the boys. But I do not believe that the troubles which
Henry Evans speaks of as ending in the imprisonment of some of the
company[54] were these of 1606; rather more likely is it that Evans
was referring to the misfortunes which came in 1608 after the presentation of Chapman's *Charles, Duke of Biron* and ended in the
dissolution of the company.

Let us pause for a moment over these two ill-considered and ill-
omened events. It is generally supposed that *Eastward Ho* lost for
the company the patronage of the queen; that they were no longer
permitted to style themselves "Children of the Queen's Revels,"
and that in consequence the plays given hereafter were printed as
played by the "Children of the Revels," or "Children at Blackfriars." Thus Day's *Isle of Gulls* and *Law Tricks* and Sharpham's
Fleire have only "Children of the Revels," with no mention of the
queen, on the title page. This is all very likely, for the plays which
are so differentiated by their title pages fall into a group which by
the dates of the first editions and by internal evidence is to be
placed after 1605.

Apparently, as another result of the *Eastward Ho* affair,[55] Edward
Kirkham left the company for a time and went over to Paul's, where
he was in charge in the early part of 1606. He brought the boys in
two plays before Prince Henry and the Duke of York, and he is

[54] Cf. *supra*, p. 192.
[55] And possibly, too, as a result of the dissentions of 1604.

called in the record "one of the Masters of the Children of Pawles."[56]
I do not understand the incident; it is not alluded to in the subsequent suits in which Evans and Kirkham engaged. Certainly this
estrangement was not a permanent one, though it may have lasted
until the Paul's boys dissolved. It was beyond doubt Kirkham who
was the means of carrying to the Paul's boys such of the Revels
plays as passed over at this time. Middleton's *Trick to Catch the
Old One* was printed in 1608 as acted "both at Paules, and the
Black-Fryers"; Marston's *Parasitaster*, printed in 1606, was acted
"at the Blacke Friars by the Children of the Queenes Maiesties
Reuels, and since at Powles."

In 1606, apparently as a result of injury upon injury, came an
unmistakable token of the displeasure the king had taken in this
company. In August of that year a writ of impressment was reissued
to Nathaniel Gyles—so far as I recall, the solitary instance of the
revocation of a former writ issued to the same person. The Privy
Seal was drawn up in August 1606; the Patent confirmed on November 7.[57] It traverses the usual formulæ of such writs, with some
important exceptions. For one thing, the class of boys subjected
to the action of the Chapel master is designated more particularly
than ever before. He may take "such and so many Choristers, or
any other whose parent*es* o*r* frinds have or shall put to learne the art
of Musicke or singing to thend to gett their lyving thereby in all
or any Cathedrall Collegiate or parish Churches Chappells and
Schooles where publique teaching of musicke is used." I can see no
reason in departing from the set phrases of former writs unless it
were to make impossible, by an exact description of the occupation
of the boy, such abuse of the privilege as had given rise to the Clifton
scandal in 1601. The patent goes on to provide in a general way
that boys whose voices have broken shall be taken care of and preferred. But the heart of the document comes at the end. "Prouided
alwaies and we do straightly charge and comaund that none of the
said Choristers or Children of the Chappell so to be taken by force

---

[56] *Decl. Accts.*, Pipe Roll 543, fol. 163b. "To Edward Kirkham one of the M^{rs} of
the children of Pawles upon the councells warr^t dated at the courte at whitehall
ultimo die Martij 1606 for bringing the said children and presenting by them two
playes or Enterludes before the Prince his grace and the Duke of Yorke upon nights
mentioned in a Schedule annexed unto the said warraunt after the rate of fyve
m*a*rks for ech play and by waye of his ma^{ts} reward fyve nobles in all the some of
xv^{li} xiij^s iiij^d."

[57] Printed in *Malone Society Collections*, I, 362.

of this Commission shalbe used or imployed as Comedians or Stage players or to exercise or act any stage plaies Interludes Comedies or tragedies for that it is not fitt or decent that such as should sing the praises of God almightie should be trayned up or imployed in such lascivious and prophane exercises." Beyond question the reason for existence of the patent is to be found in this concluding passage. There is no other conceivable motive for issuing a writ when the previous one of 1604 was perfectly good. Either the Revels company, in spite of Gyles's withdrawal, had continued all these five years to recruit their ranks by means of the master's impressment patent, or possibly the king had been moved by the events of 1605-6 to an examination of the affairs of the company, and, having discovered the abuses the writ had been put to in former years, had gone about to rectify the matter. But the wording of the new patent certainly sounds as though the offenses had been perpetrated under the authority of the patent of 1604. For the cause of issuing this new writ, we must surely look to the events of the preceding year; and we have in this document added and forcible proof of the disgrace which the Revels company had brought upon itself.

7. *The Cooke Indenture; Apprenticing Boys at Blackfriars.*

In this 1606-7 period belongs a very interesting King's Bench suit which I was fortunate enough to discover.[58] It throws no light on the history of the company, but it is unique and valuable in revealing some of the conditions which obtained at Blackfriars. The substance is that one Alice Cooke apprenticed her son to Thomas Kendall, on November 14, 1606, to remain three years with him as an actor in the company, but that in May of 1607 the boy left. Then Kendall brought suit for the forfeiture of the indenture, which Dame Cooke parried by asserting that her son had gone away by the express permission of Kendall. The suit itself conveys no great amount of information, but the indenture, which is quoted in full, is unusually interesting, as offering a unique example of a document of that nature.

The Condicion of this obligacion is suche that whereas our most gratious soueraigne lord the kinges maiestie by his letters pattentes vnder the greate seale of England bearinge date at Westminster the fourth day of ffebruary in the first yeare of his maiesties raigne of England ffraunce and Ireland

---

[58] *Coram Rege Rolls*, Michaelmas, 5 Jas. I, m. 582.

and of Scotland the seaven and Thirtith hath appointed and authorized the within named Thomas kendall among others in the sayde lettres patentes nomynated from tyme to tyme to provide keepe and bring vpp a Convenient number of Children and them to practyse and exercise in the quality of playinge by the name of the Children of the revells to the Queenes Maiestie within the Blacke ffryers in his highnes Citty of london or in any other convenient place where they should thinke fitt for that purpose as by the same letters patentes appeareth and whereas the within bounde Alice Cooke hath byn as earnest suytor vnto the saide Thomas kendall to receyve take and entertayne Abell Cooke her sonne to be one of the sayde Children of her Maiesties revells and to be practized and exercised in the sayde qualitye of playinge by the name of one of the Children of her highnes revells for and duringe the terme of three yeares now next ensuinge, And theervpon the saide Thomas kendal hath receyved and entertaynde hym the sayde Abell Cooke accordingly If therefore the sayde Abell Cooke shall from the daye of the date within written for and duringe the full terme of three yeares from thence next and immediatly ensuing continuew abide with and searve the sayde Thomas kendall and from tyme to tyme during the sayde terme when and so often as the sayde Thomas kendall requyre or commaunde the saide Abell shall practize and exercise hymselfe in the quality of playinge as one of the Queenes Maiesties Children of her revells aforesaide And allso shall to the vttermost of his power and habilitye att all tymes playe at the direccion and Commaundment of the saide Thomas kendall or his Assignes, And shall not wittingly or willingly duringe the sayde terme departe absent or prolonge hymselfe from the sayde service and practize and playinge without the consent and lycence of the sayde Thomas kendall his executors or Assignes first therevnto had obteyned in wrightinge without fraude or Covyn That then this present Obligacion to be voyde and of none effect or els to stande or remayne in full strength and vertue.

Dame Cooke's reply to the complaint of Kendall may be briefly summed up. She deposes that from November 14, 1606, until May 31, 1607, young Abell remained with Kendall and played at Blackfriars as often as he was required; that he then left the company by Kendall's express permission, had in writing. That is the sum of the suit. Judgment was postponed till the Saturday after the octave of St. Hillary, and I have been unable to find the decision.

This document supplements fittingly the suit of *Nat. Gyles v. Wm. Combes* which we have had occasion to notice in the previous chapter.[59] The latter, in revealing the pains which a father took to

[59] Cf. p. 158.

enroll his son among the choristers of St. George's, Windsor, bears witness to the popular feeling in regard to the occupation of choir boy; this suit shows how ready some parents were to apprentice their sons to the trade of player. From Gyles's evidence we learn that the royal chapels were not always filled by legalized kidnapping, and that in any case the posts were held to be desirable ones. The Kendall-Cooke suit teaches us the same thing in regard to the Queen's Revels company.

8. *Final Disgrace: Enter Robert Keysar, Goldsmith.*

Let us hasten on to the final chapter in the history of this company The catastrophe came as the consequence of another volley of satire which this time involved the dignities of King James and of a foreign country, France. We know most about the second of these insults,[60] which was committed by Chapman in one of his *Biron* plays, produced in March of 1608. M. de la Boderie, the French ambassador, wrote to M. de Puisieux at Paris on April 8,[61] saying that the Blackfriars company had given offense through a play on "Charles, Duke of Biron." The Chapman play brought on the stage the French queen and Mlle. de Verneuil engaging in an indecorous quarrel, at the close of which the queen boxed the lady's ears. "On my complaint," wrote the ambassador, "three persons were emprisoned; but the chief culprit, the author, escaped."

No doubt the king was the more willing to listen to the ambassador's protest because he had himself just been made the subject of open satire. M. de la Boderie, in the same letter, informs his correspondent, that a day or two before the *Biron* performance a play had been acted (by the same company, seemingly) in which the king, his Scotch mines, and his favorites had been ridiculed. His majesty was represented as cursing heaven over a mischance in hawking, striking a gentleman, and getting drunk at least once a day. As a result of both plays, the letter continues, the king waxed exceeding angry, ordered the players to be punished, and even went to the length of closing all the London theatres; whereat four other companies were offering 100,000 francs to lift the ban, and might possibly be successful, but only on the understanding that they should never again treat of modern events or any living person.

[60] Cf. among others Fleay, *Drama*, I, 62 ff., and Chambers, *Eliz. Stage*, II, 53-54.
[61] Cf. Chambers, *Eliz. Stage*, III, 257, using a text of this letter first published by M. Jusserand in *Mod. Lang. Rev.*, VI, 203.

Hard as it is to believe that the same company could be so fool-
hardy as to defy the censorship twice in the same week, nevertheless
it seems that the Revels children were thus guilty. M. de la Boderie
says that the same company gave both plays, and there is no doubt
that the Blackfriars company acted *Biron*. As to their responsibility
for the other play, confirmation appears in a most interesting letter
found by Mr. E. K. Chambers and printed in his *Elizabethan Stage*.[62]
It is from Sir Thomas Lake to Lord Salisbury, and is dated March
11, 1608.

His Matie was well pleased with that which your lo. advertiseth concerning the committing of the players yt have offended in ye matters of
France, and commanded me to signifye to your lo. that for ye others who
have offended in ye matter of ye Mynes and other lewd words, which is
ye children of ye blackfriars, That though he had signified his mynde to
your lo. by my lo. of Mountgommery yet I should repeate it again, That
his G. had vowed they should never play more, but should first beg their
bred and he wold have his vow performed, And therefore my lo. chamberlain by himselfe or your ll. at the table should take order to dissolve them,
and to punish the maker besides.

This letter tells us important news: that the fury of the king was
directed against Blackfriars chiefly for the affront to himself and
that his mind was set on having the company dissolved. At the
same time it introduces a slight discrepancy by implying that the
Biron play was given by another company. But inasmuch as both
Biron plays were published later in 1608 as played "at the Blacke-
Friers," this seems unlikely, and we are driven to suppose that Lake
was in error. Mr. Chambers feels sure that the play on King James
was written by Marston, and connects it with the facts that in June
of 1608 the poet was in prison,[63] and that he seems never to have
written again for the theatre. This seems a plausible deduction.

The king had vowed that the Blackfriars company should beg its
bread before he would allow them to play again, but did he keep
that vow? The facts are puzzling. We have on the one hand Henry
Evans's repeated assertion that the company fell into disgrace and
the theatre into disuse, and that after enduring such calamities for
a time he divided up the apparel and properties and turned over

[62] II, 53. First printed in *Malone Soc. Coll.*, II, 2, 1923, p. 149.
[63] Cf. *Eliz. Stage*, III, 428. Mr. Chambers cites a note in an abstract of the *Privy
Council Register* to the effect that on June 8 Marston was committed to Newgate.
This was first published by Mr. F. P. Wilson in *Mod. Lang. Rev.*, IX, 99.

the lease to Burbage;[64] in support of his testimony we have the *Biron* affair and the wrath of King James. But to upset all our conclusions that are so clearly drawn from these premises, comes the fact that the children of Blackfriars played at court during the Christmas holidays of 1608-9.[65] This is a great stumbling block, for it seems absolutely to contradict the evidence.

I see only one means of reconciling the conflicting testimony. It is surely significant that for these last performances the payee was none of the regular directors of the company, but a new man, Robert Keysar. We shall see directly how he came in, and how he played patron and backer to the tottering company. It is perfectly conceivable that we have been partly wrong in taking it for granted that the ill-will which the plays of March, 1608, had aroused in James I extended to the company; it may only, or mainly, have been directed against those men who were its sponsors and hence were really responsible. Indeed, it would be no more than just that a band of children should not be held accountable for what they were made to do. If this is so, then it is conceivable that the Blackfriars company, under a different leadership, would cease to be objectionable. Robert Keysar, a recent arrival in the partnership, might have had no hand in the deeds of 1608; he seems to have taken almost complete charge of the company in its last year or two, and from the very fact of his being received at court at Christmas of 1608-9, he was clearly *persona grata*. But Evans and Kirkham, in disgrace, may not have been able to carry on the company, and Keysar, as we shall see later, avowedly was not. And so it is comprehensible that Evans felt it necessary to sell out his stock and release the theatre to Burbage. This is only a hypothesis, but it will serve. We cannot be sure of the truth until we have more facts.

Thus ended the Children of the Revels, once Children of the Queen's Revels, once Children of the Chapel Royal. How they ultimately were reorganized into the Children of Whitefriars we shall see in a later chapter. To these familiar facts of the dissolution of the Revels company the valuable papers of the *Keysar v. Burbage*

[64] Cf. p. 192.

[65] *Decl. Accts.*, Pipe Roll 543, fol. 214. "To Roberte Keyser upon the councells warraunte dated at Whitehale x° Martij 1608 for two plaies presented before his maiestie by the Children of blackfriers in Christmas 1608 xx^{li}."

"To the same Roberte Keyser upon the councells warraunte dated x^{mo} Martij 1608 for one play presented by the children of the blackfriers before his highnes in the cockpitt at Whitehall iiij° Januarij 1608 - x^{li}."

suit of 1610[66] give some interesting information. It seems that
Robert Keysar, a goldsmith of London, had become interested in
the theatre about 1607 and wished to invest money in it. It seems
further that John Marston, the poet who had written so much for
these boys, was a share-holder in the properties of the theatre,
owning a sixth part, the whole at Keysar's valuation being worth
about £600. Keysar further asserted that Evans had made over all
or part of the remaining term of the lease to Marston, but this the
defendants one and all vigorously denied. Keysar made overtures
to Marston with the intention of purchasing his share for £100, and
in due time the bargain was consummated. But before the final
transaction, Keysar went to the Burbages and besought them not
to take any action in relation to Blackfriars which might injure his
interests, for rumor was already abroad that the Burbages were
negotiating with Evans the taking over of the lease. Thereupon the
Burbages promised that nothing of the kind should be done without
first seeing to the rights and interests of all who were concerned in
the theatre. (The Burbages, however, denied the whole interview.)
Then, says Keysar, the Burbages took over the lease and set up their
own company, and in the interval up to the present time (February,
1610) had made at least £1500,[67] of which a sixth part should have
been paid Keysar, but was fraudulently withheld. Furthermore, in
the hope of still enjoying his bargain, Keysar had kept the boys at
his own expense the last two years "of purpose to have continewed
playes in the said howse vpon the ceasing of the generall sicknes,"
and had expended thereupon £500.

Thus runs the Bill of Complaint of Robert Keysar. The Answer
of the defendants—Richard and Cuthbert Burbage, John Heminges,
and Henry Condell, acting for the whole company—dated February
12, 1610, begins by professing ignorance of the relations of Marston
to the Revels management, and then goes on to deny absolutely
that there was any interview and arrangement between them and
Keysar regarding the bargain with Marston. They say that after
the playhouse had long lain void and useless, an agreement was

---

[66] Formerly buried in the great mass of the uncalendared proceedings of the
Court of Requests, but withdrawn since its discovery by Dr. Wallace. The suit
was discussed in a fragmentary way in *Century* for Sept., 1910, and was published
in full in *Nebraska Univ. Studies* for 1910. It consists of Bill, Answer, Replication,
and Rejoinder, all in excellent preservation. The Bill is dated February 8, 1610.

[67] A grossly exaggerated estimate. Keysar's Bill is not framed in moderate terms.

concluded with Evans whereby for a consideration in money paid to Evans for his expenditures and pains in the past, the lease reverted to the hands of the Burbages. This was concluded about August 10, 1609; so that the theatre was vacant somewhat over a year (from April, 1608, to August, 1609). The defendants conclude by launching a general denial of all the other assertions contained in Keysar's Bill.

Keysar's Replication reiterates in warmer terms the charges of conspiracy to defraud and harm which had been phrased in the Bill. He charges that in pursuance of this policy the defendants were harboring Evans in secret in the playhouse and keeping him safe from the complainant; and that further to injure him, they "did . . . . privatelye Contract wth the owners of all the private playe howses wthin the cittye of Lond*o*n for one whole yeare, and for the same did satisfye and paye a dead rente to the owners theirof, to their owne great losse and hinderance . . . . and by that meanes did exceedinglie hinder this Compl*ainan*t who all that tyme had a Companye of the moste exparte and skillfull acto^{rs} wthin the Realme of England to the number of eighteane or Twentye p*er*sons all or moste of them trayned vp in that service, in the raigne of the late Queene Elizabeth for Ten yeares togeath^r and aft^{r}wardes p*re*ferred into her ma^{ties} service to be the Children of her Revells by a patent from his moste excellent Matie, but kept and mainteyned at the Cost*es* and Charges of this Compla*i*na*n*te vntill nowe by the malitious practizes of the defend^{tes} as afforesaid, they are enforced to be dispersed and turned awaye to the abundante hurte of the said young men, the disapointinge of her Maties said service, and to the losse and hinderance of this Compla*i*na*n*te at leaste of one Thousand poundes." This is extremely interesting, although it is false in details. Thus the true facts of the buying off of the private playhouses are revealed by the Rejoinder of the defendants to be quite different from Keysar's version; and Keysar's ignorance of the history of his own company is shown by his statement that they had existed for ten years in the reign of Elizabeth. Keysar's Replication ends with a general denial of the defense set up and a reaffirmation of his charges.

By the time of their Rejoinder (June 19) the defendants had evidently made inquiries more deeply into the past history of their theatre. They now deny absolutely that Evans ever made over any part of the premises or any term of the lease to Marston, alleging in confirmation that he was restrained by his lease from transferring the property to another. (We know, however, that in 1602, shortly before the articles of agreement were drawn up with Kirkham and his party on April 20, Evans had made over his interest in the theatre to Alexander Hawkins.) The defendants go on to say that they never had possession of any of the goods and properties of which Keysar claimed the sixth part, but that they understand that they are in the possession of Evans, who has appraised them and is ready to divide them equitably. From this it appears that contrary to Evans's statements,[68] the properties had not been divided among the shareholders when the lease was surrendered to Burbage. As to Keysar's charges of buying out the competition of the private houses, the facts appear to be—for the defendants' account rings truer than Keysar's—that St. Paul's company was the only one so purchased, and that it was done by Philip Rossiter, a partner of Keysar's at Whitefriars, with Keysar's consent. This extraordinary news is unquestionably the kernel of the suit—that is, of all the facts brought out, it is the most singular and valuable. It will be discussed morefully in connection with the St. Paul's troupe. As to Keysar's lamentation about the company of rare talent which he was forced to disband, the defendants have this to say: they "haue heard it credibly reported & doe verely beleeue it to be true that those Acto^rs w*h*ch he the said Comp^lt had & kept allthough none such eyther of qualety or nomber as in & by the said Replication is surmised were disperced & driven each of them to provide for himselfe by reason that the playes ceasinge in the Citty of London either through sicknes or for some other cause he the said Comp^lt was noe longer able to maynteyne them togeither." This would indicate, apparently, that the inhibition of the Revels company was not an absolute one, and that the company could have played againinother quarters; else the facts would have been too well known for any doubt about the cause of their dispersal.

Thus ends this most interesting set of documents. There is no decision recorded, and the case was probably settled outside of court. The prime facts for our history of the Revels Company are that John Marston was a shareholder in Blackfriars while he was the poet of the company, and that in or about 1607 Robert Keysar

---

[68] He had said that the appraisal and division took place about July 26, 1608; Fleay, *Stage*, 221.

entered the directorate as a business investor and did much toward financing the company in its last days. It is noteworthy that Edward Kirkham's name does not appear in this suit; nor have I been able to find him anywhere named in connection with the last years of the company. He did not bring his suit against Painton until 1612, long after the company had died away. I have a strong feeling that Kirkham's relations to the company were never close after his desertion to Paul's, that his place in the company was more or less taken by Keysar, and that he waited until all was quiet and to some extent forgotten and his erstwhile partner Kendall was dead, before stirring up old history with the hope of extracting some tidbits for himself.

9. *Plays and Playwrights.*[69]

The children of the Chapel began their renewed activities at Blackfriars with some revivals of old plays. Among these was Lyly's *Love's Metamorphosis*, originally acted by the Paul's boys about 1588. From the fact that it was registered for publication on November 25, 1600, it was probably one of their earliest ventures. In the same year, or early in 1601, they put on the *Spanish Tragedy*, which they had stolen from the King's men.

Ben Jonson began writing for them soon after their reorganization. He gave them *Cynthia's Revels* (1600), *Poetaster* (1601), and *The Case is Altered*, which was not written for them, but which they produced late in their career, not long before publication of the play in 1609.

Chapman was one of their chief purveyors. He wrote for them *The Gentleman Usher* (1601-2), *May Day* (1601-2), *Sir Giles Goosecap* (1601-2), *Monsieur D'Olive* (1604-5), possibly *Bussy D'Ambois* (1604, but see the discussion of this play in the *Appendix*), probably *The Widow's Tears*, which was acted by the Queen's Revels boys before and after their removal from Blackfriars, and which belongs somewhere between 1605 and 1608, and the disastrous *Conspiracy and Tragedy of Charles, Duke of Biron*, two plays which were on the stage in March or April of 1608.

Marston's contributions were also important. They were: *What You Will* (1601), *The Dutch Courtesan* (1601, probably during the summer), *The Malcontent* (1604), *Sophonisba* (1605-6), and *Parasi-*

---

[69] For discussions of the dating of plays in this section, cf. the *Chronological List* in the *Appendix.*

taster (1605-6:—this play was one of those which was carried over to Paul's when Edward Kirkham deserted to that company in 1606). Marston may also have been the author of the comedy of April, 1608, whose satire of King James so enfuriated that monarch.

Early in 1605 the Blackfriars company played *Eastward Ho*, written by Chapman, Jonson, and Marston.

At least two plays by Middleton were given at Blackfriars. *A Trick to Catch the Old One* was another of Kirkham's transfers to the Paul's company, who acted it at court on New Year's night, 1606. Its production at Blackfriars fell doubtless somewhere in 1605. *Your Five Gallants* belongs late in 1607.

Other performances by various authors were as follows: *Philotas*, by Daniel, was played in the summer or early autumn of 1604; *The Isle of Gulls*, by John Day, in February, 1606; and *The Fleire*, by Edward Sharpham, in 1606. I cannot agree with Mr. Chambers that Day also wrote his *Law Tricks* for this company; it should be assigned to the King's Revels at Whitefriars.

CHAPTER VIII

THE CHILDREN OF PAUL'S: 1600(1599)-1606

1. *Date of Beginning.*

I have had occasion more than once to lament the scarcity of material bearing on the history of the children of Paul's. Nowhere is that scarcity more deplorable than for the period of their revival which began about 1600. It is true that Mr. Wallace has discovered valuable evidence for the end of this period, which tells us something about the manner of their final disappearance from the London stage, but for the earlier years hardly a new fact of importance has been brought to light in the last half century. How baffling, in contrast to the noisy quarreling of the directors at Blackfriars, is the silence of Paul's!

Our first problem shall be to discover if possible when the new company at Paul's opened the doors of their playhouse. That was certainly not later than 1600; was it before? There is most unfortunately no bit of direct evidence to enlighten us. We may judge only from the fact that in 1600 plays began to be printed suddenly and rapidly as acted by the children of Paul's. We know, too, that the young adventurers turned to use in the early days of their activity certain stale and outworn inventions which had done service for their namesakes in the 1580's. Thus, to resort to a much used illustration, Brabant Senior in *Jack Drum*, speaking in approval of these same Paul's boys, qualifies his praise with this stricture:

> But they produce
> Such mustie fopperies of antiquity,
> And do not sute the humorous ages backs
> With clothes in fashion.[1]

Such a revival of old plays is easy to understand; the company was new, perhaps hurriedly prepared for the stage, possibly ill supplied with dramatists. At any rate, we may be sure that these dry bones were not brought back to rattle long upon the stage, for

---

[1] Act V, line 111.

it is evident that the public did not take well to them. Moreover, plays of a modern tone by dramatists of the time soon came into the repertory of this company.

Jack Drum was licensed on September 8, 1600; it was written and played at some time between that date and the presentation of Kemp's morris (February 11-March 11, of the same year), to which allusion is made.[2] References to Whitsuntide and spring point to a performance in spring. We may take this play, whose date of performance can be thus closely determined, as a basis from which to make our survey. Before it appeared, certain other plays had been given which offended because they were sadly antiquated. Now we may be pretty sure that at this time, when a new company was experimenting with new and old plays, few plays were kept long in reserve after their first performances. We know that in general a play was not given once, if it was at all good, but several times while patronage lasted, and was kept in hand as long as there promised to be any profit derivable from it; this happened oftentimes to be many years.[3] But when a new company, or one of lesser importance, produced plays in considerable numbers by dramatists of no great rank, we almost always find them publishing a continuous stream of plays at such regular intervals that we are obliged to conclude that the publication followed hard upon the heels of the performance. So was it in the case of the first Revels company at Whitefriars, so was it in less degree with the Queen's Revels boys at Blackfriars, and so is it very markedly with the company at Paul's. That being the case then, we may suppose that when there is such a continuous and uniform flow of publication, the dates of the *S.R.* entries give the clue in a rough way to the chronology of the plays.

With this in mind, we may now draw up a table of the first half-dozen plays at Paul's with their dates of entry and of publication.

Maid's Metamorphosis	S.R.	July	24, 1600	Pr.	1600
Jack Drum	"	Sept.	8, 1600	"	1601
Dr. Doddypol	"	Oct.	7, 1600	"	1600
Antonio and Mellida	"	Oct.	24, 1601	"	1602
Antonio's Revenge	"	Oct.	24, 1601	"	1602

[2] Fleay, *Drama*, II, 72.

[3] Heywood, in the address "To the Reader" prefixed to *The English Traveler*, said that many of his plays were "still retained in the hands of some Actors, who thinke it against their peculiar profit to haue them come in Print."

Love's Metamorphosis I do not include here because, as I have already shown,[4] I believe it to have been first produced at Paul's in 1588-90 and revived at Blackfriars in 1600.

Of the five plays listed here, two have been branded by modern criticism to be such "musty fopperies" as Brabant Senior inveighed against. Both *The Maid's Metamorphosis* and *Dr. Doddypol* show the earmarks of age. These very two may have been aimed at in *Jack Drum*. They were licensed early and almost certainly came early. That *Doddypol* was licensed a month later than *Jack Drum* is of no significance. The evidence of the *Stationer's Register*, if it can be used at all, is at least only general.

But what of the two Antonio plays? To judge from their licensing, we should put them later than the other three. But then there is that puzzling seeming-reference to these plays in *Jack Drum*:

> . . . . how like you of our moderne wits?
> How like you the new Poet Mellidus?[5]

which certainly looks like a reference to Marston under a nickname derived from the "Mellida" which his two plays had made well known. If the two tragedies came before *Jack Drum*, we can easily explain why they were published later; they were the first of the new plays acquired at Paul's and they were striking in style—two virtues which would commend any play and give it some degree of longevity. So they may have been held in reserve while Marston's less novel comedy of *Jack Drum* soon exhausted its welcome.

At the same time, two considerations give me pause. I am loath, in the first place, to believe that all four plays in the list came before *Jack Drum*, which we have placed in late spring of 1600. That would throw the earliest plays back into 1599, and there are obvious objections to that. The Marston plays were certainly not the earliest, because the progress of a new company is never from the new and popular back to the old and outmoded. *Antonio's Revenge*, moreover, was given in winter, as the prologue tells us. Now if the "musty fopperies of antiquity" were played even late in 1599, and with no response of popular approval, we wonder why they were not licensed until so much later, why they were held in reserve so unnecessarily long. Furthermore, we gather from *Jack Drum* that the general repertory of the company had been of the same anti-

---

[4] Cf. p. 140.
[5] Act V, line 37.

quated pattern. Yet would Marston have said this if either of his
two tragic plays had recently occupied the stage at Paul's? It seems
hardly a pertinent criticism.

With so many equally undecisive reasons pulling in the opposite
direction, I confess myself much puzzled as to what to think. The
"Mellidus" passage may not refer to *Antonio and Mellida,* which
may have come after *Jack Drum,* in 1600. Or it may have come
before *Jack Drum* and the *Revenge,* with its allusions to winter, may
have appeared later, in the winter of 1600. Or as Schelling thinks,
both plays may have come to birth in 1599.

It is almost hopeless to settle exactly questions of chronology for
this company. Even disregarding the Antonio plays, it seems likely
that the new company at Paul's found its beginning very close to
1599, if not actually before 1600. It is quite possible that it set up in
the winter of 1599. I have endeavored to find significance in the
fact that in midsummer of 1600 Paul's lost its old master Thomas
Gyles, or at least gained at that time a new one,[6] Edward Pierce,
who was from then on the active supervisor of plays; but I
cannot see how the commencement of dramatic activity at Paul's
can be put later than the very early months of 1600. The *Cheque
Book* is ambiguous in this matter, to be sure. It tells us when Pierce's
successor was sworn, not when Pierce left. But a glance through
the other entries in the book shows us that a man's place was not
left vacant for long, and that the period of vacancy was rarely over
twenty days at the most.

The exit of a music master from Paul's is usually taken to mean
that he has died, and this may be the case with Gyles. Yet it should
be noted that on December 23, 1605, a Thomas Gyles was appointed
music master to the Prince Henry. There is no means of identification afforded by the letters patent,[7] and the name was a common
one; at the same time, it is a little unusual that there should have
been two musicians in London of the same name. The Prince's
instructor became a prominent figure at court where masques and
revels were concerned, and we find him frequently mentioned as
supplying the music for such devices.

[6] *The Old Cheque Book,* ed. Rimbault, p. 5: "1600. Edward Pearce yealded up
his place for the Mastership of the children of Poules, and John Heatherman was
sworne in his place the 15th of August, from Westminster."

[7] The privy signet bill may be found among *Privy Signet Bills, Treas. of Receipt,*
Dec., 3 Jas. I, no. 36.

2. *The Course of Events, 1600-1606.*

The new company at Paul's was not denied the favor of court, for on New Year's day, 1601, they played there,[8] and they may have acted on February 4 a refurbished version of an old play by West-cote (?) under the name of *The Contention between Liberality and Prodigality*.[9] Before the old queen died they appeared once more, on January 1, 1603.[10] It used to be said, before the examination of the *Declared Accounts of the Treasurer of the Chamber* revealed some data hitherto unknown, that the Paul's boys found little favor at court, because they played there so seldom. As a matter of fact, though it is true they did not enjoy anything like the popularity of the major adult companies, or even so much as the Black-friars boys had, yet they played at court with as much regularity as they had any right to expect. They were summoned before the king on Shrove Monday (February 20), 1604[11]—that is, they were well enough regarded to take part in the festivities organized in the first year of the new king.

For these last two performances Edward Pierce was payee, but when next the boys played at court—on two occasions between January 1 and March 31, 1606—they were directed by the erstwhile staunch prop of the Blackfriars company, Edward Kirkham.[12] The probable causes of this man's desertion to the camp of the enemy have been dealt with in our discussion of the Chapel company; he was doubtless influenced partly by personal grudge against the partners with whom he could never work in harmony and partly by the embarrassments following the *Eastward Ho* adventure. It is

---

[8] *Acts of the Privy Council*, ed. Dasent, June 24, 1601.

[9] Cf. Chap. V.

[10] *Declared Accounts*, Pipe Roll 543, fol. 97b: "To Edward Peirs m^r of the Children of Paules uppon the counsells warraunte dated at the courte at Grenew^{ch} the last day of may 1603 for presentinge before the late Quenes ma^{tie} one play uppon Newyearsday at night laste paste x^{li}."

[11] *Same*, fol. 117: "To Edward Pearce m^r of the children of Powles upon the councells warraunte dated at the courte at Whitehall xvij^{mo} die Aprilis 1604 for presenting a playe or enterlude before his ma^{tie} uppon Shrovemonday last at nighte the some of twenty nobles and by way of his ma^{ts} reward fyve marks in all x^{li}."

[12] *Declared Accounts*, Pipe Roll 543, fol. 163b: "To Edward Kirkham one of the M^{rs} of the children of Pawles upon the councells warr^t dated at the courte at whitehall ultimo die Martij 1606 for bringing the said children and presenting by them two plays or enterludes before the Prince his grace and the Duke of Yorke upon nights mentioned in a Schedule annexed unto the said warraunt after the rate of fyve marks for ech play and by waye of his ma^{ts} reward fyve nobles in all the some of xv^{li} xiij^s iiij^d."

generally supposed that he took over with him some of the plays from the Blackfriars repertory, and that among them were Chapman's *Bussy D'Ambois* (licensed June 3, 1607), the only play of Chapman at this period not assigned by its title page to the Queen's Revels, Marston's *Parasitaster* (licensed March 12, 1606), and Middleton's *Trick to Catch the Old One* (licensed October 7, 1607)— these last two being printed as played at both theatres.

It may be that the two plays given under Kirkham's direction at court in the early part of 1606 were Middleton's *Trick to Catch the Old One* and *Phoenix*. The *Phoenix* was published in 1607 as played by the children of Paul's before the king, and the *Trick* was printed in 1608 as "presented before his Majesty on New Year's night last." The identification is Fleay's,[13] and is characteristically rash. He was acting on the conviction that the two performances in 1606 under Kirkham were the only ones by this company at court before the company ceased to act. That in itself is a questionable conclusion. The Paul's boys played once in 1606 before the king without any record getting into the *Declared Accounts*, and they may have done so again. The appositeness of printing a play in 1608 as acted on the last New Year's day when New Year's of 1606 was meant, is hard to see. That the king was present at the two performances of Kirkham is shown by his bestowing a gratuity of five nobles, the regular fee of a performance before the king himself. Yet the evidence for designating the *Phoenix* and the *Trick* as these plays is rather thin.

On Wednesday, July 30, 1606, the boys of Paul's were favored with a singular mark of esteem in being chosen to play before the visiting King of Denmark and James.[14] Their play was called *Abuses*; it has not survived to us, nor is there any record of the performance in the *Declared Accounts*. This shows that the lists furnished by the *Declared Accounts* are not accurately complete. Not since John Rightwise and the boys of Colet's school played in 1527 a Latin interlude upon the heretic Luther before the king and the French ambassadors, had a company of boys been so honored. That the children in this case were not from the grammar school is made unmistakably clear by their being called "the Youthes of

---

[13] *Drama*, under the plays in question.

[14] Cf. Nichols, *Progresses of King James I*, IV, 1074. The original account is contained in "The King of Denmarkes welcome: Containing his arivall, abode, and entertainment both in the Citie and other places . . . . London . . . . 1606."

Paules, commonlye cald the Children of Paules." No other body o
children than the actors was "commonly" called by that title.

We should like greatly to know what relations existed between
the Paul's company and the other children's companies at Blackfriars and Whitefriars. The negotiations which brought Paul's to
an end are indeed known to us, but we should like to extend our
knowledge back into the earlier years of the company. Yet search
in that direction proves vain. I have been able to find only one
suggestive reference to Edward Pierce in all the documents that
have come under my inspecton, and that is no more than suggestive.
I found that on December 2, 1604, one Edward Peerce assaulted
one Thomas Woodforde, and in Easter term, 1606, was sued in
King's Bench and fined £13-6-8.[15] That is all, and yet when we
remember that a Thomas Woodford was deeply engaged in the
King's Revels company at Whitefriars and was later interested in
the *Red Bull* playhouse, we begin strongly to suspect that he was
the same man who was thrashed by Pierce, and that the trouble
was over something theatrical.

We have no record of any performance by the children of Paul's
after July 30, 1606, and this circumstance, taken in connection with
the fact that their plays began to be licensed and published in great
numbers in the two following years, has given rise very naturally to
the hypothesis that the company ceased to act in or about 1607. A
list of their plays since *Jack Drum*, arranged in order of licensing,
will enable us to appreciate the force of this argument.

Play	Author	Licensing Date
Satiromastix	Dekker	Nov. 11, 1601
Blurt, Master Constable	Middleton	June 7, 1602
Westward Ho	Dekker & Webster	March 2, 1605
Parasitaster	Marston	March 12, 1606
Phoenix	Middleton	May 9, 1607
Michaelmas Term	Middleton	May 15, 1607
The Woman Hater	Beaumont & Fletcher	May 20, 1607
Bussy D'Ambois	Chapman	June 3, 1607
Northward Ho	Dekker and Webster	Aug. 6, 1607
Puritan	Middleton(?)	Aug. 6, 1607
Trick to Catch the Old One	Middleton	Oct. 7, 1607
A Mad World, My Masters	Middleton	Oct. 4, 1608

[15] *Coram Rege*, Easter, 4 Jas. I, fol. 536. The informative part of the document
runs thus: "London. Thomas Woodforde gen*erosus* querit*ur* de Edwardo Peerce

To these should probably be added Middleton's *The Family of Love*, which, though acted by the King's Revels at Whitefriars, seems to have been first produced in 1605, when Middleton was writing for Paul's.[16] The theatre for which it was written was round, and that agrees with Paul's.

Here it is seen that out of twelve plays licensed since 1600, seven were entered in 1607 and one in 1608. It certainly looks significant, and when we consider that no performance by the Paul's boys is known to be mentioned in any document after 1606, and no play was published by them after 1608, the conclusion becomes almost irresistible that the company ceased playing at the end of 1606 or the beginning of 1607. On this basis Fleay constructed his theory that the King's Revels company at Whitefriars was a continuation of Paul's. This we shall see to be erroneous. And now the Keysar-Burbage suit of 1610[17] comes into play, confirming our deduction that Paul's was closed in 1606-7, and giving us a most interesting glimpse of the maneuvrings that went on behind the scenes of the Jacobean stage.

The bulk of our evidence comes from the defendants' Rejoinder; but before taking that up we must note one or two other points. In the first place, the defendants (Richard and Cuthbert Burbage, John Heminges, and Henry Condell) in their Answer say that the Blackfriars theatre was given over by Henry Evans to the Burbages on or about August 10, 1609.[18] Then we must note that the long explanation in the Rejoinder which gives us our valuable information was brought forth by this charge made in Keysar's Replication:

...then allsoe did they (i.e. the defendants) in furth[r] Testimonye of their mallice privatelye Contract wth the owners of all the private playe howses

---

in Custod*ia* Marr*escalli* Mare*scalsie* dom*i*ni Regis coram ipso Rege existen*te* de eo qu*od* ip*se* secundo die Decembris Anno Regni d*omi*ni Jacobi nunc Regis Angl*ie* secundo vi & armis &c in ip*sum* Thomam Woodforde apud london .... in pace dei & d*i*cti d*omi*ni Regis adtunc & ib*idem* existen*tem* i nsult*um* fecit Et ip*sum* Thomam adtunc & ib*idem* verb*er*auit vuln*er*auit & maletratauit Ita qu*od* de vita eius desp*er*abat*ur* Et alia enormia ei intulit contra pacem d*i*cti d*omi*ni Regis nunc ad dampn*um* ip*s*ius Thome Centum librar*um*," etc.

Damages and costs awarded plaintiff of £13-6-8.

[16] Cf. p. 234.

[17] Printed in full by C. W. Wallace in *Nebraska Univ. Studies*, 1910, pp. 340 ff.

[18] Wallace, *op. cit.*, p. 347: " . . . . sithens the said surrender made by the said Evans to the said Richard Burbage as aforesaid which was about the tenth of August last past." The Answer is dated February 12, 1610.

wthin the cittye of London for one whole yeare, and for the same did satisfye and paye a dead rente to the owners theirof, to their owne great losse
and hinderance, intending nothinge theirby but the advancem^t of their
exceadinge mallice to this Complainante and his vtter overthrowe... and
by that meanes did exceedinglie hinder this Complainant.

To this definite charge the defendants made such answer in their
Rejoinder as by its very precision in details carries conviction.

And these def^{tes} further say & each of them for & by himself sayth
vnder favo^r of this ho: Co^{rt} that they much marvaile that the said Comp^{lt}
should desire soe apparently to sett forth his folly on Recorde as to charge
these def^{tes} in & by his said Replication with malice towardes him in Con-
tractinge priuately wth the owners of all the private playehouses within the
City of London for one whole yeare & for the same to paye a dead rent
to the owners thereof to these def^{tes} owne great losse & hinderance But to
the intente only thereby to aduance theire malice & to ouerthrowe the said
Comp^{lt} onely soe farre forth as by anie possibility laie in theire power:
When as the said Comp^{lt} might in truth thereby if the said suggestion were
true be perfectly perswaded & assured that these def^{tes} should be not onely
malicious as he the said Comp^{lt} most iniuriously suggesteth but allso
malicious fooles if to doe the Comp^{lt} a little hurt if they might which allsoe
must needes be vncerteyne to them they the said def^{tes} should doe themselues a farre greater & more certeine losse And when as allsoe the Con-
tracte made with the owners of the said private playe howses if any such
were hath allwaies bine soe farre from the ouerthrowe hindrance or losse of
the said Comp^{lt} that the same hath allwaies bine & yet is aswell to & for
the vse benefytte & profitte of the said Comp^{lt} himselfe & his partners
according to the said Comp^{ltes} parte & rate as to the benefyttes of these
defend^{tes} or any of them accordinge to their seuerall partes & rates as these
def^{tes} haue credibly heard & doe verely beleeue ffor these def^{tes} saye & each
of them for & by himselfe sayth that there beinge as these def^{tes} verely
thinke but onely three private playe howses in the City of London thone
of wch beinge in the Blacke fryars & in the handes of these def^{tes} or of theire
assignes One other beinge in the white ffryers in the handes or occupacion of
the said Comp^{lt} himselfe his partners or assignes & the third neere S^t
Pawles Church then beinge in the handes of one Mr Pierce But then vnvsed
for a playe howse One Mr Roseter a partner of the said Comp^{lts} delt for
& Compounded wth the said Mr Pierce to the onelye benefytt of him the
said Roseter the now Comp^{lt} the rest of theire partners & Company
(& without the preuetie knowledge or Consent of these def^{tes} or any of them
& that thereby they the said Comp^{lt} & the said Roseter & their partners
& company might aduance theire gaines & profitt to be had & made in theire
said howse in the white ffryers That there might be a Cessation of playeinge

& playes to be acted in the said howse neere St Paules Church aforesaid
for wch the said Roceter Compounded with the said Pierce to giue him the
said Pierce twenty pound*es* p*er* Ann*um* But these def^{tes} afterward*es*
Cominge to playe at their said howse in the Blacke ffryers And the said
Roceter p*er*ceyvinge that the benefytt of the said Cessation of playes at
Powles did or was likely to turne aswell to the benefytt of these def^{tes} and
theire Companie as to the benefytt of the said Comp^{lt} the said Roceter &
the rest of their Companie & yett that the whole matter of Charge for
payment of the said twenty pound*es* p*er* Ann*um* was of necessety to lye
onely on the said Comp^{lt} the said Roceter & the rest of theire Companie he
the said Roceter came vnto these def^{tes} or some of them & intreated them
that for the ease & benefytt of the said Comp^{lt} & his Company & p*art*ners
who finde themselues thereby ou*er*charged & aggreeued they the said
def^{tes} haueinge as he alleadged as great benefytt as themselues & yett were
bound to nothinge would neuertheles be content to beare & paye one
halfe of the Charge of the said rent of twenty pound*es* p*er* Ann*um* wherevnto these def^{tes} in all loue & aswell for the benefytt of the said Comp^{lt}
accordinge to his p*ar*te as of any other p*er*son or p*er*sons willingly did yeeld
& accordingly haue payed th*er*e p*ar*te of the said rent wherein alsoe the
mallice & ingratitude of the said Comp^{lt} is most p*er*spicuous & plaine whoe
Canne be Contented to receaue dayly benefytt not onely by the Cessation
of the playes in the said howse neere Powles But allsoe out of these def^{tes}
purses in ready money & yet cannot bridle his envye toward these def^{tes}.

Such is the history of the affair as the Burbages tell it, and I
repeat that it has about it the ring of truth. The date of these
negotiations can be determined pretty definitely. They were carried
on while Keysar and Rossiter were directing, or preparing to direct,
the Queen's Revels company at Whitefriars[19]—that is, after January 4, 1609, when Keysar brought the boys of Blackfriars to court
—and before August 10, 1609, when the Burbages finally took over
Blackfriars, for we are told that the defendants came to play at
Blackfriars after the bargain with Pierce was carried through. So
the date is fixed within the first half of 1609.

At that time, the theatre at Paul's was still dark. Consequently,
when the defendants speak of buying the "cessation" of plays there,
they are not quite accurate. What they mean is that Keysar paid
Pierce not to reopen his playhouse, as he may have been on the
point of doing. What the reason was for closing it in 1606-7 we
still do not know—perhaps never shall. But what is plain is that

---

[19] Cf. Chap. X.

it was never again regularly reopened, by Pierce or any one else. And so the children of Paul's pass obscurely into silence.

3. The Percy Plays.

In connection with the Paul's boys a word should be spoken of the Percy plays, which have been the subject of considerable argument.[20] They need not detain us long, for their bearing on the history of Paul's is of the slightest.

Only two of the five plays written by William Percy and preserved in a unique manuscript formerly owned by the Duke of Devonshire have been reprinted; these are *The Cuck-queans and Cuckolds Errants* (dated 1601) and *The Fairy Pastoral* (1603).[21] From the stage directions, which are unusually minute, we learn that the plays were written with a view to production at court,[22] and that the author contemplated production by the Paul's boys as well as by the unknown company (presumably adult) for which he wrote. That the plays actually came on the boards at Paul's is not sufficiently proved by the fact that various alterations are provided for in case they are produced at Paul's. At any rate, there is no evidence that these plays were written especially for the boys.

The plays have no history that we can trace. Hence some have doubted whether they were ever produced at all, regarding them as literary exercises of a gentleman of leisure. But there can be no doubt, I think, that they came to production, for all the stage directions are in the past tense, evidently referring to a particular performance; and this evident reference to a single occasion leads me to suppose that there may have been only *one* performance. The following is a typical example of the stage directions: "Here they shutt both (i.e. Orion and Hypsiphyle) into the Canopie Fane or Trophey to gether with the banquet" (*Fairy Pastoral*, V.5). But notably in the last direction of the *Pastoral* is the particularity of the reference evident: "There was no shouing here of the knaue forward, But they went on before and he followed after." All the

---

[20] Examples of such discussions are: V. E. Albright, "Two of Percy's Plays as Proof of the Elizabethan Stage," in *Mod. Phil.*, Vol. 11, Oct. 1913, p. 237; and G. F. Reynolds, "Wm. Percy and his Plays," in *Mod. Phil.*, Vol. 12, Oct. 1914, p. 109.

[21] *The Cuck-Queanes and Cuckolds Errants, and The Faery Pastorall*, by W(illiam) P(ercy), ed. for the Roxburgh Club by Joseph Haslewood; London, for the Shakespeare Press, 1824.

[22] The *Fairy Pastoral* begins with "The Prologue for the Court."

directions sound more like notes taken upon some production than general directions for all performances.

The obscurity which surrounds these plays takes from them practically all the illustrative value they might have. We cannot say, for instance, that they are typical of the plays at Paul's at any time in the history of that playhouse. The alterations suggested in case of performance there offer little information. Sometimes they are in the nature of a simplification, of action, or of properties. In the *Pastoral* one scene is made over for Paul's, the alternative reading being added in an appendix. Here the changes seem to be of two kinds: (1) the coarseness of the language is softened; and (2) words referring to people on the stage are changed from plural to singular. The meaning of the latter change seems to be that the Paul's company was smaller than the ordinary adult company.

The plays are more naive in construction and dialogue than the average play of their time, and they smack strongly of reading in the classics. A new scene is marked at each new grouping of the characters; there is little coming and going, the dialogue mainly passing among successive groups, each of which clears the stage before the next comes on; there is a great deal of Latin. Other features of interest to the student of the stage are the amount of music called for, songs within the acts and orchestral interludes between them (the latter thus marked in the text: "Here they knockt vp the Consort"); and the stage setting. The multiple stage of classic comedy and earlier Elizabethan drama was used; thus the stage of the *Cuck-Queans* represented Maldon, Harwich, and Colchester. And sign-boards were freely used. The equipment of the *Fairy Pastoral* is thus described: "Highest, aloft, and on the Top of the Musick Tree the Title The Faery Pastorall, Beneath him pind on Post of the Tree The Scene Eluida Forrest. Lowest of all ouer the Canopie NAPAIT-BODAION or Faery Chappell. A kiln of Brick. A Fowen Cott. A Hollowe Oake with vice of wood to shutt to. A Lowe well with Roape and Pullye. A Fourme of Turues. A greene Bank being Pillowe to the Hed but. Lastly a Hole to creepe in and out. Now if so be that the Properties of any These, that be outward, will not Serue the turne by reason of concurse of the People on the Stage, Then you may omitt the Sayd Properties which be outward and supplye their Places with the Nuncupations onely in Text Letters, Thus for some."

The author of these plays seems to have been William Percy, third son of Henry Percy, eighth earl of Northumberland, who was born about 1575. Mr. Chambers hazards the theory[23] that he wrote his plays for Paul's before 1590, and had them produced there. But that is hardly tenable. In the first place, he would have been too young, and in the second place the plays were not *written* for children but were *revised* for them. I think it more likely that these are school plays, possibly done at Oxford, where Percy resided in Gloucester Hall. Their academic sound lends weight to that suggestion, as well as the evidence that up to the time of revision they had had only one performance. Certainly nothing more amateurish has come down to us from the days of Elizabeth.

[23] *Eliz. Stage*, III, 464.

CHAPTER IX[1]

THE KING'S REVELS AT WHITEFRIARS

1. *The Theatre*.

Very little is known either about the theatre in Whitefriars or the companies which played there. Gradually evidences are leaking out respecting the players, but we are still in deep ignorance regarding the theatre. Of all places in London which are of interest to the student of drama and the antiquarian, the precinct of Whitefriars has been investigated and written on as little as any. Few of the many surveys and topographical histories of London even mention the place, and when they do it is hardly more than to repeat the meager facts in Stow and Maitland.

We do know that the theatre was a part of the dissolved monastery of Whitefriars, precisely in similar case to the Blackfriars theatre. Wheatley and Cunningham,[2] who alone of historians of their kind have something to say of the playhouse, submit this definite information:

> The Whitefriars Theatre was the old hall or refectory belonging to the dissolved Monastery of Whitefriars, and stood without the garden wall of Salisbury or *Dorset House*, the old inn or hostel of the Bishops of Salisbury.

This is almost a verbatim repetition of what Cunningham had said in an article on the three theatres of the precinct.[3] He is a trifle more definite; the playhouse "stood *within* the precinct of the monastery, and *without* the garden-wall of Salisbury House." We learn from a footnote that the source of this information is a very

---

[1] The substance of this chapter has been published under the title "The Children of the King's Revels at Whitefriars" in *Journ. of Eng. and Germ. Philol.*, April, 1922, XXI, 318. Unfortunately Mr. Chambers had not seen it when he wrote his chapter on Whitefriars for his *Elizabethan Stage*. Hence he has retained several of the old errors. The chapter in J. Q. Adams's *Shakespearean Playhouses* is good except that it does not have the advantage of the documents here published.

[2] *London Past and Present*, 1891, III, 504-5.

[3] "The Whitefriars Theatre, the Salisbury Court Theatre, and the Duke's Theatre in Dorset Gardens," in *Transactions of the Shakespeare Society*, IV, 89. There is no reason to doubt Cunningham's honesty in this article; he is only to be censured for having submitted to Collier's misguidance so unquestioningly.

interesting *Survey of the Precinct of Whitefriars, made in March, 1616* which tells us that the theatre was situated near the Bishop's House, was formerly the refectory of the monastery, was in a very dilapidated state, *and had been used as a theatre for more than thirty years past by the children of her Majesty!* This amazing declaration gives the hoax away. When we discover that this remarkable *Survey* has been found by Collier and is to be read only in extracts published in Collier's *New Facts regarding Shakespeare,* we realize that here is another link in the chain of lies which one of the best historians of the English stage wove to fetter his own genius. The *Survey,* with its affecting references to the "old tottered curten" and the "few worne out properties and peeces of Arras," is a forgery.

With the authenticity of the Survey destroyed, away goes our faith in Wheatley and Cunningham, and in their interestingly definite location of the theatre. All that we have left is the meager fact, sole contribution of what documents we possess bearing on the theatre, that the theatre was part of the dissolved monastery of Whitefriars, and consequently lay adjacent to the precinct of Blackfriars, just outside the city limits.

2. *The King's Revels Company; a Chapter of Lawsuits.*

When we come to the players, we are on much firmer ground. It is known that a company of children of the Revels acted there in the period 1607-9, and that they were superseded in or before 1610 by the second company to bear the title of "Children of the Queen's Revels," incorporated in 1610 under the well known patent to Rossiter and others. Various speculations have arisen in regard to this first company. Fleay's surmise[4] that they were the children of Paul's under another name has been disproved by documents that have come to light since his day. It is generally agreed, and upon seemingly good grounds, that the company known from the title pages of plays to have been called the "Children of the King's Revels" were these boys at Whitefriars.

The bulk of our knowledge of this first company comes from a Chancery suit of great interest and value—the suit *George Andrews v. Martin Slatier,* of 1609, discovered by Mr. Greenstreet and published in the *Transactions* of the New Shakespeare Society for 1887-92, Part 3. The facts brought out are so numerous and important, and the document is so little known to the general public, that a

---

[4] *Stage,* 202.

careful and fairly full summary of the various parts of the suit is necessary.

The Bill[5] of George Andrews (spelled "Androwes") begins by declaring that about February of 1608, one Lording Barry was possessed of the moyety of "a messuage or mansion howse, parcell of the late dissolved monastery called the Whitefriars, in ffleete streete," under a lease made from Robert, Lord Buckhurst, to Michael Drayton and Thomas Woodford,[6] for the term of six years, eight months, and twenty days, and at the yearly rent of fifty pounds. The moyety of the lease, together with a half part of the properties and appurtenances used there by the Children of the Revels, was, according to Barry's story, lawfully settled on him by Woodford. Barry, then being desirous to associate other men with him in the expenses and profits of his venture, and aided by Martin Slatier, citizen and ironmonger of London, and others of his confederates, persuaded Andrews to take a sixth part of the premises and properties in exchange for £70. According to Barry's sugared estimate, the properties were worth £400, and the revenue which Andrews might expect would be £100 a year clear. But after the bargain was struck, the poor dupe discovered that the valuable properties, which had been the chief cause of his action, were not worth above £5! Furthermore, charges in building, in maintaining the boys, and in other incidental matters, whereof he paid most or all (though why, we are not informed), fell so heavily on him that his losses on that account amounted to £300. Then before his sixth part was assigned him, and consequently before any remuneration had come in, the lease became forfeited by nonpayment of rent. (But just when this occurred he does not tell us.) Then he goes on to quote in full a set of articles of agreement (which doubtless were not unlike the similar articles drawn up at Blackfriars in 1602) signed on March 10, 1608, between Martin Slatier of the one party and Andrews, Lording Barry, Michael Drayton, William Trevell, William Coke, Edward Sibthorpe, and John Mason of the other party. These articles are so interesting in themselves, and so sug-

---

[5] Dated February 9, 1609.

[6] The dating is obscure here. Andrews said that Barry pretended about February, 1608, that he was possessed of the messuage "by and vnder a lease made thereof, *aboute Marche then next followinge*" from Buckhurst to Drayton and Woodford. This is puzzling, and I do not understand it, for surely the lease must have antedated the assignment of the half to Barry.

gestive of the Blackfriars set, that I shall repeat them here in full. They give an excellent idea of the plan upon which an Elizabethan playhouse, with its coterie of shareholders, worked.

Articles of agreement indented made the tenth daye of Marche, Anno Domini 1607 (1608), and in the ffiveth yeare of the raigne of our soveraigne lord Kinge James of England, ffrance and Ireland, Defendour of the faithe &c, and of Scotland the one & fortieth, Betweene Martyne Slatyar, cittizen and ironmonger, of thone partie, And Lordinge Barry, George Androwes, Michaell Drayton, Willyam Trevell, Willyam Cooke, Edward Sibthorpe, and John Mason, of the cittie of London, gentlemen, on thother partie, viz;

Imprimis it is consented, concluded, and fully agreed by and betweene the said parties, That duringe all the tearme of yeares in the lease of the plaie howse in the White ffriers, wch they hold of and from Robert, lord Buckhurst, he the said Martyn Slatyer shall have, receave, take and enioye the sixt parte, in six partes to be devided, and all such profitt, benefitt, gettings and commoditie as shall at any tyme arrise, come and growe by reason of any playes, showes, interludes, musique, or such like exercises to be vsed and performed aswell in the said playehouse as else-where, All manner of charges therevnto belonginge beinge firste defrayed and deducted.

Item it is also covenaunted, graunted, concluded and fully agreed by and betweene all the said parties That he the said Martyn Slatyar, and all his familye, shall have their dwellinge and lodgeinge in the said howse wth free ingresse, agresse, and regresse, in, to and from the same, or any parte thereof, duringe the continewance of the said lease; The roomes of w^eth howse are thirteene in number, three belowe and tenne above, that is to saie, the greate hall, the kitchin by the yard, and a celler, wth all the roomes from the east ende of the howse to the Master of the revells office, as the same are now severed and devided.

Item it is further convenaunted, graunted, concluded and fully agreed betweene all the said parties, That if any gaine or profitt canne or maye be made in the said howse either by wine, beere, ale, tobacco, wood, coales, or any such comoditie, That then he the said Martyn Slatyar, and his assignes, and none other, shall have the benefitt thereof groweinge or arrisinge duringe the continewance of the said lease.

Item it is likewise covenaunted, graunted, concluded and agreed by and betweene the said parties, That when their pattent for playinge shallbe renewed, the said Martyn Slatyar his name, wth the said Michaell Drayton shalbe ioyned therein, in respecte that if any restrainte of their playinge shall happen by reason of the plague or other wise, It shalbe for more creditt of the whole Company that the said Martyn shall travell wth the Children, and acquainte the Magistrates wth their business.

Item it is also covenaunted, graunted, concluded, and fully agreed betweene all the said parties, That if, at any tyme hereafter, any apparrell, bookes, or any other goods or commodities shalbe conveyed or taken awaye by any of the said parties wthout the consent and allowance of the said residue of his fellow shares, and the same exceedinge the value of twoe shillinges, That then he or they so offendinge shall forfeite and loose all such benefitt, profitt and commoditie as otherwise should arrise and and growe vnto him or them by their shares, besides the losse of their places and all other interest wch they may clayme amongest vs.

Item it is further covenaunted, graunted, concluded, and fully agreed by and betweene all the said parties to theis presentes, That duringe the said lease the whole chardges of the howse, the gatherers, the wages, the Childrens bourd, musique, booke keeper, tyreman, tyrewoman, lights, the Maister of the revells' Duties, and all other things needefull and necessary, whatsoever one weekes charge cometh vnto, The sixt parte of the same to be taken vpp every night; as if one weekes charge amounteth vnto tenne pounds, then to take vpp every night thirtie three shillings and fower pence, by wch meanes they shalbe still out of debte.

Item it is likewise covenaunted, graunted, concluded and fully agreed by and betweene the said parties, That whereas by the generall consent of all the whole Company all the Children are bound to the said Martyn Slatyar for the tearme of three yeares, he the said Martyn Slatyar doth by theis presentes binde himselfe to the residue of the Company in the somme of fortie pounds sterlinge, That he shall not wronge or iniure the residue of the said Companye in the partinge wth, or puttinge awaye any one or more of the said younge men or ladds to any person or persons, or otherwise, wthout the speciall consent and full agreement of the residue of his fellow sharers, Excepte the tearme of his or their apprenticeshipp to be fully expired.

Item it is also covenaunted, graunted, concluded and fully agreed betweene the said parties, That all such apparrell as is abroad shalbe imediatly brought in, And that noe man of the said Company shall at any tyme hereafter put into print, or cause to be put in print, any manner of playe booke now in vse, or that hereafter shalbe sould vnto them, vpon the penaltie and forfeiture of ffortie pounds sterlinge, or the losse of his place and share of all things amongest them, Except the booke of Torrismount, and that playe not to be printed by any before twelve monthes be fully expired.[7]

[7] It is of at least passing interest here to note that this same Martin Slatier was sued in King's Bench in 1598 by another actor, Thomas Downton, for the value of a play book lost by him and found and kept by Slatier. Downton valued the book at £13-6-8; it was lost on Dec. 1, 1597, found on Dec. 10, and on March 1 staged by Slatier's company (for so I take the words "in vsum & Commodum suum proprium disposuit & convertit") to the damage of Downton of £30. Damages and costs of eleven guineas were awarded the plaintiff. The digest of the suit will be found in *Placita Coram Rege*, roll 1351; Trinity Term, a° 40 Eliz., part 2, m. 830 b.

Item it is finally convenaunted, graunted, concluded and fully agreed by and betweene all the same parties, That if at any tyme hereafter the same Company shalbe restrayned from playenge in the said howse by reason of the plague, or otherwise, and that thereby they shalbe inforced to travell into the Countrye for the vpholdinge of their Company, That then the said Martyn Slatyar duringe the tyme of such his travell shall have an allowance of one full share and a half.

Item all the said parties before mencioned, in testimony hereof, have interchaungeably sett their hands and seales to theis presentes the daye and yeare first above written.

These articles of agreement set forth in such detail and so full of interest for us, are of minor importance in the suit. They serve but to introduce the prime factor, which was a bond of £200 drawn up March 10, 1608, by which the parties in the agreement bound themselves to Slatier not to break any of the covenants therein set forth. This bond had become forfeit, according to Slatier, through the violation of some of the articles by some of the sharers, and so he had instituted suit in the King's Bench to recover his £200. But Andrews declares, in the first place, that the infractions had not in any case been caused by him, that on the contrary he had strictly observed all the agreements, and in the second place that he had been assured by Slatier and the scrivener who drew up the bond that he could not be held responsible for the misdeeds of the other sharers, but only for his own. The present suit is brought to check Slatier's suit in common law.

In his Answer[8] Slatier admits Barry's half interest in the playhouse, but denies that he ever solicited Andrews to buy a sixth part, alleging that the bargain was made before he knew either Andrews or Barry. He professes ignorance of the appraisals of the goods which Andrews says had deluded him, again for the reason that he had not at that time joined the company or seen the properties. He scoffs at Andrews's complaints about his excessive building expenses, saying that the work was undertaken long after the purchase of the share, and hence could not have been done without Andrews's consent or at a greater expenditure on his part than fell to the rest. He admits the losses sustained by Andrews at the failure of the enterprise, but declares that his own losses were greater, and that the calamity was in no way his fault. He admits the drawing up of the articles of agreement and the £200 bond, and marvels that the

[8] Dated Feb. 17, 1609.

plaintiff should offer "soe fryvolous, false and weake a plea for his reliefe as ignorantiae legis." He says that even if he did assure Andrews that it was in no way his intention to hold him responsible for any acts but his own, yet that agreement is beside the point, because the plaintiff has shielded himself against such a possibility by a deed made with the defendant; so that if it is true that Andrews has not broken any of the articles of agreement, he is protected by his deed. He accuses Andrews of conspiring with the others "ryotouslie, willfullie, violentlie & vnlawfully" to keep him and his family out of his rooms and deprive him of his livelihood, "therebie leavinge this defend^t and his whole famelie, beinge tenne in nomber, to the worlde, to seeke for bread." A hint of some disputes lying behind these suits is given in the closing lines of the Answer, which are for the most part, as is usual, given up to a general denial of the assertions of the plaintiff. "And further saith, that this defend^t hath, or should have a sufficient estate to satisfie any thinge the compl^t could justlie demaunde of him this defend^t, in case the saide compl^t, and others, did not willfully, vnlawfullie, & vnconscionablie witholde the same from this defendant." This looks as though the action of the sharers, whatever it was, in shutting Slatier out of his rooms had come as a consequence of Slatier's failing to satisfy some demands which they had made upon him.

Thus end the only two pleas on record of this highly important suit. The decision is not preserved, or was not rendered,—at any rate was not found by Mr. Greenstreet. We need not concern ourselves with the legal merits of the arguments put forward by either party, or speculate on the probable moral characters of the two men. We do know, from the suit over the play book which I have referred to in a recent note, that Slatier was a tricky man, found guilty in times past for misappropriating the property of another, and he is therefore to be suspected in the present case. It looks, moreover, as though the ultimate cause of the trouble lay at his door, because of his failure to satisfy certain demands on the part of the sharers. They retaliated by locking him out of his house, and then he brought suit against them in King's Bench.

Further evidence, at the same time corroborative and contradictory, in the history of this enterprise is offered by a document which has strangely enough remained unpublished and unnoticed, though it is referred to by Cunningham in the same article in which he cites the *Survey of Whitefriars*. This is what he says: "The theatre in the Whitefriars was not, I believe, rebuilt, though the case of Trevill v. Woodford, in the Court of Requests, informs us that plays were performed at the Whitefriars Theatre as late as 1621; Sir Anthony Ashley, the then landlord of the house, entering the Theatre in that year, and turning the players out of doors, on pretence that half a year's rent was yet unpaid him." Cunningham is grossly and inexcusably wrong in his date, but the rest of his facts are accurate. For some reason he did not print the document, contenting himself with this short résumé and a note referring the reader to "Trevill v. Woodford, in Court of Requests, 18 Charles I." No one since his time has had the interest to look up the suit and publish it. I found the document in the *Decrees and Orders* books;[9] it turned out to be a statement of the judgment of the Court preceded, fortunately, by a long recapitulation of the case. The original pleas of the case, could they be found, would doubtless contribute many more details; but in the present state of the Court of Requests *Bills and Answers* it is impossible to find the records of a suit without searching for weeks or months through a vast, uncalendared chaos of documents. It was an undertaking from which the exigencies of time debarred me; I can hope only that an investigator more gifted with leisure will some day hunt out the papers of this suit, along with the many others of equal or greater interest which lie there.

The major part of the document is taken up with aspects of the case which have no interest whatever for us; therefore I shall quote here only so much as bears on the history of the Whitefriars theatre. It will be seen that Andrews was not the only man to suffer from the ill-fated venture in Whitefriars, but that Trevill endured more persecution than he. Indeed, the enterprise seems to have given birth to an enormous amount of litigation, as scraps and notices of suits in my possession show. It was an ill-advised and ill-managed affair from the outset. The reader will notice too that in this document Sir Anthony Ashley is named as the landlord of the playhouse, instead of Lord Buckhurst; but except in this point, the present document agrees with the Andrews-Slatier suit.

It is sufficient for our present purpose to know that in 1608-9 William Trevill was sued by Thomas Woodford for the forfeiture of two bonds—the commonest of all causes of litigation in the theatrical world. "The consideracion wch induced the sd Willi*am*

---

[9] *Court of Requests (Books)*; *Orders and Decrees*, 17 & 18 Chas. I, fol. 247.

Trevill to become bound in the sd bonds beinge only for a sixt p*a*rte
of the Lease of a Playhouse in the Whitefryers whereunto the sd
Will*i*am Trevill was drawne by the p*e*rswasion of Sr Anthony
Ashley kn^t & one Mr Smith & the Def^t who likewise preuailed wth
the sd Trevill (beinge ignorant in the course of sharers in a Playhouse) to become ingaged in seu*e*rall other bonds & bill*e*s to diuerse
p*e*rsons for paym^t of diuerse som*m*es only to make a stocke for
supply of the Playehouse And although that the sd Sr Anthony
Ashley beinge Landlord of the Playhouse by combinac*i*on with the
Def^t vppon pr*e*tence that halfe a yeares Rent for the Playhouse was
unpaid entred into the Playhouse & turned the Players out of doors
& tooke the fforfeiture of the Lease whereby the sd Will*i*am Trevill
was frustrated of all benefitt wch he was to haue by the sd Lease,"
etc.[10]

[10] This was not the only suit in which Trevill became involved as a consequence
of the failure of the Whitefriars theatre. In the *Decrees and Orders* of the Court of
Requests are notes on these two suits.

29 June, a° 8 Jas. I; Trevill v. Methold.

William Trevill of London, tallow chandler, together with Hugh Fountayne, Esq.,
Emanuel Fenton, Thos. Savage, Margaret Deborse, widow, Edward Cowlin,
Henry Crathorne, and divers others of the creditors of Trevill, have complained
against William Methold, William Cooke, Felix Wilson, Thomas Woodford, George
Androwes, Richard Brogden, Richard Jobber, Martin Slatier, John Marks, Michael
Drayton, Elizabeth Browne, Richard Black, and Richard Hunter, others of his
creditors, to be relieved in equity concerning certain debts which Trevill owes the
said defendants upon bonds and otherwise. The complainants, because Trevill was
very poor and they had pity on him, consented on the mediation of Sir Edmund
Bowyer to remit part of the debts and give long terms of payment. But the defendants would not agree, and, with the exception of John Marks, have gone about
to vex and annoy Trevill in common law upon "diverse bonds and other specialties
wherein or in the most whereof the said Trevill is onely suretie for others although
there are diverse others more sufficient then hee bound wth him in the same," and
although the most part of the sums due is satisfied, as is alleged. If they persist,
they will ruin Trevill and do the complainants out of any realisation of their debts.
The defendants, again with the exception of Marks, were summoned to appear
before the Court on a certain day and contemptuously neglected to do so, and still
persist in their unjust course. The Court orders that the defendants be stayed in
their suit at common law until they have appeared before the Court and decision
has been rendered.

(This case enables us to understand how it was that Woodford could pursue his
persecutions of Trevill over so long a space of time and at such long intervals. With
so many creditors and with so much extra time in which to pay his debts, Trevill
was doubtless pestered to the end of his life, and forgot which men he had paid off
and when.)

11 Nov., a° 8 Jas. I; Trevill v. Andrews.

Whereas in the suit of William Trevill against George Andrews and others, an
injunction was heretofore awarded against the defendants in respect they had not

We can now make some attempt to gather our threads together and reconstruct the history of the Whitefriars playhouse. It is impossible to say just when the enterprise was conceived, or when the alterations were begun in the theatre, or when the company was installed. The original landlord was Robert, Lord Buckhurst (who became the second Earl of Dorset on April 19, 1608, and died February 27, 1609); but when the company was dispossessed the ownership had passed to Sir Anthony Ashley. We do know that the theatre was some part of the group of buildings comprising the old Whitefriars monastery. I do not think the company can have been organized much before the early part of 1607, for in all the suits I have gathered together, none of the numerous bonds entered into by the shareholders dates earlier than August, 1607. Moreover,

---

answered the complainant's bill, thereupon, upon motion made on behalf of the defendants and on information that the defendants had demurred, it was ordered that for the reasons exhibited in the demurrer the matter should be dismissed and the injunction dissolved, if the complainant on Nov. 3 next should not show good matter to the contrary, as by the order dated Oct. 13 last it does appear. The plaintiff has failed to show any such matter, and so the suit is dismissed, the injunction made void, and the plaintiff ordered to pay 20s. costs.

Lording Barry, too, had his share of litigation. The following are notes of suits I have found in the *Coram Rege Rolls*, in which he is always the defendant.

Easter, 6 Jas. I, m. 483.

Two suits for debt brought by Anthony Wilkins. First for £7 on a bond dated Aug. 15, 1607, to be paid 20s. a week, beginning Oct. 3 next. Not contested, and plt. awarded £8-6-8. Second for £4-6-9 on bond of same date. Plt. awarded £5-13-5.

Easter, 6 Jas. I, m. 483b.

Suit for debt of Thomas Woodford, for £120 on a bond dated Aug. 12, 1607. The indorsement of the bond reads: "The Condicion of this obligacion is such that if the within bounden lordinge Barrye William Treveele Edwarde Sybthorpe & Michaell Drayton or any of them theire or any of their executors administrators or assignes doe well and trulie pay or cause to be payde vnto the within named Thomas Woodforde his executors or Assignes the somme of three score poundes of lawfull money of England on the ffyve and Twentieth day of November now next cominge att or vn the ffont stone in the Temple Churche neere ffleetestreet london att one entire payment without delay That then this present obligacion to be voyde and of none effecte Or els to stande and abide in full force and vertue." It was finally proved that the money was not paid. Complainant awarded, for debt and costs, £122.

This, of course, was the same bond on which Woodford had sued Trevill and won £121.

Trinity, 6 Jas. I, m. 1312.

Three suits of debt on the part of Thomas Woodford, all successful. First for £40, bond dated Aug. 15, 1607; £41 awarded. Second for £7 on bond dated Nov. 16, 1607; £8-10-0 awarded. Third for £10 on bond dated Aug. 15, 1607; £11 awarded.

none of the plays written for this company bears indubitable evidence of belonging earlier than 1607.

George Andrews said that the lease of the premises was made to Thomas Woodford and Michael Drayton, and that about February of 1608 a half interest was sold to Barry. Thomas Woodford stands throughout as the promoter of the enterprise, the financial backer, and the nemesis which pursued the shareholders for years after the theatre had closed. It was he who furnished most of the loans, and it was he who enticed William Trevill and probably Lording Barry into the scheme. This Woodford is a man hitherto almost unknown in theatrical annals, and yet he promises to take an important place in the future, when we have unearthed more facts about his activities; for he was fond of dabbling in theatrical affairs, and had his finger in more than one pie. He owned an eighteenth share in the *Red Bull* playhouse, and the decrees in his suit in 1613 against Aaron Holland for the recovery of his dues there may be read in Fleay's *History of the Stage*.[11] I have already referred to a tantalizing notice of a dispute between him and one Edward Pierce, whom I take to have been the master at Paul's. It seems that on December 2, 1604, Pierce fell upon Woodford *vi et armis* and beat him. For that injury Woodford brought suit in 1606 and received balm to the extent of £13-6-8.[12] I have not been able to find the cause of the assault, or to connect the two men by any other suit; yet there seems to be a promising history behind the affair, if we could but find it.

By August of 1607 many or most of the shareholders had been gathered in. On August 12, Lording Barry, William Trevill, Edward Sibthorpe, and Michael Drayton signed an obligation to Thomas Woodford; so these men at least were then in the venture. In February, 1608, George Andrews was drawn in, and later Martin Slatier. I am not sure when Slatier entered. He says in his Answer to Andrews's Bill that he could not have told Andrews in February, when Barry and Andrews were negotiating, about the value of the properties at Whitefriars, or indeed have had any hand in the deal, because he had not at that time met the two men or taken any part in the affairs of the theatre. Yet on March 10 following he was signing articles of agreement with the shareholders. This does not sound quite straight; but is a hopeless knot to untangle—we do not know which of the men may have been lying. In the articles of

[11] Pp. 196-7.
[12] *Vide* p. 213.

agreement, signed March 10, 1608, appear the names of Martin Slatier, who had charge of the children and was, I imagine, brought in for his long experience as an actor to take expert charge of the producing of plays, Lording Barry, George Andrews, Michael Drayton, William Trevill, William Cooke, Edward Sibthorpe, and John Mason. I do not know whether these were all the people interested in the theatre, or whether some or all the names recited in the Trevill-Methold suit are to be counted in. They were, in addition to those in the articles of agreement, Hugh Fountayne, Emanuel Fenton, Thomas Savage, Margaret Deborse, Edward Cowlin, Henry Crathorne, William Methold, Felix Wilson, Richard Brogden, Richard Jobber, John Marks, Elizabeth Browne, Richard Black, and Richard Hunter.

3. *The Dissolution.*

The date of the closing of the theatre can be found pretty closely. Andrews, who purchased his share about February, 1608, says that the lease was forfeited before any assignment of his share in the proceeds was made him, that is, at least before the end of the year following the purchase, if the assignments were made yearly, and not later than the end of summer, if they were made half-yearly. It is most probable that the crash came soon after the articles of agreement were drawn up, for the lawsuits began to rain in 1608. Thus Woodford and Wilkins brought suits against Barry in Easter Term of 1608, and Woodford sued again in Hillary Term of the same year. To judge from the evidences of these documents, the existence of the company was about a year and a half, from the early part of 1607 till the middle of 1608. I am not convinced in regard to the earlier date, but I am certain that the theatre closed about the middle of 1608—that is, not long after the inhibition of the Revels children at Blackfriars which followed the presentation of Chapman's *Biron* plays. Perhaps the catastrophe was hastened by the plague, which raged from July to December of 1608. Perhaps, too, the inhibitions brought on by the *Biron* plays may have helped. This company was one of four—of which the others were the King's, Queen's, and Prince's companies—mentioned by de la Boderie as petitioning against this restraint.[13]

The theatre was not long unoccupied. Within a year Robert Keysar, together with Philip Rossiter and others, had moved in

[13] *Vide* Chambers, *Mod. Lang. Rev.*, 1910, p. 162.

with their company of boys, which may have been in part recruited from these same Whitefriars children, but was more likely the boys from Blackfriars transported bodily. But we shall come to that when we take up the second Whitefriars company.

4. *A Lawsuit Over Hats.*

A suit of secondary importance in the history of the company, but of real interest, is one brought in Trinity Term, 1608, in King's Bench by one Richard Edwards against Thomas Woodford, who for once is defendant. It is brought for debt incurred for various properties used in plays, and besides giving some particulars about these pieces, brings in the names of some of the shareholders and fixes the date of at least one performance at Whitefriars on December 23, 1607. The gist of it is as follows.[14]

On August 30, 1607, Edmund Sharpham[15] became indebted to Edwards in the sum of 17s. 2d. for "quatuor galeris anglice felt hat*tes* & tribus legaminib*us* galer*i* anglice hatband*es*" bought at some time previous; and on the same day Edward Sibthorpe became similarly indebted in 6s. 6d. "p*ro* vno galero Anglice a felt hatt & vno legamine galer*i* anglice a hat band." Then Thomas Woodford, on December 23, 1607, persuaded Edwards to accommodate him with "vnu*m* galeru*m* phrigiatu*m* cu*m* argento anglice a felt hatt embrodered with silver & vnu*m* ligamen galer*i* cum margaritis ornat*um* anglice a pearle hatt band" for use in a play to be given that day; promising that within three days after the present date he would pay Edwards the combined debts of the other two men, amounting to 23s. 8d. Listening to the wiles of Woodford, Edwards supplied the articles of apparel; but the money was not for all that forthcoming, in spite of frequent demands, and thus arose the occasion of the present suit. Woodford did not contest, and costs and damages were finally set at £5-6-8. It is worthy of passing note that Felix Wilson, named in the Trevill-Methold suit as one of Trevill's creditors, appeared as Woodford's attorney.

The proof brought forward by this document of the connection of Edmund Sharpham with Whitefriars settles almost definitely that the company there was the one called "Children of the King's

[14] I have not thought it important enough to print *in extenso.* The reference is *Placita Coram Rege,* Trinity 6 Jas. I, m. 1032.

[15] The author, of course, of *Cupid's Whirligig* and *The Fleire,* at this time writing plays for the Whitfriars boys.

Revels," for his *Cupid's Whirligig* was published in 1607 as acted by the children of His Majesty's Revels, and there was no other Revels company at this time except that at Blackfriars, which bore the name of the queen.

5. *Plays at Whitefriars.*

Seven plays are shown by their title-pages to have been acted "by the children of the King's Revels" at Whitefriars, and may with enough certainty be assigned to the company we have been discussing. They are:

Cupid's Whirligig (Sharpham).....	S.R. June 29,	1607,	pub. 1607
The Family of Love (Middleton)....	S.R. Oct. 12,	1607,	pub. 1608
Humor out of Breath (Day)	S.R. Apr. 12,	1608,	pub. 1608
The Dumb Knight (Markham)	S.R. Aug. 6,	1608,	pub. 1608
Two Maids of Mortlake (Armin)....	S.R. ?		pub. 1609
The Turk (Mason)..............	S.R. March 10,	1609,	pub. 1610
Ram Alley (Barry)..............	S.R. Nov. 9,	1610,	pub. 1611

To these we must add the unknown *Torrismount*, mentioned in the Slatier-Andrews suit.

Of these, *The Turk* and *Ram Alley* were without doubt written for this company, because Mason and Barry were shareholders. Almost as surely, *The Family of Love* and *Two Maids of Mortlake* were not written for it; but were revived plays, as I shall show presently. *Cupid's Whirligig* I believe to have been written for the company, and in the absence of any clew to the contrary we may assume the same for *Humor out of Breath* and *The Dumb Knight*. A brief glance at each of these will reveal some facts of interest.

Robert Armin's *Two Maids of Mortlake*, to begin with the oldest, was written in Elizabeth's reign and before the death of Dean Nowell who is mentioned as alive. One limit of composition is thus fixed in 1602, when Nowell died. The other may be fixed in 1597, if I understand an allusion correctly. Toward the end of the play Sir William Verger says:

> "Yet remember Donington's man, Grimes,
> Who for an heir so stolne and married,
> Was hanged, and the sergeant at armes,
> For assisting them did loose his place."

The *Acts of the Privy Council*, under date June 14, 1597, record that Alice Stoite, a young woman of Dorset, was abducted by one Dinington and others. No further particulars are given, but it seems likely that this abduction is the one referred to by Sir William. Otherwise the coincidence would be singular. The movements of Armin within the years in question are too uncertain to hazard more than a guess at the company for which he wrote the play. It was probably not written for the Lord Chamberlain's company, at the Globe, because in an address "To the friendly peruser" Armin says that the play "in part was sometime acted more naturally in the Citty." It may have been done for Lord Chandos's company.

Fleay guessed, on quite inadequate grounds,[16] that Middleton's *Family of Love* had been first produced at Paul's about 1604, but in this case I think he guessed luckily. In Act IV, Scene 3, Gerardine says: "I am, if it please you, of the spick and span new-set-up company of porters." I do not know the precise date when this company was instituted, but it cannot have been much before 1605 to judge from a ballad licensed on June 15 of that year, entitled: "A newe ballad Composed in commendacon of the Societie or Company of the porters."[17] Gerardine's emphasis on the newness of the company points to composition shortly after the event. I therefore would date the play about the middle of 1605, and in that case it was probably given by the Paul's boys for whom Middleton was then writing. Indications in the text that the theatre was round would fit the Paul's playhouse.

Cupid's Whirligig by Edmund (or Edward) Sharpham, was licensed so early in the career of the King's Revels as to give rise to the supposition that it was a revived play. He had previously written *The Fleire* for the Blackfriars boys. But Sharpham, as I have shown above, was connected in 1607 with the King's Revels, and may have written his *Whirligig* for them. In Act II Nan says that Sir Timothy Troublesome's heart beats "for all the world like the Denmarke Drummer," a reference to the visit of the King of Denmark in July of 1606, when one of his drummer boys astonished London.

Day's *Humor out of Breath* belongs without much doubt to the spring of 1608. This is determined on the one hand by the date of licensing (April 12) and on the other hand by a reference to the great frost of December, 1607. In III, 4, Aspero says: "For my

---

[16] *Drama*, II, 94.
[17] Cf. *Stationer's Register*, under that date.

beard, indeed that was bitten the last great frost, and so were a number of Justices of the peace besides." Though Fleay is not accurate in saying that there was no frost between 1598 and 1607-8, it is nevertheless true that no other frost approached in vigor that which began on December 8, 1607, and returned more violently on December 22, freezing the Thames and keeping it frozen through most of January.[18] In the address "To Signior No-body" we read: "Being to turn a poore friendlesse child into the world, yet sufficiently featur'd too, had it been all of one mans getting (woe to the iniquitie of Time the whilest) my desire is to preferre him to your service." This has been taken to mean that Day had help in writing the play, but his name stands alone on the title page, and more conclusively, there is no deviation in the style of the play from Day's known manner.

Not without plausibility is the suggestion that Day's *Law Tricks* was also acted by the Whitefriars boys. The 1608 quarto states that the play had been "divers times acted by the Children of the Revels," which would ordinarily mean the Queen's Revels at Blackfriars. Fleay so understood it, and dated the play 1606. But Bullen, in his edition of Day, shows references to speeches in *Pericles*, which is generally assigned to 1607-8. The Blackfriars boys had acted *The Isle of Gulls* in 1606, with results that nearly proved disastrous. Therefore it seems a little unlikely that they would stage another play by the same author in the same satirical vein. In IV, 2, the page Joculo tells a rigamarole about recent events in England, mentioning in particular a flood in July so great that the boatmen caught fish in the Exchange. This may be an echo of the mighty wind which in January of 1607 caused an inflooding of the sea.[19]

The Dumb Knight by Lewis Machin and Gervase Markham was another play with a satirical tinge. The address "To the Understanding Reader" says that "Rumour . . . . by the help of his intelligencer Envy, hath made straunge constructions on this Dumb Knight," but what caused these strange constructions is not easy to see. Possibly the offense lay in the savage attacks on law and lawyers which are put into the mouth of Mechant. Berating the law was a favorite pastime at Whitefriars.

Neither John Mason nor Lording Barry had any known connection with the company which came over to Whitefriars from Black-

---

[18] See Stow's *Chronicle*, under date.
[19] See Stow's *Chronicle* under date.

friars early in 1609, and therefore their plays were amost certainly written for the King's Revels. Of Mason practically nothing is known. Mr. J. Q Adams, who has edited his play,[20] supposes that it was written in 1606-7, which cannot be far wrong. In *Ram Alley* there are allusions to the statute of 4 Jac. I, c. V (1606-7), which authorized stocking a man for drunkenness. This proves that the play was not written before the organization of the King's Revels. Like the others of the same company, the play is hard on the legal profession.

Now this little group of plays fully bears out my contention that the first Whitefriars company was a piece of unsound, not to say rotten, speculation. In the first place, they had, with the exception of Middleton and Day, no connection with the better class of dramatists. And Middleton should be discounted because the one play of his which they used was probably borrowed from another company, and he wrote no more for them. As for Day, although he enjoys a little reputation to-day it is certain that he had very little in his own time and should be counted among the obscure. In the second place, if one considers quality of play rather than prominence of author, the conclusion is equally unfavorable. In all seven plays, only Day's *Humor out of Breath* can be read with any sense that one is conversing with a writer of literary taste. All the rest are dull, imitative, second-hand material, cut on patterns popular in the first decade of the seventeenth century, but without style.

It is quite plain what Thomas Woodford and his coadjutors were up to. They meant to capitalize the great popularity of the theatre in London, and the success which the two great children's companies had enjoyed, by founding a similar company in the unsavory liberty of Whitefriars. And because their purpose was dishonest (at least in the case of Woodford) they set about selling as many shares as possible and putting on a bold front, while at the same time they gathered a shoddy repertory of plays, partly from old plays given elsewhere, partly from amateurs on their own board of shareholders, and partly from a few hangers-on of the writing profession. The result was what everyone might have foreseen. At least one did see it, and saved himself from the crash. That man was the wily promoter of the enterprise, Thomas Woodford.

[20] In Bang's *Materialen zur Kunde des ält. Eng. Dramas.*

CHAPTER X

LAST YEARS OF THE QUEEN'S REVELS

1. *The New Company under Rossiter at Whitefriars.*

Some time after the company financed by Thomas Woodford came to grief in the middle of 1608, the Whitefriars theatre was occupied by a company of boy actors under the direction of Robert Keysar. The Burbages, in their Rejoinder in the *Keysar v. Burbage* suit, stated that at the time when Keysar and his partner Rossiter were buying off the children of Paul's these men were in possession of Whitefriars, and that this bargain preceded the entry of the King's Men into Blackfriars.[1] And this entry, as they plainly say in their Answer of the same suit, took place about August 10, 1609.[2] But Keysar was still directing the children of Blackfriars on January 4 of 1609, when these children played at court.[3] Therefore the transfer must have been made at some time between January and August. There is hardly any question that the new company at Whitefriars was the old company at Blackfriars—the association of Keysar as manager of both companies assures that. Furthermore, the 1616 quarto of Jonson's *Epicœne* declares that the play was acted in 1609 by the Children of her Majesty's Revels, and the prologue refers to Whitefriars in such a way as to indicate that the play was produced there. It seems clear, then, that following the disturbances of 1608 Keysar had drawn into partnership one Rossiter (Philip Rossiter, a lutenist among the royal musicians) and possibly others, and in the spring of 1609 had moved his company from Blackfriars to the house abandoned by the King's Revels. There they played through the year under their old title of "Children of the Queen's Revels."

Then on January 4, 1610, a new patent was secured, reaffirming to the translated company its precious title.[4] But the management had changed. The names which now stood at the head were those of Philip Rossiter, Robert Daborne, John Tarbock, Richard Jones,

[1] See p. 204.
[2] See p. 203.
[3] See p. 201.
[4] Frequently printed. See Chambers, *Eliz. Stage*, II, 56.

and Robert Brown—Keysar does not appear. Yet he had not severed connection with the company, because he was the payee for no less than five performances in the first third of that year.[5] But what the nature of that connection was, or how long it continued, I am unable to say. The last we hear of him is the suit which he brought in 1610 against the Burbages, and which gives us so many interesting facts about his short but eventful career as manager.

The newly incorporated company made an excellent start, on the flood tide of court favor. They played several times yearly at court, their next appearances after April of 1610 being on December 13, 1610, and February 2, 1611,[6] when they acted before the king and John Tarbocke was their payee. They played next on April 14 of the same year, again under the direction of Tarbocke.[7] Then, sometime before November 24, 1612, they played Beaumont and Fletcher's *Coxcomb*[8] before the king, the Princess Elizabeth, and the County Palatine.[9] As Fleay says, the play must have been given

[5] *Declared Accts., Treas. of the Chamber, Pipe Office*, Roll 543, fol. 235 b. "To Roberte Keysar uppon the Counsells warraunt dated at Whitehall decimo die Maij 1610 in the behalfe of himselfe and the reste of the children of the whitefryars for presenting fyve severall playes before his ma^tie and the Prince on severall nights menconed in the said warraunt xxxiij^li vj^s viij^d and by waye of his ma^ts rewarde xvj^li xiij^d In all L^li."

[6] *Accts. of the Treas. of the Chamber, St. Michael, 1610, to St. Michael, 1611*, in Bodleian, *Rawlinson* A 204.

[7] *Declared Accts., Treas. of the Chamber, Pipe Office*, Roll 543, fol. 265:"To John Tarboxe upon the Counsells warraunte dated at whitehall x° die Octobris 1611 for himselfe and the children of her Ma^ts Revells for presenting one Playe before the Prynce highnes the xiiij^th day of Aprill vj^li xiij^s iiij^d."

[8] Among the actors whose names are prefixed to the printed play are Cary and Barkstead. These men, or lads, left the company on Aug. 29, 1611, to join the Lady Elizabeth's men; so the play came before their departure. Since Beaumont and Fletcher were busy with the King's men in 1611, the play probably was written and given in 1610, but before March 30, when Taylor, another member of the cast, left to play with the Duke of York's company.

[9] The particulars for this and the following performances are more fully given in the *Accts. of the Treas. of the Chamber* for 1612-13, preserved in the "Vertue MS.," which is *Rawlinson* A 239 in the Bodleian. It has been published in the *Shakes. Soc. Papers*, II, 124. These are the entries which relate to the Revels company.

"Itm paid to Phillipp Roseter uppon the Councells warra*nt* dated att Whitehall xxiiij^to die Novembris 1612 for himself and the Children of the Queenes Ma^tes Revells, for presentinge before the Princes highnes: the La: Eliz: grace, and the Cownt Pallatyne; a Comedye called the Coxcombe the some of—vj^li xiij^s iiij^d.

Itm paid to the said Phillipp Roseter vppon the lyke warra*nt* dated att Whitehall vltimo die Maij 1613 for presentinge two severall playes, before the Princes highnes, One vppon the ix^th of Januarie last called Cupides

between October 16, when the Palsgrave arrived, and October 24, when Henry was taken fatally ill.[10] Oldys says that it was given again in 1613, but I think he is confusing this play with *Cupid's Revenge*, which was played twice.[11] This latter play was performed on January 1, 1613, before the king and again on January 9, before the Prince Charles. Fleay has it dated wrongly 1612,[12] but the *Declared Accounts* corroborate the *Vertue MS*. in putting it in 1613. Fleay would date the writing of it 1610, for the same reasons as applied to *The Coxcomb*. Chapman's *Widow's Tears*, originally produced at Blackfriars in 1605-6, was revived before Prince Charles on February 27, 1613.

This was nearly, if not quite, the last performance of this company under their old title. In March of 1613 they amalgamated with the Lady Elizabeth's men under Henslowe to form a new company, still under the patronage of Lady Elizabeth.[13] But with them in their new capacity we have no concern.

The following plays are known to have been produced at White-friars during the tenancy of Rossiter:

> Chapman's *Widow's Tears* and *Revenge of Bussy D'Ambois*, the first and probably the second, revived from the repertory of the Black-friars boys.
> Marston's *Insatiate Countess*.
> Jonson's *Epicœne* (played in 1609).
> Field's *Woman is a Weathercock*.
> Beaumont and Fletcher's *Knight of the Burning Pestle* (probably from the Blackfriars repertory; cf. E. K. Chambers, *Mod. Lang. Rev.*, 1910, p. 160), *Coxcomb*, *Cupid's Revenge*.

These boys played occasionally in the Provinces between 1610 and 1613. These performances are recorded in Murray:[14]

---

revenge: And the other called the Widdowes Teares, vppon the xxvij[th] of ffebru*ary* followinge the some of—xiij[li] vj[s] viij[d].

Itm paid to Phillipp Roseter vppon the Cowncells warr*ant* dated at White-hall vltimo die Maij 1613 for presentinge a Playe before his Ma[tie] the first daye of Janu*ar*ie last 1613 Called Cupides Revenge twentie Nobles, And by waye of his Ma[tes] reward fyve M*ar*kes In all the some of x[li]."

[10] Fleay, *Drama*, I, 185.
[11] MS. notes on Langbaine; cf. Dyce, *Beaumont and Fletcher*, III, 117.
[12] *Drama*, I, 185.
[13] Malone's *Shakespeare*, 1821, XXI, 416.
[14] *Eng. Dram. Comp.*, I, 364.

1609-10 (c.March, 1610 .... Maidstone)[15]
1610-11; Aug. 10, 1611 .... Norwich
1612-13; May 20, 1612 .... Norwich
1612-13....................... Coventry

2. *Provincial Excursions.*

The second Queen's Revels company at Whitefriars gave rise to various ramifications, which appeared in a more or less erratic transit across the Provinces. For our information in regard to these branches of the parent stem, we are indebted almost entirely to Murray. Thus we discover[16] that on August 10, 1611, a company under Ralph Reeve arrived in Norwich and showed to the Mayor's Court Rossiter's patent, as their authority for playing. At first Reeve declared that he was Rossiter, but was discovered, and on failing to show any "letters of deputation" from Rossiter, was ordered out of town, the bitterness of dismissal being poulticed with the salve of 40s. Murray assumes that this company was part of the Queen's Revels, but it is significant that the Chamberlain who gave them their reward called them "Children of the King's Revells."

On May 20, 1612,[17] a company of boys turned up at Norwich under the guidance of Nicholas Long. They showed the Queen's Revels license and a proper deputation from Rossiter, but the Mayor's Court decided that the license gave Rossiter the right only to "teach and instruct" children, and therefore refused to allow the boys to play, solacing them with a reward of 20s. The Chamberlain recorded them as children of the King's Revels; this looks as though they were the same company as had travelled the year before under Reeve. In 1614[18] we find a company travelling under the direction of Long called the Princess Elizabeth's men. I suppose that it was the same as the preceding one, and was simply a duplicate company maintained by Rossiter to tour the country with a competent director while he took charge in London. In that case, their title would change with the title of the London company. They played on March 2, 1614, at Norwich, and probably at various times during the next two years. Murray thinks that this Princess Elizabeth's company was organized from the remnants of the Revels Company

[15] This item is puzzling. The boys are called in the record of payment "Children of the Chappell," but there was no company of that name at this time.
[16] Murray, *op. cit.*, I, 259; II, 339, 370.
[17] Murray, II, 339.
[18] Murray, II, 339.

at Whitefriars when the amalgamation with Henslowe's men took place in March, 1613; but I incline to regard it as the same company which had been touring the year before under Long as the children of the Revels, from the fact that Long directed both companies and that the appearances of the two companies form a continuous chain. Of course recruits may well have come in at the breaking up of the Whitefriars company.

Murray attempts to draw up a list of the performances by this company which are recorded in Provincial annals, but I cannot regard his conclusions as justifiable. He assumes, as I am willing to grant, that the traveling company of Lady Elizabeth's men under Long came into existence after March 1613, when the second Lady Elizabeth's company was formed in London, and used an "exemplification," or duplicate, of the original patent granted on April 27, 1611, to Joseph Moore and John Townsend.[19] That such a duplicate did exist is proved by its being displayed in Norwich in May of 1615.[20] The date of the exemplification was May 31, 1613—just about the right time for Murray's theory. Murray is also doubtless right in concluding that this company cannot have been in existence after July, 1616, or at latest March, 1618. On the former date the Earl of Pembroke issued an order revoking all duplicate patents such as this one to the Princess Elizabeth's company.[21] Although her companies are not specified in the order,[22] yet the provisions are so sweeping in their nature that no company could have escaped. Certainly by March 20, 1618, there was only one Lady Elizabeth's company in existence, because on that day a new patent was issued to the company in which it was provided that there should be one and only one company of that name.[23]

Murray simply lumps together all the Provincial performances by players of the Lady Elizabeth which fell between March, 1613, and July, 1616, and assigns them to this company under Nicholas Long; so that his list reads as follows:

[19] I find that neither Murray nor Fleay shows any first-hand knowledge of the original patent to Townsend; Murray is familiar with it from references in Provincial records. The document is filed among *Chancery Warrants, Privy Seals*, Ser. II, file 1799, P.R.O.

[20] Murray, II, 340.

[21] Murray, II, 343.

[22] The companies mentioned were: two Queen's companies, one children of the King's Revels, one Prince's company, and one Prince Palatine's.

[23] Murray, II, 344.

1612-13.	April 9, 1613.......................	Norwich
	Betw. Nov.25,1612, and Nov.23,1613...	Coventry
		Shrewsbury
	Spring, 1613	Bristol
		Marlborough
	July 4, 1613	Canterbury
	July 12, 1612-August 7, 1613	Dover
		Shrewsbury
	October 13, 1613....................	Leicester
1613-14.	March 2, 1614.......................	Norwich
		Marlborough
		Shrewsbury
1614-15.	March, 1615	Nottingham
	March, 1615	Coventry
	April 7, 1615........................	Marlborough
	May 27, 1615.......................	Norwich
	(June 5, 1616.......................	Norwich)
	(July 1, 1616	Leicester)

These last two items do not stand in Murray's list, but they ought to, because Pembroke's restraining order was not issued until July 16, 1616. Murray's great fault is that he does not remember that there were two companies traveling at this time as the Lady Elizabeth's players. One of them, as we have seen, possessed an exemplification of the original patent, dated May 31, 1613, and the other carried the original patent of 1611. This seems to be the necessary conclusion from the Norwich records, though the records themselves are contradictory. Thus on May 27, 1615, a company appeared with the exemplification; then on June 5, 1616, a company headed by John Townsend, one of the original patentees, came with the patent of 1611; yet the clerk who noted their visit expressly said that they had "bene formerly here vpon the xxvij[th] of May 1615."[24] This contradiction, however, may be simply due to carelessness on the clerk's part. In any case, we are sure that there were two copies of the patent and equally sure that they were both in use, else we misjudge the express wording of the new patent of 1618, which provides that there shall be only one company of the Princess Elizabeth's men.

We naturally assume that the original patent was held by Townsend and Moore and the duplicate by the second company, that is,

[24] Murray, II, 340, 341.

the one headed by Long. Now of all the list of performances gathered by Murray and transcribed above, in only three cases is any indication of the personnel of the company given. The company playing on March 2, 1614, at Norwich was headed by Long, and the company playing there on May 27, 1615, and June 5, 1616, was headed by Townsend, if we are to believe the June 5 entry in the Mayor's Court Books. In none of the other cases is the designation any clearer than "the Lady Elizabeth's players." It is a confusing mess. One thing we may be certain of, which is that not all the performances in Murray's list were given by Long's company. It is impossible to distinguish between the two companies except in the three cases noted. A glance through the documents in Murray's second volume will show that the players of the Lady Elizabeth toured the country consistently and with few breaks from 1611 till 1630. It would be silly to suppose that the parent company withheld itself in London during the hypothetical existence of Long's company from 1613 to 1616, and we have positive evidence as well of the existence of two patents and consequently of two companies.

3. *The Queen's Revels at Puddlewharf Theatre, Blackfriars.*

It has been known since the appearance of Collier's *Annals of the Stage* that the Queen's Revels children under Rossiter did not end permanently upon the amalgamation of Rossiter's and Henslowe's companies in March of 1613, but that they were revived under another patent on June 3, 1615.[25] This patent has been under suspicion on the part of Fleay, but its genuineness is not to be disputed. The original Privy Seal may be found among *Chancery Warrants, Privy Seals*, Ser. II, file 1855, in the Public Record Office. The provisions of the patent are so well known that only a brief rehearsal is necessary. After reviewing the first patent of 1610, the present one goes on to say that Rossiter's lease of Whitefriars is now expired, and that he, together with Philip Kingman, Ralph Reeve, and Robert Jones, has taken a lease of divers "buildings, cellers, sollers, chambers and yards" in the precinct of Blackfriars, near Puddle Wharf, with the purpose of erecting a playhouse there in which to exercise his boys. The premises are known as "Lady Saunder's house," otherwise "Porter's Hall," and are in the occupation of Robert Jones. Permission is granted these men to build their house and to exercise therein not only the children of the Revels, but also the companies of the Lady Elizabeth and the Prince.

[25] *Annals*, 1879, I, 381.

The brief history of this company is also well known. Just as the inhabitants of Blackfriars protested against the erection of a theatre there in 1596 and again in 1619, so they did with regard to this new playhouse. They doubtless felt that two houses in one precinct were too much, and we cannot blame them. The effect of their remonstrance was that the Privy Council called Rossiter before it, listened to the arguments of the mayor and aldermen[26] and to the opinions of Lord Chief Justice Coke, and ended by issuing an order on September 26, 1615, forbidding the continuance of building. The reason which clinched the matter was the expressed opinion of Coke that Rossiter's license extended to building a playhouse *outside* the liberties of London and not within.[27] In the light of the patent to Rossiter, which defines beyond doubt the Blackfriars as the field of operation, this interpretation of the Lord Chief Justice is rather staggering. Evidently Rossiter did not regard it with great respect, for he kept bravely on with his work. Finally, on January 26, 1616, a peremptory order was issued directing that the theatre, which was described as "lately erected" and "almost if not fully furnished," be torn down.[28]

Thus much of the history of the Puddle Wharf theatre has long been common property. It is also known that at least one play came to its boards before the last blow fell. This was Nathaniel Field's *Amends for Ladies*, which was printed in 1618 as "acted at the Blacke-Fryers, both by the Princes seruants, and the Lady Elizabeth's."

I can add some new particulars to this history from a Chancery suit of 1623, showing that Henslowe was associated with Rossiter in this venture (thus upsetting Murray's rather natural guess that the enterprise was a breaking away on Rossiter's part resulting from Henslowe's ill-treatment of the company)[29] and showing that Edward Alleyne was drawn into the affair in 1617, thus explaining

---

[26] That the part the city officials took in suppressing the house was an active one, is shown by an entry in the *Repertories of the Court of Common Council*, 32, fol. 182 b, Sept. 28, 1615. "Item it is ordered by this Court that m^r Chamberlen shall pay vnto m^r Dyos the Cities Remembrancer the some of iij^{li} xvij^s vj^d by him disbursed about the restraint of building of the playhouse at puddle wharfe as by his bill of particulars allowed heere in Court may appeare."

[27] Malone, *Shakespeare*, 1821, III, 493.

[28] *Shakespeare Jahrbuch*, Vol. 48, 1912, p. 105.

[29] *Vide* the "Articles of Grievance against Mr. Henchlowe" and the following "Articles of Oppression," Malone, XXI, 416.

several entries in his notebook. It is a matter for wonder that this
document has not yet been put before the general public, for it was
known to Halliwell-Phillips in 1884 and was referred to then by
him.[30] A copy of Alleyne's Bill of Complaint is preserved among the
Alleyne papers at Dulwich, but there is no hint in the Bill of theatrical matters to awaken the curiosity of a Collier or a Fleay. It is
not my intention to transcribe the whole document, for only a small
portion of it discusses the theatrical history of the buildings concerned, and the greater part can be sumed up briefly.

The suit was brought in 1623 by Edward Alleyne against Edward
Travis, citizen and haberdasher, of London.[31] The Bill, which is
dated June 18, begins by saying that about six years ago (1617)
Travis was, as he still is, seized of certain "old decayed and ruined
messuages" late in the tenures of Thomas Thorpe, baker, David
Evans, and divers others, lying in the parish of St. Anne's, Blackfriars. Travis, aware that unless they were repaired soon, the
tenements would come to utter ruin, and knownig that the needed
repairs would be expensive, was ready to listen to Alleyne when
he proposed to take a lease of the premises. Alleyne, in his turn,
knowing that the repairs would cost upward of £1,000, and not
being sure what estate the defendant or his wife had in the premises,
was unwilling to take the lease except for a long term and unless he
could be guaranteed a strong title. It was finally arranged that a
fifty year lease should be made out at the huge rental of £160 the
year, with the provisions that in recompense for Alleyne's repairing
the buildings no fine was to be levied upon him, that Susanna,
Travis's wife, was to join with her husband in the lease, and that to
prevent any title of dower or jointure which Susanna might have
in the premises, Travis was to levy a fine *surconcessit* on the said
premises. The indenture was signed on March 26, 1617. Therein
Alleyne agreed to repair the buildings thoroughly and keep them
in good order, and by another obligation of the same date Travis
pledged himself to the levying of the fine before the second return
of the following Easter term. Then the plaintiff took possession of
the premises and expended in their regeneration more than £1,500,

---

[30] In *Memoranda intended for the use of Amateurs, who are sufficiently interested
in the pursuit, To make searches in the Public Record Office*, Brighton (for private
circulation), 1884. This book is full of valuable and concise data, and yet seems
very little known.

[31] *Chancery Proceedings*, Jas. I, A 1/16.

and has paid the agreed rent ever since the commencement of the lease. But the obligation relating to the fine coming into the defendant's hands, so that Alleyne could not compel him to levy the fine, the defendant has taken advantage of the circumstance and refused to carry out his part of the agreement under color of a jointure made to Susanna Travis by her husband before the lease to Alleyne. Alleyne thereupon sues in Equity for relief which he cannot get by process of Common Law.

To this Bill the defendants submitted on June 30 their Demurrers and Answers, in which some interesting facts regarding the premises come to light. After rehearsing their reasons for demurring, they go on in this fashion:

.... they saie, and ffirst the Def᛫ Edmund Traves for himselfe saith, that he taketh it that he this Def᛫ was and is seised of diuers Messuages, or Tenem᛫ᵉˢ wᵗʰ their appurtenaunces together wᵗʰ diuers wayes, passages, yardes, gardens, backsides and other easem᛫ᵉˢ and Comodities there vnto belonging sometimes in the tenures of Thorpe, Evans, and others, as in the bill is sett forth and that some of the same were auntient, and some parte thereof ruinous, and decayed, but most parte thereof auntient and strong building, and some parte thereof Demised vnto one Iones for certaine yeares by one Dawborne, or some others, before this Def᛫ had anie absolute estate, or interest in the same, and somme parte thereof this Def᛫ did demise vnto one Phillipp kingman wᶜʰ said Iones, and kingman as this Def᛫. hath heard, did transferr theire estate, or some parte thereof vnto one Hinslowe the Compˡᵗᵉˢfather in lawe wᶜʰsaid Iones, kingman, and Hinslowe, or some of them, by the advice, expences, and ayde of the said Hinslowe did cause some parte of the said Messuages, or Tenem᛫ᵉˢ to be pulled downe, and indeavoured to build a playhouse there, the wᶜʰ, some of the parishoners dislikeing, did cause stay to be made thereof,[32] and afterwardes the said Hinslowe dyed and as this Def᛫. hath Credibly heard, in the time of his sicknes or before, made the Compˡᵗ. his executour after whose decease the Compˡᵗ. came vnto this Def᛫. to treate wᵗʰ him aboute the sameMessuages, or Tenem᛫ᵉˢ. and implored this Defˡᵗᵉˢ. ayde to be relieved for the monyes wᶜʰ the said Hinslowe had dispended and laide forth in building the said playhouse wᶜʰ as the said Compˡᵗ. affirmed was much, and there vpon this Def᛫. was contented to make the Compˡᵗ. at his earnest request a Lease of the same Messuages or Tenem᛫ᵉˢ. for the terme of ffiftie yeares vpon like reservacions, paiem᛫ᵉˢ. and Covenauntes as in the said Bill of Compˡᵗ. is expressed.

[32] The Council's order was issued Jan. 26, 1616. It is printed in Boswell-Malone (1821), III, 494, with the date 1617; but Mrs. Stopes's transcripts of the Privy Council Registers (*Shakes. Jahrbuch*, 1912, p. 105) show this to be incorrect.

This is all of the document that concerns us. Travis goes on to say that Susanna, his wife, was fearful that the levying of the fine agreed on would injure her rights of jointure, and so was unwilling that it should be done. And so Travis and Alleyne made a new agreement together, by which Alleyne received £5, the cost of the fine, in lieu of the fine itself, and Travis acknowledged a statute of £1,000 for discharge of the jointure, to protect Alleyne in his possession of the lease. The defendants deny having possession of any obligation according to Alleyne's charge, and further disclaim any intent to conspire against him. The consequences of the suit I have been unable to discover.

Thus it appears that Henslowe was the active party in the deal, and that the operations in Blackfriars were conducted on a large scale. I take it that the £1,500 and more that Alleyne speaks of expending in repairs were paid in greater part by Henslowe, as Travis implies. This is a large sum to lay out on a playhouse, and the rent of £160 is enormous. We recall that the rental of the Blackfriars house was £40. What Alleyne intended to do with the property when he took it over, or what use he did put it to, I cannot clearly understand. He had paid the rent regularly until shortly before the event of the suit of 1623, as Travis witnesses, but how he derived his profits is a puzzle. Did he operate the house as a theatre? The order of suppression from the Council was absolute, and we have no evidences of the existence after 1616 of a playhouse in Blackfriars other than the one possessed by the King's men. Did he reconvert it into dwelling houses? I cannot imagine what else he could have done, and the money he speaks of having paid out may have gone in this way. It seems likely, judging from the none too clear phrasing of the lawsuit papers, that Alleyne was associated with Henslowe in the business from the beginning. Thus Travis says that Alleyne did not acquire the property until after the suppression order and Henslowe's death, when the theatre should have been finished, and yet Alleyne speaks as though he had taken it over when it was still in a ruinous state.

There are various references to this property and this transaction among the Alleyne papers at Dulwich, which go to bear out strongly the likelihood that Alleyne was associated with Henslowe. Thus there are two quittances from Edmund Travis to Alleyne for £3-10-0 for "a quarters rente of a howse in the blacke Fryers late in the occupasone of Roberte Jones," one dated October 9, 1616, the other

January 7, 1617.[33] An entry from Alleyne's diary of August 27, 1618, reads: "Pole brought me word y^t ye building[34] would be puld downe, so I went to London."[35] He is referring here not to any edict against the playhouse, but to the act against new buildings. His buildings were spared, for we learn from a return of houses demolished according to this act, rendered by Sheriff Robert Johnson on September 20, 1618, that "In Swan Alley, near the Wardrop, Edward Allen his houses are respited by warrant."[36]

That Alleyne built over or added to the buildings in 1617, when he acquired full title to them, is suggested by another entry from his diary, of September 28, 1618:

> ....more disbursed for ye building in ye Blackfriars for this yeare and in a^o 1617, when itt first began w^t ye 200^l first disbursed by my father: bueying in off leases: chargis in lawe: and ye building itt selfe, w^t making meanes to kepe them from being puld downe, is 1105^l 00^s 02^d.[37]

Whatever became of the theatre which Henslowe built, it was not pulled down as the Council had directed. Doubtless the Lords were satisfied that it should be put to "some other good use," as they had been thus satisfied in the case of the *Curtain* in 1600.

4. Children of the Revels after 1615.

During the years following the patent to Rossiter reconstituting the Queen's Revels children in 1615, there are various references to the companies of Revels boys in the Provinces, while at the same time there is no record of their appearance in London. For these notices we are indebted to Murray. A company of Queen's Revels children played in Coventry on October 7, 1615, and in Nottingham in February, 1616, and sometimes during 1616-17.[38] They were probably the company from Blackfriars. We cannot be sure that the Revels boys who played at Leicester in or before February, 1616, at Coventry on June 21, 1616, and at Leicester on the following day were the same, for they are only called "Children of the Revels."

[33] G. F. Warner, *Catalogue of Dulwich MSS.*, p. 142.
[34] Warner says that the words "of the playhouse" inserted at this point are patent forgeries, probably to be laid at Collier's door.
[35] Warner, *op. cit.*, p. 172.
[36] *Cal. S. P. Dom.*, *Jas. I*, 1611-18, p. 574.
[37] Warner, *op. cit.*, p. 174.
[38] Murray, *op. cit.*, I, 365.

Yet Murray gives all these performances to the same company, though he is forced to comment on the fact of one company playing in two places on two successive days. I am sure that one or two of these notices belong to a company of King's Revels children whom Murray shows[39] to have existed for a short time under an exemplification made out to William Hovell, William Perry, Nathan May, and others and dated February 27, 1615. They were named in the order issued July 16, 1616, by Pembroke revoking all such exemplifications, and doubtless ended their career then. This company appeared at Norwich on June 17, 1615, and probably is referred to in one or more of the vague notices of 1616. We can get a hint from the towns visited. It is not unreasonable to suppose that these traveling companies kept to certain more or less restricted routes, revisiting towns where they had already made themselves familiar and avoiding as far as possible crossing the circuit of another company. We know that the Queen's Revels boys played in Coventry on October 7, 1615, and so I think it most likely that the company which played again in Coventry on June 21, 1616, was the same. The remaining two doubtful performances fell in Leicester, and I should give them to the King's Revels boys. The date of the first is doubtless February, 1616, for although that entry is undated, the next one is dated February 22, and from the close relation between the two entries implied by the phrasing,[40] I believe they were written at the same time. One more reference to a Revels company which Murray has overlooked in making his tables belongs to Leicester and is dated February 6, 1617.[41] It belongs either to the Queen's Revels company, since the King's Revels were done away with in July 1616, or else to a combination of the two companies.

On October 31, 1617, a new Queen's Revels company was organized under the leadership of Rossiter, Robert Lee, William Perry, and Nicholas Long. They exhibited the patent in Norwich on August 29, 1618.[42] Since William Perry, who had erstwhile been directing the King's Revels children, was a member of the managing board, I suspect that the new company was simply a combination of Rossiter's and Perry's companies. The amalgmation may well

[39] II, 10.
[40] "Itm given to a Companye . . . . etc."
   "Itm the xxijth of ffebruarie given to one other Companye," etc.
[41] Murray, II, 312.
[42] Murray, II, 345.

have come before the patent was issued, thus accounting for the performance in Leicester of 1617.

This new company played in the provinces until 1623. After 1619 they were known as "Children of the Revels to the late Queen Anne."[43] Before 1619 Robert Lee returned to the Queen's players[44] whence he came, and by February, 1620, Nicholas Long must have gone too, for in that month he received a patent for a company of his own.[45] On April 9, 1623, a confirmation of the license of October 31, 1617, was granted Perry for one year.[46] With him were named as associates George Bosgrave, Richard Backster, Thomas Band, James Jones, Walter Barrett, James Kneller, and Edward Tobye. The reason for procuring this confirmation was possibly the failing health of Rossiter. He died on May 5, 1623, as his nuncupative will in Somerset House tells us.[47] Until 1627 there are scattering notices of Revels children in the Provinces. They disbanded before September 18, 1629, when Perry set up "His Majesty's Servants of the City of York."[48]

The list[49] of performances in the Provinces by the Queen's Revels, the King's Revels, and later the combined companies, would appear as follows, doubtful performances being bracketed:

Queen's Revels	King's Revels
1615, October 7 . . . . Coventry	1615, June 17 . . . . Norwich
1616, February . . . . Nottingham	1616, before Feb.22 Leicester
1616, June 21 . . . . Coventry	1616, June 22 . . . . . Leicester
1616-17 . . . . Nottingham.	

1617, before Feb.6....Leicester (probably a company formed from the two Revels companies after the inhibition of Perry's King's Revels).

Queen's Revels (formed of the two preceding)
1618, August 29 . . . . Norwich
1618, before February 22 . . . . Leicester
1619 . . . . Leicester
(1620 . . . . Leicester)

[43] Murray, I, 362.
[44] Same, I, 196.
[45] Same, II, 345. Long exhibited his patent in Norwich on May 20, 1619, and that is the only notice we have of this company.
[46] Same, II, 272-3.
[47] Prerog. Court of Canterbury, Swan 41. There is no information provided in the will. Everything is left to the wife. Present were Hugh and Dudley Rossiter and Elizabeth, wife of Wm. Simpson. Proved May 21, 1623.
[48] Murray, II, 8.
[49] Varied in many details from the lists in Murray, I, 365. Cf. also II, 10.

```
        1622, April 12.....................Leicester
        1622, June 8......................Norwich
        (1623, after January 25..............Leicester)
        1623, May 4......................Norwich
        1623-4...........................Exeter
        (1624, March 18...................Leicester)
        (1627, July 8.....................Leicester)
        (1627, after July 8.................Leicester)
```

The bracketed items are under question because there seems good evidence that another company of children of the Revels was abroad at the same time.[50] In September of 1619 the "Children of the Kinges Revelles" acted in Nottingham. So there was another King's Revels company in existence at this time. In most of the items bracketed in the list above, the company is no more clearly identified than as children of the Revels. This company most probably played in Leicester in 1618, for there are two payments registered there in that year to "one other Companye of Playors called the Children of the Revells." One of these was certainly the Queen's Revels boys, who were visiting Leicester regularly. The item of 1623-Leicester is dubious because the company is called only the company of the Master of the Revels.[51] If this was the Queen's Revels company, as Murray supposes, [52]then doubtless it was identidentical with the company of "Sir George Buck's players" which appeared in Bristol in 1618. But Murray supposes that *they* were the King's Revels boys—why it is hard to discover.

Murray's list[53] of the performances of these King's Revels boys is open to much question. These performances are specially labeled as given by the children of the King's Revels. (The first is assigned them on strong likelihood; cf. above.)

```
        1618, after February 22.............Leicester
        1619, September...................Nottingham
        1621, Spring.....................Dover
        1623-4...........................Nottingham
        1624, July 9-October 22............Leicester
```

The other items on Murray's list are all dubious. Some [as Dover, 1620, Leicester, 1622 (January 10), Coventry, 1626 (December 21),

---

[50] Murray, II, 10-12.
[51] *Same*, II, 315.
[52] I, 365.
[53] II, 12.

Leicester, 1627 (July 8)[54] and 1628] designate the company as "Children of the Revels," or simply as "Company of the Revels." In one case (Canterbury, 1621-2) Murray gives the performance to the children because the company was called King's players and was headed by William Daniel, and because Daniel is found in 1634 organizing a King's Revels company of *men*. This is straining circumstantial evidence too far. Other items [Norwich, 1623 (June 14), and Coventry, 1628 (April)] are questionable because their identification rests on the fact that in each case the company was led by Nicholas Hanson and in the second case it was called the company of the King's Revels. In neither case is it known that the actors were children, and we know too much about the confusion and license which attended the regulation of companies in the Provinces and too little about the actual doings of such companies to draw hasty conclusions like these.

One of Murray's children of the Revels companies can be disposed of in short order. He shows[55] that on December 30, 1629, a license was granted Robert Kimpton and others to conduct a company of the King's Revels, and that they played in the Provinces until about 1623. But in no place is the company said to be composed of boys, and why Murray calls it so I cannot comprehend. He even connects this company by the evidence of synchroneity, with the London Revels company at Salisbury Court, and that was made up of men.

[54] This assignment is more likely than the others because the two payments were entered for the children of the Revels, one on July 8 and one some time after; probably not the same company.

[55] II, 13.

CHAPTER XI

PLAYS AND INFLUENCES

Hitherto we have been concerned almost entirely with historical facts and aspects, in the effort to trace as accurately and as completely as possible the rise and fall of our boy actors; but let us not leave them without casting a glance, however summary, over the literary product of their energies, their plays. During the full century in which these youngsters flourished, did they leave no impress on English drama? Are there no effects which we can attribute to their influence, and which would not have come to pass but for them? These are inquiries which it is fitting we should answer as well as we may.

Two questions arise, or rather two divisions of the same question: How did the fact of writing for children affect the dramatist—that is, what are the characteristics, if any, of children's plays? And how did this body of plays affect the great body of Elizabethan drama? Neither of these questions has ever met with discussion—possibly because the difficulties which attend them are forbidding. Indeed I can recollect only one statement of one critic which touches upon the matter. Sir Walter Raleigh, in his book on Shakespeare[1] says: "With the disappearance of the boy-players the poetic drama died in England, and it has had no second life." This is a bold thought, perhaps too bold, but it raises a quantity of doubts and inquiries which deserve debate. Certainly, considering how active children were in the field of drama during the hundred years between 1515 and 1616, we ought not to be surprised to find them exercising a marked influence on plays and players. If we find that they do not, it is proper to inquire why and how a natural consequence has been prevented.

Our period breaks readily into two halves at the decade 1590-1600, before and after which children were busy in the theatre, but during which they were inactive; and each of these halves has characteristics of its own. To begin with the first period, we shall find that before 1580 practically no distinction can be traced between the

[1] *English Men of Letters* series, p. 120.

work of children and of men; that they produced the same kinds of plays; and that as a matter of fact the boys led the way because they had the best playwrights working for them. This is a stimulating and in many ways a surprising discovery, that the sixty-five years between 1515 and 1580 belong to the children of the Elizabethan theatre, yet it is one which I believe is capable of proof. As to the succeeding period from 1600 to 1616, that is a different matter. Then, we shall find, children were on a far different status both with playwright and public, for they were no longer serious competitors with men, but apes imitating without equaling, transforming tragedy into bombast, and meeting their adult rivals only on the plane of light satirical comedy. In a word, the art of the child actors was hardy and vigorous before 1590, and decadent after 1600.

We should come to the period of 1515-1580 with one fact in mind which is frequently lost sight of, namely, that the drama was mainly an affair, first of the court, and secondly of the schools, or if we wish to speak only of drama in the vulgar tongue we may neglect the schools. Consequently the term "popular drama," as we apply it to *Ralph Roister Doister, Gammer Gurton's Needle*, and the interludes of Heywood, is only partially accurate. If, as I fear it is often used, it means drama written for and inspired by the people, the term is quite wrong, for more often than not these rough, hearty products of mirth were designed for the gorgeous audience of Eltham and were written by men educated in school and court. This is true particularly of plays until about 1560, when as far as I can judge the children of Paul's and the Chapel began to play before the people in houses of their own. Thereafter these boys presented many pieces in the town which never saw court, but nevertheless their plays continued to be written by men who in occupation and training were courtiers.

This assertion that the mid-sixteenth century drama belongs to the court will appear more reasonable when we reflect upon the conditions under which plays were produced, particularly upon the status of the actors. At court there were the children of the Chapel, acting through an almost unbroken chain of years from 1515 to 1584; there were also the children of Paul's, almost an appendage of the court, as we have seen, acting from about 1552 till 1590; there was the royal company of interlude players, who were only four in number and do not appear to have had much of importance to do;

and there were various noblemen's companies who came and went. At such schools as Eton, Westminster, Shrewsbury, Merchant Taylors, and at some chapels like Windsor the boys were exercised in Latin and English interludes by masters who were industrious in composing material for their practice. Elsewhere, the country at large was supplied by unnumbered bands of roving players whose identity and relationships it is now impossible to discover. Doubtless many plays were written for the consumption of the Provinces, but more often, I think it is safe to say, these wanderers carried abroad plays which had been presented at court. Whether or not this is true, it nevertheless is certain that if there was any large body of plays written for consumption outside of London, it has almost totally disappeared and hence must be treated as non-existent.

The greater number of extant plays of this pre-1580 period, then, belong directly or indirectly to the court; that is, they were written for production at court, or they were written by men who lived there. Some few, it is well to remember, like *Gammer Gurton* and *Thersites*, belong to the universities and schools. The truth of this contention is supported by the fact that at court were to be found conditions best suited for production,—i.e. established companies, money, and the institution of the Revels. It is further supported by what we know of the dramatists, for it appears that the best known and most admired writers of plays dwelt and labored at court. And what is still more surprising, a large proportion, it is almost safe to say the majority, of this select body wrote solely for the children of the Chapel. A brief survey will make these points clear.

Beginning early in the century we come upon the names of John Skelton and Bishop John Bale, both of whom wrote interludes which have survived. Neither of these can be connected with children's companies, but neither can they be connected with men. That is a fact which hampers our comparisons constantly, that many plays bear about them no evidences to tell us who acted them. If we knew all, we should undoubtedly find that many of these neutral plays ought to be credited to children. Yet to be quite fair, I shall assume, unless we have good reason to suspect the contrary, that they were acted by men. Neither Skelton nor Bale appears in the *Books of King's Payments* or *Revels Books* as writing for court performances, and the circumstances of the production of their plays remain a mystery. Contemporary with and succeeding them we meet with the names of John Heywood and William Cornish. The case of Heywood is much like that of Bale and Skelton—we are not sure that he wrote for boys; yet there is thus much evidence, that he is known to have acted a couple of times before Mary, as princess and queen, with an anonymous company of children, thereby opening at least a reasonable doubt that all his work was done for children. We know at any rate that he lived until his exile at court and that all his interludes were written for presentation there. Cornish is the first name which can be connected definitely with children. As master of the children of the Chapel and assistant director of Revels, he wrote a constant succession of pageants and plays which have all perished. He was the first Chapel master, apparently, to organize the children into a regular acting company. For them he wrote his interludes and parts of his pageants; it was they who acted in 1515 *Troilus and Pandor*, the first recorded play on a medieval romantic subject. Though none of this man's dramatic work survives, his predominance in the theatrical life of Henry VIII's court until his death in 1523 shows undeniably in the records of payments. After him William Crane took up the work and wrote, but in no great quantity, and all his writings too are lost. Then came Richard Bower, another shadowy figure, who held his mastership in four reigns and wrote occasional plays; but none of his work remains, unless he is the R. B. who wrote *Appius and Virginia*. Contemporary with him was a notable man, Nicholas Udall, who directed the Revels for Queen Mary, and whose three plays— *Ralph Roister Doister*, *Jack Juggler*, and *Respublica*—all bear internal evidence of having been written for children. *Roister Doister* is now dated 1552 and *Respublica* belongs to Christmas, 1553, so that these two at least were written for production at court, whether or not by the Chapel Royal. *Jack Juggler* may belong to the Eton days before 1543, but the fact that it appears to discuss certain conditions in common with *Respublica*[2] leads me to place it near the latter play, in Edward's reign. After Bower, as master of the Chapel Royal, came Richard Edwards, a man extravagantly praised in his own day, who was flattered with having carried the art of comedy to its highest point and of whom the fear was expressed that he would run mad if he wrote more plays. Strained as these threnodies sound to us who possess only one of his plays, the uneven *Damon*

---

[2] See my review of Williams's ed. of *Jack Juggler* in *Journal of Eng. and Germ. Phil.*, XV No. 2, April 1916, p. 317.

and Pythias, there yet can be no doubt that in 1565 Edwards was an admired dramatist. How far he was ahead of his contemporaries in his treatment of a romantic subject shows even through the summary which has come down to us of his famous pair of plays on the subject of the *Knight's Tale.*[3] Edwards is still a dark horse in the history of English drama. Many things are possible in this man of whose work we know so little, and it is quite likely that if we discover more of his plays, and particularly the *Palemon and Arcite,* we shall sympathize far more with the praises of Twine and Googe. After Edwards as Chapel master came William Hunnis, also highly praised by contemporary criticism. It matters not that none of the plays by him or Cornish and only one by Edwards have come down to us; the fact which matters is that they wrote copiously and aroused the enthusiasm of their contemporaries and successors.

The history of Paul's boys within the present limit of discussion presents to us only two dramatists. One of them, Sebastian Westcote, is on the whole a shadowy figure, not so well known as Edwards or Hunnis; yet I believe that the unassigned moral interlude of *The Contention between Liberality and Prodigality* came originally from his pen. He must have written many plays between 1550 and 1582, and the *Declared Accounts of the Treasurer of the Chamber* show that his company was even more popular at court than the Chapel boys; so that the loss of his plays is a matter for much regret. If Westcote is largely a subject for guess, that cannot be said of John Lyly, the other writer for Paul's, the greater part if not all of whose work we possess. It constitutes by all odds the most important body of plays produced by any children's company. More will be said of it later.

Besides these men, who wrote exclusively for children, should be mentioned the names of a few dramatists who wrote ordinarily for men, but occasionally for boys. Thus Peele's *Arraignment of Paris* was played by the Chapel at Blackfriars; Nash wrote *Summer's Last Will and Testament* for the Paul's boys; and Marlowe's and Nash's *Dido* was played by the Chapel.

The conclusion of this summary is that despite the existence of a large body of plays about whose authorship and production we known nothing, it is nevertheless safe to say that most of the known dramatists between 1515 and 1580-90, and indeed the most important of them, wrote exclusively for children. Some exceptions

[3] In the Latin of John Bereblock. Cf. W. Y. Durand, "Palemon and Arcyte," in *Pub. of the Mod. Lang. Assoc.,* 1905, New Series, Vol. 13, pp. 520 ff.

there are. The reader recalls at once Sackville and Norton, Mr. S.
of *Gammer Gurton's Needle*, William Baldwin, the ambiguous Lawrence Bariona, or Johnson, of *Misogonus*, and some others. But the
congregation of these names does not equal in fame or significance,
real or potential, that which includes Cornish, Heywood, Edwards,
Udall, Westcote, Hunnis, and Lyly. Of the large body of anonymous drama little can be said. Certain plays, like *Nice Wanton*, *Tom
Tiler*, and *Thersites*, bear clear internal evidences that they were
played by children. Some others, like *Youth* and *Lusty Juventus*,
bear less certain evidences which nevertheless constitute a probability. And of the others, it is certainly safe to say that some were
written for children, though it is impossible at present to know
which and how many. And so I repeat that by all indications the
child actors of the mid-sixteenth century led their adult rivals in
the production of plays, because conditions of presentation favored
them and because they had the dramatists.

   When we find the plays of children occupying so large a space in
the theatre of this period, we are naturally curious to know what
traits characterized them. Were they different from the plays
written for men? The question is a difficult one because we know
in so few instances which plays *were* written for men. But so far
as this obscurity will permit me to judge, I can see no vital respect
in which the obvious limitations of the young actors were reflected
in their plays. *The Nice Wanton* is not different in kind from *Hyckes-
corner* and *Mundus et Infans* (supposing these were played by men);
it is only a better play. *Roister Doister* is not essentially different
from *Gammer Gurton's Needle*, which again I grant to be a men's
play. Indeed, in *Respublica* Udall has given us a political morality
absolutely unaffected by any concession to childish limitations, a
play which is vigorous in comic delineaton, lively in spirits, and
keen in satire. The student will have to search well the list of
sixteenth century moralities before he will find its match. If the
youth of the actors did impose any restriction, it was to keep the
plays of children in the channels of farce and morality—light or
didactic. Children seem rarely or never to have ventured anything
serious like *Gorboduc* or *Calisto and Meliboea*. But the tendencies
of the day were nearly always toward farce and morality, so that
they directly favored the talent of the children. Herein lies, as we
shall see presently, a vital fact in the success of child actors.

A glance through the *Revels Accounts* shows that there is no great difference perceptible in the period under discussion between the titles of plays given by men and those given by boys. If they do not sound classical, they suggest a romantic story from the medieval chronicles. The children of various companies produced, for example, in the decade of 1570 these plays among others: *Alcmeon, Quintus Fabius, Timoclea at the Siege of Thebes, Perseus and Andromeda, The History of Mutius Scevola, The History of Titus and Gisippus, The History of Loyalty and Beauty, The History of Alucius.* At the same time companies of men were playing these: *Predor and Lucia, Mamillia, Herpetulus the Blue Knight and Perobia, Philemon and Philecia, The History of Phedrastus and Phigon and Lucia, The Painter's Daughter, The History of the Solitary Knight, A Pastoral or History of a Greek Maid, A History of the Four Sons of Fabius, A History of the Duke of Milan and the Marquis of Mantua.* Except that there was a greater tendency among the men toward romantic plays of adventure, and among the children toward plays of classical inspiration (a generalization which a more extended comparison would bear out), these lists are not greatly different. The prevailing drama of this time at court was all of a kind, either medieval-romantic, or, if.I may be allowed the term, classical-romantic.

Now there is pretty good evidence that the impulse which sent the drama in this direction came from the children's plays. Before the advent of *Calisto and Meliboea*, hitherto considered the first romantic play in English, and long before *Thersites* and *Roister Doister*, which marked the successful transplanting of classic modes to English soil, Cornish was turning from the traditional morality and interlude to new models. In 1515 he produced his *Troilus and Pandor*, drawn from Chaucer's mighty romance, the first known English play of medieval inspiration. And Cornish at least had an eye on the classics, for in the *Triumph of Love and Beauty*, played in 1514, Venus was a character. Again, the interlude by the Chapel which formed part of the brilliant revels of May 6, 1527,[4] made use of classical machinery, the debate being introduced by Mercury, who reported himself as sent down by Jupiter, and the two participants being called Cupid and Plutus (Love and Riches). Powerful aid in fixing the classical tradition came from the grammar school masters, who between 1540 and 1580 were training their boys with

[4] Cf. p. 62.

plays drawn from the classics. But chief among the men of influence must be counted Nicholas Udall and Richard Edwards. In
Jack Juggler and more especially in *Roister Doister* Udall established
a model of classical adaptation into English. Edwards, in this
extant play of *Damon and Pythias* and his pair of plays on *Palemon
and Arcite* (so far as our scanty knowledge may be relied upon), had
just the modernized classicism and the medieval romanticism which
was then dominant in the plays at court.

So it is possible to trace the classical and romantic tradition in
the Chapel plays from the early years of Henry VIII to 1590. We
find reinforcements on the classical side in the plays of Udall and
in such interludes as *Thersites*, and we find the other children's
companies following in the same tradition. It is not unreasonable,
then, to credit the introduction and popularization of this kind of
drama to the child actors, since they were in possession of it first
and played it most continuously. Indeed it is not at all impossible
that the entry of classical principles into English drama was mainly
due to children's plays, and this for two special reasons. First,
more importance than we have yet allowed may belong to the work
of the grammar school masters, who produced a large part of the
drama, in Latin and English, between 1540 and 1570, and who made
the recitation of plays of classical antiquity or plays imitated from
antiquity a part of their theory of education. Secondly, we cannot
rightly estimate the influence of Richard Edwards, who was the
earliest English dramatist to declare allegiance to Latin principles
of dramatic art,[5] and that influence, as I have frequently said, must
have been great if it was in proportion with the general admiration.
I do not mean, it is perhaps needless to say, that classicism would
not have come to England without the assistance of the children's
companies. It was on the way and nothing could keep it out. But
it does appear that those elements of classical art which belong to
drama found in the grammar schools and in the main children's
companies a particularly sympathetic medium which facilitated
greatly their entry and naturalization. In this case the adult actors
were content to follow the lead of their young rivals.

Where the children, prior to 1580, did not lead, they kept abreast.
As I have said, their interludes and moralities were neither inferior
to those of men's companies, nor appreciably cramped by the his-

[5] Cf. p. 81.

trionic limitations of the actors. To explain this state of affairs I find two closely related reasons, both depending upon the more primitive and uncritical relations of men to drama which obtained in those days. In regard to audiences, this simplicity of attitude bred an omnivorous and unsophisticated appetite. People were glad to see plays because they were plays, and they did not particularly care who acted them. The eager satisfaction with which nobles and commons alike witnessed performances which would now be laughed at is testified to again and again in the annals of the Tudor theatre. At the close of an elaborate pageant in the days of Bluff King Hal the common people, railed off at one end of the room, burst through their barriers and raided nobles and princes, even stripping the king himself of his gold ornaments.[6] The admiration of the Venetian ambassadors at the composite revels of 1527 which included the dialogue of Love and Riches, the eulogies of Edward's *Damon and Pythias,* and indeed every critical opinion of the mid-sixteenth century displays a simplicity of standard and a readiness to be content with the trivial so long as it is amusing which is not only below our own criteria of today, but far below those of the post-1600 period. Not much is demanded of a theatrical performance when the spectator is eager to be amused. The art of acting had not yet developed ideals, except possibly in broadly farcical parts. We do not hear of actors before 1580 as we hear of Alleyne and Burbage and Field and Pavey after. And not only does our evidence all go to prove that the public of the earlier period welcomed all kinds of adult actors with a generous and uncritical appreciation, but it shows also that they welcomed children as readily as men. This I have taken pains to establish in my first chapter, so that further proof is unnecessary here.

In the second place, this uncritical simplicity in the relations of men to drama showed in the plays of the period precisely as it showed in the audiences. We must not forget that the drama was still in its childhood, although it was lusty and approached adolescence. The prevailing modes were morality and farce, hybrid combinations, neither of which made anything more than elementary demands upon the technique of the actors. There was nothing in the average play of the period which transcended the abilities of a boy of twelve. Even the comparative intricacies of *Respublica* and

---

[6] See Hall, *Chronicles,* ed. 1809, p. 518 ff.

Nice Wanton could be easily handled by the trained companies of the Chapel Royal and St. Paul's. Consequently in the rivalry between boys and men the natural handicaps of the boys were counteracted by the dramatic simplicity of the times, which made no difference between plays suited to men and plays suited to boys.

But in time such a separation did take place, as the force of masculinity inevitably began to express itself and as the conceptions of dramatic power deepened beyond anything which had been entertained before. Gradually the plays of men's companies drew away into a group by themselves, passing towards rough and wholesome comedy, as in *Misogonus* and *Common Conditions*, or through plays of crude violence like *The History of Murderous Michael* toward real tragedy, as in *The Spanish Tragedy* and the plays of Marlowe; while the boys went on with their farces and their moralities and their classical comedies until they culminated in a set of plays stamped as no others are with their virtues and their limitations—the plays of Lyly. Just when this split began it is impossible to say. Doubtless the germs of it were present early in the century and can be found at work in such plays as *Calisto and Meliboea* and *Gorboduc*. But it was not until about 1575 that the difference between "men's plays" and "children's plays" began to make itself felt, and the split was not finally accomplished before 1580.

The plays of Lyly deserve at this point special attention, for not only are they the culminating achievement in this period of child actors, as I have said, but they are practically the only body of plays of which one may say: "These were written for children and could have been written for none but them." They bear the children's stamp unmistakably upon them; and yet to regard them simply as the product of catering to children would be to make a serious error, for they are to a remarkable degree the product of cooperation, in which the dramatist found actors who were particularly suited to his talents, and the players found a dramatist who could give them better than anyone else the thing which they could do well. The result of this cooperation was a group of plays which not only were popular in their own day, but brought new elements into English drama and gained a place as one of the important formative influences on the great playwright who was to follow. For several reasons, then, the plays of Lyly deserve to be held a landmark in the history of children's companies.

We must not underestimate the debt which Lyly owed to the children of Pauls. His plays required not acting which was vivid or powerful, or even true to life, but the kind of stage presence which delivered the lines with clarity and point and which possessed the cardinal virtue of vivacity. These qualities the children had in greater degree than the men, for their shrill, well trained voices could launch the speeches with just the piquancy that was needed, and their pert and graceful bearing would show off to the fullest advantage the mischievous pages who today hold what sparkles of life remain in the plays. The children had, in short, just what the plays needed—charm and vivacity. And most fortunately for Lyly, their very inability to portray passion or any deep emotion agreed with the same notable lack in their dramatist. In one more respect, I believe, the boys aided Lyly. Just as after 1600 the managers of the Queen's Revels children made deliberate use of the immunity which the youth of their actors supposedly furnished to fill their plays with scandalous satire, so it is not unlikely that Lyly made some use of the same license of action to indulge in rather daring allusions to court histories and to give his plays the topical cast which we recognize as part of their very fibre and which furnishes so much of the matter for discussion when Lyly's plays are studied. I doubt if such familiarity would have been tolerated in a company of men. In a word, then, the boys of Paul's offered a special set of conditions particularly well adapted for a special set of plays. In no company of men could Lyly have found a medium so sympathetic.

Thus abetted in his own inborn tendencies by his young stars, Lyly developed a style in drama which was radically new. While keeping to the subject matter which had been traditional with the children's companies, he discarded verse altogether and wrote in prose, with a degree of polish, finesse of thought and expression, and play of words which had hitherto appeared nowhere save in his own *Euphues*. It is not my purpose to raise so platitudinous a question as the debt of English style to Lyly. We know how much the earlier comedies of Shakespeare owed to him. It is true that Lyly was only a stepping-stone, and that his successors soon progressed far beyond and above him, but as an inspiration toward contrivance and refinement in style he cannot be much overestimated. And so far as his plays are concerned, it was largely through his finding a company of actors which aided him in indulging his genius that he was enabled to accomplish this result.

While the plays of Lyly are the fine flower of the children's drama before 1590, they are at the same time a decadence. In them for the first time we can clearly observe cropping out the effect of the limitations of the actors. If the lads had sprightliness, vivacity, pertness, and charm, they lacked power to portray serious and deep emotions. And accordingly we find none of the deeper emotions in Lyly. His main figures are animated marionettes, endowed with beautiful speeches but no action. The only figures which are in any way characterized and give scope for acting are the scallawag pages and an occasional Sir Thopas. Doubtless the utter lack of real feeling in Lyly was due in large part to the man's temperament, but doubtless also the nature of his actors guided him a good deal. We shall never know just how much his plays owed to himself for their faults and virtues and how much to the actors; but I have no doubt that the actors had a considerable share in his post-Euphuesian development.

His plays, then, mark a growing break between the drama of the juvenile and of the adult companies. As Lyly is the flower of the one group, so were Greene, Kyd, and Marlowe the flower at this time of the other, and the differences between the work of these groups are typical of the tendencies of the two classes of actors. The children could not, or would not, follow where the drama was leading. It is a significant illustration of the reality of this schism that when the new school of dramatists wrote for children, as they occasionally did, they departed from their usual style to write down to the abilities of the actors. This is not so clearly evident in Peele's *Arraignment of Paris*, because Peele's genius was never very masculine, but it does appear in Nash's *Summers Last Will and Testament* and Marlowe's and Nash's *Dido*. The children of Paul's were lucky in finding a man who by the freshness of style of his plays gave them a vogue in their own class of drama; but that class was fast dying, and by 1600 it was so dead that when the resuscitated companies of the Chapel and St. Paul's revived some of their old successes they were laughed off the stage.

As we look back over the period of 1515-1590, we see that so long as the children kept pace with the drama, they led in it, but that as soon as the drama grew beyond their powers they fell behind. The plays of the period were seldom such that children could not satisfactorily perform them. If they were not moralities of elementary characterization, they were farces like *Jack Juggler* and *Tom Tiler*, or pageants like *Loyalty and Beauty*, or comedies of modified classicism like *Damon and Pythias* and *The Arraignment of Paris*, or comedies of modified romanticism like *Common Conditions*. These plays, with certain exceptions, did not go deeply enough into the souls of men to make demands in acting which the children could not satisfy. In the case of the moralities, it must have been particularly appropriate to see them acted by youths of the very age to profit by them. The children could do this kind of drama, which after all was itself a youthful and immature thing; and they did it so well that they led the country in the production of important plays. But the drama grew and the children did not, with the result that they were left finally behind. After the interval of dissolution between 1590 and 1600, they again matched themselves with men in the plays they gave, but the conditions which made this possible were peculiar, and the boys no longer commanded the best talents of the best writers of the time.

When the children of St. Paul's and the Chapel returned to the stage in 1599-1600, their relations to their fellow actors and to the drama were far different from what they had been before 1590. The change is marked by the appearance of two new elements—commercialism and imitation.

The split which was an accomplished fact in 1590 did not cease to be effective during the ten years banishment which the main children's companies suffered, and when the Paul's and Chapel boys returned at the close of the century they began by continuing in the tradition which had been established in the decade of 1580-90 with the plays of Lyly, Peele's *Arraignment of Paris*, and Marlowe's *Dido*. The first plays they put on were such "musty fopperies of antiquity" as *The Maid's Metamorphosis*, *Doctor Doddipole*, and Westcote's (?) *Contention between Liberality and Prodigality*. But the public would have none of them, for the taste for "children's plays" had gone out, and Lyly was now quite dead as a literary force. The wisdom, and to some extent the daring, of the managers of the children's companies now manifested itself, for instead of attempting to carry the boys on in the kind of play experience had declared to be most suitable, they bent to the popular will and boldly launched forth in direct rivalry with the great men's companies, meeting them upon their own dramatic ground. Both Paul's and the Chapel companies looked about among the young generation of dramatists for men whom they could enlist in their service, and both were singularly fortunate in discovering talents which were suited to their needs. Paul's at once found in young John Marston, whose *Scourge of Villainy* and *Pygmalion* had in 1598 created a *succès de scandale*, a dramatist whose plays offered the high seasoning needed to titillate the public palate. The Chapel was happy in securing for a time the aid of another young, though more experienced dramatist, Ben Jonson, who was already a personality in literary London and whose two controversial plays, *Cynthia's Revels* and *Poetaster*, launched the company upon the course of satire whose reward was publicity and whose penalty, as it turned out, was imprisonment and dissolution. In another young dramatist, though experienced poet, George Chapman, the Chapel found a man who was to be faithful to them through many years, to their special glory, and Paul's found an assistant to Marston in young Middleton.

In appropriating the services of these three men—Marston, Chapman, and Middleton,—the children put upon the stage a body of plays which occupies an important share of Jacobean drama and is not generally separated in the minds of critics from the plays written to be acted by men. On a hasty survey, accordingly, it might appear that child actors had returned to the status they enjoyed before 1580 as the worthy rivals of men; yet such a conclusion would be wrong. To this point I shall return later. For the present I wish to point out that the hiring of Marston, Jonson, Chapman, and the rest of the professional writers meant a significant change from previous methods of conducting children's companies— they had become *commercialized*. And this is another way of looking at the difference between the period of 1515-1590 and the period of 1600-1615. It would be useless to deny that before 1590 the idea of profit-making had entered into the children's theatre. The boys of Paul's and the Chapel had places for public performances, wherever they were, and charged admission. The building of the first Blackfriars theatre was a thoroughly commercial venture. But the *raison d'être* of both companies was still to prepare and present plays at court, and the writing and producing of plays was still in the hands of the choir masters. Thus the companies, headed by their masters, were self-supplying and self-sustaining. To some extent, it is true, the plays of other dramatists were bought, as in the cases of Lyly, Peele, and Nash, but such outside work is not to be compared in amount with the work of Cornish, Edwards, Farrant, and Hunnis. After 1600, however, the reliance on professional dramatists, which showed sporadically before 1590, became a custom. No longer were the children managed by men who wrote plays. Not one play has ever been heard of from the pen of Edward Pierce, master of Paul's, nor from any of the several directors of Blackfriars—Nathaniel Gyles, Edward Kirkham, Thomas Kendall, or Robert Keysar.

And so the companies of Paul's and the Chapel were now, after 1600, commercial companies hiring their dramatists and (in the case of the Chapel, at least) guided no longer by a single master, but by a board of directors, banded together in accordance with strictly business principles. If anything were needed to prove the commercialization of the children's stage, a glance would serve through the history of the Chapel-Revels company from 1600 to 1605, filled as it is with bonds, deeds, letters patent, lawsuits and pleas. Even more to the point, as I have shown, is the history of the first Whitefriars company, a purely commercial venture from first to last. As to the management of Paul's, there is considerable doubt because of our almost total ignorance, yet sufficient indication exists that Pierce, the choir master, retained the management;[7] nevertheless, in the hiring of dramatists Paul's fell in line with the Chapel. And in conclusive witness of the trend of the times, the miscellaneous companies of children which previous to 1590 had flourished spontaneously and in the middle of the century were active all over the kingdom, had by 1600 died almost completely away. Occasionally thereafter a grammar school may be traced playing before the magistrates of a country town, but such performances are few, and they never appear in London records.

The first Whitefriars company I have referred to as exhibiting *par excellence* the commercial spirit. In the early months of 1607, and by successive negotiations through that year and into 1608, a company of children was organized to act at a new theatre in the Whitefriars precinct, just outside the city limits. For its guidance a board of directors was gathered together on a profit sharing basis, including the promotor Thomas Woodford, the actor Martin Slatier, who was to have charge of the boys, a few amateur dramatists like Lording Barry and John Mason, and a miscellaneous group of men who desired an easy investment. These were bound by various obligations, and an elaborate set of Articles of Agreement was drawn up and signed. The first thing which strikes the observer is the

---

[7] The negotiations in 1609 to buy out Paul's were carried on with Pierce.

number of men who anticipated deriving profit from this one company; the next is the complete failure of the enterprise, for within a
year and a half the company had been evicted for failure to pay
rent, and for many years thereafter the courts of London were filled
with suits to recover damages. From the business point of view the
Whitefriars venture presents the familiar spectacle of inflated inception and quick collapse. When we look at the plays, our impression
is fortified that the company was started purely from desire to rival
the success of the two main companies, for imitation is strong in
them. In Machin's and Markham's *Dumb Knight*, Barry's *Ram
Alley*, Armin's *Two Maids of Mortlake*, Day's *Humor out of Breath*
and possibly *Law Tricks*, we find comedies which are little more
than hodge-podges of popular situations, plundering English drama
from *Ralph Roister Doister* to *Eastward Ho*, filled with literary allusions and burlesques. There is hardly a situation in *Ram Alley* or
Cupid's Whirligig which cannot be duplicated in plays of the day.
Two facts stand out in relation to these Whitefriars plays. The first
is their general mediocrity; the second is their readiness to absorb
the popular elements of contemporary drama.

The commercialization of the children's theatre bore fruit in
many ways, all of which it is impossible to trace. The effect on the
drama I am reserving for final consideration. At the present moment
I wish to present one aspect of this fruition which is sufficiently
striking, I mean the part played by children's companies in the
satirical drama of the decade 1600-1610. The mingling of the Chapel
and Paul's in the War of the Poets—through *The Poetaster, Cynthia's
Revels*, and *Satiromastix*—is a case in point, but I refer particularly
to political, and therefore dangerous, satire, for which the directors
of the Chapel-Revels company seem to have had an uncontrollable
appetite. We have seen how they courted disaster in Daniel's
Philotas, in Day's *Isle of Gulls*, in Chapman's and Jonson's *Eastward
Ho*, in Chapman's *Biron* plays, and in one or two pieces which we
know by reference only. Besides these important instances, there
were minor shots in other plays. One is astonished at the persistence
with which the masters at Blackfriars indulged in this dangerous
pastime and at the lengths to which they dared go—as in the bitter
denunciation of legal injustice at the end of *The Widow's Tears*, the
unveiled thrusts at the king in *The Isle of Gulls*, *Eastward Ho*, and
the unknown play of 1608 in which the king was brought on the
stage drunk, quarrelsome, and foul mouthed. One explanation for

the recourse to satire suggests itself at once—sensationalism. There is no surer way of gaining the public ear than by abusing prominent people. Lyly catered in his plays to the taste for topical allusiveness, prevalent as well at court as in the City, and thereby helped their vogue. That the managers of the Chapel company found the spicy satire of *Poetaster* and *Cynthia's Revels* an effective aid in their early efforts to capture the public ear, and that their subsequent daring flights made for them fame and patronage, I cannot doubt. Whether their own quarrelsomeness and the bitterness engendered by successive reproofs may not have sharpened their pens, is a reasonable conjecture; but I believe that primarily the Chapel plays strove for notoriety in the most effective of all ways—personal satire.

This explanation does not, of course, make clear why the adult companies did not have recourse equally to the same expedient. The answer can be made that after the passing of the children's companies the men *did* make frequent use of satire (as in the *Game of Chess*), and that anyhow they had not so much need as the children of violent means of publicity. Yet neither explanation touches upon the real reason why the satirical plays of 1600-1610 belong far more to the children than to the men. Thomas Heywood has given us the clue we want. In his *Apology for Actors*,[8] in which he speaks for the men of the profession, he writes as follows:

Now to speake of some Abuse lately crept into the Quality as an inveighing against the State, the Court, the Law, the Citty, and their Governements, with the particularizing of private Mens Humors (yet alive) Noble-men, and others, I know it distastes many; neither do I any way approve it; nor dare I by any Meanes excuse it The liberty which some arrogate to themselves, Committing their Bitternesse, and liberall Invectives against all Estates, to the Mouthes of Children, supposing their juniority to be a Priviledge for any rayling, be it never so violent, I could advise all such, to curbe and limit this presumed Liberty within the Bounds of Discretion and Government. But wise and Juditiall Censurers, before whom such Compliments shall at any time hereafter come, wil not (I hope) impute these Abuses to any Transgression in us, who have ever been carefull and provident to shun the like.

The explanation offered here is, I believe, a true as it certainly is a plausible one. Children dared go farther than men in their satirical attacks because their youth gave them a fancied immunity, "a

---

[8] Published in 1612. Reprinted in Lord John Somers's *Second Collection of Scarce . . . . Tracts*, 1750; this extract appears on p. 202 of Vol. I.

privilege for railing." It was the screen behind which the hunter lay.
Heywood implies that the reason which prompted the satire was
the pure spirit of negation and misrule. Perhaps so, and yet I fear
that such an explanation savors too much of seventeenth century
polemic to be trustworthy. But whatever the explanation, the fact
remains that the children, and especially the Chapel boys, pursued
an unrelenting and unparalleled course of satire in which poets,
public men, institutions, and royalty itself were besmirched. This
body of plays is perhaps the most definite and striking, if hardly the
most creditable, contribution of the child actors to English drama
after 1600. It could not, I believe, have been made before 1600; it
would not have been made but for the existence of the children's
companies; and it is very doubtful if it would have been made had
the children's theatre remained uncommercialized, in the hands of
the choir masters.

We now approach the plays which were acted by children between
1600 and 1615, with the question: How are these plays related to
the actors who gave them and to the rest of contemporary drama?
The list of children's plays after 1600 is a long one. It includes
most of the work of Chapman and Marston, nearly half of Middleton's, several of Jonson's (with *Epicœne*), several of Beaumont and
Fletcher's (with *The Knight of the Burning Pestle*), and a great many
by lesser men, of whom some wrote entirely for children. Hardly
a dramatist, high or low, but wrote some piece of work for one or
another children's company. In this respect Shakespeare, with
possibly Heywood, stands almost alone. In running through the
list one encounters, besides the two famous plays mentioned above,
such names as *Satiromastix*, *Eastward Ho*, *Bussy d'Ambois*, *Malcontent*, *A Trick to Catch the Old One*, *The Puritan*, *All Fools*, *The
Turk*, *The Isle of Gulls*, *Philotas*, *Woman is a Weathercock*. These
exhaust Elizabethan drama; there are no kinds of plays which are
not represented here. It looks as though the effort of the children
to rival the men had succeeded, and that the split which for a time
had divided English drama into "children's plays" and "men's
plays" had been obliterated. Yet such is not the case, for as long
and as notable as is the list of children-acted plays, the split proved
nevertheless to be incurable, and its effects persisted in the plays
we have listed.

To understand what these effects were and how they showed, one
must appreciate the changed relations of the children to the public

of the theatre. In the earlier decades of the sixteenth century, as I have repeatedly tried to make clear, boy actors were listened to with respect, with an enthusiasm which is hardly comprehensible if respect were lacking. Then the drama was younger and cruder, and so likewise was the art of acting; then there was not the wide gulf which our twentieth century prejudices might infer between the young actors and the old; then the boys were abetted by a drama and style of acting which were yet unfinished, and by a public which was yet untrained in criticism. But in 1600 these conditions no longer held. The drama had made tremendous strides toward maturity and complexity; the art of acting had been enriched by the labors of Tarleton, Alleyne, and Burbage; the public was becoming rapidly trained to the fine points of dramaturgy and acting, and was inevitably bound toward finer sophistication, aided by the great decade which had opened. London in 1600 was a far different place from what it was in 1585, even in 1590. How could people now feel toward child actors as they had felt before? Even admitting that the Jacobean spectators were as satisfied of the fitness of boys to play women as the Elizabethans had been, surely they found no illusion when boys impersonated men, they who knew Burbage and Alleyne. Boys on the stage must have seemed to them largely what boys on the stage now seem to us—masqueraders They had charm, of course, the charm of piquant strangeness and the genuine charm of delightful music, nimble dancing, the vivacity of rattling comedy, often precocious skill, as in Salathiel Pavey's old men; but granting all that, and making allowances for the perpetuating instincts of an old tradition, I cannot help feeling that the fundamental attraction of the boy actors for the Jacobean public was the whimsical charm of a masquerade. "The apes in time will do it finely," said Brabant Senior of the boys of Paul's, most happy in his descriptive noun. Hamlet's "little eyases that cry out on the top of the question" is a commentary from an unfriendly source, bearing witness to a popularity which throve in spite of limitations as clearly perceived as they could be to-day.

The boys of post-1600 were no longer leading the way for men to follow; they were now apes, copying the matter and manner of the men. That granted, the part these lads played in the drama of the time becomes clear. Because they were simply copyists, who did not inspire the best talents of the best men, that part was small; with certain exceptions which had nothing to do with their histrionic ability, they had no appreciable influence on the course of the drama. It is true that besides Shakespeare there was hardly a dramatist who did not write for them; true that they possessed Marston and Chapman and for a time Middleton; true that some charming and brilliant comedies, notably *Epicœne*, were acted by them; but it is equally true that no play of real depth of feeling and of artistic purpose, two exceptions always made, was brought upon the boards of their theatres. Instead they played rattling comedies, like *All Fools* and *Two Maids of Mortlake*; or satirical comedies, like *Eastward Ho*, *The Isle of Gulls*, and *The Widow's Tears*; or swelling fustian, like *Sophonisba*, *Antonio's Revenge*, and *Bussy d'Ambois*. Furthermore, although the greater dramatists wrote for them, yet none of these men, except in the one unexplainable case of *Epicœne* (we cannot count the *Knight of the Burning Pestle*, which was refused by many companies before being accepted by Robert Keysar), wrote their best plays for boys. Jonson is represented by *The Case is Altered*, *Poetaster*, and *Cynthia's Revels*; Middleton by several of his comedies but *not* by *The Changeling* or *The Chaste Maid in Cheapside*; Beaumont and Fletcher by *The Coxcomb*, *The Woman Hater*, and *The Scornful Lady*.

Upon careful study of the list of plays acted after 1600 by children, it becomes clearly apparent that the same effect of limitation exists which we observed in Lyly's plays, though a great deal more scope is allowed than Lyly could compass. There was still one road which was irretrievably barred to children, the road to emotional depth and tragic intensity. For the boys no great dramatist, except the obstinate Jonson, would do his sincerest work. That does not mean that the children acknowledged their limitations and avoided tragedy. To do so would have been a violation of their principle of rivalry in all things. But in attempting tragedy, at the hands of their own dramatists, they proved conclusively the hollowness of that rivalry, for in their hands tragedy turned to melodrama and tragic declamation to swelling bombast. The tragedies of Marston and Chapman, of *Sophonisba*, *Antonio and Mellida*, and even of *Bussy D'Ambois*, are "children's tragedy," just as truly as Lyly's plays a decade before had been "children's comedy." They are a playing with fire and thunder, in which fine passages and noble lines cannot successfully combat the general unreality. The relations of children to tragedy cannot be better illustrated than in the following incident. About 1585 Kyd's *Spanish Tragedy* was brought out, and in its day it was a play of exceptional and moving power. The year before had seen the production of Peele's *Arraignment of Paris* and Lyly's *Campaspe* and *Sapho and Phao*, in which the boys of Paul's and the Chapel Royal virtually declared their determination not to transcend their limitations. I do not believe that at this time a company of children would have dreamt of acting Kyd's play or anything like it. Shortly after 1600 the Chapel company, being in need of a play, got hold of *The Spanish Tragedy*, then in the possession of Burbage's company, probably had Jonson write a number of new scenes, and produced it.[9] But in the fifteen years since its birth, the play, while retaining a large measure of popularity with the crowds, had become completely outmoded with the *conoscenti* and had long been a source of jest for its fervid and meretricious pomp. Within a year or two of this revival London saw *Hamlet* and *A Woman Killed with Kindness*. The incident is full of meaning.

If we can deny to children any important participation in Jacobean tragedy, we must allow them an honorable share in comedy. Herein their limitations are far less perceptible. This does not surprise us, for we have seen from the beginning that the genius of children lay on the side of the comic, and it is there at all times that their real successes were made. All that agility, audacity, grace, and pertness can bring to the stage belonged to these boys, and these are the graces of comedy. In such light characterizations the boys of Paul's and the Queen's Revels doubtless attained skill often amounting to brilliancy. Salathiel Pavey's old men, so praised by Jonson, were the old men of comedy. It is to be expected that as in the case of tragedy the children's genius should lie away from depth of feeling; and hence it is that we find practically no serious or romantic comedies—no *Philasters* or *Shoemaker's Holidays*—but a great many which are farcical, cynical, and satiric. Thus the old limitations show again, but within their generous limits the "children's comedies" of post-1600 are not to be distinguished from the men's. Though it is true that most of them are second- and third-rate, yet many are important in the catalogue of Elizabethan and Jacobean drama, and we must not forget that to the children belong most of the comedies of Chapman and Marston. For these alone the boy actors would be noteworthy. As we have seen, the rather unsavory comedy of public satire was their peculiar property.

[9] Cf. Induction by Webster to Marston's *Malcontent* in the version of the King's men, who took the play in revenge for the Chapel theft.

The whole course of the children's companies after 1600 bears witness to the artificial basis of their relations to the public. It is the characteristic of fads that they flourish and die quickly. Whereas children had acted in an almost unbroken course from 1515 to 1590, their post-1600 history lasts a bare sixteen years. By 1616 the Chapel Revels company had vanished from the London stage after its brief revival at the Puddlewharf theatre. Paul's boys had been bought out in 1609. The King's Revels company had bloomed for a year and a half. After 1616, it is true, children went on for years traveling the Provinces, where custom had not staled their variety and where taste kept some of its Tudor simplicity. In London, too, boys reappeared occasionally, as in 1637 under the guidance of Christopher Beeston, but these resurrections are sporadic and without meaning, save as marking the dying sputters of an old fire. For the purposes of our history we have accepted the year 1616 as marking the end of children's companies in London. The Cromwellian interregnum put a permanent end to boy actors as a serious factor in English drama. During the reign of Charles II was established the Nursery, or training school of young actors, but its life was short and uneventful, and no plays were written for these artists. After their demise we must pass to the early nineteenth century before we meet again with a child on the stage. The furor which greeted the young tragedian Master Betty[10] remains a curious phenomenon in the history of the English theatre. Undoubtedly Betty had talent which was far in advance of his age and which appeared genius for being so. But his triumph was brief. It was over in two years, and his case justly deserves the term I have applied—phenomenon. In the nineteenth and twentieth centuries children have been seen not infrequently on the stage—in the once-popular Sunday school performances of *Pinafore*, for a few months in New York as a company acting fairy plays for children, and occasionally in special performances.

But the virtue has gone out of children's companies. We no longer know how to look at them, as our ancestors knew in the days when Elizabeth was still young. We would have to put ourselves in the frame of mind of an audience of Italian laborers at a marionette show, lose our sense of unreality in a deep interest in the play, and forget that the puppets are not the heroes they pretend to be. Such

[10] Cf. p. 37.

an attitude requires three things which our Elizabethan ancestor had in common with the modern Italian laborer: keen appetite for drama of all kinds, critical sense which demands little and is satisfied with little, and the familiarizing effect of a long tradition. Without these three aids, child actors, like marionettes, cease to be a living force in art and become a fad. For that reason it is impossible that children shall ever return in earnest to the stage. They died about 1616.

APPENDIX I
THE CHILDREN OF THE PRIVY CHAMBER

Besides the Chapel boys, there was another body of singing children in the Royal Household about whom a word should be spoken. It was the custom, from how early times I cannot determine to maintain among the musicians at court six singing boys. They were usually under the supervision of one of the luters, who exercised over them much the same control and care as did the master of the Chapel over his children, and they were acquired by the same expedient of impressing. The first writ of impressment we have knowledge of was granted in 1456 to Walter Halyday, Robert Marshall, William Wykes, and John Clyffe.[1] In order to supply vacancies caused by death, these men were instructed to take up "quosdam Pueros, Membris Naturalibus Elegantes, in Arte Ministrellatus instructos," wherever they could be found, as well within liberties as without. This writ has been much discussed in relation to the custom of impressment, but it has never before been connected with the body of singing boys here under consideration.

They appear in various account sheets of the court from the end of Henry VIII's reign on, always among the musicians. Their duties are easy to guess; they doubtless took part in the concerts provided by the musicians, and they make it apparent that the compositions then given were not confined to instruments. Whether they were used in any other way is not clear. We should like to know, for instance, if they followed the example of the Chapel boys in performing plays. There is at least a possibility that they may have, under Heywood. Their existence, at any rate, has given rise to some confusion about the supposed connection of Philip van Wilder with the Chapel.

This Philip van Wilder, gentleman of the Privy Chamber, first appears in the *Household Expense Book* of Henry VIII[2] under February 3, a° 29 (1548): "philip Welder luter wag*es* lvj*s* viij*d*." Another payment[3] was made in the next year to "Philip van Wilder,

[1] Rymer's *Foedera*, XI, 375.
[2] *Arundel MSS.* 97, fol. 3.
[3] Brewer and Gairdner, XIII, p. 101.

276

Luter, £70 allowance for six singing children." In 1550 he was authorized to impress for the King's use "in any churches or chappells within England . . . . such, and as many singing children and choristers as he or his deputies should think good."[4] He must have died before the seventh year of Edward VI, because his Inquisition Post Mortem was taken then.[5] His son Peter inherited his place as luter and with it the charge of the six children. The following note is taken from a book of certificates of the Treasurer of the Chamber from 37 Henry VIII to 2 and 3 Philip and Mary.[6] It is part of a longer list of musicians and court officers.

xxiiijto Octobris Annis Regnor*um* R*egis* et Regine Phi*l*ipi et Marie S*ecun*do et Tertio

	Peter van Welder lewter, by the	
	yere xviij[li] v[s] in the	
lewters &	rowme of Phelip van Welder luter	
syngynge	decessed by the yere xl[li]. And	cxxxviij[li]
Children	also xx iiij[li] to hym more for	v[s]
	fyndynge of six synginge Children	
	belongynge to the privye Chamber	

Philip van Wilder's title and duties are outlined in the following order for payment, dated September 18, 1550:[7] "A warrant . . . . to deliver LX (sic) to Philip Vanwilder, oone of the Kinges Majesties Privie Chambre and Master of his Hignes Singinge Children, for wages for iij quarters of a yere endinge at mighelmas." The wages (£80) paid Wilder for his services are extraordinarily high, especially in view of the fact that he had but six boys to take care of. No doubt he had to support the boys on that sum, for there are no records of payments for the purpose, either directly or through the Wardrobe.

The existence of a body of singing children enrolled among the musicians, and so highly thought of that a writ of impressment was granted their supervisor to replenish their number, raises interesting suppositions. Were they ever drafted into an acting company? Were these the boys whom Heywood used in putting on his interludes before Edward VI and Mary? Did the regular Chapel company ever draw upon them in cases when the number of acting

---

[4] *Lansdowne Mss.* 171; *Stowe MSS.* 571; Stopes's *Hunnis*, p. 12, and elsewhere.
[5] Stopes's *Hunnis*, p. 12.
[6] *Exchequer Accounts*, 429/9, p. 195.
[7] *Acts of the Privy Council, New Series*, 1550-52, p. 26.

parts exceeded their number? Perhaps some day a document will be found which will inform us more thoroughly on these and other questions.

Seemingly the Privy Chamber boys were kept up until well into the next century, for in a list of officers of the court, apparently of the time of James I,[8] I found, among musicians and players:

		£	s	d
Singers..........8	ffee a peece	6	13	4
	Allow: for Chil-			
	dren for singinge	50	-	-

And in a similar list contained in *Sloane MSS.* 3194 (fol. 38) of the year 1585, I found:

Luters	3	ffee.....................40[li]
		ffor 6 singinge Children
		ffee.....................18[li] 5[s].

[8] *Rawlinson MSS.* B. 161, fol. 91ff (Bodleian).

APPENDIX II

A CHRONOLOGICAL LIST OF CHILDREN'S PLAYS

The interludes of John Heywood.

Title pages,   *A play of loue, A newe and a mery enterlude concernyng*
head-pieces,   *pleasure and payne in loue, made by Jhon Heywood.*
and   *The players names.* (names follow)
colophons:
    Col: Prynted by .W. Rastell M. CCCCC. XXXIIII. Cum
    priuilegio Regali.
    (There is also an edition, the earliest, of 1533.)

    The play of the wether A new and a very mery enterlude
    of all maner wethers made by John Heywood, The
    players names. (names follow)
    Col: Prynted by W. Rastell 1533. Cum priuilegio.

    A mery play betwene the pardoner and the frere. the
    curate and neybour Pratte.
    Col: Imprynted by Wyllyam Rastell the .v. day of Apryll,
    the yere of our lorde .M. CCCCC. XXXIII.
    Cum priuilegio.

    The playe called the foure P.P. A newe and a very mery
    enterlude of A palmer. A pardoner. A potycary. A
    pedler. Made by Iohn Heewood.
    Col: Imprynted at London in Fletestrete at the sygne of the
    George by Willyam Myddylton. (n.d., but c.1545)

    A mery play betwene Johan Johan the husbande, Tyb
    his wyfe, & syr Jhan the preest.
    Col: Imprynted by Wyllyam Rastell, the .xii. day of Feb-
    ruary the yere of our lord .M.CCCCC. and .XXXIII.
    Cum priuilegio.

Date: Only one of the interludes has in it a reference to date; *The Pardoner* mentions Pope Leo X, who died in 1521. Otherwise we have only the dates of printing, the span of Hewyood's life, and the æsthetic values of the plays themselves to guide us. For a more thorough balancing of these elements, I refer the reader to my paper on *The Interludes of John Heywood* in *Modern Philology*, XIII, No. 5, September, 1915, the conclusions of which I may thus summarize. The *Play of Love*, clearly the effort of a young man, I place first, with *Weather*, which bears a family likeness to *Love* but is technically more advanced, not long after. *John the Husband*, if indeed it is Heywood's, belongs last because it seems in all respects the most mature product of his dramatic genius. Between *Love* and *John the Husband* come the other two, *The Pardoner and the Friar* and the *Four PP*, both showing influence from France, which may have come in by way of the Field of the Cloth of Gold (1520); of these two *The Four PP* certainly came last, for reasons which I have elaborated in my article. My tentative chronology of the interludes goes then as follows: *Love* (c. 1518), *Weather*, *The Pardoner* (c. 1521), *The Four PP* (1525 or earlier), and *John the Husband* (before the outbreak of the Anglican Reformation).

Remarks: I do not include these plays in my list because I am convinced that children played them, but out of deference to opinion, which though it acts in this case with little foundation, cannot be disproved. No reason exists for believing that these plays were acted by the Chapel boys (or any others) except that Heywood is known to have played at least once before the Princess Mary with a company of unidentified children and more than once before Elizabeth, and that one character in his plays (Little Dick in *Weather*) is known to be a child. Against the assumption that Heywood put on his interludes with the children of the Chapel, who were the only company of boys known to be playing at court at this time, we may charge that Hewyood was in no way connected with the Chapel at the time he was writing his plays, but was enrolled among the musicians, and that the Chapel boys were engaged regularly in playing under their own masters; furthermore, that there is nothing in the plays, with the possible exception of *Weather*, which suggests that they were written for children.

Thersites, anon.

Title page: *A new Enterlude called Thersytes Thys Enterlude
                  Followynge Dothe Declare howe that the greatest boesters
                  are not the greatest doers.* (names of players follow)

        *Col: Imprinted at London, by John Tysdale and are to be
              solde at hys shop in the upper ende of Lombard strete,
              in Alhallowes church yarde neare vnto grace church.*

Date: The prayer for the queen, Lady Jane, and the new born prince, fixes the date at October, 1537. But, as has been frequently pointed out, there are indications in the lines of the play that the time of production was Christmas. (For a discussion of these matters, see Pollard, *English Miracle Plays*, 1904, p. 214.) A compromise theory is usually held that the play was revived at the occasion of the birth of the prince.

Remarks: Mr. Boas, in his *University Drama in the Tudor Age* (Oxford, Clarendon Press, 1914), p 20, brings pretty sound evidences from allusions in the play that *Thersites* was acted at Oxford and suggests that it was one of the Magdalen Christmas plays written between 1530, when Textor's *Dialogi*, the source, was published, and 1537. That the play was written for children, either young scholars or choir-boys, is witnessed by the epilogue, with its admonition "to youre rulers and parentes be you obediente."

Tom Tiler, anon.

Title page: *Tom Tyler and His Wife. An excellent old Play, as It was Printed and Acted about a hundred Years ago. Together, with an exact Catalogue of all the playes that were ever yet printed. The second Impression. London, Printed in the Year, 1661.*

Date: All the guide we have is critical opinion based on the text. Of course Kirkman's (the publisher) "hundred Years ago" is used in the most general sense. While no other edition than this is known, there are hints of editions in 1551, 1578, 1598 (see J. S. Farmer, *Hand List to the Tudor Facsimile Texts*, under *Tom Tiler*). Ward dates the play, or the publication thereof, 1578; Schelling judges that it belongs about 1540, or at the latest early in the reign of Elizabeth. The prayer to the queen (unnamed) at the end is no certain evidence, because early interludes were often brought up to date in their references to the sovereign when they were published, e.g. *Nice Wanton*.

Remarks: That the play was written for boys is witnessed by the prologue:

> I humbly come.... to make report
> That after me you shall hear merrie sport.
> To make you joy and laugh at merrie toyes,
> I mean a play set out by prettie boyes.

The kinship of this rollicking and risky interlude to the work of John Heywood had been noticed.

Lusty Juventus, by Wever.

Title page: *An Enterlude called lusty Juuentus, Lyuely discribing the frailtye of youth: of nature, prone to vice: by grace and good counsayle, trayneable to vertue. The names of the players.* (names follow)

Col: *Finis. Quod. R. Weuer.*

Imprinted at London by John Awdely dwelling in little Britayne strete without Aldersgate. (n.d.)

Date: Temp. Edward VI, in all probability. And see p. 66.
Remarks: There are no incontrovertible evidences that *Lusty Juventus* was acted by children; yet the strongly disciplinary nature of the teaching raises that probability, and the ardent Protestantism points to the reign of Edward VI, when plays by children, occasionally with the king in the cast, were popular at court.

The Nice Wanton, anon.

Title page: *A pretie Enterlude called Nice Wanton.*

> *Wherin ye may see,*
> *Three braunches of an ill tree:*
> *The mother and her Children three,*
> *Two naught and one godly.*

> *Early sharp that wilbe thorne,*
> *Soon ill that wilbe naught:*
> *To be naught better vnborne,*
> *Better vnfed then naughtily taught.*

> *Et magnum magnos, pueros puerilia decus.*

> *Imprinted at London at the long Shop adioyning vnto Saint Mildreds Church in the pultrie, by John Allde.* (n.d.)

This is the title page of the facsimile in the Tudor Text series. The earliest dated 4to is from 1560.

Date: Reign of Edward VI. See pp. 125 ff.

Jack Juggler, by Nicholas Udall.
Title page: *A new Enterlued for Chyldren to playe, named Jacke Jugeler, both wytte and very playsent. Newly Imprented.*
(names of the characters)
Col: *Imprinted at London in Lothbury by me Wyllyam Copland* (n.d.)

S.R. 1562 (?)
Authorship and date: Mr. W. H. Williams, in his edition of the play (University Press, Cambridge, 1914), adduces excellent reasons for ascribing the play to Nicholas Udall, a conclusion at which I had already arrived and with which I am in perfect sympathy. As to date all that we can say with surety is that *Jack Juggler* precedes *Ralph Roister Doister* (q.v.), which probably dates 1552.

Ralph Roister Doister, by Nicholas Udall.
Title page: Lacking. The one extant copy is supposed to have been published about 1566.
S.R. undated; c. 1566.
Date: Formerly it was customary to ascribe *Roister Doister* to Udall's Eton days, before 1543; now, however, and with more reason, it is placed in 1552-3, before the 1553 edition of Thomas Wilson's *Rule of Reason*, which quotes the famous letter with acknowledgement to the play, and after the first two editions of 1550-1, 1552, which omit the letter; certainly the play belongs after 1546, when Heywood's *Proverbs* appeared, for it echoes Heywood's work in many ways. Udall is known to have been active at the court of Mary in the capacity of revels manager and producer of plays, sometimes at least with children as actors. *Ralph Roister Doister*, as a child's play, is then to be given rather to the Chapel Royal than to the boys at Eton.

Respublica, by Nicholas Udall (?)
Title page: (The play exists only in MS., and has been reproduced for the Tudor Text series): *A merye enterlude entitled Respublica made in the yeare of oure Lorde. 1553. and the first yeare of the moost prosperous Reigne of our moste gracious Soverainge Quene Marye the first. The partes and names of the plaiers.*
(names follow)
Date of performance: For the evidences that the play was written

for children, and was probably acted by the children of the Chapel at the Christmas revels of 1552-3, see p. 69.

Youth, anon.
Head-piece: The Enterlude of Youth.
    Col: Imprinted at London in Lothbury ouer against Sainct Margarytes church by me Wyllyam Copland. (n.d.)
Date: The strong Catholicism of the play points to the reign of Queen Mary.
Remarks: It is with considerable hesitation that I include this play among children's plays, for there are no other evidences of its performance by boys than that it is obviously aimed at the instruction of youth. In view of the facts that a large percentage of the plays at court during the first seventy-five years of the sixteenth century were acted by children, and that nearly all the extant plays of that period were written for presentation at court, I believe it to be very probable that plays which bear clearly the stamp of instruction to youth were acted by children.

Damon and Pythias, by Richard Edwards.
Title page: *The excellent Comedie of two the moste faithfuliest Freendes, Damon and Pithias. Newly Imprinted, as the same was shewed before the Queenes Maiestie, by the Children of her Graces Chappell, except the Prologue that is somewhat altered for the proper vse of them that hereafter shall haue occasion to plaie it, either in Priuate, or open Audience. Made by Maister Edvvards, then beynge Maister of the Children. 1571. Imprinted at London in Fletelane by Richard Iohnes, and are to be solde at his shop, ioyning to the Southwest doore of Paules Churche.*
S.R. 1567-8.
Date: The play is generally ascribed to Christmas, 1564.
    See pp. 77ff. and W. Y. Durand in *Journal of English and Germanic Philology*, IV, p. 348.

The Bugbears. A manuscript play of uncertain authorship, possibly by one John Jeffrey, preserved in the British Museum (*Lansdowne MSS.* 807). Dependence on Grazzini's *La Spiritata* (1561) and J. Weier's *De Praestigiis Daemonium* (1563) gives a backward limit for dating the play; its style suggests that it cannot have been written much later than these dates. Mr. R. W. Bond, who has reprinted it (in *Early Plays from the Italian*) sets the date at 1564-5, which is probably not far wrong.

That it is a children's play is shown by the last chorus, in which the actors refer to themselves as "we boyes." But there is no way of identifying the company. Chambers rightly rejects Wallace's theory that because Iphigenia is the name of a secondary character, this is the play *Effiginia* which the Paul's boys brought to court on December 28, 1571. The caption of one of the songs "Giles peperel for Iphiginia" may mean that Giles was the composer of the song or the actor of the part. If the latter is the true case, it helps no whit, because no Giles Peperel occurs on any company roster that we possess.

The play has also been reprinted by Carl Grabau in *Archiv für das Studium der neuren Sprachen u. Literaturen*, Vols. 98, 99.

The Wars of Cyrus, anon.
Title page:	*The Warres of Cyrus King of Persia, against Antiochus King of Assyria, with the Tragicall ende of Panthæa. Played by the children of her Maiesties Chappell. London Printed by E. A. for William Blackwal, and are to be sold at his shop ouer against Guild-hall gate. 1594.*

Date: No indication of date other than the title page has been suggested. The Chapel boys cannot be traced as a regularly playing company after 1584, so that unless the play was given by them before that date, it must have appeared at a private performance or during their obscure flittings about the country. Mr. W. J. Lawrence (in the *Times Literary Supplement* of August 11, 1921) suggests that the play may have been written by Farrant during his Chapel mastership. Mr. Chambers (*Eliz. Stage*, III, 311, and IV, 52) thinks that it came after *Tamburlaine* and hence cannot have been written by Farrant, but that it may have been based on a play by him. The evidence is all very slight.

The Arraignment of Paris, by Peele.
Title page:	*The Araygnement of Paris A Pastorall. Presented before the Queenes Maiestie by the Children of her Chappell. Imprinted at London by Henrie Marsh. Anno. 1584.*

Date: We have no means of fixing upon the date of the performance of this play, except in a general way. In 1583 Peele made a deposition at Oxford in which it appears that he was twenty-five years old and had been at London about two years (Fleay, *Biog. Chron.*, II, 151). Between 1580 and 1584 the Chapel children played on Shrove Sunday and December 31, 1581, Shrove Tuesday, 1582, and Twelfth and Candlemas days, 1584 (cf. pp. 99-100). It is impossible to tell which of these dates is the right one.

Campaspe, by Lyly.

Title page: *A moste excellent Comedie of Alexander, Campaspe, and Diogenes, Played beefore the Queenes Maiestie on twelfe day at night by her Maiesties children, and the children of Poules. Imprinted at London for Thomas Cadman 1584.*
                  Two other 4tos of 1584 have "newyeares day at night."

S.R. April 12, 1597.

Date: Presented to the queen January 1, 1584. See p. 134.

Sapho and Phao, by Lyly.

Title page: *Sapho and Phao, Played beefore the Queenes Maiestie on Shrouetewsday, by her Maiesties Children, and the Boyes of Paules. Imprinted at London for Thomas Cadman. 1584.*

S.R. April 6, 1584.

Date: Performed Shrove Tuesday, 1584. See p. 134.

Endimion, by Lyly.

Title page: *Endimion, The Man in the Moone. Playd before the Queenes Maiestie at Greenewich on Candlemas day at night, by the Chyldren of Paules. At London, Printed by I. Charlewood, for the widdowe Broome. 1591.*

S.R. October 4, 1591.

Date: February 2, 1586 ? or February 2, 1588 ? See pp. 140-141.

Galathea, by Lyly.

Title page: *Gallathea. As it was played before the Queenes Maiestie at Greene-wiche, on Newyeeres day at Night. By the Chyldren of Paules. At London, Printed by Iohn Charl-woode for the Wid-dow Broome. 1592.*

S.R. April 1, 1585.

Date: Probably presented to the queen at Greenwich on January 1, 1588. See pp. 139-140.

Love's Metamorphosis, by Lyly.
Title page: Loves Meta-morphosis. *A Willie and Courtly Pastorall, Written by Mr. John Lyllie. First playd by the Children of Paules, and now by the Children of the Chappell. London Printed for William Wood, dwelling at the West end of Paules, at the signe of Time. 1601.*
S.R. November 25, 1600.
Date: c. 1588-90. See p. 140.

Mother Bomby, by Lyly.
Title page: Mother Bombie. *As it was sundrie times plaied by the Children of Powles. London, Imprinted by Thomas Scarlet for Cuthbert Burby. 1594.*
S.R. June 18, 1594.
Date: The play is in style and workmanship late, and may well have come after *Midas* (cf. p. 142). Note that it is not stated to have been presented at court.

Midas, by Lyly.
Title page: Midas. *Plaied before the Queenes Maiestie vpon Twelfe Day at night, By the Children of Paules. London Printed by Thomas Scarlet for I. B. and are to be sold in Paules Churchyard at the signe of the Bible. 1592.*
S.R. October 4, 1591.
Date: Probably composed between May and November of 1589 and produced at court on Twelfth Day, 1590. See p. 141.

Dido, by Marlowe and Nash.
Title page: The Tragedie of Dido *Queene of Carthage: Played by the Children of her Maiesties Chapell. Written by Christopher Marlowe, and Thomas Nash. Gent.* (List of characters) *At London, Printed, by the Widdowe Orwin, for Thomas Woodcocke, and are to be solde at his shop, in Paules Church-yearde, at the signe of the black Beare. 1594.*
Date: Fleay guesses "perhaps at Croydon, in 1591." His guess is worthless, but there seems to be no ground on which to make a better one.

The Woman in the Moon, by Lyly.

Title page: *The Woman in the Moone. As it was presented before*
               her Highnesse. By Iohn Lyllie maister of Artes. Im-
               printed at London for William Iones, and are to be
               sold at the signe of the Gun, neere Holburne Conduit.
               1597.

S.R. September 22, 1595.

Date: The play is described in the prologue as:

"The first he had in Phœbus holy bower,
But not the last, unless the first displease."

This cannot mean that *The Woman in the Moon* was the first of
Lyly's plays, because the absence of euphuism and the excellence
of the blank verse show that the author was in his maturity. The
date is hard to settle, and in many ways the play is puzzling. Although the play is said to have been given before Elizabeth, there
is in it distinct satire of the queen. This, and the absence from the
title page of the name of the children of Paul's, who were "put down"
about 1590, has led Bond, the editor, Baker (ed. of *Endimion*), and
Feuillerat (*John Lyly*) to date the play 1591-3. For the literary
relationships of this play, with its possible influence on *Midsummer
Night's Dream*, the reader is referred to Bond's edition of Lyly, III,
231.

Although nothing is said on the title page about the play's being
acted by children, the authorship of Lyly and the presence of numerous songs and dances point to presentation by children. The play
is not different in theme from other plays of Lyly, only different in
style. The difficulty is that in 1591, so far as we know, no children
were playing in London. Hence we are driven to suppose that the
performance was a special and private one, like that which presented
Summer's Last Will and Testament, in 1592,

Summer's Last Will and Testament, by Thomas Nash.

Title page: *A Pleasant Comedie, called Summers last will and*
               Testament. Written by Thomas Nash. Imprinted at
               London by Simon Stafford, for Walter Burre, 1600.

S.R. October 28 (1600).

Date and performance: The play was privately acted, probably, at
Croydon in August or September of 1592, by the children of Paul's.
See p. 148, note.

The Case is Altered, by Jonson.

Title page:　　*A Pleasant Comedy, Called: The Case is Alterd. As it hath beene sundry times acted by the children of the Black-friers. Written by Ben. Ionson. London, Printed for Bartholomew Sutton, and William Barrenger, and are to be sold at the great North-doore of Saint Paules Church. 1609.*

S.R. January 26 and July 20, 1609.

Date: Probably 1598. This play is mentioned in Nash's *Lenten Stuff*, entered *S.R.* on January 11, 1599. But as to the question of its being played by the Chapel boys then, see p. 154.

Antonio and Mellida, by Marston.

Title page:　　*The History of Antonio and Mellida. The first part. As it hath beene sundry times acted, by the children of Paules. Written by I. M. London Printed for Mathewe Lownes, and Thomas Fisher, and are to be soulde in Saint Dunstans Church-yarde. 1602.*

S.R. October 24, 1601.

Date: A line in *Jack Drum's Entertainment*, act IV: "How like you the new Poet Mellidus?" is generally taken to refer to Marston under a pseudonym taken from this play. Since *Jack Drum* was acted in April of 1600, *Antonio and Mellida* must then have appeared earlier in the spring, or late in 1599. There is, however, no direct evidence that Paul's was open in 1599.

From the stage directions of IV, 1 we learn that two of the actors were named Cole and Norwood. For the names of other boys in the company at this time see p. 111.

The Old Law, by Middleton.

Title page:　　*The Excellent Comedy, called The Old Law, or A new way to please you.*

　　　　　　　　　　　　　⎧ *Phil Massinger.*
　　　　　　　By ⎨ *Tho. Middleton.*
　　　　　　　　　　　　　⎩ *Wlliam Rowley.*

Acted before the King and Queene at Salisbury House, and at severall other places, with great Applause. Together with an exact and perfect Catalogue of all the Playes, with the Authors Names, and what are Comedies Tragedies, Histories, Pastoralls, Masks, Interludes,

more exactly Printed then ever before. London, Printed
for Edward Archer, at the signe of the Adam and Eve,
in Little Britaine. 1656.

Date: Fleay, Dyce, and others agree that the play was first produced
in 1599, because in III, 1 the Clerk reads from the church-book
"Agatha, the daughter of Pollux—born in an. 1540" and adds "and
now 'tis 1599." But the evidence is largely discounted by the fact
that the date 1540, or some date ending in a 0, is necessary to the
plot of the play, for the entry in the church-book must be altered by
changing the 0 to 9. Granting that had the play been written in
or after 1609 the authors would probably have used 1550, all that
we can deduce from this evidence is that the play was not written
before 1599 or after 1608. There seems to be no other guide to a
more precise dating.

The ascription of the play to the Paul's repertory depends on
assuming that it was written in 1599 or shortly thereafter. In that
case its sole author was Middleton, who was then devoting himself
to Paul's. For a consideration of its date, authorship and successive
revisions, cf. E. E. Morris, "On the Date and Composition of The
Old Law," *P.M.L.A.* XVII, 1.

Antonio's Revenge, by Marston.
Title page: *Antonios Reuenge. The second part. As it hath beene*
                   sundry times acted, by the children of Paules. Written
                   by I. M. London Printed for Thomas Fisher, and are
                   to be soulde in Saint Dunstans Church-yarde. 1602.
S.R. October 24, 1601.
Date: Probably shortly after *Antonio and Mellida.* Marston had
already planned the second part before the first was finished; Antonio, in the induction to *Antonio and Mellida,* says: " . . . . I have
heard that those persons, as he and you, Feliche, that are but
slightly drawn in this comedy, should receive more exact accom-
plishment in a second part; which, if this obtain gracious acceptance,
means to try its fortune."

Cynthia's Revels, by Jonson.
Title page: *The Fovntaine of Selfe-Loue. Or Cynthias Revels. As*
                   it hath beene sundry times priuately acted in the Black-
                   Friers by the Children of her Maiesties Chappell.
                   Written by Ben: Iohnson.

Quod non dant Proceres, dabit Histrio.
Haud tamen inuideas vati, quem pulpita pascunt.
Imprinted at London for Walter Burre, and are to be
solde at his shop in Paules Church-yard, at the signe
of the Flower de-Luce and Crowne. 1601.
S.R. May 23, 1601.
Date: 1600.
The following list of actors is given in the folio:
    Nat. Field
    Sal(athiel) Pavy
    Tho. Day
    J(ohn) Underwood
    Rob. Baxter
    John Frost.

Doctor Doddipole, anon.
Title page: *The Wisdome of Doctor Dodypoll. As it hath bene*
    sundrie times Acted by the Children of Powles. London
    Printed by Thomas Creede, for Richard Oliue, dwelling
    in Long Lane. 1600.
S.R. October 7, 1600.
Date: I have no quarrel with the accepted theory that *Doddipole*
was revived by Paul's at the beginning of their activities in 1599-
1600 from their older repertory of before 1590; that it was one of the
"musty fopperies of antiquity" sneered at in *Jack Drum.*
Author: Fleay suggests Peele, mainly on the strength of the inclu-
sion in this play of a lyric taken from the *Hunting of Cupid.* Schelling, however, mildly dissents from this dictum, and the play still
awaits thorough critical examination.

Jack Drum's Entertainment, by Marston.
Title page: *Iacke Drums Entertainment: or The Comedie of Pas-*
    quill and Katherine. As it hath bene sundry times
    plaide by the Children of Powles. At London Printed
    for Richard Oliue, dwelling in Long Lane. 1601.
S.R. September 8, 1600.
Date and authorship: The play was given about Whitsuntide (I, 1)
of 1600, a leap year (V, 1). To clinch the matter, Kemp's morris
(February-March, 1600) is mentioned (I, 1). Thus Fleay, and
rightly. It is now generally agreed that the play is by Marston;
indeed the vocabulary alone practically establishes the fact.

Allusions: Fleay believed that in the cuckolding of Brabant Senior by M. John fo de King he had discovered the circumstance alluded to in Jonson's conversations with Drummond (ed. Laing, p. 20), that "Marston represented him in the stage, in his youth given to venerie. . . . . He said that two accidents strange befell him; one, that a man made his own wyfe to court him, whom he enjoyed two years ere he knew of it, and one day finding them by chance, was passingly delighted with it"; and thereupon concluded that John fo de King must be Jonson, in spite of the facts that in no other respect is there any similarity between the dramatist and the swashbuckler, that the incidents, anyway, are only broadly alike, and that there is legitimate question as to the pointing of the sentence which ends "in his youth given to venerie" (cf. J. H. Penniman, *War of the Theatres*, p. 40). These objections are too strong for Fleay's slender analogy, and if Jonson is present in the piece, we must look elsewhere for him. Several critics have suggested Brabant Senior, an identification with which I am ready to agree. This gentleman is represented primarily as a carping and arrogant critic, such as Jonson is constantly censured in the *Poetomachia*. After the brief conversation in act IV concerning poets, in which Brabant Senior has said a bad word for every one, the dialogue thus goes on:

Planet.	*Brabant* thou art like a paire of Ballance,
	Thou wayest all sauing thyselfe.
Bra. Sig.	Good faith, troth is, they are all Apes & gulls,
	Vile imitating spirits, dry healty Turffes.
Bra. Jun.	Nay brother, now I thinke your iudgement erres.
Planet.	Erre, he cannot erre man, for children & fooles
	speake truthe alwaies.

Later on in the act, Planet voices his hopes that John fo de King has succeeded in his plans of cuckolding Brabant:

> o that twere lawfull now
> To pray to God that he were Cuckoled.
> Deare *Brabant* I do hate these bumbaste wits,
> That are puft vp with arrogant conceit
> Of their owne worth, as if *Omnipotence*
> Had hoysed them to such vnequaled height,
> That they suruaide our spirits with an eye
> Only create to censure from aboue,
> When good soules they do nothing but reproue.

Finally, in the last scene Planet forces Brabant Senior to wear the horn in token of his cuckoldry, upbraids him for his "arrogance" and "glorious ostentation" of wit, and adds: "Now you Censurer Be the ridiculous subiect of our mirth."

The only other satirist than Jonson to whom Marston is known to have addressed the same reproofs was Hall, but with Hall Marston had no quarrel in 1600, whereas he was then entering into his conflict with Jonson. Of other bits of satire in the play, only one can be identified with fair certainty; John Ellis, with his obvious parodies of euphuistic similes, is John Lyly, as Fleay has observed. Fleay's other interpretations are so obviously guesses that they do not require consideration. One, however, that Brabant Junior is Marston, is at least possible.

The Spanish Tragedy, by Kyd.

Title page: (of the amended version): *The Spanish Tragedie: or, Hieronimo is mad againe. Containing the lamentable end of Don Horatio, and Belimperia; with the pittiful death of Hieronimo. Newly corrected, amended, and enlarged with new Additions of the Painters part, and others, as it hath of late been diuers times acted. London, Printed by W. White, for I. White and T. Langley, and are to be sold at their Shop ouer against the Sarazens head without New-Gate. 1615.*

Date of performance: The Spanish Tragedy does not properly form part of the history of children's companies. Nevertheless it deserves a place here because, as we learn from the induction to Webster's version of Marston's *Malcontent* (q.v.), the children of the Chapel acquired this play in or about 1600, by some means, and played it. In revenge the king's men in 1604 put on the *Malcontent,* which was written for the Chapel boys.

The Maid's Metamorphosis, by Lyly (?) and —?

Title page: *The Maydes Metamorphosis. As it hath bene sundrie times Acted by the Children of Powles. London Printed by Thomas Creede, for Richard Oliue, dwelling in long Lane. 1600.*

S.R. July 24, 1600.

Date and authorship: Definite evidence as to date is given in the play. The performance took place in leap year (IV, 1), in a time of dearth (II, 1), at a marriage (last lines). These all agree with 1600; it was leap year; in May or June wheat went from 3s. to 6, 7, and 8s. the bushel, and the queen issued a proclamation holding grain within England and forbidding extortion (Stow's *Chronicle*, in Howe's continuation). On June 16, 1600, Lord Herbert married Lady Anne Russel at Lord Cobham's house, Blackfriars, when eight ladies danced to Apollo's music and invited the queen to make up nine (Nichols, *Progresses*, III, 499). It is to this concluding ceremony, according to Fleay, that the final lines of the play refer:

"When their wedding chanced
Phoebus gave music and the Muses danced,"

and I believe that in this case Fleay is right. The fairy, masque-like quality of the play is well suited to a marriage, and the harmony of the evidences almost definitely settles the matter.

Fleay, apparently carried away by a misquotation of a line from Daniel's first sonnet:

"Unto the boundless ocean of thy beauty,"

which is rendered:

"Then to the boundless ocean of thy worth,"

assumes that Daniel wrote all but the prose parts, of the pages and the fairies; these he assigns to Lyly. But Bond (*Lyly's Works*, III, 337-9) rightly points out that neither Daniel's early drama, *Cleopatra*, of 1594, nor *Philotas* of 1605 is anything like *The Maid's Metamorphosis*, nor is there a parallel in Daniel's treatment of Juno, Iris, and Somnus in *The Vision of Twelve Goddesses*, of 1605. Daniel has clearly no claim upon the metrical portions of our play; Bond suggests Day, a more likely identification, but still lacking in convincing evidence. It seems to be generally conceded that the parts of the pages and fairies are in Lyly's vein, but the author of the rest, if indeed it was not Lyly exhibiting a "later manner," remains to be found.

The Malcontent, by Marston.

Title page: *The Malcontent. By Iohn Marston. 1604. At London printed by V. S. for William Aspley, and are to be solde at his shop in Paules Church-yard.*

The Malcontent. Augmented by Marston. With the Additions played by the Kings Maiesties servants.

295] THE CHILD ACTORS

*Written by Iohn Webster. 1604. At London Printed
by V. S. for William Aspley, and are to be sold at his
shop in Paules Church-yard.*

S.R. July 5, 1604.

Date and stage history: Definite indication of date is given in the
play, viz. the reference in III, 1 to "the horn growing in the woman's
forehead twelve years since," a phenomenon which is described in a
pamphlet licensed *S.R.* October 15, 1588, thus fixing the date of the
play between October 1600 and October 1601 (Fleay). The year
1601 agrees with the numerous echoes of *Hamlet* which abound in
the play, of which not the least is the character of the foolish old
marshall Bilioso, strongly reminiscent of Polonius. From the Induction to the version used by the King's men we learn that the play
was first produced by the Revels children at Blackfriars, and was
afterwards taken up by the King's men in revenge for the appropria-
tion by the boys of *The Spanish Tragedy.*

Sly.	.... I would know how you came by this play?
Condell.	Faith, sir, the book was lost; and because 'twas pity so good a play should be lost, we found it, and play it.
Sly.	I wonder you would play it, another company having interest in it.
Condell.	Why not Malevole in folio with us, as Jeronimo in decimo-sexto with them? They taught us a name for our play; we call it *One for another.*

In reply to Sly's inquiry: "What are your additions?" Burbage
replies that they are slight, only enough "to entertain a little more
time, and to abridge the not-received custom of music in our theatre."
The Induction was written by Webster. Marston's "additions"
seem rather to be restorations, and the first edition has the look of a
copy cut down for stage purposes. For the King's men the entire
part of Passarello, the clown, was added or restored, together with
several scenes involving Bilioso, and these changes are about all.
The first edition contains the Shakespeare allusions.

In the address To The Reader the author issues warning against
reading unintentional meanings, as has been done; there is no
attempt to satirize persons. What these interpretations were it is
hard to discover, unless the constant animadversions upon *Hamlet*
offer a clue.

Chambers (*Eliz. Stage*, III, 431) thinks the play was not written until 1604, but the reasons he gives for objecting to the current opinion seem to me slight.

Blurt, Master Constable, by Middleton.
Title page: *Blurt, Master-Constable. Or The Spaniards Night-walke. As it hath bin sundry times priuately acted by the Children of Paules.*
                                        Patresq:severi
              Fronde comas vincti coenant, et carmina dictant.
              London, Printed for Henry Rockytt, and are to be solde at the long shop vnder S. Mildreds Church in the Poultry. 1602.
S.R. June 7, 1602, for Edward Aldee.
Date: No evidences. Fleay guesses 1600-1. The play is a poor comedy, with many allusions to other plays, chiefly to those acted by the Admiral's men; also to *Romeo and Juliet,* and possibly *Macbeth.*

What You Will, by Marston.
Title page: *What You Will. By Iohn Marston. Imprinted at London by G. Eld for Thomas Thorppe. 1607.*
S.R. August 6, 1607.
Date and allusions: It is clear from the induction that the play was given at Blackfriars; the frequent mention of feathers would alone settle that. Since it clearly belongs to the War of the Poets group of plays, it falls in the period of 1600-1603; Fleay suggests 1601, before Marston had patched up his quarrel with Jonson, and this date will do as well as any. It agrees with other scraps of evidence, such as the reference to the "moral play" of Dame Temperance to be given at the revels in the last act, whch seems to be an animadversion upon Chapman's *May Day,* produced c. 1601. For the time of year cf. V, 1: "I may go starve till Midsummer Quarter."
   The interest of this play lies for the modern commentator not in the main action, but in the counter-plot, an ill-regulated mass of incidents centering about Quadratus, a peppery gentleman, Lampatho Doria, with whom he is perpetually quarreling, and Lampatho's simple-minded admirer Simplicius Faber. The problem of identifying these persons is made difficult by the contradictory nature of the evidence the play affords. To Fleay, however, there are no obscurities; Quadratus is Johnson, and Lampatho is Marston.

The latter identification is fixed by Lampatho's being called "Don Kynsader" in II, 1. As to Jonson, his papist belief is alluded to in IV, 1: "He and I are of two faiths"; he writes epithalamiums like Horace in *Satiromastix*, II, 1. The Signor Snuff, Monsieur Mew, and Cavaliero Blirt of the Induction are meant for Armin, Jonson, and Middleton (but *why?*). Philomuse is Daniel, whose *Musophilus* was written in 1599 (this is more reasonable). Furthermore, *Twelfth Night, or What You Will*, which introduces Marston as Malvolio (i.e. Malevole, the Malcontent) and addresses him in an anagrammatic way as M.O.A.I. (i.e. Jo. Ma.), is Shakespeare's rejoinder to the two plays *What You Will* and *The Malcontent*. Query: rejoinder to *what?* Even Fleay's sibyl could not pierce this mystery.

Thus Fleay, and he seems to have a good deal of reason. Jonson's captiousness under criticism is censured in the induction. Lampatho is certainly a writer, and a writer of satires. In II, 1 he threatens Quadratus:

> So Phoebus warm my brain, I'll rhyme thee dead.
> Look for a satire: if all the sour juice
> Of a tart brain can souse thy estimate
> I'll pickle thee.

Quadratus is incensed with him for using foppish and effeminate language: e.g. protest, vehemently enamoured, passionately dote, most complete phantasma; calls him "a fusty cask, Devote to mouldy customs of hoary eld"; and accuses Simplicius Faber, "yon chamlet youth, ... that hermaphrodite, ... that bastard mongrel soul," of toadying to Lampatho. Unfortunately for Fleay all this does not suit Marston, and especially inapplicable is the fact that Lampatho is the most derided man in the play, whereas Quadratus is represented merely as a man of impatient and rough humor. The calling Lampatho "you Don Kynsader" in II, 1 is the strongest argument that he was Marston. Quardatus more nearly fits Jonson, and yet there are contradictions here too. In act IV, where the ladies are discussing the gentlemen, Meletza thus describes Quadratus: "Fie, fie! Speak no more of him: he lives by begging. He is a fine courtier, flatters admirably, kisses 'fair madam,' smells surpassing sweet; wears and holds up the arras, supports the tapestry, when I pass into the presence, very gracefully." Later on: "Then there's my chub, my epicure, Quadratus, that rubs his guts, claps his paunch, and cries Rivo! entertaining my ears perpetually with a

most strong discourse of the praise of bottle-ale and red herrings."
This hardly fits Jonson. Bullen has gathered in his notes (cf. his
edition of Marston) a suspiciously large number of phrases which
are paralleled in the then extant plays of Jonson; but note that
hardly one of these is used in ridicule.

Certain apparently definite hints as to the identify of Lampatho
and Simplicius are given in the play, particularly of Lampatho, if
we could but interpret them. Simplicius is represented (II, 1) as the
syncophantish friend of Lampatho, forever admiring in extravagant
language:

> Doth he but speak, 'O tones of heaven itself.'
> Doth he once write, 'O Jesu admirable.'

Note that farther in the scene Quadratus gets into a quarrel by
inducing Simplicius to repeat "O tones of heaven itself," though
the scene is obscure. The hints for Lampatho are more precise.
Lampatho tells all about himself at the end of II, 2. Note that
Quadratus starts him on his tirade by quoting, apparently, a line,
"In Heaven's handiwork there's naught," and Lampatho, taking
the cue, goes on to an abuse of man and especially scholars. Then
Lampatho goes on to say that Simplicius never vented a syllable
of his own creating since Lampatho could see and hear.

> I was a scholar: seven useful springs
> Did I deflower in quotations
> Of crossed opinions 'bout the soul of man.

He exhausted Zabarell, Aquinas, Scotus, and Donatus. He began by
asking "an sit anima," then if it were mortal, then corporeal, local,
fixed, extraduce; whether it had free will or no; how it was created,
how it exists.

> One talks of motes, the soul was made of motes;
> Another fire, t'other light, a third
> A spark of star-like nature;
> Hippo water, Anaximenes air,
> Aristoxenus music; Critias I know not what!
> A company of odd phrenetici!
> Did eat my youth; and when I crept abroad,
> Finding my numbness in this nimble age,
> I fell a-railing.

Cf. III, 2. In IV, 1 Lampatho reads two lines of his poetry. Note
in II, 1, 169 an apparent confirmation that Quadratus is Marston.

He says that if Mastigophorous or Cinaidus should chide him, he would observe their censure; cf. similar mention of Mastigophorus in the author's comment on *Pygmalion*, 1, 38.

Whatever may be right, there certainly is personal satire in the play, and it provides the moving cause. There are evidences in the plentiful confusions of names that the play has been patched. The pages' names are almost hopelessly entangled, and there is confusion between Celia and Lucea, Adrean and Andrea. Was the play written to be a vehicle for satire, or was it remade for that purpose, thus bringing about chaos in the *dramatis personæ*?

The Contention between Liberality and Prodigality, by Sebastian Westcote (?)

Title page: *A Pleasant Comedie, Shewing the contention betweene Liberalitie and Prodigalitie. As it was playd before her Maiestie. London Printed by Simon Stafford for George Vincent: and are to be sold at the signe of the Hand in hand in Wood-street ouer against S. Michaels Church. 1602.*

Authorship and date: See pp. 128 ff.

Poetaster, by Jonson.

Title page: *Poëtaster, Or His Arraignement. A Comicall Satyre. Acted, in the yeere 1601. By the then Children of Queene Elizabeths Chappel. The Author B. I.*
                    Mart.
        Et mihi de nullo fama rubore placet.
    London, Printed by William Stansby, for Matthew Lownes. M.DC.XVI.
    This is the title page of the folio. There was a 4to issued in 1602.

S.R. December 21, 1601.

Date: 1601.

The following list of actors is appended to the play in the folio:

    Nat. Field.
    Sal. Pavy
    Tho. Day
    Joh. Underwood
    Will Ostler
    Tho. Marton

Satiromastix, by Dekker.

Title page: *Satiro-mastix. Or the vntrussing of the Humorous Poet. As it hath bin presented publikely, by the Right Honorable, The Lord Chamberlaine his Seruants; and priuately, by the Children of Paules. By Thomas Dekker. Non recito cuiquam nisi Amicis idq; coactus.*
London, Printed for Edward White, and are to bee solde at his shop, neere the little North doore of Paules Church, at the signe of the Gun. 1602.

S.R. November 11, 1601.

Date: As every one knows, this play was Dekker's reply to the *Poetaster*, and was performed in the same year, 1601. It probably also followed Marston's *What You Will*, for Asinius's declaration (I, 2): "No, faith, ever since I felt one hit me ith teeth that the greatest clarkes are not the wisest men, could I abide to goe to schoole; I was at *As in presenti* and left there," looks like a reference to *What You Will*, II, 2, where Holofernes Pippo leaves school just after he had got into difficulties over *as in presenti*. For what is on the whole the most satisfactory brief summary of the War of the Poets and the relation of this play thereto, the reader is referred to J. H. Penniman's edition of *Poetaster* and *Satiromastix* in the Belles Lettres series of Elizabethan plays.

The Percy plays: *The Cuck-Queanes and Cukolds Errants, and, The Færy Pastorall, by W(illiam) P(ercy).*   Ed. for the Roxburgh Club by Joseph Haslewood; London, the Shakespeare Press 1824.

These two alone out of the five contained in the Percy *MSS.*, have been reprinted. They are dated in the manuscript respectively 1601 and 1603, but were probably written earlier. For a discussion of them cf. pp. 217 ff.

The Gentleman Usher, by Chapman.

Title page: *The Gentleman Usher. By George Chapman. At London. Printed by V. S. for Thomas Thorppe, 1606.*

S.R. November 26, 1605.

Date: There is very little to go on. There is in II, 1 a clear reference to *Sir Giles Goosecap*, and in Marston's *Malcontent* a less clear reference to *The Gentleman Usher* (see Fleay, *Drama*, I, 58). The dates of these two plays are in themselves conjectural; still the general consensus of opinion that *The Gentleman Usher* was brought out in 1601 or 1602 is in every way reasonable.

Company: While there is no indication of company on the title page, the chances are all that the Chapel boys had the play, for Chapman was at this time writing for them, and the amount of music, dancing, and masquing which is brought in argues for that company, which paid special attention to those things.

May Day, by George Chapman.

Title page: *May-Day, a witty Comedie, divers times acted at the Black Fryers. Written by George Chapman. London. Printed for John Brown e dwelling in Fleetestreetein Saint Dunstones Church-yard, 1611.*

No *S.R.*

The date is fixed by references in the play and by comparison with the author's other comedies to be late 1601 or early 1602. See IV, 1, 18-19, a mock quotation from *Antonio's Revenge*; and III, 3, an imitation of *Twelfth Night.* Passages parallel to *Gull's Hornbook* make it appear that the play was touched up subsequently to 1607, when the satire was printed. (See Parrott's notes on the play in his edition of Chapman.) Chambers (*Eliz. Stage*) holds for 1609, on the grounds that the imitation of the *Gull's Hornbook* is "a little arbitrary to explain by revision." But to my thinking the style of the play forbids putting it so late.

Sir Giles Goosecap, by Chapman.

Title page: *Sir Gyles Goosecappe Knight. A Comedie presented by the Chil: of the Chappell. At London: Printed by John Windet for Edward Blunt.* (The date was 1606; there was another quarto in 1636.)

S.R. January 10, 1606.

Date: The title page shows that the play was acted before the Chapel company changed its name in the early part of 1604; allusion to Elizabeth in I, 1, 140 puts the play before her death on March 24, 1603. In III, 1, 46, Rudesby's remark: "I have seen none of the French dames, I confess, but your greatest gallants, for men, in France were here lately," is taken by Parrott to be directed at the Biron embassy of Sepember 5-14, 1601, and this seems likely. For details of the embassy, see Stow's *Chronicle.* The play, then, may be put at the end of 1601, or early in 1602. There is a reference in

Satiromastix to Lady Furnifall, which may be the lady of our play. *Satiromastix* was registered in *S.R.* November 11, 1601.

The main plot, deriving from Chaucer, has substance, but the comic plot, where Goosecap belongs, is almost without action, and bears signs either of being hastily and carelessly put together, or of being made over from a former state. For example, there is talk of a fool who is to be procured for the fianl reuniting dinner in the last act given by Momford, but nothing comes of it; there is promise of showing Lady Furnifall, who is a shrew when sober, amorous when drunk, but she never appears. The likelihood is that the play has suffered revision, presumably because the part of Lady Furnifall had given offense, or perhaps because Chapman intended to transfer it to *The Gentleman Usher*, where she appears as Cortezza. Clarence, with his praises of scholarship, is taken to represent Chapman; Fleay would identify other of the characters, but the grounds are slight. The play is full of Chapman's characteristic situations: there is Momford, a rattlepated philanthropist much like Lodovico in *May Day*; there is Clarence with his sublimated love, like the almost platonic Aurelio in *May Day* and the quite platonic Vandome in *D'Olive*; there is a characteristic letter-writing scene; there are foolish gentlemen to be gulled by the help of pages. Jonson's influence shows in the evident humor basis of the main comic characters and in the preference for dialogue over plot. The influence of Lyly shows in the predominance of the pages in the comic intrigue, and in flashes of euphuism. Compare, for example, this speech of Momford (I, 4):

"Wilt thou not shine in the world anew, and make those that have slighted thy love with the austerity of thy knowledge dote on thee again with thy commanding shaft of their humors?"

Sophonisba, by Marston.

Title page: *The Wonder of Women Or The Tragedie of Sophonisba,*
                as it hath beene sundry times Acted at the Blacke Friers.
                Written by Iohn Marston. London. Printed by Iohn
                Windet and are to be sold neere Ludgate. 1606.

S.R. March 17, 1606.

Date: Fleay asserts categorically 1602-3, without proof. Chambers, on the grounds that the title page points to a performance after Anne's patronage had been withdrawn from the Revels boys, late in 1605 or early in 1606, suggests 1606. And because the staging smacks somewhat more of the manner of Paul's than of Blackfriars, he thinks it possible that the play may have been first produced at Paul's. This is all very tentative.

The Dutch Courtesan, by Marston.
Title page: *The Dutch Courtezan. As it was playd in the Blacke-Friars, by the Children of her Maiesties Reuels. Written by Iohn Marston. At London, Printed by T. P. for Iohn Hodgets, and are to be sould at his shop in Paules Church-yard. 1605.*
S.R. June 26, 1605.
Date: Fleay dates the play in the summer of 1601. But the title page suggest a performance after the company received its new patent in 1605, and there are allusions to Florio's Montaigne, published in 1603. It would seem that the play was popular, for it was revived in 1613, when the Lady Elizabeth's men played it as *Cockledemoy* (from the comic character) before Prince Charles.

The Family of Love, by Middleton.
Title page: *The Familie of Love. Acted by the Children of his Maiesties Reuells.*
Lectori.
Sydera iungamus, facito mihi Iuppiter adsit,
Et tibi Mercurius noster dabit omnia faxo.
At London Printed for John Helmes, and are to be sold in Saint Dunstans Churchyard in Fleetstreet. 1608.
S.R. October 12, 1607.
Date: In the address "To the Reader" Middleton says that the play is printed too soon and too late; "too soon, in that it was in the press before I had notice of it, by which means some faults may escape in the printing; too late, for that it was not published when the general voice of the people had sealed it for good and the newness of it made it much more desired than at this time." There are two references to the new company of porters (I, 3 and IV, 3), and there is also talk in I, 3 of a visit to a play where was seen "the most excellent Sampson excell the whole world in gate-carrying." "Believe it, we saw Sampson bear the town-gates on his neck, from the lower to the upper stage, with that life and admirable accord, that it shall never be equalled, unless the whole new livery of porters set (to) their shoulders."

The date of the performance at Whitefriars by the King's Revels children can be set with tolerable accuracy, for the company cannot be traced earlier than the opening months of 1607, and the play was licensed on October 12. But there are signs of alteration, as though the play had been made over from an earlier version. Thus Shrimp is substituted for Smelt, and in one place Poppin for Exigent. I have opined that the play was first performed at Paul's in 1605. See p. 234.

Philotas, by Daniel.
Title page: *Certaine Small Poems Lately Printed: with the Tragedie of Philotas. Written by Samuel Daniel. G. Eld for Simon Waterson. 1605.*
S.R. November 29, 1604.
Date: Probably the autumn of 1604. See pp. 192-3.
Played by the Children of the Revels at Blackfriars.

Westward Ho, by Dekker and Webster.
Title page: *West-Ward Hoe. As it hath beene diuers times Acted by the Children of Paules. Written by Tho: Decker, and Iohn Webster. Printed at London, and to be sold by Iohn Hodgets dwelling in Paules Churchyard. 1607.*
S.R. March 2, 1605.
Date: Fleay is this time correct. The play was begun before the fall of Ostend and finished after it, that is, before and after August, 1604. In *Northward Ho* we learn that *Westward Ho* was brought out before Christmas. Cf. *Biog. Chron.*, II, 269.

Bussy D'Ambois, by Chapman.
Title page: *Bussy D'Ambois: A Tragedie: As it hath been often presented at Paules, London. Printed for William Aspley, 1607.*
S.R June 3, 1607.
Date: There has been much dispute, and the question cannot be said to be definitely settled. Opinion varies mainly between 1609 and 1604, the former date being upheld by Stoll (*Mod. Lang. Notes*, Nov., 1905), and the latter by the editor of the standard edition of Chapman, Parrott (*Mod. Lang. Review*, January, 1908). The curious reader will find the arguments well summarized in Parrott's article. A good case can be made out for either date; I am inclined to stand

by Parrott, who ought to be recognized as the authority in Chapman and whose arguments for 1604 are pretty convincing. In the prologue to the 1641 edition of the play we are told that:

"Field is gone
Whose actions first did give it (the play) name."

If this really means the first of all performances, then it proves that the play was brought out at Blackfriars, where Field was a leading actor from 1600 until and after the company moved to Whitefriars. Parrott, however, believes that the first performance after the play was revised was meant, and this seems likely. There is some reason for thinking that *Bussy* may have first trod the boards at Blackfriars, namely, that in no other case is Chapman known to have composed for Paul's boys—his connection with that company rests entirely upon the title page of this play, and all of his other work from 1600 to 1610 was done for the Queen's Revels. One explanation that has received favor is that the play was one of those which Kirkham carried over to Paul's with him when he abandoned Blackfriars in 1605 (cf. *Parasitaster*); but this is mere conjecture.

One hypothesis of Parrott's deserves mention: that Chapman revised *Bussy* in 1610 for Field at Whitefriars, before writing *Bussy's Revenge*. While the theory is not impossible, the evidence is too slight to be convincing.

Monsieur D'Olive, by Chapman.

Title page: *Monsieur D'Olive. A Comedie, as it was sundrie times acted by her Maiesties children at the Blacke-Friers. By George Chapman. London. Printed by T. C. for William Holmes, and are to be sold at his Shop in Saint Dun-stons Church-yard in Fleet-streete, 1606.*

S.R. 1606.

Date: The play belongs after 1603 at least, because the title page fits the name of the company after the granting of their patent and because there are numerous references to matters of James's reign. Thus there are allusions to the creation of knights and the fees thereto attaching in I, 1, 263-7, and IV, 2, 77-80, and to the proclamation calling in monopolies in 1603 in I, 1, 284-5. The preparations of D'Olive to go on his embassy are parodies of the preparations made in 1604-5 for the embassies of Lenox to France, Hertford to the Archduke in the Low Countries, and Northampton to Spain (see Parrott's notes to the play). The satire would be most effective

in the winter of 1604-5, and we may date the play then, before the
appearance of *Eastward Ho* in April, 1605.

The following passage (II, 267 ff.) is clearly directed toward James.
D'Olive is received at the court by the Duke.

> D'Ol. But sure, my honour'd Lord, the times before
> Were not as now they be, thanks to our fortune
> That we enjoy so sweet and wise a prince
> As is your gracious self; for then 'twas policy
> To keep all wits of hope still under hatches,
> Far from the Court, lest their exceeding parts
> Should overshine those that were then in place;
> And 'twas our happiness that we might live so;
> For in that freely choos'd obscurity
> We found our safety, which men most of note
> Many times lost; and I, alas, for my part,
> Shrunk my despised head in my poor shell;
> For your learn'd Excellence, I know, knows well
> *Qui bene latuit, bene vixit*, still.

Jonson was at this time a great friend of Chapman, and an enemy of
Northampton. Northampton had lived apart from the court in the
preceding reign (Parrott, p. 774 and note 2). Query: can Chapman
be championing Jonson by directing his satire especially at Northampton?

Michaelmas Term, by Middleton.

Title page: *Michaelmas Terme. As it hath been sundry times acted
             by the Children of Paules. At London, Printed for A. I.
             and are to be sould at the signe of the white horse in
             Paules Churchyard. An. 1607.*

S.R. May 15, 1607.

Date: There is, in II, 3 a distinct reference to a recent event in the
speech of Mrs. Quomodo:

> Why stand I here (as late our graceless dames,
> That found no eyes), to see that gentleman
> Alive, in state and credit, executed,
> Help to rip up himself does all he can?

Dyce, (the editor) suggests that the reference applies to the execution of Sir Everard Digby, who, for his share in the Gunpowder
Plot, was hanged, drawn, and quartered January 30, 1606; but

Fleay thinks the execution of Clarke and Watson at Winchester on November 29, 1604, is meant. Fleay is more consistent with Dyce's evidences than Dyce himself, for the editor, in commenting on the line (II, 1): "Let's search him, gentleman: I think he wears a smock," interprets this as meaning "is a knave," and quotes a passage showing that there was a saying to the effect that in leap year "knaves wear smocks." If this speech has significance, it is more likely that the leap year was 1604 than 1600, for there is no evidence that Middleton had begun to write for the Paul's boys before 1601-2.

A Mad World, My Masters, by Middleton.
Title page: *A Mad World, my Masters. As it hath bin lately in Action by the Children of Paules. Composed by T. M. London, Printed by H.B. for Walter Bvrre, and are to be sold in Paules Church-yard at the signe of the Crane. 1608.*
S.R. October 4, 1608.
Date: Satirical references to knighthood prove that the play was written in James's reign. In IV, 5, an indication is given in the speech of Follywit: "He makes a great feast upon the eleventh of this month, Tuesday next." Fleay, going on the assumption that the Paul's boys ceased to act about the end of 1606, opines that the play was probably produced in March of 1606, when Tuesday fell on the eleventh. But Tuesday was also the eleventh in November, and in August of 1607; and there is no reason why the play might not have appeared in 1605 or 1604.

All Fools, by Chapman.
Title page: *Al Fooles A Comedy, Presented at the Black Fryers, And lately before his Maiestie. Written by George Chapman. At London, Printed for Thomas Thorpe. 1605.*
No *S.R.*
Date: It is generally agreed that Chapman's play is meant in an entry in Henslowe's diary of July, 1599: "Lent . . . . to pay Mr. Chapman in full payment for his Boocke called the world Rones a whelles and now all foolles but the foolle some of xxx^s," and also in a previous reference to *The World Runs on Wheels* of January, 1598. The conclusion is obvious that before passing to the Chapel boys, the play was performed by the Admiral's men. Chapman began

writing for the Chapel in or before 1600, but there is no telling how soon afterwards *All Fools* was played there.

According to the much debated list of performances at court in 1604-5 (first published by Cunningham in his *Extracts from the Accounts of the Revels at Court*, Shakespeare Soc., 1842, p. 203), *All Fools* was presented New Year's night, 1605. In spite of pronouncements of forgery, these lists of Cunningham have been ably championed by Ernest Law (*Some Supposed Shakespeare Forgeries*, 1911, and *More about Shakespeare Forgeries*, 1913), and are accepted as genuine by Chambers (*Eliz. Stage*, IV, 136-141).

Northward Ho, by Dekker and Webster.

Title page: *North-ward Hoe. Sundry times Acted by the Children of Paules. By Thomas Decker, and Iohn Webster. Imprinted at London, by G. Eld. 1607.*

S.R. August 6, 1607.

Date: Allusions to the play in Day's *Isle of Gulls*, which was produced in February of 1606, give one limit. The other it is difficult to determine, except that the play belongs in James's reign. Probably Fleay's guess of 1605 is near enough.

Eastward Ho, by Chapman, Jonson, and Marston.

Title page: *Eastward Hoe. As It was playd in the Black-friers. By the Children of her Maiesties Reuels. Made by Geo: Chapman. Ben: Iohnson. Ioh: Marston. At London Printed or William Aspley. 1605.*

S.R. September 4, 1605.

Date: 1605, before April. See p. 194.

The Widow's Tears, by Chapman.

Title page: *The Widdowes Tears A Comedie. As it was often presented in the blacke and white Friers. Written by Geor. Chap. London, Printed for John Browne, and are to be sold at his shop in Fleetstreet in St. Dunstanes Church-yard. 1612.*

S.R. 1612.

Date: The title page shows that the play was acted by the Queen's Revels boys both before and after their removal from Blackfriars in 1609. Otherwise there is little to guide us. I have explained my reasons for rejecting Wallace's identification of this play with the *Casta Vidua* which the Duke of Stettin-Pomerania saw at Black-friars on September 18, 1602 (cf. p. 172 and also see Parrott's intro-duction to his notes of the play), and testified my agreement with those who see in the savage arraignment of legal chicanery in the last act a protest against the *Eastward Ho* arrests. Accordingly I date the play after the spring of 1605; more definite it is impossible to be.

This play was revived at court before Prince Charles on February 27, 1613, as we learn from the *Accounts of the Treasurer of the Chamber* for 10-11 Jas. 1 (*Rawlinson* A 239, in Bodleian):

> Item paid to the said Phillipp Roseter vppon the lyke warr*ant* dated att Whitehall vltimo die Maij 1613 for presentinge two severall playes, before the Princes highnes, One vppon the ixth of Janu*a*rie last called Cupides revenge: And the other called the Widdowes Teares, vppon the xxvijth of ffebr: followinge the some of — xiii^{li} vj^{s} viij^{d}.

Parasitaster, by Marston.

Title page: *Parasitaster, Or The Fawne, As It Hath Bene Divers times presented at the blacke Friars, by the Children of the Queenes Maiesties Reuels. Written by Iohn Marston. At London Printed by T. P. for W. C. 1606.*

(Another quarto of the same date has these significant additions): *As It Hath Bene Divers Times Presented at the blacke Friars, by the Children of the Queens Maiesties Reuels, and since at Powles. Written by Iohn Marston. And now corrected of many faults, which by reason of the Author's absence, were let slip in the first edition.*

S.R. March 12, 1606.

Date: The title page tells us that the play was one of those which were carried from the Blackfriars to Paul's when Edward Kirkham transferred himself thither, presumably as the result of a schism arising in the Revels company out of the *Eastward Ho* troubles. The precise date of the shift cannot be fixed, but we know that Kirk-ham was helping to manage the Paul's boys in 1606,[1] and doubtless he went to them soon after the disastrous experiences of the spring of 1605. It is not likely that the play was written earlier than 1604, but the title page is for me sufficient evidence that it was written before the execution of Sir Everard Digby, on January 30, 1606,

---

[1] Cf. p. 211 ff.

to which some have supposed that reference is made (in IV, 1). The
Kirkham schism must have taken place by then. Nor is it likely
that a play would be written, played by two companies, and printed
all in one year.

A Trick to Catch the Old One, by Middleton.

Title page: *A Tricke to Catch the Old-one. As it hath beene often
in Action, both at Paules, and at the Blacke-Fryers.
Presented before his Maiestie on New-yeares night last.
Composde by T. M. At London Printed by G:E. and
are to be sold by Henry Rockytt, at the long shop in the
Poultrie vnder the Dyall. 1608.*

Another quarto of the same date mentions only the
children of Paul's.

S.R. October 7, 1607.

Date: The evidence of the title page is not trustworthy, unless the
official record of performances of plays at court is incomplete, for
there is no record of plays by children between the Christmases of
1606 and 1609. That New Year's night of 1606 was meant is made
probable by the following entry from the *Declared Accounts of the
Treasurer of the Chamber* (Pipe Office, Roll 543, fol. 163b):

> To Edward Kirkham one of the M^{rs} of the children of Pawles upon
> the councells warr^t dated at the courte at whitehall ultimo die Martij 1606
> for bringing the said children and presenting by them two playes or enter-
> ludes before the Prince and his grace and the Duke of Yorke vpon nights
> mentioned in a Schedule annexed unto the said warraunt after the rate of
> fyve marks for ech play and by waye of his Ma^{ts} reward fyve nobles in all
> the some of xv^{li} xiii^s iiii^d.

Although the king is not specifically said to have been present, yet
his gift of five nobles argues either that he was a spectator, or that
he had intended to be. The information that Kirkham was directing
the children of Paul's is significant in connection with the title page
of the play, which tells us that the play was produced both at Paul's
and Blackfriars. Doubtless it was carried over to Paul's by Kirkham
along with Marston's *Parasitaster* (q.v.) when he abandoned the
Revels company in 1605.

The date of first production, at Blackfriars, we have no sure means
of telling. According to Fleay, this play was on the stage in 1605,
because it is alluded to in the *Isle of Gulls;* we could have deduced
as much, however, from the rest of our evidence.

Chambers (*Eliz. Stage*, III, 439) interprets 1608 of the quarto as 1608-9, or early 1609, and thinks that the Revels children took the play over from Paul's and played it at court on January 1, 1609. But I see no great plausibility in this theory.

The Isle of Gulls, by John Day.

Title page: *The Ile of Gvls. As it hath been often playd in the blacke Fryars, by the Children of the Reuels. Written by Iohn Day. Imprinted at London, and are to bee sold by Iohn Hodgets in Paules Church-yard. 1606.*

S.R. ?

Date: February, 1606. See p. 194.

The Fleire, by Sharpham.

Title page: *The Fleire. As it hath beene often played in the Blacke-Fryers by Children of the Reuells. Written by Edward Sharpham of the Middle Temple, Gentleman. At London, Printed and are to be solde by F. B. in Paules-Church-yard, at the signe of the Flower de Luce and the Crowne. 1607.*

S.R. May 13, 1606, "Provided that they are not to printe yt tell they bringe good aucthoritie and license for the Doinge thereof"; November 21.

Date: There is no satisfactory evidence. Herr Nibbe, the editor (in Bang's *Materialen* series, Louvain, 1912), declares for 1606, but since he claims Marston's *Parasitaster* for an important influence and dates that play after the Gunpowder Plot executions of January, 1606, which is certainly too late, we cannot rely too strongly on his authority. From the fact that Sharpham was writing for the king's revels at Whitefriars in 1607, (see *Cupid's Whirligig*) and this is the only other play of his we know anything about, I think that 1606 is nevertheless likely to be correct.

The Puritan, anon.

Title page: *The Pvritaine or The Widdow of Watling-streete. Acted by the Children of Paules. Written by W. S. Imprinted at London by G. Eld. 1607.*

S.R. August 6, 1607.

Date: We are told that July 15 falls on Tuesday (III, 6); this fits 1606, as Fleay has pointed out. This diligent scholar finds many references to Shakespearean plays, and declares the author to be unquestionably Middleton; these are at least matters which should serve for a basis of study. There are certainly many allusions to scenes in Jacobean drama which elude us today. For instance, Nicholas (sig. C2, in the Tudor Text edition) says: " . . . . our Parson railes againe Plaiers mightily I can tell you, because they brought him drunck vppo'th Stage once,—as hee will bee horribly druncke"; and later on (sig. E and E2) the sergeants scold the players for staging them: (E2) "Youle rayle againe Sariants, and stage 'em."

The Phoenix, by Middleton.
Title page: The Phoenix, as it hath beene sundrye times Acted by the Children of Paules, And presented before his Maiestie. London Printed by E. A. for A. I., and are to be solde at the signe of the white horse in Paules Churchyard. 1607.
S.R. May 9, 1607.
Date: There seems to be no clear hint to work on. Fleay finds satire of Jonson. He believes that Proditor is meant for Jonson, apparently because in V, 1 Proditor is likened to a raven; but where the likeness to Jonson comes in it is difficult to discover. The last scene, says Fleay, is a travesty of the *Poetaster*, and the "oil of quiet" therein derives from the Oglio del Scoto in *Volpone*. This would put our play after 1605, when *Volpone* was produced. But we are treading dangerously thin ice.

Chambers (*Eliz. Stage*) would assign the performance before James I to February 20, 1604, as the "only available" one. Perhaps.

The Woman Hater, by Beaumont (and Fletcher?).
Title page: The Woman Hater. As it hath beene lately Acted by the Children of Paules: London Printed, and are to be sold by John Hodgets in Paules Churchyard. 1607.
S.R. May 20, 1607.
Date: Fleay puts the play categorically at Easter of 1607, on the ground that the "favorite on the sudden" of I, 3 refers to Robert Carr, Earl of Somerset, who first came into notice at a tilt on March 24, 1607. But there is some doubt that the Paul's boys were playing then. Thorndike believes that in the prologue the arrest of Jonson and Chapman for *Eastward Ho* is glanced at, and therefore is in-

clined to move the play nearer to 1605. Thorndike's case is the
stronger, but we cannot date the play closer than 1605-7.

Cupid's Whirligig, by Sharpham.
Title page: *Cupids Whirligig. As it hath bene Sundrie times Acted,
                  by the Children of his Maiesties Reuels. London,
                  Printed by T. H. for R. Meighen, and are to be sold at
                  his shop, next to the Middle-Temple Gate, and in S.
                  Dunstans Church-yard in Fleet-street, 1630.*
S.R. June 29, 1607.
Date: In Act II Nan says that Sir Timothy Troublesome's heart
beats "for all the world like the Denmarke Drummer." If, as seems
likely, this be a reference to the visit of the King of Denmark in
July of 1606, then the play falls between then and the date of licensing. Since there seems no evidence that the King's Revels company
existed prior to 1607, the date of performance can be still more
narrowly circumscribed.

Your Five Gallants, by Middleton.
Title page: *Your fiue Gallants. As it hath beene often in Action at
                  the Blackfriers. Written by T. Middleton. Imprinted at
                  London for Richard Bonian, dwelling at the signe of the
                  Spred-Eagle, right ouer-against the great North dore of
                  Saint Paules Church.* (n.d.)
S.R. March 22, 1608 (*Fyve Wittie Gallants*).
Date: Fleay is in this case sound. Indications of dating within the
play agree with November, 1607; the Mitre nights are Fridays,
November 6, 13, 20, 27; a new moon comes on Thursday, November
5, which fixes the year as 1607. The plague returns of that year fell
below forty on November 26 (cf. I, 1); hence we may suggest December as the probable month of presentation.

The Dumb Knight, by Machin and Markham.
Title page: *The Dumbe Knight. A. historicall Comedy, acted sun-
                  dry times by the children of his Maiesties Reuels.
                  London, Printed by Nicholas Okes. for Iohn Bache, and
                  are to be sold at his shop in Popes-head Palace, neere to
                  the Royall Exchange 1608.*
S.R. October 6, 1608.
Date: There are no guides except the title page and the date of
publication, which put the play clearly in the year and a half be-

tween January of 1607 and August of 1608 (see discussion of Barry's *Ram Alley*). The writer of the address "To the understanding Reader" tells us that "strange constructions" have been put on the *Dumb Knight*, laughs at them, and says that his "partner in the wrong" can answer for himself. Fleay believes that the subplot of Prate, the Orator, Alphonso, who cuckolds him, Drap, Velours, and Mechant (clients of Prate) gave offense, though he cannot suggest who is satirized in the person of Prate. I rather incline to find the offense in the savage attacks which are made on the delays and bribes of law-suits, especially from the mouth of Mechant. In this respect the play falls in line with others of the period, notably Chapman's *Widow's Tears*.

Ram Alley, by Lording (Lodowick) Barry.

Title page: *Ram-Alley: Or Merrie-Trickes. A Comedy Divers times here-to-fore acted by the Children of the Kings Reuels. Written by Lo: Barrey. At London Printed by G. Eld, for Robert Wilson, and are to be sold at his shop in Holborne, at the new gate of Grayes Inne. 1611.*

S.R. November 10, 1610.

Date: The title page tells us that the play was acted by the "King's Revels" children, who are now known to be the boys playing at Whitefriars. Fleay brings together much circumstantial evidence to prove that the play was brought out in the Christmas holidays of 1609-10. The main objection thereto is that no scrap of evidence shows the company to have been in existence then. Therefore the play must have appeared originally in the year and a half between January, 1607, and August, 1608.

It is not impossible that the play was *revived* in 1609-10, for there are some evidences that the play was made over: e.g. Captain Face of the *dramatis personæ* is also called Captain Puff; and in that making over current allusions may have been introduced.

Two Maids of Mortlake, by Robert Armin.

Title page: *The History of two Maids of More-clacke With the life and simple maner of Iohn in the Hospitall. Played by the Children of the Kings Maiesties Reuels. Written by Robert Armin, seruant to the Kings most excellent Maiestie. London, Printed by N. O. for Thomas Archer and is to be sold at his shop in Popes-head Pallace, 1609.*

S.R. ?

Date: We have nothing to go on but the title page, which indeed puts the play between January of 1607 and August of 1608 so far as Whitefriars is concerned. But it was not written for the King's Revels. Some information about the antecedents of the play, though by no means clear, is given in the address "To the friendly peruser," which I shall quote entire. We learn that previous to its acquisition by the revels boys, the play was put on in the city (Whitefriars was just outside the walls).

Gentlemen, Cittizens, Rustickes, or quis non, I haue boldly put into your hands, a Historical discourse, acted by the boyes of the Reuels, which perchaunce in part was sometime acted more naturally in the Citty, if not in the hole. Howsoeuer I commit it into your hands to be scan'd, and you shall find verse, as well blancke, as crancke, yet in the prose let it passe for currant, I would haue againe nacted Iohn my self, but *Tempora mutantur in illis*, & I cannot do so as I would, I haue therefore thought good to diuulge him thus being my old acquaintance, Iack, whose life I knew, and whose remembrance I presume by appearance likely. Wherein I whilome pleased: and being requested both of Court and Citty, to shew him in priuate, I haue therefore printed him in publike, wishing thus much to euery one, so delighting, I might put life into this picture, and naturally act him to your better contents; but since it may not be, my entreaty is, that you would accept this dumbe show, and be well wishing to the substance.

I have dated the play 1597-1602. Cf. p. 233.

The Turk, by Mason.

Title page:　　*The Tvrke. A Worthie Tragedie. As it hath bene diuers times acted by the Children of his Maiesties Reuels. Written by Iohn Mason Maister of Artes.*
　　　　　　Sume superbiam quesitam meritis
　　　　　　　　　　Horat.
　　London. Printed by E. A. for Iohn Busbie and are to be sold at his shop in S. Dunstons Church-yard in Fleete-streete. 1610.

S.R. March 10, 1609.

Date: The title page tells us that the play was acted at Whitefriars. The author, John Mason, was one of the signers of the articles of agreement drawn up with Martin Slatier on March 10, 1608 (see p. 223). Mr. J. Q. Adams, the editor of the play (Bang's *Materialen* series, Louvain, 1913), decides for 1606-7, but we do not know that the company was in existence in 1606.

Law Tricks, by John Day.

Title page: *Law-Trickes or, Who Would Have Thought It. As it hath bene diuers times Acted by the Children of the Reuels. Written by Iohn Day. London Printed for Richard More, and are to be solde at his Shop in S. Dunstanes Church-yard Flete-streete. 1608.*

S.R. ?

Date: Fleay says that the play was acted "at Blackfriars, of course" by the children of the Queen's Revels, and guesses 1606. But Bullen, in his notes to his edition of Day, shows references to speeches in *Pericles,* which is generally put in 1607-8. Moreover, I think it unlikely that Day would have written another play for the Black-friars boys, and a satirical one too, immediately after the disastrous adventure with the *Isle of Gulls* in February of 1606. Indeed, there is no direct evidence that Day wrote at all for this company there-after. But we do know that in 1608 Day was writing *Humor out of Breath* for the King's Revels boys, and I suggest that to them is also to be assigned *Law Tricks.* Like other Whitefriars plays, this is a hodge-podge of popular situations, with numerous literary refer-ences and burlesques.

Humor Out of Breath, by John Day.

Title page: *Humour out of breath. A Comedie Diuers times latelie acted, By the Children Of the Kings Reuells. Written by Iohn Day. Printed at London for Iohn Helmes, and are to be sold at his shop in Saint Dunstons Church-yard in Fleet-street. 1608.*

S.R. April, 1608.

Date: The play was brought out either in the Christmas holidays of 1607-8 or between then and April following. Cf. p. 234.

The Conspiracy and Tragedy of Biron, by Chapman.

Title page: *The Conspiracie And Tragedie of Charles Duke of Byron, Marshall of France. Acted lately in two playes, at the Black-Friers. Written by George Chapman, Printed by G. Eld for Thomas Thorppe, and are to be sold at the Tygers head in Paules Churchyard. 1608.*

S.R. June 5, 1608.

Date: The plays were on the stage in March or April of 1608, when the French ambassador made his complaint about them and brought the company into trouble (cf. p. 199). They must have been written after the appearance in 1607 of Grimeston's *General Inventorie of the History of France,* which Chapman made use of (Boas, in *Athenæum,* January 10, 1903).

The Knight of the Burning Pestle, by Beaumont and Fletcher.

Title page: *The Knight of the Burning Pestle.*
*Quod si
Iudicium subtile, videndis artibus illud
Ad libros & ad hæc Musarum dona vocares:
Bæotum in crasso iurares aëre natum.*
Horat. in Epist. ad Oct. Aug.
London, Printed for Walter Burre, and are to be sold at the signe of the Crane in Paules Church-yard. 1613.
A second 4to of 1635 assigns the play to Beaumont and Fletcher.

No *S.R.*

Date: There has been considerable argument upon this subject, Thorndike holding for 1607 and Fleay and Murch (ed. of the play in *Yale Studies in English,* N. Y., 1908) maintaining, with more reason, 1610. In the oft-quoted dedication "To his many waies endeered friend Maister Robert Keysar," the publisher Burre gives the history of the play:

Sir, this vnfortunate child, who in eight daies (as lately I haue learned) was begot and borne, soone after, was by his parents (perhaps because hee was so vnlike his brethren) exposed to the wide world, who for want of iudgement, or not vnderstanding the priuy marke of Ironie about it... vtterly reiected it: so that for want of acceptance it was euen ready to giue vp the Ghost, and was in danger to haue bene smothered in perpetuall obliuion, if you...had not bene moued both to relieue and cherish it:...You afterwards sent it to mee, yet being an infant and somewhat ragged; I haue fostred it priuately in my bosome these two yeares, and now to shew my loue returne it to you, clad in good lasting cloaths, which scarce memory will weare out, and able to speake for it selfe, &c.

The stage history of Robert Keysar is easy to trace. He first became interested in the Blackfriars company in 1606-8, but we first hear of him as a director when he brought the boys to court in Christmas and January of 1608-9 (cf. pp. 201-205). It was he who carried the children to Whitefriars, but when the new patent was issued on January 4, 1610, Keysar's name was absent, and he vanishes from sight soon thereafter. Keysar was a producer, then, from 1608 to 1610, and the play must have been brought to him within that period.

When we remember that 1608 was a lean year for Blackfriars because of the troubles resulting from the *Biron* plays and that Keysar was out of the company by January 4, 1610, this seems to narrow the period in which he was likely to receive the play to the year 1609, possibly the end of 1608.

Of course the Citizen's statement in the Induction that "This seuen yeares there hath beene playes at this house" conflicts with any dating except 1607, for we cannot trace the Whitefriars theatre before 1607, and the Blackfriars boys were established in 1600. Nevertheless, the arguments for a later date than 1607 are to me convincing, and I must decline even to attempt to solve the Citizen's crux.

Epicœne, by Jonson.

Title page: (the play is first printed in the 1616 folio of Jonson): *Epicœne, or The silent Woman. A Comœdie. Acted in the yeere 1609. By the Children of her Maiesties Revells. The Author B. I.*

Horat.

Vt sis tu similis Cæli, Byrrhiq; latronum,
Non ego sim Capri, neq; Sulci. Cur metuas me?
London, Printed by William Stansby. M.DC.XVI.

S.R. September 20, 1610.

Date: The title page gives us the date and the company, and the Prologue tells us that the play was acted at Whitefriars. This has caused many to date the play 1610, after the patent of January 4 granted to the ex-Blackfriars company; but we know now that these boys had been playing at Whitefriars since the first half of 1609. Mr. Thorndike (*Influence of Beaumont and Fletcher on Shakespeare*, 16-7) has made out a good case for Jonson's using the new system of dating in the 1616 folio; if this is true, the play is to be assigned to 1609.

A list of actors is printed in the folio:

> Nathaniel Field
> Will Barkstead
> Giles Carey
> Will Pen
> Hugh Attawell
> Richard Allin
> John Smith
> John Blaney

The Scornful Lady, by Beaumont and Fletcher.

Title page: *The Scornful Ladie. A Comedie. As it was Acted (with great applause) by the Children of her Maiesties Reuels in the Blacke Fryers. Written by Fra. Beaumont and Io: Fletcher, gent. London Printed for Myles Partrich, and are to be sold at his Shop at the George neere St. Dunstons Church in Fleete-streete. 1616.*

S.R. March 19, 1616.

Date: Though the title page is explicit in stating that the play was given at Blackfriars by the Revels children, references in the play to the Cleve wars and to the "cast Cleve captain" point to the latter half of 1609 (Fleay) or 1610-11, after fighting had begun (Thorndike, *Influence of Beaumont and Fletcher on Shakespeare*, 86). But the Revels boys had ceased to act in Blackfriars before the Cleve troubles had begun. Thorndike argues that the play belongs, as far as references go, to 1610-11. But a reference to the negotiations for a Spanish match with Prince Charles in 1613 points at least to later revision. Probably the various references which have so puzzled the editors are accountable to retouching. The play may have been first acted in 1610, in which case Blackfriars was not the place. Most likely Thorndike and Chambers are right in thinking that the second Blackfriars theatre of 1616 is referred to by the title page.

The Coxcomb, by Beaumont and Fletcher.

First printed in the Folio of 1647.

Date: In the *Account Book* of the Treasurer of the Chamber for 1612-13 (see *Cupid's Revenge*) occurs the following entry:

> Item paid to Phillipp Roseter vppon the Cowncells warrant dated att Whitehall xxiiijᵗᵒ die Novembris 1612 for himself and the Children of the Queenes Maiestes Revells, for presentinge before the Princes highnes: the La: Eliz: grace, and the Cownt Pallatyne, a Comedye called the Coxcombe the some of - vjˡⁱ xiijˢ iiijᵈ.

Oldys says (MS. notes to Langbaine) that the play was acted before the king in March of 1613, but the Treasurer of the Chamber says nothing about it. In the second Folio of 1679 appears the following list of actors:

Nathan Field	Joseph Taylor
Giles Gary (Cary)	Emanuel Read
Rich. Allen	Hugh Atawell
Robert Benfield	Will. Barcksted

As Fleay points out, the list belongs before August 29, 1611, because on that date Cary and Barkstead left the Revels company to join the Lady Elizabeth s men; and according to Thorndike the same kind of argument puts it before March 30, 1610, because on that date Taylor left the company to join the newly constituted company of the Duke of York. Both Oliphant and Thorndike date the play before 1610.

The Revenge of Bussy D'Ambois, by Chapman.

Title page: The Revenge of Bussy D'Ambois. A Tragedie. As it hath beene often presented at the private Play-house in the White-Fryers. Written by George Chapman, Gentleman, London. Printed by T. S. and are to be solde by John Helme, at his shop in S. Dunstones Church-yard, in Fleetstreet, 1613.

S.R. April 17, 1612.

Date: No more definite evidence can be found than the title page, which tells us that the play was acted at Whitefriars; that it was by the ex-Blackfriars company there can be no shadow of doubt, for Chapman wrote almost exclusively for them. That puts the play between spring of 1609, when the children moved into Whitefriars, and April, 1612, unless as Fleay hypothecates it was first brought out at Blackfriars—but there is no evidence for that.

Cupid's Revenge, by Beaumont and Fletcher.

Title page: Cupids Revenge. As it hath beene divers times Acted by the Children of her Majesties Revels. By John Fletcher. London Printed by Thomas Creede for Josias Harison, and are to bee solde at the Golden Anker in Pater-Noster-Row. 1615.

S.R. April 24, 1615.

Date: The *Account Book* of the Treasurer of the Chamber for 10-11 James I (1612-13) at the Bodleian (*Rawlinson* A, 239) has the following entries:

> Item paid to the said Phillipp Roseter vppon the lyke warrant dated att Whitehall vltimo die Maij 1613 for presentinge two severall playes, before the Princes highnes. One vppon the ix[th] of Januarie last called Cupides revenge: And the other called the Widdowes Teares, vppon the xxvij[th] of ffebr: following the some of xiij[l] vj[s] viij[d].

Immediately following is an entry of the same date recording a performance before the king on January 1 of the same play. Oldys tells that the play was acted on January 5, 1612, before Prince Henry and the Princess Elizabeth and again on January 1, 1613. I do not know where he got the authority for his first dating, and I prefer the authority of the Treasurer of the Chamber.

As to the date of composition of the play, nothing definite can be said. If it was written for Rossiter's Queen's Revels company, then it belongs in or after 1610, when he came into the company.

A Woman is a Weathercock, by Field.

Title page: *A Woman is a Weather-cocke. A New Comedy, As it was acted before the King in White-Hall. And diuers times Priuately at the White-Friers, By the Children of her Maiesties Reuels. Written by Nat: Field. for Iohn Budge. 1612.*

S.R. November 23, 1611.

Date: Between 1609, when the Revels company moved to Whitefriars, and the date of licensing. Fleay's argument for 1610 carries persuasion.

The Insatiate Countess, by Marston.

Title page: *The Insatiate Countess. A Tragedie: Acted at White-Fryers. Written by Iohn Marston. London: Printed by T.S. for Thomas Archer, and are to be sold at his shop in Popes-head-Pallace, neere the Royall-Exchange. 1613.*

Another 4to in 1616 with no name; two in 1631, one with Marston's name and one with William Barkstead's. The play is not in the collected edition of M. in 1633.

Date and authorship: Bullen finds that the play is printed in a very corrupt condition, and that the hand of another is clear in it, and this hand he takes to be Barkstead's. There are many imitations of Shakespeare, more than in any other play of Marston's. Fleay, agreeing that the play is in bad shape, is of the opinion that modern editing has only made matters worse. He supposes that the play is a condensation by Barkstead from two other plays, a comedy and a tragedy; and from the abuses resorted to liberally by the Jew and the Apothecary, he guesses that the comedy was the *Abuses* acted before James by the Paul's boys in 1606. It is hardly necessary to comment that this bold guess has not the slightest grounds of proof; in fact, it rests partly on another hypothesis which Fleay upholds, but which we know now to be wrong, that the Whitefriars boys were a continuation of the Paul's troupe, disbanded c. 1606. Fleay dates the original play, or plays, c. 1604, another guess. The Apothecary Claridiana's satirical book on women called *The Snarl* he identifies with *Microcynicon, Six Snarling Satires,* published in 1599 by T(homas) M(offat), who also wrote *Father Hubbard's Tale, The Black Book,* and others.

The observations of Fleay and Bullen do little more than emphasize the need for a thorough studying of this play, in the effort to untangle its confusions,—a need which, indeed, applies to all Marston's plays. Such investigation will probably confirm the opinion that Barkstead made over a play of Marston, possibly fusing it with another play, or more likely adding parts of his own composition. The tragic plot, with its combination of violence and lust, is characteristic of Marston, and should be credited to him; the comic plot is the familiar story of the husbands who, thinking that they are cuckolding each other, lie with their own wives, and this portion of the play might have been done by anyone—it is not distinctly Marston. A reasonable conjecture is that the present play was put together by Barkstead for performance in 1613 at the time when the revival of Marston's *Dutch Courtesan,* under the name of *Cockledemoy,* by the Lady Elizabeth's men, to whom Barkstead belonged, made Marston live again for an hour upon the stage. Barkstead joined this company on its inception in April, 1611.[2] But if he prepared the play for the Whitefriars company, whose name stands upon the title page, then the date is fixed between the limits of April, 1611, and the summer of 1609, when the Queen's Revels company was deprived of their theatre at Blackfriars, through the entry of the King's men, and moved to Whitefriars. Barkstead was a member of this company, at least in 1610.[3]

[2] Cf. Murray, *Eng. Dramatic Cos.,* I, 243.
[3] Murray, *op. cit.,* I, 358-9.

The Faithful Shepherdess
Philaster
Monsieur Thomas } by Beaumont and Fletcher.
Four Plays in One

No direct evidence connects any of these plays with any company of children. But both Fleay and Thorndike suggest that they *may* have been written originally for the Children of the Queen's Revels at Blackfriars, the argument being that *if* they were written before 1609 they *probably* were produced by these children, for whom the dramatists were *probably* doing most of their work. Evidently there are too many if's here to build upon; nevertheless, I present the plays for the bare possibilities in them.

The case of *The Faithful Shepherdess* is the strongest because that play presents some internal evidence of being written for children. Thus Thorndike, while hesitating to assign it to a definite company, says that it was "evidently written for a company of children." From the fact that *The Scornful Lady*, *The Woman Hater*, and *The Knight of the Burning Pestle* were written for children, some likelihood is raised for other plays of the same period.

APPENDIX III

DOCUMENTS ILLUSTRATIVE OF THE HISTORY OF CHILDREN'S COMPANIES AND THE STAGE

I.

Cornish's "Troilus and Pandor."

From the Revels Books of Richard Gibson; *Records of the Exchequer, Miscellaneous Books, Treasury of Receipt,* Vol. 229, p. 139.

Vide p. 54

The kynge*s* grace holdyng hys crystmes at hys maner Elltham y⁰ vii^th yer of hys rayen wher for then and ther hys plesyer was to have reuells for yoyvs pastym in y⁰ sayd feest of crystmes as well by y⁰ avyes of mast Wyll^a kornyche as by y⁰ avyes of y⁰ mast of y⁰ revelle*s* wher for by cvmmandment of our sayd sov*e*rayn lord i rechard gybson resayvyd instroccyvn of our sov*e*rayn lorde*s* plesyer for weche revelle*s* was provydyd a castel of tymbyr fyx and fast in y⁰ kyngs hall garnechyd aft*er* seche devyes as shall in sew & allso in ye sayd tym of crystmes for solas by mast kornych and other and by y⁰ chylldyrn of ye chappell was played y⁰ storry of troylous and pandor rychely inp*a*relled all so kallkas & cryssyd inp*a*rylld lyke a wedow of onour in blake sarsenet and other abelemente*s* for seche mater dyomed and ye greke*s* inp*a*rylld lyke men of war a kordyng to y⁰ intent or porpoos aft weche Camedy playd and doon an harroud Cryd and arad an oy y^t iii strange knygte*s* wer cum to do batall w^t weche out of ye sayd Castell yssvd iiij men of arme*s* w^t punchyng spere*s* redy do (sic) do feets at y⁰ barryer inp*a*rylld in whyghthe saten and greeyn saten of bregys lynd w^t gren sarse-net and whyght sarsenet and y⁰ saten kut ther oon to ye sayd iij men of arme*s* enterd other iij men of arme*s* w^t lyke wepune*s* and inp*a*rylld in slope*s* of reed sarsenet and yelow sarsenet and w^t speere*s* arad sartayn stroke*s* and aft y^t doon w^t nakyd swerde*s* fawght a fayer batayll of xii strooke*s* and so departyd of foore*s* then out of y⁰ Castell ysseud a qvyen and w^t her vi ladye*s* w^t spechys aft y⁰ devyes of m^t kornyche and aft thys doon vii mynstrelle*s* inp*a*rylld in long garmente*s* and bonete*s* to y⁰ saam of saten of brcgys whyght and greeyn on y⁰ walle*s* and towrys of y⁰ sayd Castell played a melodyus song then cam out of y⁰ Castell vi lorde*s* and gentyllmen inp*a*relld in garmente*s* of whyght saten of bregys and greyn browdyrd w^t counterfyt stouf (or stons?) of flandyre*s* makyng as bruchys

THE CHILD ACTORS

ovchys spang*es* and seche and all so vi ladyes inp*arylld* in vi garment*es* of ryght saten whyght and greeyn set w*t* h and k of yelow saten etc.

Items
It spent and in ployed in a goun for m*t* harry of ye chappell y*t* playd in thys dysgysyng and a bonet - xv yerd*es*
It spent and in ployd in a dobelet for oon of y*e* chappell chylldryn yt playd eulyxes - ii yerd*es* etc.
It spent and in ployed in a mantell and a bechop*es* surkoot for mast kornyche to play kallkas in and a bonet to ye saam and a long gyrdyll-xii yerds etc.
It in a garment (of black sarsnet) for m*t* kornyche y*t* he played y*e* haurood in and other dyver*es* besenes - ix yerd*es*
..ii pec*es* of florens coton y*e* iiii*s* spent and inployd for and on ye ap*ar*ell of lady kryssyd by ye dyscrecyun of y*e* ladyes of y*e* koort.
It for inp*ar*ell of ye lady y*t* playd faythe...
(7 ells of linen) spent by y*e* avyes of mast kornyche for dyomed and hys felow*es* for shert slevys wyd hangyng out at y*e* hand and other plac*es* so spent - vii ell.
(for points for) troylus pandor dyomed eulyxes...
It ii chyllderne troyllus and pandor ii dobelet*es* saten.

For y*e* play xv p*er*sonag*es*
for y*e* Castell vii ladyes
It vii mynstrell*es*
y*e* nombyr of p*er*son*es* It vi lord*es* and gentyllmen dysgysyd.
It vi ladyes for ye dysgysyng
It vi men of arm*es*
It iii tamboryn*es*

2.
Note of Excommunication of Sebastian Westcote, 1563.
Records of the Consistory Court of London, In the Principal Probate Registry, Somerset House, London; *Libri Vicarii Generalis, Huick 1561-1574,* Vol. 3, fol. 77. *Vide* p. 120.

Offic*ium* dom*i*ni c*ontra*
  Sebastianu*m*
  Wescott

Sexto die mens*is* Julii in loco capit*u*lari ecclesie cath*edra*lis s*anc*ti Pauli london cora*m* mag*ist*ro huyck vicario gen*er*ali &c inpre-*s*entia mei Petri Johnson Reg*ist*rarij.

Quo die idem venerabilis vic*arius* Thomas huyck eundem Sebastianum Wescott p*er*conizat*um* et non comp*ar*end*um* in no*n* parend*o* certis mon-nitionib*us* iustis et le*gi*timis p*er* Reuerend*um* p*a*trem london ep*iscop*u*m* ali*a*s sibi fact*is* et

iniu*nct*i*s* pronu*n*ciauit contumace*m* et in pena*m*
contumacie sue hu*iu*smod*i* excom*mun*icauit
p*ro*(ut) in schedula.

Westcote's Bond of Good Behavior, 1564.

St. Paul's Cathedral library; A. Box 77/2059. The document is
badly written, and mutilated so that two or three words on each
line of one margin are lŏst.

Vide p. 123.

Sciant Omnes p*er* pr*e*sentes me Sebastian*um* Westcote de London gen-
*er*osum teneri et firmiter obligari Reuerendissimo in *Christo* patri Edmundo
p*er*missione diuina London Ep*iscop*o in Centum marcas legalis monete
Anglie Soluend*as* eidem Ep*iscop*o aut successor*ibus* suis Ad quam quidem
soluc*i*o*n*em bene et fidel*iter* faciend*am* Obligo me heredes & executor*es*
meos p*er* pr*e*sentes Sigillo meo sigillat*os* Dat*os* Octavo die Novembr*is* Anno
Regni d*omi*ne n*os*tre Elizabeth dei gr*atia* Anglie ffrancie et hib*er*nie Regine
fidei defensor sexto

(The) Condic*i*on of this obligac*i*on is such that if the aboue bounden
Sebastian Westcot at and from . . . (fea)st oof Easter next comynge after
the date hereof shall not frame his consciens so as the same (shall c)onforme
it self agreable to all and singler such poynt*es* and articles of Relligion as
are nowe . . . aswell by the Lawes and statutes made in the tyme of o*ur*
sou*e*reign Lady the Queenes ma*i*estie . . . s as by her graces ordyn*an*c*es* and
Iniunc*i*ons That then if the said Sebastian after . . . (p)ast and notice given
that his consciens cannot agree unto the same shall give th. . thexercise
and mynystery aswell of all such Romes offices p*ro*moc*i*ons chardges and . .
wh*i*ch he hath w*i*thin the Cathedral church of S Paule w*i*thin the Cittie of
(london a)s also from the vicars Rome there and also of and from all such
fees stipends (emolument)es and other com*m*odities p*ro*fitt*es* and advantages that from thenceforth should or might . . . to hym by reson of any of
the said offic*es* or Romes And also if the said Sebastian (at a)ll tymes on
this side the said feast of Easter next comynge shalbe discreet and . . .
words and behavior toward*es* the Quenes maiestie That then this pr*e*sente..
be voide and of none effect Orels to stand and abide in full strength and
vertue . . . alwaies and neu*er*theles it is agreed that thissues p*ro*fitt*es* Reven-
ewes stypends and . . (wh)atsoeu*er* they be beinge due unto the said Sebastian for his said roomes and offices . . . annunciac*i*on (of) o*ur* Lady next
comyng after the date hereof shall . . . and holy belonge . . unto the said
Sebastian and his assignes w*i*thout let or denyall any thinge before . . .
(c)ondic*i*on to the contrary not w*i*thstandinge.

3.

Will of Sebastian Westcote.

Somerset House, Prerogative Court of Canterbury, 14 Tirwhite.

Vide p.119.

In the name of the most glorious and blessed Trinitie the father the sonne and the holy ghoste, so be it. I SEBASTIAN WESTCOTE Almener of the Cathedrall Churche of Sainte Paule in London beinge greved withe sickenes, beinge yet of perfecte minde and memorye (to god I geve praise therefore) this thirde daie of Aprill in the yere of oure Lorde god 1582. And in the xxiiij^th yeare of the raigne of oure most gracious soveraigne Ladye Queene Elizabeth etc. make my last will and testamente in manner and fourme ensewinge, hereby revokinge all other will*es* and testament*es* whatsoever by me heretofore made...my worldlye good*es* I geve and dispose as followeth viz ffirst I geve and bequeathe to and amoungest the Petycannons of the saide Cathedrall churche of St Paule to bringe my body to the Churche fyve poundes. And amoungest the vicars of the same Churche to bringe my body likewise to Churche fower poundes. And to the tenne Chorasters of the same churche fyve poundes Item I geve to Gyles Clothier and Iohn Boult viz Gyles three poundes sixe shilling*es* eighte pence And Boulte I geve fower poundes. To everye of the Vergers of the same Churche tenne shillinges a peece to bringe me to Churche. To the keeper of the Churche vestrye three shillinges fower pence, To everye of the Bellringers there three shilling*es* fower pence, To the poore of the p*a*rishe of Chimley where I was borne in the Countie of Devon three poundes, To the poore within the Towne of Tawnton in the Countie of Somer*s*^t fortie shilling*es*. To the poore of kyrton in Devon fiftie shilling*es*. To the poore of kingestone neere Tawnton aforesayde fyve shilling*es*, To the poore of the p*a*rishe of St Gregoryes neere Pawles churche in London twentye shilling*es* To the poore prisonners within the severall howses and prisons called the fflete, the Marshallsye, the king*es* benche, the white Lyon in Southwark, the twoe Cownters, Newgate, Ludgate, Bethelem, and the gatehowse in Westminster to euerie prison sixe shillinges eighte pence a peece. Item I geve and bequeathe to the vse of the Almenrye howse of the said Cathedrall Churche of St Pawle where I nowe dwell to be and remayne vnto the same Almenrye howse to the vse of the Almener there for the tyme beinge forever toward*es* the furnishinge of the same howse, my cheste of vyalyns and viall*es* to exercise and learne the children and Choristers there. And also one Table in the hall withe the frame, a settle of ioyned work, a payre of great iron Aundirons, there, the table, frame and settl*es*, hanging*es*, wainscott, and Cupborde in the p*a*rlour there, The hanging*es* in mine owne chamber, the hanging*es* in the Chamber over the kytchen,

The great chest and greate presse there the Cupboard and the greate chest at the stayers heade fyve bedsteed*es* fyve mattress*es*, fyve paire of blank-ett*es*, fyve bolsters of floxe fyve coverled*es* suche as are accustomablie vsed for the Tenne Choresters, together withe all suche wood and coales as shalbe lefte in the howse exceptinge some necessarye fewell, for my ex-ecto*ur* for the tyme beinge there vntill suche tyme as the reste of the stuffe be ryd owte of the howse, a pestle and morter, the thirde brasse pott, a water Chaffer, the worser Chaffingdishe, fyve latten candlestick*es* the second and thirde spitt*es* the second paire of Aundirons, one paire of Tong*es* and a fyer shovell of the worser sorte a drippinge panne, twoe paire of hang-ers, a trevitt, three of the worser plater*es* fower of the worser dishes, the worste skom*m*er (?), fower porringers, sixe of the worst Sawcer*es* of pew*ter* one of the worser basons a pottle and a quarte potte of pewter, Twoe pynte pott*es*, the worste Chamberpott. More I geve to the saide Almenerye howse to remayne forever as aforesaide, twoe Mazers bounde abowte withe sylver one bigger and the other lesser, sixe silver spoones of the smaller sorte withe slype*es* All wch saide plate and howshold stuff so by me as afore-saide geven to the saide Alme*n*erye howse (necessarye waste onelye ex-cepted) I will that an Inventary Indented thereof to be made, one parte whereof I will shalbe and remayne in the safe custody of the worshipfull Deane and Chapter of the saide Cathedrall Churche and their Successor And the other parte thereof to be delyvered vnto the Almener of the saide Cathedrall Churche for the tyme beinge, to thentente the saide Deane and Chapter maye at their pleasures call the Almener for the tyme beinge to an Accompte. And for the suer delyverie of the same to his Successors forever. Item I geve and bequeath to my brother George Westcote ffortye shilling*es*, And to everie of his children Twentie sixe shilling*es* eighte pence. Item I geve and bequeathe vnto my Sister Iaquet Goodmowe Tenne poundes, And forgeve all suche debt*es* as she oweth me. Item I geve and bequeathe vnto Elizabeth Westcote widowe my sister in lawe twentye poundes, togeather with the Lease of Westgrene wch I nowe have, and all ye howshold stuffe and kyene and cattell there. Item I geve and bequeathe vnto my brother Robert Westcote Thirtene pownd*es* six shilling*es* eighte pence. And I forgeve him all suche Debt*es* as he oweth me. To Andrew Westcote his Sonne Tenne pound*es*. And to eurie of his other children thirtie shilling*es*. Item I geve vnto Roger Westcote, Sebastian[1] & ffrancis Westcote sonne of my late brother William Westcote, to everye of theme tenne poundes, allowinge suche thing*es* or som*m*es of monneye as I owe theme. Item I geve to the daughters of my sister Iaquet Goodinowe Three poundes

---

[1] There is a signature "Sebastian Westcot" affixed to a petition for arrears of pay of certain poor knights of St. George's, Windsor, in *Ashmole MSS.* 111, fol 53 (Bodleian). The petition is undated, but belongs in the reign of Charles I, after the outbreak of the Civil War.

a peece beinge fower of theme. Item I geve and bequeathe to my sisters Daughter wch was married of late towardes thee buyldinge of her howse wch was burnt sixe poundes thirteene shilling*es* fower pence, And to her twoe children twentie shilling*es* a peece. Item I geve and bequeathe vnto ffrydiswide Clunye widowe nowe beinge in howse withe me, the Somme of Tenne pound*es* and the fowrthe featherbed perfourmed. Item I geve to Margaret Riche my sister in lawe fortie shilling*es* in money. Item I geve to Iohn Thorneleye and his sister ffraunc*es* thirtie shilling*es* a peece. Item I geve to henrye Redforde and to Elizabethe ffarthinge dwellinge at Bierton in the Countie of Buck if theie be lyving at the tyme of my decease Twentie shilling*es* a peece. Item I geve to Batholomewe Redforde Thirtie shillinges. Item I geve to katherine my mayde Servaunte three poundes. Item I geve to Thomas Bluet, Thomas Barsey, Robert and Iohn Aunderson nowe remayninge in my howse, to eu*er*ye of theme fyve poundes a peece. *Item I giue to Richard my man xxx s.* Item I geve to Peter Phillipp*es* likewise remayninge withe me sixe poundes thirtene shilling*es* fower pence. Item I geve to Thomas Venge three pound*es* Item I geve to Bromeham, Richard Huse, Robert knight, Nicholas Carleton Baylye   Nasion, and Gregorye Bowringe, sometymes children of the saide Almenery howse to everye of theme twentie shilling*es* a peece. Item I geve and bequeathe to the righte worshipfull m^r Iustice Sowthcote my especiall good frende my guilte cuppe withe the cover havinge on the cover St Sebastian. Item to my loving frende M^r henerye Evans sixe pound*es* thirtene shillinges fower pence, and a little cuppe of silver and a cou*er* withe twoe litle winges on the cover. Item I geve to Westcote that is blinde three poundes. Item to my frende Iustinian kyd gent a square Salte gilted wroughte. And whereas I the saide Sebastian Westcote haue in this my last will and testament geven and bequeathed vnto divers of the childrenne of my brothers and sisters and to other my frend*es* children all or the moste parte of theme nowe beinge verye younge, and so by lawe not hable to discharge my executor of the receipte of suche legacies, as I have geven vnto theme, My will and meaninge is, That if it shall happen anye of the saide children to be putt forth apprentices, that the M^r and Parent*es* of everye suche childe puttinge in sufficie*n*t assuranc*es* to my execut*our* to discharge him against theme and everye of theme for the same, shall have the legacie of everie suche childe, as by good discrecion of my executor shalbe thought best for the benefitt of suche childe and children. Item I geve and bequeathe to M*is*tres Good latelye the wife of Doctor Good Phisitian a ringe of gold withe a blewe stone, And to her daughter kynborowghe a ringe with three Iemmowes small, to my mistris Sowthcote a golde ringe of some pretye fashion to be made for her to the valewe of fortye shilling*es*.

* . . . .*, a marginal note.

To m^r Iohn Sowthcot*es* wife the younger a like ringe of golde of fortie shilling*es* price. The residue of all my good*es*, cattell*es* monneye plate, Iewelles with my debt*es* to me owinge not heretofore geven and bequeathed (my debt*es* paide and this my Testament accomplished and perfourmed and all other necessarye expenc*es* and charg*es* from tyme to tyme that my executor shall be at satisfied allowed and paide) I wholie geve and bequeathe porcion and porcion alike amongest thee children of my brethren and Sisters. And thexecutor of this my last will and testament I make and ordaine my lovinge frende Iustinian kydd gent, to whome for his frendelye paynes herein to be taken I geve Tenn pound*es*. And overseer of the same I make my foresaide deere friende Mr Henrye Evans, prayinge him to be assistinge to my executoure withe his good councell, and likewise to be carefull for my sister Elizabeth Westcote widow in her affayres and busynes as tyme shall serve. It witnes whereof I the saide Sebastian Westcote to this my last will and testament have putte my hande and Seale the daye & yere abovewritten. Witness*ed* at the sealinge and delyveringe hereof. Signed sealed and delyvered as his last will and testamente the daie and yere abovesaide as his will & testamente deede in the presence of m^r Creake, Robert Nycholl*es*, Iohn Ore, and Raphe Parys gent. by me Thomas Creak.

(A codicil adds these following legacies: John Ore, 10s; Edward Cooper "the Innocent in my howse" £6-13-4; William Gafford,5s; Mother Alyce, 10s; Mother Smaleye,10s; Mother Walter,10s; "To Pole the keper of the gate," 10s; each of Ralph Paris's children, 10s; "To Shep*ard* that kepeth the doore of playes," 10s; George Parys, 10s; "more to make up 20s"; Catherine the maid, for her great pains with him in his sickness, 40s.)

(Proved April 14, 1582. The will was contested by Robert Westcote and others of the beneficiaries, but was upheld in court. It does not seem worth while to transcribe the Latin digest of these proceedings, which contains no items of interest.)

4.

Suit in Chancery: Nath. Gyles v. Wm. Combes.

Chanc. Proc. Ser. II, Bdl. 240, no. 91.

Vide p. 158.

Evelyn. vicesimo nono Apr*ilis* 1594   To the ryght honorable
d   Sr John Puckeringe Knyght
                                                Lord Keep*er* of the
                                     greate seale of Englande.

In most humble wyse Complayninge sheweth unto you^r honorable good Lordshippe you^r poore and daylye Orator Nathanyell Giles bachelor of Musycke and M^r of her Maiestyes Chyldren of the Chapell of Saynt George w^thin her hyghnes Castle of new Wyndsor That whereas one Wyllyam

Combes of the parysh of gregory Stoke w^{t}hin the County of Somersett
Carpenter dyd in Consyderacyon that your sayde Orator should take and
for the space of ffower yeares keepe and well instruct and teach in the Art
of musycke one Wyllyam Comes sonne of the aforesayde Wm Combes And
in consideracion also of a certayne some of mony payde by your Orator agre
to and wyth your sayde Orator to buy one fayre breedinge Mare for the use
of your sayde Orator, And the sayde Mare so bought as aforesaide and all
the Coltes wch should so come of her wyth in the same ffower yeares at the
Charges of the same Wyllyam Comes to feede and Depasture and the sayde
Mare and Coltes to delyver unto your sayde Orator or his Assignes when-
soeuer your sayde Orator w^{t}hin the sayde terme of ffower yeares should
requyer the same of hym, the sayde Wyllyam Combes, wch agreement or
the lyke in effect was sett down in wrytinge under the hand and seale of the
sayde Wm Combes Accordinge to wch agreement your sayde orator dyd not
only paye sayde Mony mencyoned in the same agreement but dyd also
take and at hys owne Charge hath euer synce hetherto kept and instructed
in the art of Musycke the sayde w^m Combes soone of the sayde Wm Combes
to your poore orators Charge of twenty markes at the least But so yt is yf
it please your good Lordshyppe That the sayde w^m Combes hauinge by
casuall meanes gott into hys handes the sayde wrytinge of agreament And
knowinge then that your sayde Orator hath no wyttnesses to proue the
same, He the sayde w^m Combes hath utterlye neglected not to performe his
parte of the same agreament contrary to all equyty and good Conscyens In tender consyderatyon whereof and because your sayde orator ys
remedyles for the premysses by cowrse of the Comon Lawe aswell for that
he hath neyther the sayde wrytinge wherein the same Agreament ys conteyned nor can for want of the same wrytynge, sett downe the same agreament so precysely and stryctly as the Cowrse of the Comon Lawe requyreth
May yt therfore please your good Lordshyppe the premysses consydered
to grant to your sayde orator her Maiestyes Most gratyous wrytt of Spec-
iali to be dyrected unto the sayde w^m Combes the elder Comaundinge hym
therby at a certayne daye and under a certeyne payne there in by your
Lordshyppe to be lymyted personally to appeare before your good Lordshyppe in her Maiestyes Hyghe Cowrt of Chauncery then and ther to
Aunswere the premysses upon hys corporall oth And further to stand to
and abyde such further order and dyrectyon therein as to your good Lordshyppe shall seme to stand wth equyty and good Conscyens And your
orator shall pray unto god for the longe health of your honorable good
Lordshyppe longe to contynew wth much increase.

Ley.

5.

Suit in King's Bench: Henry Evans v. Thomas Kendall, 1608.
Coram Rege Rolls, Easter, 6 Jas. I, m. 303.
Vide pp. 186 ff.

Memorandum quod alias scilicet Termino sancte Trinitatis Anno regni domini Jacobi nunc Regis Anglie secundo coram eodem domino Rege apud Westmonasterium venit henricus Evans de london generosus per Willelmum langhorne Attornatum suum Et protulit hic in Curia dicti domini Regis tunc ibidem quandam billam suam versus Thomam kendall alias dictum Thomam kendall Ciuem & haberdasher london in Custodia Marrescalli &c de placito debiti Et sunt plegii de prosequendo scilicet Johannes Doo & Ricardus Roo Que quidem billa sequitur in hec verba// london// henricus Evans de london generosus queritur de Thoma kendall alias dicto Thoma kendall Ciue et haberdasher london in Custodia Marrescalli Marescalsie domini Regis Coram ipso Rege existente de placito quod reddat ei quinquaginta libras bone & legalis monete Anglie quas ei debet & iniuste detinet pro eo videlicet quod cum predictus Thomas vicesimo die Aprilis Anno regni domine Elizabeth nuper Anglie quadragesimo quarto apud london videlicet in parochia beate Marie de Arcubus in Warda de Cheape london per quoddam scriptum suum obligatorium sigillo ipsius Thome sigillato Curieque dicti domini Regis nunc hic ostensum cuius datum est eisdem die & Anno cognoscit se teneri & firmiter obligari prefato henrico in predictis quinquaginta libris soluendis eidem henrico cum inde requisitus esset predictus tamen Thomas licet sepius requisitus &c predictas quinquaginta libras prefato henrico nondum soluit sed illas ei hucusque soluere omnino contradixit & adhuc contradicit ad dampnum ipsius henrici viginti librarum Et inde producit sectam &c.

Et modo ad hunc diem scilicet diem Sabbati proximum post Octabas Sancti hillarij isto eodem Termino vsque quem diem predictus Thomas kendall habuit licenciam ad billam predictam interloquendum Et tunc ad respondendum &c Coram domino Rege apud Westmonasterium venerunt tam predictus henricus Evans per Attornatum suum predictum quam predictus Thomas kendall per Ricardum Bretton Attornatum suum Et idem Thomas defendit vim & iniuriam quando &c Et petit auditum scripti obligatorij predicti et ei legitur &c petit eciam auditum Indorsamenti eiusdem scripti Et ei legitur in hec verba // The Condicion of this obligacion ys suche That yf the within bounden William Rastell Edwarde kirkham and Thomas kendall or any of them theire or any of their executors, administrators or assignes everye weeke weekly on Saturdaye duringe the space of fifteene yeres next ensuinge the date within written when & soe often as anye enterludes playes or showes shalbe playde vsed showed or published in the greate hall and other the Roomes scituat in the Blackfriers london or any parte thereof menci*o*ned to be demysed by one Richard Burbage gent to the within named henry Evans in and by one Indenture of lease bearinge date the second daye of September in the twoe and fortith yere of the raigne of our Sou*e*raigne ladye Elizabeth the Queenes maiestie that nowe ys or els where by the children or any called by the name of the children of the queenes Maieste*s* Chappell or by any other Children which by the consent of the sayd Will*i*am Edward Thomas henrie and one Alexander hawkyns gent theire executors or Administrators or any three of them whereof the saide henrie or Alexander theire Executors or Administrators to be one shalbe dyeted kepte or retayned for the exercize of the saide en*ter*lud*e*s or playes doe and shall well & trewlie paye or cause to be paide vnto the saide henrie Evans his Executors or assignes att or in the saide great hall the som*m*e of eighte shilling*e*s of lawfull money of England The first payment thereof to begynne and to be made on Saturdaye beinge the fower & twenteth daye next com*m*ynge of this instant moneth of Aprill within written That then this p*r*esent obligac*i*on to be voide & of none effect Or els yt to stande in full force and vertue Quib*us* lec*t*is & audit*i*s idem Thomas kendall dicit q*u*od p*re*dic*t*us henricus Evans acc*i*onem suam p*re*dic*t*am inde v*er*sus eum ha*b*ere seu mauntenere non debet quia dic*it* q*u*od ip*s*e post datum scripti p*re*dic*t*i scil*i*cet p*re*dic*t*o die Sab*b*ati vicesimo quarto die p*re*dic*t*i Mensis Aprilis & sic qualib*et* septimana septimanatim sup*er* diem Sab*b*ati vsque diem impetrac*i*onis bille p*re*dic*t*e tocies quoties aliqua ludicra anglice enterludes ludi vel spectacula anglice showes fuerunt lusta vsa ostens*a* siue publicat*a* in p*re*dic*t*a magna aula & aliis locis anglice roomes scituat*is* in le Blackfriers london vel aliqua parte inde menc*i*onat*is* fore dimiss*is* p*er* p*re*dic*t*um Ricard*u*m Burbage p*re*fat*o* henrico Evans p*er* p*re*dic*t*am Indenturam in Condic*i*one p*re*dic*t*a superius spec*if*icat*am* vel alibi p*er* pueros vel aliquos voc*atos* p*er* nomen puero*rum* Capelle regie maiestatis Anglice children of the queenes maiesties Chappell vel p*er* aliquos alios pueros qui p*er* Concensum p*re*dic*torum* Will*e*lmi Edwardi Thome henrici & Alex*andr*i vel eor*um* trium fuer*unt* Comensal*ati* anglice dyeted servat*i* siue retent*i* anglice retayned p*ro* exerc*i*one p*re*dic*t*orum ludicror*um* vel ludor*um* bene & vere soluit p*re*fat*o* henrico Evans in p*re*dic*t*a magna aula scil*i*cet in parochia sanc*t*e Anne in le Blackfriers in warda de ffaringdon infra london p*re*dic*t*a sum*m*am octo solidor*um* leg*a*lis monet*e* Anglie sec*und*um formam & effec*t*um indorsamenti p*re*dic*t*i Et hoc p*ara*t*us* est verificare vnde pet*it* iud*icium* si p*re*dic*t*us henricus Evans acc*i*onem suam p*re*dic*t*am inde v*er*sus eum ha*b*ere seu mauntenere debeat &c.

Et p*re*dic*t*us henricus Evans dicit q*u*od ip*s*e p*er* aliqua p*er* p*re*dic*t*um Thomam kendall sup*er*ius pl*a*citando allega*t*a ab acc*i*one sua p*re*dic*t*a v*er*sus ip*s*um Thomam ha*b*end*a* p*er*cludi non debet quia p*ro*testando q*u*od p*re*dic*t*us Thomas kendall non soluit eid*e*m henrico aliquas denarior*um* sum*m*as in indorsamento p*re*dic*t*o sup*er*ius spec*if*icat*as* sec*und*um formam &

effectum indorsamenti predicti modo & forma prout idem Thomas superius placitando allegauit pro placito idem henricus dicit quod post confeccionem scripti obligatorij predicti & ante diem impetracionis bille predicte scilicet super diem sabbati existentem sextumdecimum diem Junij Anno regni domini Jacobi nunc regis Anglie secundo quoddam ludicrum anglice an interlude lusum fuit in predicta magna Aula in Indorsemento predicto mencionata scituata in le Blackfriers london predicta videlicet in predicta parochia sancte Anne in le Blackfriers in warda de ffaringdon infra london predicta per pueros qui per Concensum predictorum Edwardi henrici & Alexandri fuerunt retenti pro exercicione ludorum predictorum quodque predictus Thomas kendall super eundem diem sabbati scilicet predictum sextumdecimum diem Junij Anno dicti domini Regis nunc secundo supradicto non soluit eidem henrico Evans summam octo solidorum quam ei ad eundem diem soluisse debuit secundum formam & effectum Indorsamenti predicti modo et forma prout predictus Thomas superius placitando allegauit Et hoc paratus est verificare vnde petit iudicium Et debitum suum predictum vnacum dampnis suis predictis occasione detencionis debiti illius sibi adiudicari &c.

Et predictus Thomas kendall dicit quod nullum ludicrum anglice enterlude lusum fuit in predicta magna Aula in Indorsamento predicto superius specificata super predictum diem sabbati existentem septumdecimum diem Junij Anno regni dicti domini Regis nunc secundo supradicto per pueros qui per Concensum predictorum Edwardi henrici & Alexandri fuerunt retenti pro exercitione ludorum predictorum modo & forma prout predictus henricus Evans superius replicando allegauit Et de hoc ponit se super patriam Et predictus henricus Evans similiter &c Ideo preceptum est vicecomiti quod venire faciat Coram domino Rege apud Westmonasterium die Jovis proximo post mensem Pasche xij^cim &c de visu de predicta parochia sancte Anne in le Blackfriers in warda de ffarringdon infra london predicta per quos &c Et qui nec &c Ad recognoscendum &c Quia Tam &c Idem dies datus est partibus predictis ibidem &c.

7.

Suit in Chancery, 1609.

Edward Kirkham v. Samuel Daniel; *Chancery Bills and Answers,* Ser. I, Jas. I, K. 4/33.

Vide p. 177.

Nono die Maij 1609
    Saunders
To the Right Honorable Thomas Lord Elsemere
    Lord Chauncelour of England.

In most humble wise Complayninge sheweth vnto your good Lor^pp your dayly Oratour Edward Kyrkham of the Strand in the County of

Midd*lesex* gentlema*n* and Anne Kendall Widowe Executrix of the last will
and Testament of her late husband Thom*a*s Kendall Cityzen & haberdasher of London deceased that whereas o*ur* Sou*er*igne Lord the King*es*
Ma*iestes* that now is by his L*ett*res Patent*es* beareinge date at Westminst*er*
the ffourth day of ffebruary in the ffirst year*e* of his Ma*iestes* reigne of
England ffraunce and Ireland and Scotland the Seaven and Thirteth did
authorise & appointe the foresaid Edward Kirckha*m* & Thomas Kendall
w*i*th Allexand*er* Hawkins and Rob*er*te Payne from tyme to tyme to pr*o*uide
and bringe vpp a Convenyente number of Children & them to Exercise &
practise in the qualitie of playinge by the name of the Children of the Revells to the Queene w*i*thin the Blackeffryers in the City of London, or
w*i*thin any other Convenyent place where they shoulde thinke fitt for that
p*ur*pose: Provided that noe such playes or shewes should be pr*e*sented be-
before the Queene or by them any where publiquely Acted but by the
Approbac*i*on & Allowance of Samuel Danyell as by the said L*ett*res Patent-
es more at large appearethe. And whereas afterward*es* aboute the Twenteth
Eighte day of Aprill then nexte followinge in Regard of the paines to be
taken by the said Samuell Danyell aboute the Approbac*i*on and Allowance
of such Playes and shewes as shoulde be Acted and pr*e*sented by the said
Children as aforesaid the said Edward Kyrkham and Thomas Kendall by
one Obligac*i*on or writeinge Obligatorie beareinge date the said Twentie
Eighth day of Aprill in the second year*e* of his Ma*iestes* Reigne became bound
vnto the said Samuell Danyell in the some of One hundred pound*es* of Law-
ful Englishe Monie w*i*th Condic*i*on thereon Indorsed for the true paym*en*t
vnto the said Danyell everie yeare that the said Edward Kyrkham, Thomas
Kendall, Allexand*er* Hawkins and Robert Payne shoulde by vertue of his
Ma*iestes* l*ett*res patent*es* aforesaid keepe and maintayne any Children
according to the teno*ur* of the said l*ett*res patent*es* one Annuity or yearely
Some of Tenne pound*es* of lawfull mony of England at the ffeastes of S*t*
John Baptiste, S*t* Michaell Tharchangell, the birth of our Lord god, and the
Annunciac*i*on of the blessed Lady S*t* Marie the virgine or w*i*thin Tenne
dayes nexte after eu*er*y of the same ffeast*es* by even p*or*c*i*ons, yf the said
Children shoulde play, or make any shewes eyth*er* publiquely or privately
the full tyme Sixe Monethes in euerie yeare· And yf the said Children
shoulde not play or make any showes the full tyme of Sixe moneths in
eu*er*y yeare by reason of any pr*o*hibic*i*on or pestilence in the City of
London that then the said Kyrkha*m* and Kendall shoulde paye vnto the
said Danyell after the rate of Sixteene shilling*es* and Eighte pence a moneth
for such longer or shorter tyme as the said Children shoulde pr*e*sente or
doe any playes or shewes eyth*er* publiquely or privately as aforesaid
beinge not the full tyme of sixe moneths in one yeare as by the said Obligac*i*on and Condic*i*on thervppon Indorsed more at large yt doth and may
appeare: After w*hi*ch bond soe made the said Danyell havinge occasion to

vse monye woulde still importune and Request the said Kyrkham and
Kendall to pay to him his mony before the day did come that the same was
due and somtymes to pay the same to others to whom the said Danyell did
stande indebted, the which thinge to doe the said Kyrckham and Kendall
soe to pleasure the said Danyell weare very willyinge and did, soe that the
said Kyrkham and Kendall were neuer behinde hand in payinge the monie
due vnto him by the said obligacion, but allwayes paid the same to the said
Danyell or to others by his appoint(m)ent before the same was due; vntill
the ffive and Twenteth day of October in the second yeare of his Maiestes
Reygne that nowe is, at which tyme there was a new Composicion and
Agreamentat the Requestof the said Danyell, made betweene the said Danyell,
and the said Kyrkham and the said Kendall and others then partners in the
same business that the same bound shoulde be deliuered vpp by the said
Danyell to the said Kyrkham and Kendall to be Cancelled, and that the
said Danyell shoulde haue weekely paid vnto him, by the said Kyrkham
and Kendall and others partners in that business ffive shillinges of lawfull
money of England dureinge such tyme as the said Kyrkham and Kendall
or any others shoulde keepe or maintayne any such Children by vertue of
the foresaid lettres patentes, euery weeke that they the said Children did
make or showe any exercises or shewes privately or publiquely vnto which
the said Danyell did agree and for a longe tyme after receyved the said ffive
shillinges weekly according to the said Agreement And confessinge that
the said bond was fully satisfyed and discharged did promise to deliuer the
same to the said Kyrkham and Kendall to be Cancelled: Yet not with-
standinge soe yt is maye yt please your good Lorᵖᵖ that allthoughe the
said Danyell doth verie well knowe all and singuler the premisses to be
true, yet havinge a greedy and Covetous minde, and knoweinge that your
Oratours cannot dircetly proue the somes weare payde in pryuate betweene
themselues, and some of them weare at the request of the said Danyell and
by his appointement payd to others, and not to the said Danyell himselfe:
And for that the said Danyell doth likewise knowe that your said Orator
haue noe remedy by the Course of the Common Lawe to get the said bond
out of his handes the said Danyell hath nowe lately Commenced suyte
vppon the said Obligacion against the said Kyrkham in his Maiestes Courte
of kinges benche meaninge to take the whole forfeyture of yᵉ said Obligacion against the said Kyrkham and likewise doth giue out that he will
Commence suyte against the said Anne Kendall vppon the same Obligacion, and doth seeke with all the expedicion he canne to recouer the
penallty of the said obligacion against your said Oratour Kyrkham contrarie to all righte equitie and good Conscience: And albeit your said
Oratours haue diuerse and sundrie tymes earnestly required of the said
Danyell to deliuer the said obligacion to your said Oratours accordinge to
his promise, and to surcease his suyte vppon the same yet that to doe he

hath denyed and refused, and still doth deny and refuse contrarie to all Equity, right and good Conscience. In Consideracion whereof may yt please your good Lor^pp to award aswell the kinges Maiestes most gratious write of Iniunction to be directed to the said Samuel Danyell, and all and euery his Counsellours Attorneyes, solicitours and ffactours Commaundinge them therby noe further to proceed in the suyte vppon the said Obligacion against your said Oratour Kyrkham vntyll your Lor^pp shall haue taken further Order and direction therein: As allsoe the kinges Maiestes writ of Subpena to be directed to the said Samuell Danyell Commaundinge him thereby at a certaine day and vnder a certaine paine therein to be Lymited by your good Lor^pp to be and personally to appeare before your good Lor^pp in his Maiestes highe Courte of Chauncerie then and there to Aunswere vnto the premisses, and further to abide such Order and direction therein as to your good Lor^pp shall seeme to stand with right, equity, and good Conscience, And your said Oratour shall dayly pray to god for the preservacion of your good Lor^pp in all happines longe to Continue.

                                                      Darcey.

Jur. 12 Maij 1609 Mat. Carew.

The Aunswere of Samuel Danyell deffend^t to the Bill of Complaynte of Edward Kerkham and Anne Kendall Complaynantes.

This deffend^t saving to himselfe nowe and at all tymes hereafter all aduantages and benefytt of exception to the incerteyntie and insufficiency of the said Bill for Aunswere there vnto this deffend^t sayeth That true it is as he taketh it that the Kinges Maiestie that nowe is by the earneste suite, meanes & indeavor of this deffend^t which he performed with his greate labor costes & expences did by his Lettres Pattentes dated the ffowerth of ffebruary in the ffirste yere of his highnes Reigne aucthorize & appoynte the said Edward Kirkeham and others in the said Bill mencioned to trayne and bring vp certeyne children in the quality of Playinge by the name of the children of the Reuells in such sorte or to such effect as in the said Bill is expressed. ffor more certeyntie whereof this deffend^t referreth himselfe to the said Letters Pattentes And further sayeth that for and in consideracion of his greate paynes & travell therein formerly taken aboute the tyme in the Bill mencioned the said Compl^t Edward Kirkham & one Thomas Kendall deceased became bounde vnto this deffend^t in the some of One hundred Poundes with condicion therevppon indorsed to such effect as in the Bill is declared, to which bond & condicion of the same this deffend^t for more certeyntie referreth himselfe And further sayeth that after the said Compl^t and Kendall had entred into the said bond he this deffend^t thinketh that he had satisfaccion to his contentement for all suche some & somes of money as were dewe and payable yerly or monthely vnto him this deffend^t by the true intente & meaninge of the condicion of the said bond vntill the Eight & twentith of Aprill in the Third yere of his Maiestes reigne aboute which tyme this deffend⁺ by Letter of Attourney or otherwise by his deede or writinge as he thinketh for good consideracion did assigne & sett over the benefitt of the said obligacion & all such somme or sommes of money as he should or ought to receive by the same: from thensforth As also the said bond vnto one John Gerrard synce which tyme this deffend⁺ neaver intermeddled or had to doe with the said Complainantes or Lettres Pattentes or eaver demaunded any thinge of the Complainantes as dewe apperteyninge vnto him for the same And this deffend⁺ further sayeth that true it is that there was a speech of communicion betwene this deffend⁺ & the Compl⁺ Kirkham in the bill mencioned, that the said Compl⁺ Kirkeham and the others in the Bill mencioned should paye ffive shillinges weekelye to the said deffend⁺ as in the Bill is expressed ffor security whereof they the said Kirkham and others should become bounde by their obligacion and that vppon Seallinge & deliuery of the said bond he this deffend⁺ would deliuer his bond of One hundred Poundes but for that that noe such security was entred into the said Communicacion & speech Cessed & became voyde loung before his assignement of the said bond to the said Gerrard. But this deffend⁺ hath heard that forasmuch as the said Complainantes haue not satisfyed and payd the said Annuity since the said Assignement in such manner as they ought to haue done accordinge to the condicion of the said bonde he the said Gerrard hath vsed this deffendantes name and put the same bond in siute by force of the said Letter of Attourney as this deffend⁺ thinketh it lawfull for him to doe and hopeth with the favor of this honorable Court he may prosecute the same for his juste satisfaccion Without that that the said obligacion of the somme of One hundred Poundes was made by the Compl⁺ Kirkeham & the said Kendall in regarde of the paynes to be taken by the said deffend⁺ but for & in respecte of his paynes formerly taken in procureinge the said Pattentes And with out that there was any agreemente concerninge the said ffive shillinges weekely other then this deffend⁺ before in his Aunswere hath confessed And without that that the deffend⁺ confessed that the said bond was fully satisfyed and discharged & did promisse to diliuer the same to the said Kirkeham & Kendall to be cancelled in such sorte as in the said Bill is vntruely alleadged, And without that that any other matter or thinge materyall or effectual in the Lawe to be Aunswered vnto & not herein confessed or avoyded traversed or denyed is true to this deffendantes knoledge All which matters this deffend⁺ is ready to averr and prove as this honorable Court shall award and prayeth to be dismissed with costes & charges her in this behalfe wrongfully susteyned.

Saunders   Rande

BIBLIOGRAPHY

Adams, J. Q. *The Conventual Buildings of Blackfriars London, and the Playhouses Constructed therein.* In *No. Carolina Studies in Philol.*, XIV, 1917.
Shakespearean Playhouses, Boston and N. Y., 1918.
Albrecht, H. A. *Das Englische Kindertheater.* Inaug. Dis. Halle, 1883.
Alleyn, Edward, Memoirs of. Ed. J. P. Collier for the *Shakespeare Society*, 1841.
Alleyn Papers, The. Ed. J. P Collier for the *Shakespeare Society*, 1843.
Antiquary, An. *The Historical Charters and Constitutional Documents of the City of London.* Lond. 1884.
Arber, Edward. *Introductory Sketch to the Martin Marprelate Controversy.* Lond. 1879.
Arber, Edward, editor. *A Transcript of the Register of the Company of Stationers of London 1554-1640.* Lond. 1894.
Baker, D. E. *Biographia Dramatica*, rewritten by J. O. Halliwell. Lond. 1860.
Baker, G. P. Introduction to his edition of Lyly's *Endimion*. N. Y. 1894.
Bale, John. *Scriptorum Illustrium Maioris Brytannie . . . . Catalogus.* Basel, 1557-9.
Bang, Willy. *Acta Anglo-lovaniensia; John Heywood und sein Kreis.* In *Englische Studien.* XXXVIII, 1907.
Benham, William (Canon). *Old St. Paul's Cathedral.* Lond. and N. Y. 1902.
Benndorf, Cornelie. *Die Englische Pädogogik im 16. Jahrh.* In *Wiener Beiträge*, 1905.
Binz, Gustav. *Londoner Theater u. Schauspieler im Jahre 1577.* In *Anglia*, XXII, 1899.
Birch, Thomas. *The Court and Times of James I.* Lond. 1849.
Birt, H. N. *The Elizabethan Religious Settlement.* Lond. 1907.
Blanch, W. H. *Dulwich College.* Lond. 1877.
Ye Parish of Camerwell. Lond. 1875.
Bloxam, J. R., and Macray, W. D. *A Register of the Members of St. Mary Magdalen College, Oxford.* Oxf. 1853-58.
Bolingbroke, L. G. *Pre-Elizabethan Plays and Players in Norfolk.* In *Norfolk Archæology*, XI, 336.
Bond, R. W. *The Works of John Lyly.* Oxford, 1902.
Early Plays from the Italian. Oxford, 1911.
Bonnard, G. *La Controverse de Martin Marprelate.* Paris, 1916.
Boy Bishop, Two Sermons of. Ed. E. F. Rimbault, in *Camden Miscellany*, VII, 1875.
Brandl, Alois. *Quellen des Weltlichen Dramas in England vor Shakespeare.* In *Quellen u. Forschungen.* Strassburg, 1898.
Brewer, J. S., and Gairdner, J. *Letters and Papers, Foreign and Domestic, of the Reign of Henry VIII.* Lond. 1862.
Brodmeier, Cecil. *Die Shakespeare Bühne nach dem alten Bühnenanweisungen.* Weimar, 1904.
Browne, Carleton. *English Grammar Schools*; thesis for the degree of Ph.D., Harvard, 1903.
Bumpus, J. S. *Organists and Composers of St. Paul's Cathedral.* Lond. 1891. (privately printed)

Burney, Charles. *A General History of Music.* Lond. 1782.
Cambridge History of English Literature, VI and VII. Cambridge, 1910.
Camden, William. *Annales.* Lond. 1625.
Campbell, W. *Materials for a History of the Reign of Henry VII.* For the *Royal Soc.* Lond. 1873-77.
Castelain, Maurice. *Ben Jonson, l'homme et l'œuvre.* Paris, 1907.
Catholic Record Soc., Pub. of. Lond. 1905—.
Cavendish, George. *Life of Wolsey.* Lond. 1885.
Cayley, A. *Memoirs of Sir Thomas More . . . . and his Latin Poems.* Lond. 1808.
Chalmers, George. *Apology for the Believers in the Shakespeare Papers.* Lond. 1797.
　　　Supplementary Apology, etc. Lond. 1797.
Chambers, E. K. *Court Performances before King James I.* In *Modern Language Review,* II, 1906-7.
　　　Dramatic Records from the Lansdowne MSS. In *Malone Society Collections,* II, 1908.
　　　The Elizabethan Stage. Oxford, 1923.
　　　The Medieval Stage. Oxford, 1903.
　　　Notes on the History of the Revels Office under the Tudors. Lond. 1906.
　　　Remembrancia. In *Malone Society Collections,* I, 1907.
　　　Review of Ordish's *Early London Theatres.* In *Academy,* Aug. 24, 1895.
Chapman, J. K. *Complete History of Theatrical Entertainments . . . . at the English Court from Henry VIII to the Present Day.* Lond. 1894.
Chappell, William. *Some Account of an Unpublished Collection of Songs and Ballads by King Henry VIII and his Contemporaries.* In *Archæologia,* XLI, p. 371.
　　　Popular Music of the Olden Time. Lond. 1855-59.
Cheque Book of the Chapel Royal, The Old. Ed. E. F. Rimbault for the *Camden Society, New Series,* Lond. 1872.
Churchyard, Thomas. *The Worthiness of Wales* (1587). In *Pub. of the Spenser Society,* XX, 1876.
Churton, Ralph. *Life of Alexander Nowell.* Oxford, 1809.
Clapham, Alfred W. *On the Topography of the Dominican Priory of London.* In *Archæologia,* 1912, p. 57.
Clode, C. M. *The Early History of the Guild of Merchant Taylors.* Lond. 1888.
　　　Memorials of the Merchant Taylors Company. Lond. 1875.
Collier, J. P. *A Booke of Plaies and Notes thereof.* Lond. 1836.
　　　History of English Dramatic Poetry. Lond. 1879.
　　　Memoirs of the Principal Actors in the Plays of Shakespeare. In *Shakes. Soc. Pub.,* 1846.
　　　New Facts Regarding Shakespeare. Lond. 1835.
Collins, Arthur. *Letters and Memorials of State.* Lond. 1746.
Collinson, John. *History of Somersetshire.* Bath, 1791.
Cooper, Charles H, and Cooper, Thompson. *Athenæ Cantabrigienses.* Cambridge, 1858-1913.
Cornish, William. *A Treatise between Trowthe and Enformacion.* Ed. F. J. Furnivall in *Archiv. f. d. Stud. d. n. Sprache u. Litt.* 1908, CXX.
Cox, J. C. *Churchwardens' Accounts from the Fourteenth Century to the Close of the Seventeenth Century.* Lond. 1913.
Cox, J. E. *The Annals of St. Helen's Bishopgate, London.* Lond. 1876.
Creizenach, W. *Geschichte des Neueren Dramas.* Halle a. S., 1911.
Cunningham, Peter. *Extracts from the Accounts of the Revels at Court.* In *Shakes. Soc. Pub.,* 1842.

Daniel, Samuel. *Works.* Ed. A. B. Grosart. Lond. 1885-96.

Dekker, Thomas. *The Whole Magnificent Entertainment: Given to King James, Queen Anne his wife, and Henry Frederick the Prince. . . . the 15. of March. 1603.* Lond. 1604.

De la Fontaine, H. C. *The King's Music.* Lond. 1909.

Devon, Frederick. *Issues of the Exchequer.* Lond. 1836.

    Pell Records. Lond. n.d.

Devrient, Hans. *Das Kind auf der antiken Bühne.* Weimar, 1904.

Dictionary of National Biography.

Dixon, R. W. *History of the Church of England.* Lond. 1878-92.

Dodsley, Robert. *Fugitive Pieces.* Lond. 1765.

Dodsworth, William. *An Historical Account of the Episcopal See and Cathedral Church of. . . . Salisbury.* Salis. 1814.

Dugdale, Sir William. *History of St. Paul's Cathedral.* Lond. 1818.

    Monasticon Anglicanum. Lond. 1718.

Durand, W. Y. *Notes on Edwards.* In *Journal of Germ. Philol.,* IV, 1902.

Durham Abbey Account Rolls. Ed. J. T. Fowler for the *Surtees Society,* 1898-1901.

Durham Household Book. In *Pub. of the Surtees Society,* 1844.

Dyer, T. F. Thistleton. *Old English Social Life as told by the Parish Register.* Lond. 1898.

Excerpta Historica. Lond. 1831.

Fabyan, Robert. *Chronicles.* Lond. 1811.

Fairholt, F. W. *Catalogue of a Collection of Works on Pageantry.* Lond. 1869.

    Introd. to ed. of Heywood's *Dialogue on Wit and Folly,* for the *Percy Society.* Lond. 1846.

    Lord Mayor's Pageants, for the *Percy Society.* Lond. 1843.

Farmer, J. S. *Handlist of the Tudor Facsimile Texts.* Lond. 1911.

Feuillerat, A. *Blackfriars Records.* In *Malone Soc. Coll.* II, 1, 1913.

    Le Bureau des Menu-Plaisirs (Office of the Revels) et la Mise en Scène a là Cour d'Elizabeth. Louvain, 1910.

    Documents Relating to the Office of the Revels in the Time of Queen Elizabeth. Louvain, 1908.

    Documents Relating to the Revels at Court in the Time of King Edward VI and Queen Mary. Louvain, 1914.

    John Lyly: contribution à l'histoire de la Renaissance en Angleterre. Cambridge, Univ. Press, 1910.

    The Origin of Shakespeare's Blackfriars Theatre. In *Shakespeare Jahrbuch,* XLVIII, 1912.

Field, Nathaniel. *Remonstrance to a Preacher in Southwark who has been arraigning the Players of the Globe Theatre in 1616.* Ed. J. O. Halliwell. Lond. 1865.

Fisher, G. W. *Annals of Shrewsbury School.* Lond. 1899.

Fitzjeffrey, H. *Notes from Black-fryers.* Lond. 1620.

Fleay, F. G. *Biographical Chronicle of the English Drama 1559-1642.* Lond. 1891.

    Chronicle History of the London Stage 1559-1642. Lond. 1890.

    Queen Elizabeth, Croyden, and the Drama, a Paper read before the Balham Antiquarian and Natural History Society, Jan. 24, 1898. Lond. 1898.

Flood, W. H. G. *Master Sebastian.* In *Musical Antiquary,* III, p. 149; IV, p. 187.

Forshall, F. H. *Westminster School Past and Present.* Lond. 1884.

Foster, Jas. *Alumni Oxonienses. . . .* 1500-1714. Oxford, 1891-2.

Frere, W. H. *Visitation Articles and Injunctions of the Period of the Reformation.* Lond. 1910.

Froude, J. A. *History of England from the Fall of Wolsey to the Death of Elizabeth.* Lond. 1856-70.

Fuller, Thomas. *The Church History of Britain.* Ed. J. S. Brewer. Oxford, 1846.

G., I. *Refutation of the Apology for Actors.* Lond. 1615.

Gardiner, R. B. *Admission Register of St. Paul's School.* Lond. 1884.

Gayley, C. M. *Representative English Comedies.* N. Y. and Lond. 1903.

Gildersleeve, Virginia C. *Government Regulation of the Elizabethan Drama.* Col. Univ. Press, N. Y., 1908.

Googe, Barnaby. *Eclogs, Epytaphs, and Sonettes.* In Arber's *Reprints.* Lond. 1895.

Gosson, Stephen. *Playes confuted in five actions.* In W. C. Hazlitt's *The English Drama and Stage . . . . 1543-1664.* Lond. 1869.

    School of Abuse. Ed. Edward Arber. Lond. 1868.

    A Second and Third Blast of Retrait from Plaies and Theatres (1580). Ed. W. C. Hazlitt, *The English Drama and Stage.* Lond. 1869.

Goulding, R. W. *Louth Old Corporation Records.* Louth, 1891.

Greenstreet, J. *Documents relating to the Players at the Red Bull, Clerkenwell, and the Cockpit, Drury Lane.* New Shakes. Soc. Trans., 1885.

    Blackfriars Playhouse, its Antecedents. In *Athenæum,* Nos. 3064 and 3141, 17 July, 1886, and 7 January, 1888.

    Blackfriars Playhouse in the Time of Shakespeare. In *Athenæum,* Nos. 3154 and 3156, 7 April, 1888, and 21 April, 1888.

    The Whitefriars Theatre in the Time of Shakespeare. In *New Shakes. Soc. Trans.,* 1888.

Greg, W. W. *A List of English Plays written before 1643.* Lond. 1900.

    A List of Masques, Pagents, etc. Lond. 1902.

Gregory, John. *The Works of . . . . J. G.* Lond. 1683-4.

Gregory, William. *Chronicle.* Ed. James Gardiner for the *Camden Soc., New Series,* XVII, 1876.

Gutch, John. *Collectanea Curiosa.* Oxford, 1781.

Hackett, Maria. *Documents and Authorities Respecting the Ancient Foundation for the Education of the St. Paul's Choristers, etc.* Lond. 1812. (privately printed)

    A Popular Description of St. Paul's Cathedral. Lond. 1828.

Hales, J. W. *The Date of the "First English Comedy."* In *Englische Studien,* XVIII, 1893.

Hall, Edward. *Chronicle.* Lond. 1809.

Halliwell-Phillips, J. O. *A Collection of Ancient Documents respecting the Office of Master of the Revels, etc.* Lond. 1870.

    A Dictionary of Old English Plays. Lond. 1860.

    Memoranda intended for the Use of Amateurs who are sufficiently interested in the Pursuit, to make searches in the Public Record Office. Brighton, 1884. (privately printed)

    Outlines of the Life of Shakespeare. 8th ed., Lond. 1889.

Hampson, R. T. *Medii Aevi Kalendarium.* Lond. 1841.

Harrington, Sir John. *A Brief Apology for Poetry.* Lond. 1591.

Harrison, William. *Description of England in Shakespeare's Youth.* Ed. F. J. Furnivall, 1877-81.

Harvey, Gabriel. *Works.* Ed. A. B. Grosart. Lond. 1884-5. (privately printed)

    Foure Letters, and Certaine Sonnets &c. London, 1592.

    Strange Newes of the intercepting certaine Letters, &c. Lond. 1592.

    Letter Book of. For the *Camden Soc.* Lond. 1884.

    A New Letter of Notable Contents, etc. Lond. 1593.

Haslewood, Joseph. *Account of the Old London Theatres,* appended to *Roxburghe Revels* (James Maidment, ed.), 1837.

Hawkins, Sir John. *A General History . . . . of Music.* Lond. 1776.

Hazlitt, W. C. *The English Drama and Stage under the Tudor and Stuart Princes, 1543-1664.* Lond. 1864.

Hearne, Thos. *Liber Niger Scaccarii.* Oxford, 1728.

Hennessy, G. *Novum Repertorium Ecclestiacum Parochiale Londinense.* Lond. 1898.

Henry, Aurelia. *Epicœne.* In *Yale Studies in English.* N. Y. 1906.

Henslowe, Philip. *Diary.* Ed. W. W. Greg. Lond. 1904-8.

Heywood, Thomas. *An Apology for Actors.* In *Shakes. Soc. Pub.,* 1841.

Holinshed, Raphael. *Chronicle of England, Scotland, and Ireland.* Lond. 1807-8.

Holthausen, F. *Zu Heywood's Wetterspiel.* In *Archiv.f. d. Stud. der neueren Sprachen u. Litt.* CXVI, 1906.

　　Studien zum älteren englischen Drama Thersites. In *Eng. Studien,* XXXI.

Hone, William. *Ancient Mysteries, etc.* Lond. 1823.

Hunnis, William. *The Hive full of Honey.* Lond. 1578.

Jeaffreson, J. C. *Middlesex County Records.* Lond. 1886-92.

Jebb, J. *Choral Service of the United Churches of England and Ireland.* Lond. 1843.

Jonson, Ben. *B. Jon. His Part of King James and his Royal and Magnificent Entertainment through his Honorable Cittie of London, Thursday the 15. of March, 1603 . . . .* Lond. 1604.

Jonson, Ben, and Chapman, George. *Letters from Prison, 1605, relating to their Disgrace.* Ed. Bertram Dobell, in *Athenæum,* March 30, 1901.

Jusserand, J. J. *Le Théâtre en Angleterre.* Paris, 1881.

Kempe, A. J. *The Losely Manuscripts.* Lond. 1836.

Kirby, T. J. *Annals of Winchester College.* Lond. 1892.

Kittredge, G. L. *The "Misogonus" and Laurence Johnson.* In *Journ. of Germ. Philol.* III, No. 3, 1901.

　　Source of Sir Giles Goosecap. In *Journ. of Germ. Philol.* II, No. 1, 1898.

Knight, Samuel. *Life of Dr. John Colet.* Lond. 1724.

Langbaine, Gerard. *An Account of the English Dramatic Poets.* Oxford, 1691.

Law, Ernest. *Supposed Shakespeare Forgeries.* Lond. 1911.

　　More about Shakespeare Forgeries. Lond. 1913.

Lawrence, W. J. *Early French Players in England.* In *Anglia,* XXXII, 1909.

　　The Elizabethan Playhouse and other Studies. Philadelphia and Stratford-on-Avon, 1912.

　　The Elizabethan Playhouse and other Studies. Second Series. Shakespeare Head Press, Stratford, 1913.

Leach, A. F. *Early Yorkshire Schools.* In *Yorkshire Archæological Soc. Record Series.* Lond. 1899.

　　St. Paul's School before Colet. In *Archæologia,* LXII, Pt. 1, 1910.

　　The Schoolboys' Feast. In *Fortnightly Review, New Series,* LIX, 1896.

Leland, John. *Collectanea.* Lond. 1770.

Liber Famelicus of Sir James Whitelocke. Ed. John Bruce, for the *Camden Soc.* 1858.

Liber Rubeus de Scaccario. Ed. H. Hall in the *Rolls Series,* No. 99, 1896.

Lincoln's Inn Records. Lond. 1896.

Lincoln's Inn, The Records of the Honorable Society of. The Black Books. Ed. W. P. Baildon. Lond. 1897.

Longman, William. *The three Cathedrals dedicated to St. Paul in London.* Lond. 1818.

Lupton, J. H. *Life of John Colet.* Lond. 1887.

Lysons, Daniel. *Environs of London.* Lond. 1811.

Lyte, H. Maxwell. *History of Eton College.* Lond. 1899.
Maas, H. *Aeussere Geschichte der englischen Theatertruppen in dem Zeitraum von 1557 bis 1642.* In Bang's *Materialen zur Kunde des älteren Engl. Dramas,* XIX. *Die Kindertruppen.* Göttingen, 1901.
Machyn, Henry. *Diary.* Ed. J. G. Nichols for the *Camden Soc.,* XLII, 1848.
Madden, Sir F. M. *Privy Purse Expenses of the Princess Mary.* Lond. 1831.
Magnus, Leonard A. *Respublica.* In *Early Eng. Text. Soc., Extra Series,* XCIV, 1905.
Maitland, William. *History and Survey of London.* Lond. 1803.
Malcolm, James P. *Londinium Redivivum.* Lond. 1803.
Malone, Edmund. *Variorum Shakespeare.* Ed. Jas. Boswell, Lond. 1821.
Malone Society. *Collections.* Lond. 1907-23.
Martinist Tracts, in the Lambeth Palace Library, London:
    Admonition to the People of England. 1589.
    An Almond for a Parrat (Thomas Nash?). n.d.
    A Countercuffe given to Martin Junior, by the venturous, hardie, and renowned Pasquill of Englande, Cavaliero. (1589)
    The First parte of Pasquils Apologie. 1590.
    Martins Months Minde. 1589.
    Pappe with an Hatchet (John Lyly, 1589-90).
    The Returne of . . . . Pasquill of England. n.d.
    Theses Martinianæ. (1589)
    A Whip for an Ape. n.d.
    See also Bonnard, and Pierce.
Milman, Henry Hart. *Annals of St. Paul's Cathedral.* Lond. 1869.
Monkmeyer, Paul. *Prolegomena zu einer Darstellung der englischen Volksbühne zur Elizabeth- und Stuart-Zeit.* Hanover, 1905.
Mulcaster, Richard. *The First Part of the Elementarie which Entreateth Chefelie of the Right Writing of our English Tung.* Lond. 1582.
    Positions, wherein those Primitive Circumstances be examined which are Necessary for the Training up of Children. Ed. R. H. Quick. Lond. 1888.
Munday, Anthony. *Camp-bell, or the Ironmongers Faire Feild.* Lond. 1609.
Murray, J. T. *English Dramatic Companies.* Lond. 1910.
Nash, Thomas. *Works.* Ed. R. B. McKerrow. Lond. 1904.
New Shakespeare Society. *Transactions.* 1874-1904.
Newcourt, Richard. *Repertorium ecclesiasticum parochiale londinense.* Lond. 1708-10.
Nicolas, N. H. *Privy Purse Expenses of Elizabeth of York.* Lond. 1830.
Nichols, J. G. *Literary Remains of King Edward the Sixth.* Roxburghe Club, 1857.
    London Pageants. Lond. 1831.
Nichols, John. *Progresses of King James First.* Lond. 1828.
    Progresses and Processions of Elizabeth. Lond. 1823.
Nixon, F. R. *History of the Merchant Taylors School.* Lond. 1823.
Nixon, Rev. Robt. *Note on the Priory of White Carmelites at Hitchins, Herts.* In *Archæologia,* XVIII, p. 447.
Ordinances, A Collection of, for the Government of the Royal Household. Pub. by the Soc. of Antiquaries. Lond. 1790.
Ordish, T. F. *Early London Theatres.* The Camden Library, 1894.
    Shakespeare's London, New Edition. Lond. 1904.
Overall, W. H. and H. C. *Analytical Index to . . . . Remembrancia, 1579-1664.* Lond. 1878.
Owen, Hugh, and Blakeway, John B. *History of Shrewsbury.* Lond. 1825.

Paradise of Dainty Devices, The.   Reprinted with *England's Helicon*, with an introduction by Sir Edgerton Brydges. Lond. 1812.

Park, Thomas, ed. *Heliconia, Comprising a Selection of the English Poetry of the Elizabethan Age; written or published between 1595 and 1605.* Lond. 1815.
    Nugæ Antiquæ. Lond. 1804.

Parrott, T. M. *The Plays and Poems of George Chapman,* N. Y. 1910.

Patent Rolls, Calendar of, Ed. I to Rich. III. Pub. for the Public Record Office, London.

Peele, George. *Works.* Ed. A. H. Bullen. Lond. 1887.

Penniman, J. H. *The War of the Theatres.* In *Pub. of the Univ. of Penna.,* IV, No. 3, 1897.

Percy, Bishop, ed. *The Regulations and Establishment of the Royal Household of Henry Algernon Percy, the Fifth Earl of Northumberland.* Lond. 1770.

Percy, William. *Cuck-Queans and Cuckolds Errants, or, The Bearing down of the Inne.* Ed. J. R. Lloyd, for the *Roxburghe Soc.* 1825.
    Fairy Pastoral, or, Feast of Elves. Ed. Joseph Haslewood for the *Roxburghe Society.* 1825.

Pierce, William. *An Historical Introduction to the Marprelate Tracts.* Lond. 1908.
    The Marprelate Tracts. Lond. 1911.

Pits (Pitseus), John. *Relationum historicarum de rebus anglicis tom. i, quatuor partes complectens.* Paris, 1619.

Plummer, Charles, ed. *Elizabethan Oxford.* For *Oxf. Hist. Soc.,* at Clarendon Press, 1887.

Privy Council, Acts of the. Ed. J. R. Dasent. Lond. 1890-5.

Privy Council, Proceedings and Ordinances of. Ed. Sir Harris Nicolas. Lond. 1834-7.

Raine, James. *History and Antiquities of the County Palatine of Durham.* Lond. 1816-40.

Rankin, W. *Mirror of Monsters, wherein is shown the vices caused by the sight of plays.* Lond. 1857.

Raumer, Fred von. *Briefe aus Paris zur Erläuterung der Geschichte des sechszehnten Jahrhunderts.* Leipzig, 1831.

Reed, A. W. *John Heywood and his Friends.* In *The Library,* 3 Ser. VIII, 1917.
    The Canon of John Heywood's Plays. In *The Library,* 3 Ser. IX, 1918.

Register of the University of Oxford. Pub. by the *Oxford Hist. Soc.,* Oxf. 1885-9.

Reyher, Paul. *Les Masques Anglais.* Paris, 1909.

Ritson, Joseph, *Ancient Songs.* Lond. 1829.
    Bibliographia Poetica. Lond. 1802.

Rotuli Parliamentorum. Lond. 1767-77.

Rushworth, John. *Historical Collections.* Lond. 1659-1701.

Rye, W. B. *England as seen by Foreigners in the Days of Elizabeth and James.* Lond. 1865.

Rymer, Thomas. *Fœdera.* Lond. 1726-35.

Sargeant, J. *Annals of Westminster School.* Lond. 1898.

Schelling, F. E. *Elizabethan Drama.* Boston and N. Y. 1908.
    The Queen's Progress. Boston, 1904.

Scott, E. J. E. *The Westminster Play Account of 1564 and 1606.* In *Athenæum,* Feb. 14, 1903. Cf. also further notes on the same subject by Mr. Scott and Mr. E. K. Chambers in *Athenæum* of November 17 and November 24, 1900.

Shakespeare Society. *Papers.* 1844-49.

Sharpe, R. R. *Wills in the Court of Husting.* Lond. 1899.

Sheppard, J. E. *The Old Royal Palace at Whitehall.* Lond. 1902.
    Memorials of St. James' Palace. Lond. 1894.

Simpson, William Sparrow. *Chapters in the History of Old St. Paul's.* Lond. 1881.
   Documents Illustrating the History of St. Paul's Cathedral. Lond. 1880.
   Gleanings from Old St. Paul's. Lond. 1894.
   Registrum Statutorum. . . . Ecclesie. . . . Sancti Pauli. Lond. 1873.
   St. Paul's Cathedral and Old City Life. Lond. 1894.
   St. Paul's Library, Catalogue of. Lond. 1893.
Sinclair, William. *The Chapels Royal.* Lond. 1912.
Small, R. A. *The Stage-Quarrel between Ben Jonson and the So-called Poetasters.* Lond. 1899.
Somers, John, Lord. *Second Collection of Scarce. . . . Tracts.* Revised and augmented by Sir Walter Scott. Lond. 1810.
State Papers, Domestic, Calendar of. Ed. M. Lemon and Mary A. E. Green. Lond. 1865-72.
State Papers. . . . King Henry the Eighth. Pub. by the Record. Com. of Gt. Britain. Lond. 1830-52.
State Papers, Venetian, Calendar of. Pub. for the Public Record Office, London.
Stettin-Pomerania, The Diary of the Duke of. Ed. G. von Bülow and W. Powell. In *Trans. Royal Hist. Soc., N. S.,* VII, 1892.
Stopes, C. C. *Extracts from the Lord Chamberlain's Office.* In *Shakespeare Jahrbuch,* XLVIII, 1912.
   Mary's Chapel Royal and her Coronation Play. In *Athenæum,* Sept. 9, 1905.
   William Hunnis. In *Athenæum,* March 31, 1900.
   William Hunnis and the Revels of the Chapel Royal. In Bang's *Materialen zur Kunde,* etc. XXIX, 1910.
Stow, John. *Annales.* Lond. 1631.
   Survey of London. Reprinted from the text of 1603 by C. L. Kingsford. Oxford, 1908.
Strutt, Joseph. *Sports and Pastimes of the People of England.* Ed. J. C. Cox. Lond. 1903.
Strype, John. *Annals of the Reformation.* Lond. 1725.
   Ecclesiastical Memorials. Lond. 1721.
   Historical Collections of the Life and Acts of John Aylmer. Lond. 1701.
   The History of the Life and Acts of the Most Reverend Father in God, Edmund Grindal. Lond. 1710.
   The Life and Acts of Matthew Parker. Lond. 1711.
   The Life and Acts of John Whitgift. Oxford, 1718.
Symmes, H. S. *Les Débuts de la Critique dramatique en Angleterre jusqu'à la mort de Shakespeare.* Paris, 1903.
Thompson, E. M. S. *The Controversy between the Puritans and the Stage.* N. Y. 1903.
Thorndike, A. H. *The Influence of Beaumont and Fletcher on Shakespeare.* Worcester, Mass., 1901.
Tolman, A. H. *Select Bibliography of Drama in English before Elizabeth.* Chicago, 1896.
Trevelyan Papers. Ed. J. P. Collier for the *Camden Soc.,* 1857.
Tuberville, J. *Epitaphs, Epigrams, Songs and Sonets.* Lond. 1570.
Van der Velde, Alf. *Englische Bühneverhältnisse im sechszehnten u. siebzehnten Jahrhunderten.* Görlitz, 1894.
Vatke, T. A. *Das Theater und das Londoner Publicum in Shakespeares Zeit.* In *Shakespeare Jarhbuch,* XXI.
Venn, John and J. A. *The Book of Matriculations and Degrees . . . in the University of Cambridge from 1544 to 1657.* Camb. Univ. Press, 1913.
Wallace, C. W. *The Children of the Chapel at Blackfriars, 1597-1603.* In *Nebraska Univ. Studies,* 1908.

The Evolution of the English Drama up to Shakespeare, with a History of the First Blackfriars Theatre. Berlin, 1912.

Shakespeare and his London Associates as revealed in recently discovered Documents. In Nebraska Univ. Studies, 1910.

Ward, A. W. History of English Dramatic Literature to the death of Queen Anne. Lond. 1899.

Warner, G. F. Catalogue of the MSS. and Muniments . . . . at Dulwich. Lond. 1881.

Warton, Thomas. History of English Poetry. Ed. W. C. Hazlitt. Lond. 1871.

Wilkins, David. Concilia. Lond. 1737.

Wilson, H. B. History of Merchants Taylors School. Lond. 1812-14.

Withington, Robert. English Pageantry: An Historical Outline. Harvard University Press, 1918-20.

Wood, Anthony à. Athenæ Oxonienses. Lond. 1813-20.

Fasti Oxonienses. (Printed with Athen. Oxon.) Lond. 1813-20.

Woodruff, C. E., and Cape, H. J. Schola Regia Cantuariensis: A History of Canterbury School. Lond. 1908.

Wordsworth, C. Ceremonies and Processions of the Cathedral Church of Salisbury. Salis. 1909.

Wright, James. Historia Histrionica: an Historical Account of the English Stage. In Colley Cibber's Apology, ed. R. W. Lowe, Vol. I, and in Hazlitt's Dodsley, Vol. XV.

Wright, Thomas. Queen Elizabeth and her Times. Lond. 1838.

Young, Karl. Influence of French Farce on the Plays of John Heywood. In Mod. Philol., June, 1904.

Young, W. The History of Dulwich College. Lond. 1889.

DOCUMENTS

Public Record Office:
  Books of the Court of Requests.
  Chancery Bills and Answers.
  Placita Coram Rege (Cases in King's Bench).
  Close Rolls.
  Feet of Fines.
  Recovery Rolls.
  Documents in the Lord Chamberlain's Office.
  Miscellaneous Books, Treasury of Receipt.
  Declared Accounts of the Treasury of the Chamber, Pipe Office.
  Patent Rolls.
  Privy Signet Bills.
  Privy Seals, Chancery Warrants.
  State Papers.
  Warrants for Issue, Exchequer of Receipt.
British Museum:
  Miscellaneous MSS.
Bodleian:
  Rawlinson, Malone, Ashmole Collections.
Guildhall, London:
  Remembrancia.
  Repertories of the Court of Common Council.
  Letter Books of the Court of Aldermen.
Lambeth Palace:
  Miscellaneous MSS.
St. Paul's Library:
  Muniments and Miscellaneous MSS.

INDEX